TO :

Dear Srie
presentation & dedicated
Worker :

Dilip Thatte

with love .
&
respect

[signature]

अजय सिंह
9 3 oct. 2019

MESSENGERS OF HINDU NATIONALISM

WALTER ANDERSEN AND SHRIDHAR D. DAMLE

MESSENGERS OF HINDU NATIONALISM

How the RSS Reshaped India

HURST & COMPANY, LONDON

First published in the United Kingdom in 2019 by
C. Hurst & Co. (Publishers) Ltd.,
41 Great Russell Street, London, WC1B 3PL
© Walter Andersen and Shridhar D. Damle, 2019
All rights reserved.

Printed in India

Distributed in the United States, Canada and Latin America by
Oxford University Press, 198 Madison Avenue, New York, NY 10016,
United States of America.

The right of Walter Andersen and Shridhar D. Damle to be identified
as the authors of this publication is asserted by them in accordance with
the Copyright, Designs and Patents Act, 1988.

A Cataloguing-in-Publication data record for this book
is available from the British Library.

ISBN 978-1-78738-025-7

This book is printed using paper from registered sustainable
and managed sources.

www.hurstpublishers.com

Photographs courtesy of the Rashtriya Swayamsevak Sangh, from the
Panchjanya and Organiser archives

To the late Lloyd I. Rudolph and Susanne H. Rudolph

Contents

Introduction

Some fifteen months into Narendra Modi's new Bharatiya Janata Party (BJP) government, his party's ideological godfather, the Hindu nationalist Rashtriya Swayamsevak Sangh (RSS), held a widely reported 'coordination' meeting with some two dozen of its affiliates in New Delhi in September 2015; their purpose was to consider a wide range of significant—and sometimes controversial—public policy issues facing the Indian nation.[1] At the end of this conclave, several of the most senior government ministers, including Prime Minister Modi, arrived to discuss these issues in person. What is analytically interesting about this event is not the mere fact of its occurrence, as these 'coordination' meetings have been a regular feature of RSS–BJP relations for some time (dating back to the 1998–2004 Vajpayee-era coalition government). Rather, what lent this meeting its singular significance was the confluence of three unprecedented factors: the unusually wide spectrum of often-contentious policy issues that were included in the discussions, the organizers' willingness to publicize these meetings, and the differences of opinion on display, both among the RSS's various affiliates (collectively referred to as the *sangh parivar*—or 'RSS family') and between them and the government proper. Interlocutors from the 'family' tell us that compared to the Vajpayee government, the Modi government has shown a greater willingness to discuss the policy concerns of affiliates.[2] The breadth and intensity of the discussions reflected a significant shift from the RSS's earlier reliance on making a policy impact through individuals who had undergone a training programme it referred to as 'character-building'.[3] This programme envisioned training thousands of young men who, endowed with the discipline and ideology taught in the RSS, would on their own play a significant role in shaping the new India. At the apex of this system is the full-time worker (*pracharak*) who has typically participated at the local daily meetings for several years, attended the three-year officer-training courses and worked as an intern before entering the ranks. (See Appendix V for RSS organization.) In 2017, there were about 6000 pracharaks and they play a key role in the parivar or family. There are thirty-six affiliates designated as full affiliates (see Appendix II) and well over a hundred more that are either their subsidiaries or, for a variety of reasons, not yet designated as affiliates. Almost all the affiliates have pracharaks at their most senior administrative positions. They work among a wide variety of groups that include India's ruling party, BJP, its largest university student group, the Akhil Bharatiya Vidyarthi Parishad (ABVP) and its largest trade union, the Bharatiya Mazdoor Sangh (BMS), as well as among farmers, journalists, entrepreneurs, health workers, elementary and high school teachers and so on. The top levels of the RSS itself are similarly drawn from their ranks. But, especially with the increasingly complex policy activism and the expanded breadth of their activities, the role of householders[4] in the affiliates has grown. The role of pracharaks has also changed somewhat. They focus on organizational issues, especially since householders cannot devote the time to travel, and on interfacing with ministers.

This study builds on our earlier book almost three decades ago on the RSS. We decided to write another study because of the significant changes in the RSS, especially the growing importance of the affiliates as its messengers of Hindutva. The growth of the 'family' coincides with and may be related to the social and economic changes in India that followed the introduction of economic reforms in the early 1990s. The socio-economic changes have both transformed the RSS and led to its increased popularity in the Indian social milieu. Yet another reason to revisit the topic is the political surge of the BJP, which seems to have replaced the long-dominant Congress party as the pre-eminent political force in the country. To understand India therefore requires an understanding of the RSS.

We decided to analyse the subject for this project in a very different way from the first book. We adopted the case-study approach and selected nine issues which illustrate the decision-making of the RSS and its affiliates. We decided to turn the analytical searchlight on how it handled several different challenges on the assumption that multiple probes of RSS decision-making would provide a rounded picture of the RSS 'family'.[5] Utilizing the case-study method, we focus on a few 'how' and 'why' questions:

1. Why has the RSS increasingly relied on the affiliates to convey its message?
2. How does the RSS manage the links between itself and its affiliates, particularly with its political affiliate?
3. Why has the RSS 'family', despite different policy perspectives among its constituents, been able to stay together?
4. How has the growing social inclusiveness of the sangh parivar shaped its perception of democracy, secularism and Hindutva?

The RSS since the early 1990s has grown into one of the world's largest non-government associations, with an estimated 1.5–2 million regular participants in its nearly 57,000 local daily meetings (referred to as *shakhas*), 14,000 weekly shakhas and 7000 monthly shakhas, taking place across 36,293 different locations nationwide as of 2016.[6] In addition, there are some 6 million alumni and affiliate volunteers.[7] The number of daily shakhas (see Appendix III) has grown at an unprecedented rate in 2015 and 2016, expanding from 51,332 daily in March 2015 to almost 57,000 a year later.[8] The RSS in addition has about 6000 full-time workers (pracharaks), about one half of whom forms the bureaucratic framework of the organization, with the other half on loan to affiliated organizations.[9] The daily shakhas form the structural foundation of the RSS, as it is there that the sangh aims to foster and inculcate its ideology of Hindutva—a brotherhood above caste, class and regional identities.

The RSS was founded in 1925 by Dr Keshav Baliram Hedgewar—a Telugu Brahmin medical doctor from the central Indian city of Nagpur—who believed that the deep social divisions among the Hindus of India were responsible for what he considered a thousand years of foreign domination on the subcontinent.[10] What a truly independent India required, he felt, was a system of training (referred to by the RSS as 'character-building' or *'chaaritya nirman'*, to use the Sanskrit term favoured by the organization) that would create a cadre of men who would unify a highly pluralistic country, using their own perfected behaviour as a model for other Indians. Independence in 1947, however, did not bring about the India imagined by the RSS's founders. The subcontinent was divided by the British into a Hindu-majority India and a Muslim-majority Pakistan, with the RSS left powerless to prevent this partition. Moreover, they believed that the new Indian Prime Minister Jawaharlal Nehru's Fabian socialist views on the central role of the state in development were alien to Indian traditions. Perhaps the ultimate blow to the utopian ambitions of the RSS was the national ban placed on it on 4 February 1948, driven by suspicion of RSS involvement in the assassination of Mahatma Gandhi; Gandhi's killer, Nathuram Godse, was a former RSS member.[11] This ban resulted in the virtual exclusion of RSS members from the ruling Congress party and its various affiliated organizations.[12]

Following the lifting of this ban on 11 July 1949—for lack of evidence—the RSS found itself in a much-weakened condition, and for many Indians, it was a pariah organization to be avoided at all costs. The social sanctions of associating with the RSS dissuaded many potential sympathizers from being involved. Phoenix-like, it gradually revived in the 1960s and established dozens of affiliated groups that came to penetrate virtually all areas of Indian society. It has since grown rapidly, especially from the early 1990s onwards. The largest political party in the Indian Parliament, the BJP, is the political affiliate of the RSS, and Prime Minister Modi began his public-service career as a full-time RSS worker. Both the largest students' group and the largest trade union in India are RSS affiliates, as are dozens of other organizations across the country.

At the time of our earlier study of the RSS in the late 1980s, the organization was in the initial stages of a fundamental shift away from its previously exclusive focus on 'character-building', a training system that takes place mainly in the daily shakhas of its local branches, to increasing reliance on affiliates to spread its message. It was sufficiently self-confident to provide a substantial number of its pracharaks to those affiliates which it saw as critical for mobilizing support among important groups, especially the Akhil Bharatiya Vanvasi Kalyan Ashram (ABVKA) for tribals, the Vishva Hindu Parishad (VHP) for the Hindu religious establishment, and the Bharatiya Jana Sangh (BJS) for politics.[13] The RSS was at that time establishing new ways to sustain the participation of its traditional membership, especially college students and professionals, and the affiliates provided an avenue for activity to spread its message.[14] They were also beginning to strengthen an RSS presence in rural India, where previously it had only been weakly represented. There were then only a few affiliated organizations, referred to collectively as the 'family' (sangh parivar).[15] The RSS's decision in the early 1950s to support the BJS was prompted by the demands of activist RSS members who desired a political vehicle through which their Hindu nationalist views could be expressed nationwide. Another motive was to protect the RSS from restrictions or repression, such as the aforementioned ban of 1948–49. That ban had a devastating impact on the RSS, whose members were already demoralized by the partition of India which flew in the face of their central goal of a territorially unified India (referred to in Hindi as *Akhand Bharat*).

Despite the debate within the RSS over its mission in an independent India, those pracharaks who remained tended to support the efforts of Madhav S. Golwalkar (1940–73) to sustain the shakha system and its accompanying 'character-building' programmes, with no significant changes in the organization's core mission. According to RSS biographer C.P. Bhishikar, Golwalkar believed that as a relative newcomer to the RSS (he had been a full-time worker for only four years before taking charge in 1940), it was his duty to preserve the organization as he had received it—and to hand it over virtually unchanged to his successor, Madhukar D. Deoras (1973–94), one of the earliest pracharaks trained by Hedgewar.[16] Deoras, for his part, put the RSS on a much more intense activist path in such varied arenas as education, tribal uplift, rural development and social service NGOs. Deoras's enthusiasm for greater activism was a recognition of the fact that the RSS's Brahmanical conception of self-improvement through training did not appeal to India's non-elite. He also opened the RSS to Muslim and Christian participation.

During and after the tenure of Deoras, the RSS's range of service projects, mostly in areas of health and education and largely managed by the affiliates, expanded at a rapid pace (from 5000 service projects in 1989 to ten times that number in 1998, approximately 1,40,000 in 2012,[17] and an estimated 1,65,000 in 2015[18]). Deoras assigned RSS pracharaks to work exclusively for service activities. Addressing journalists after touring the tribal belt of his native Maharashtra state, Deoras announced that 'two all-Bharat and 45–48 provincial karyakartas shall exclusively bear responsibility of seva work'.[19] While RSS *swayamsevaks* had previously been involved in ad hoc relief efforts after natural disasters, Deoras systemized the RSS's service activities. There has also been a simultaneous shift away from the RSS's formerly cautious approach to the public policy process to an active interest in it, partly due to the expansion of its affiliates that address issues like education (Vidya Bharati) and foreign direct investment (Swadeshi Jagran Manch [SJM]), both directly impacted by government policy. A related change that was demonstrated in the 2015 RSS–BJP conclave noted above is that the RSS, formerly averse to publicity, is now much more transparent about its interest in policy issues and the policy process.[20] Its most senior figures have told us that this greater transparency reflects a growing sense of self-confidence, which in turn stems from their perception that they are now part of India's political and cultural mainstream.[21]

This change in the RSS, we contend, is related to the major social and economic upheavals that have taken place in the country over the past two decades. In our earlier work, we argued that it was the RSS's intensive training system that produced a cadre of adherents dedicated to Hindu nationalism and (perhaps more importantly for the sangh as a whole) to each other. Based on extensive interviews with cadre members in three different regions of India, our data at that time suggested that 'RSS socialization had a greater effect on the cadre's ideological orientation than such socioeconomic variables as age, income, caste, occupation.'[22] Our current research indicates the continuing importance of the RSS experience in shaping ideological orientations and cohesion among its members. But of increasing importance in shaping opinion, and a potential source of internal tension, is the greater social and regional diversity that has come with the rapid expansion of the RSS and its affiliates since the early 1990s. Interviews suggest a growing variance between the views of pracharaks from north and south India on social issues, such as gender norms or LGBT rights.[23]

The India of the twenty-first century is radically different from the India of the past and that has had an impact on the RSS, on both its membership and its policy orientation. In the wake of the fiscal reforms of the early 1990s, the national economy had expanded, in real terms, over 400 per cent.[24] Along with that, according to the World Bank, the urbanization rate almost doubled between 1960 and 2015: from 18 per cent in 1960 to 26 per cent in 1990 to 33 per cent in 2015.[25] The McKinsey Institute reports that the middle class in India has grown from 14 per cent in 2005 to 29 per cent in 2015, and estimates it will grow further still, all the way to 44 per cent in 2025.[26] Access to cell phones has increased phenomenally and, more recently, access to the Internet has exploded as well. There are (in 2018), according to the Telecom Regulatory Authority of India (TRAI), over 1.1 billion cell phone subscribers across the country.[27] The Internet and Mobile Association of India (IAMAI), estimates that almost 500 million will access the Internet from their mobile phones by mid-2018.[28] The rapid adoption of mobile phones and the enhanced use of the Internet undermine traditional social hierarchies and provide individuals and groups an autonomy that is socially disrupting. Ronald Inglehart, building on Max Weber's assertion that secularization and bureaucratization are among the most important consequences of modernization, argues that such key variables as industrialization, urbanization and literacy produce predictable changes in the way people think about themselves and their governments.[29] India's recent and rapid social and economic development, we propose, is positively related to the growth in the number of RSS shakhas, as well as increasing participation rates in the various affiliates. We argued in our earlier study that the bonds of community and family advocated by the RSS 'have a salience to those who feel rootless', and this is especially true in the case of 'developing countries where new economic and administrative systems have rapidly undermined institutions and moral certitudes which traditionally defined a person's social function and relationship to authority'.[30] This thesis, we think, can still explain the appeal of the RSS and its affiliated organizations in a socially complex and diverse country undergoing rapid societal and economic changes. Amidst the diversity of India—with its dozens of languages and associated cultures, countless permutations of the hierarchical Hindu caste system and vast economic gulfs—the proliferation of affiliates provides many different avenues by which to mobilize support for the Hindutva message of unity among those seeking stability in an inherently tumultuous environment. Erik H. Erikson, in his analysis of Martin Luther's attack against the corruption and improprieties of the sixteenth-century Roman Catholic Church, argues that Luther's dramatic actions were rooted in his 'crisis of identity' as he searched for his 'real self', a search that was triggered by the rapid social and technological changes of his age. His reformation of the church succeeded in mobilizing significant support precisely because his response to his personal 'crisis' mirrored the experiences of many others of his time.[31] The RSS and its affiliates have also sought to provide messages that appeal to those searching for a new identity in a new world. These organizations conceive of themselves as the messengers of dharma, the Hindu ideal of duty and righteous conduct. They act, to borrow a phrase from David D. Laitin, as cultural entrepreneurs who seek 'buyers' for their message.[32] The recent successes of the BJP may also provide an explanation for the growing appeal of the RSS and its affiliates. Thomas Schelling's analysis of what he terms as 'tips' and 'cascades'—open political support or involvement triggered by the belief that those around you think and act similarly—may account for at least some of the growth of the RSS that has occurred over the past three decades, as the BJP has become increasingly successful at the state and national levels.[33] Leaders in the 'family' certainly believe that the 'normalization' of the RSS has something to do with the political victories of the BJP, which could explain their firm support for the party, despite key differences on several significant policies (which we will discuss later). 'Cascading' might also account for the public's acceptance—especially outside the Hindi-speaking heartland where the RSS has its core support base—of an idealized Hindu homeland that incorporates considerable cultural variety in its nationalistic milieu. Reflecting its current willingness to accept this diversity, the RSS has virtually abandoned efforts to make Hindi the sole national language, reflecting popular support for English in the Dravidian-speaking south and in the Northeast. The RSS's evolution, especially as it sought to expand outside the 'Hindi-Hindu-Hindustan' culture of north India, has included the shedding of many age-old verities. Manmohan Vaidya, the former RSS spokesperson, has stated that the organization was not interested in enforcing dietary practices and that those who consume beef can become its members.[34] Sunil Deodhar, RSS pracharak and the BJP's strategist for the 2018 Assembly elections in the north-eastern state of Tripura, declared that the BJP has no intention of imposing a cow-slaughter ban in states where beef consumption is not a cultural taboo.[35] These shifts are only a few among the many—some of which we will describe in our case studies—that demonstrate the willingness of some senior figures to reshape the sangh, ideologically and organizationally, to win mass appeal in a changing India. The shifts also represented increased divergence of views among the sangh parivar cadre—a consequence of rapid growth and the changing social composition of its membership.

From the perspective of the RSS, the most damaging threat to India's national integrity since independence in 1947 had been efforts by the Congress leadership to impose what RSS ideologists consider a radical form of Western enlightenment, one that saw tradition as an impediment to progress and the state as the most effective agency of that progression. RSS writers argue that change should come primarily from below, and that most significant transitions are effected by private rather than public endeavour. Yet, the organization's enthusiastic support of the BJP in recent elections and their efforts to gain an official platform for the parivar's views underscore that the RSS, if only implicitly, also views the state as vital to shaping a stable society. As Dattatreya Hosabale, the RSS's joint general secretary, asserted, 'We [the RSS] would want the BJP to win all the state elections because only then can significant social, political and cultural changes take place in this country . . . The 2014 election victory should be seen as the starting point of a long term mission.'[36] While the sangh parivar has become something similar to the long-dominant Congress (with a left, centre and right as it accommodates groups seeking to influence the policy process), the RSS continues to view politics as only one of several factors shaping society, and not necessarily the most important one. Several of our case studies analyse this divergence between the RSS and the BJP regarding the role of the state as the arbiter of social values and development.

RSS writers repeatedly point out that they have a vision for an India that operates contrary to such Western-inspired models as capitalism and communism—such systems only serve, they say, to weaken respect for traditional cultural values, and thus undermine the very integrity of the Indian state.[37] We suspect that the adamant opposition to the RSS from a large part of India's intellectual left wing may have something to do with the RSS's central argument that ethno-nationalism plays a far more important role in shaping Indian society than does the notion of economic class struggle. RSS chief Mohan Bhagwat's 30 September 2017 Vijayadashami speech—his most important annual policy statement of the year—took a swipe at Western 'isms' among Indian intellectuals that focus attention on what he considers the wrong issues. In the context of ethno-nationalism, the RSS's goal is a harmonious society that is assimilationist, but also rejects both special cultural privileges for minorities and the adoption of Western cultural values.[38] One can practise any religion, it argues, as long as worship is done within the framework of cultural Hinduism and with respect for national traditions, broad categories that we will show involve a self-conscious effort to assimilate aspects of local traditions into the larger framework of Hindu culture. On the frontiers of Hinduism, especially in India's Northeast, the RSS has tried to assimilate local tribal culture into mainstream Hinduism, often by designating local deities as incarnations of popular Hindu gods.[39] Since the late 1970s, the RSS has opened its doors to Muslim and Christian participants in the shakhas and within the affiliates, but accepts them only on its own terms. The RSS has also initiated service activities as a means of outreach to minority communities in India's Northeast.[40]

The RSS and the ideologues of the sangh parivar have in the past concentrated their writing on identity issues, analysing what makes Hindus *similar* to each other on the one hand, and different from other groups on the other.[41] This approach required enumerating and categorizing those common features which bind Hindus together as a community, quite a challenge in a country as socially and economically diverse as India. This search for similarity compelled the traditionally high-caste RSS leadership to openly appeal to groups at the lower end of the traditional caste spectrum through pan-Hindu campaigns for the construction of the proposed Ram Janmabhoomi (a temple at the site believed to be the place where Lord Ram took human form) at Ayodhya in the state of Uttar Pradesh. However, these pan-Hindu appeals were often phrased in high-caste terms, the language too elitist to appeal to many non–high-caste Hindus, who comprise a majority of the population and who have become increasingly politicized over the past three decades. Led by the BJP's effort to mobilize votes, the parivar in the 1990s began to incorporate what Christophe Jaffrelot refers to as 'social engineering' (positive discrimination for non–high-caste Hindus) into their earlier model of 'sanskritization' (that is, the emulation of high-caste behaviour) aimed at achieving the social assimilation of all Hindu groups.[42]

We argue that an additional tactic has recently been added to get around the dilemma of backing strategies that seem to have a high-caste bias. That new element is economic growth, which creates jobs and benefits all groups—and, by implication, enhances social unity in an increasingly politicized society. Modi, as chief minister of Gujarat, vigorously advocated economic growth as the core policy of his administration, and thus virtually abandoned the classic RSS pan-Hindu approach, with its single-minded focus on identity. This was much to the chagrin of Gujarat's more hard-line ideologues, especially the VHP. He also pushed this economic development line in his successful 2014 election campaign. In an interview with us, in fact, Modi went so far as to imply that economic development was now a central element of Hindutva.[43] Social solidarity is a key component of the RSS's vision, which Prime Minister Modi has internalized. While the RSS rejects Marxism as culturally alien, it prefers an egalitarian and less hierarchical society. Improving India's creaky welfare state is a key part of the Modi government's agenda. Even while pursuing liberal economic reforms, the Modi government has focused on both improving the efficiency of India's safety net through Aadhaar-linked[44] direct cash transfers and expanding the welfare state through new programmes, such as free cooking-gas cylinders and subsidized power to the poor, and proposed something close to a universal health system. The virtue of this new orientation on economic development and more efficient welfare delivery is that it reduces the criticism that accompanied the previous 'social engineering' and 'sanskritization' strategies, while still keeping intact the RSS's traditional call for social unity; simultaneously, by spurring an improvement in living standards and fostering social solidarity, it diminishes the nationalist impulse to distinguish the 'us' from the 'other' (which all too often is defined as Muslims and Christians, who together form some 17 per cent of the population). As Prime Minister Modi has noted frequently, the provision of *bijli* (electricity), *sadak* (roads) and *paani* (water) is non-discriminatory.

By diminishing the economic salience of an implicitly xenophobic dichotomy (for example, Hindus vs Muslims) in the population, it is easier for the various members of the parivar to cooperate with traditionally 'otherized' groups, an especially important consideration for the BJP as it seeks regional electoral allies that rely on Muslim and Christian support. Some observers note that the BJP's success in getting votes from Muslim women is owed to the government's campaign against instant divorce by decree (triple talaq) and the provision of free cooking-gas cylinders.[45] Economic development also provides the party with an argument to rein in the often-embarrassing demands of the hard-line Hindutva fringe that relies on identity politics to justify its occasionally outrageous behaviour towards those it considers the 'other'. Such identity politics in a plural society carries the potential to complicate economic development and job creation. Further, this reliance on economic development gives the BJP, the RSS and other members of the 'family' a better opportunity to counter those major opponents who rely on identity politics for votes, such as the many regional and caste parties that have proliferated over the past three decades, and even some elements of the Congress party.[46] However, it is not at all assured that economic liberalism will predominate within the parivar, as there are many activists and intellectuals who subscribe to and advocate for their own version of the Hindu identity. A pan-Hindu identity strategy as well as economic nationalism have been employed in political campaigns, and some groups, like the VHP, still focus almost exclusively on pan-Hindu identity issues. However, as we will try to show in our chapter on Hindutva, Hindu identity has so many interpretations—and those interpretations themselves are often so amorphous—that it may not provide a useful core of ideas around which to rally.

A major interest of ours in this study is to discover how the rapid expansion of the RSS and its affiliates over the past twenty-five years has affected the ways in which it operates and presents itself to the nation. Related to this is the question of what mechanisms it has in place to reconcile the oft-conflicting interests of its increasingly diverse 'family'.

We advance a set of propositions to explain RSS growth and the impact of that growth on its ideology and decision-making:

(1) The expanding appeal of the RSS may be related to a homogenizing of society that has accompanied modernization, as well as a more inclusive ideological message.

(2) While the RSS's success in establishing a vast organizational network appealing to often-conflicting interest groups has put a significant strain on the cohesion of the parivar, the RSS has worked out a mediation strategy that has maintained cooperation among them. In short, none of its 'children' have yet truly seceded from the 'family'.

(3) The relative autonomy of these organizations—and an emphasis on consensus among the members of the parivar—has so far abetted the expression of a wide range of ideological and social opinions without tearing the parivar apart.

(4) Perhaps a major factor holding this complex set of organizations together is the intensive socialization provided by the RSS in its 'character-building' process, which includes attending RSS training camps and participating in a wide range of service activities. Full-time RSS workers (pracharaks) at the administrative helm of the organization and its affiliates provide the glue that keeps the parivar together.

Our goal is to test these propositions by using a case-study approach to analyse how a much-expanded RSS has handled a number of recent challenges. In terms of presentation, the first five chapters are a general overview of the RSS over the past three decades. The first chapter analyses the growing involvement of the parivar in the public policy debate. The second is a study of RSS-affiliated groups and how they have nudged the RSS towards an interest in influencing public policy because many of the affiliates are directly affected by public policy. The third is a study of the RSS overseas and the long-distance nationalism that the RSS encourages among the overseas diaspora, with a focus on the United States, home to the largest and wealthiest element of the diaspora. The fourth is an analysis of the parivar's focus on education and the challenges it faces in shaping an educational philosophy relevant to the many changes taking place in India. The fifth chapter examines the shifting conceptions and definitions of Hinduism within the parivar. Following these general chapters is a set of nine case studies, each of which looks at how and why the RSS addresses a significant issue. We have chosen the case-study method to shine a spotlight on the RSS from different angles on the assumption that the more probes you have, the more rounded a picture of the organization you will get. The first two case studies (chapters six and seven) analyse the RSS approach to Muslims as a people and Islam as a religion, with a focus on the internal debate over this outreach effort. Chapter Six is a study of the RSS-inspired quasi-affiliate, the Muslim Rashtriya Manch (MRM), which was created to mobilize Muslim support for Hindu nationalism. Chapter Seven looks at the RSS's acceptance of the coalition government in the state of Jammu and Kashmir between the BJP and a party that draws its support almost exclusively from the state's Muslim majority. This decision forced the sangh parivar to broaden its definition of Hindu to mean all those who reside in the state, largely devoid of a conventional religious context. The following two chapters focus on economic issues. Chapter Eight studies the SJM, an RSS affiliate that has had an often-contentious relationship with the Modi government over its progressive liberalizing and globalizing of the Indian economy. Chapter Nine evaluates the RSS's cautious response to the border tensions with China so as not to undermine the Modi government's important economic ties to China. The next three chapters analyse the RSS's manoeuvring between the pious and the profane to maintain a balance among various affiliates that take somewhat different stands on conversion (Chapter Ten), cow protection (Chapter Eleven) and a Ram Temple (referred to as the Ram Janmabhoomi—or birth site of Lord Ram) in the holy city of Ayodhya that would be built on land contested by Muslim and Hindu groups (Chapter Twelve). The final two case studies address what are basically issues of political process. Chapter Thirteen delves into a rare instance of an internal rebellion within the RSS in Goa due to deep differences in the state's sangh parivar over the Goa BJP government's language policy. Chapter Fourteen considers the nature and context of RSS involvement in the elections and personnel management of its political affiliate, the BJP, with a focus on the state of Bihar. The RSS's involvement in the Bihar state election campaign was rooted in the weak BJP party organization in that state, while its intervention in the political affairs of the BJP, such as through selection of party office-bearers and candidates, is extensive in times of a leadership vacuum in the BJP.

Running through all these issues is the search for compromise so that a consensus can emerge. This affirms a conclusion from our earlier study that the RSS is a very cautious group that slowly evolves, a generalization that one could make about India itself. The RSS has never been revolutionary and is not likely to be so any time soon. Its goal is social harmony and cultural assimilation. However, it does change and it is this change that prompted us to take another look at the RSS and its family.

We would like to make special mention of the late Lloyd I. Rudolph and Susanne H. Rudolph, whose many books on India and whose advice provided us a theoretical context for our original work and this one as well. On their advice, we adopted the case-study approach for this book. We also thank Gautam Mehta who was a reliable source of information, analysis and constructive criticism. Gautam, in addition, did field work for us on three case studies: 'Bihar Elections, 2015' (Chapter Fourteen), 'A Debate on Economic Self-Sufficiency' (Chapter Eight) and 'A Ram Temple in Ayodhya' (Chapter Twelve). We very much appreciate the statistical work done by our other research assistant, Sharad Sharma. We want to thank Professor Philip Oldenburg for reading the complete manuscript and giving us advice on how to improve it. We also appreciate several other scholars who read parts of the draft: Partha Ghosh, Allison Burland and Dargesh Kasbekar.

Finally, we want to thank Erik Andersen for reading and editing the text to ensure that it makes sense to a non-specialist of India.

ONE

A Growing Involvement in the Policy Process

When asking the senior RSS leadership in the summer of 2015 about the organization's major changes since our previous book was published some three decades ago, we usually received one of four answers—all of which noted a greater interest in public policy and the political decision-making process. Those we questioned were, however, adamant that the RSS is not a political organization, and that its primary focus—as it was when we did our first study—remains its schedule of 'character-building' programmes.[1] The first change noted by almost everyone is that the RSS is no longer a political pariah perpetually operating under the threat of another ban; thus, it is more willing to speak out and be transparent. Second is the rapid growth of affiliated groups, penetrating almost all areas of society. Third, and related, is that the spread of these affiliates into areas directly impacted by public policy has prompted the RSS to take an interest in influencing government decision-making. This development, they admitted, presents the RSS with the growing challenge of coordinating the many parts of the ever-expanding parivar, whose members have different and often-competing interests. The fourth change is the expansion of the RSS's work to social groups among which they were previously weakly represented, such as farmers, tribals and low-caste Hindus, especially Dalits; this development in particular has altered not only the demographics of

1

the RSS, but also its policy face. What seems most interesting about the changes identified is the manner in which they reflect the RSS's commitment to and interest in the national political process.

Two events of the past few years underscore this reinvigorated political interest. The first was Bhagwat's 30 September 2017 Vijayadashami speech, an annual statement that traditionally lays out the goals and priorities of the RSS for the following year and is usually delivered in only the most general of terms.[2] This address, however, differed in the specificity of its policy proposals. The second was the RSS's decision to throw its full weight behind the BJP's 2013–14 parliamentary campaign and, consequently, behind Modi's candidacy for prime minister.

The 2017 Vijayadashami speech stands out as both a critique of the Modi government's policies and a statement about India's developmental priorities. Given the close relationship between Bhagwat and Modi, the Indian press minutely analysed this document for clues about the issues the RSS was pressing the government to adopt.[3] Reflected in the speech are such traditional RSS values as support for small business owners and the small-scale farmer, viewed as major providers of jobs and as the prime upholders of conventional morality and the family unit, which the RSS considers the bedrock of Indian society. Bhagwat's advocacy of public policies that strengthen families and the independent farmer reflects RSS efforts to reprioritize these institutions through public programmes. His emphasis on the importance of small industries, tradesmen and the self-employed may have been informed by criticism from such groups—historically the cornerstone of the RSS's support base—regarding the hardships created by the Goods and Services Tax (GST), introduced with the intention to make India a unified common market, as well as demonetization. The RSS weighing in on this issue may have had some influence on the significant revisions to the tax made by the GST Council in November 2017.[4] Bhagwat also devoted a large part of his address to the plight of Indian farmers: he suggested the adoption of a minimum support price which would guarantee farmers the money to support a family and to finance their next year of farming, as well as better implementation of existing schemes like crop insurance, soil testing and e-marketing. He also discussed the environmental advantages of organic farming, water management and cow-based animal husbandry. Bhagwat framed the issue of cow protection as both a cultural and an economic matter, and called for tough state action against vigilantism arising from the controversy. He not-so-subtly criticized both the central and state governments for relying on economic advisers committed to 'economic "isms"' that are divorced from ground realities and national traditions, advocating instead a buy-in-India programme aimed at economic self-sufficiency (swadeshi). Towards the beginning of the speech, he argued that it was a 'prerequisite that our intellectuals and thinkers get rid of the ill-effects of the colonial thought and mindset'. This resembles the Chinese government's official advice that academics take into consideration the unique Chinese characteristics of history and the social sciences.

A senior BJP figure told us that on only two occasions has the RSS fully engaged in parliamentary elections: once in 1977 for the Janata Party and then again in 2014 for the BJP.[5] This does not mean that the RSS has not been involved in other elections, but those two elections were the only ones in which it permitted its pracharaks and other high-level officials to take part in the campaigns. In both instances, there was a fear that the RSS's programme of Hindu unity could suffer a severe setback if the Congress retained power. The RSS, in the first instance, feared that the Congress, having banned the organization and imposed the Emergency just two years earlier—during which Indira Gandhi virtually suspended the democratic process and imprisoned many of her opponents[6]—would never allow the RSS to officially reform.[7] During this time, the outlawed RSS under Madhukar D. Deoras took the unprecedented political step of actively involving itself in the Opposition movement.[8] It organized, for example, a two-month national protest, starting mid-November 1975 and involving some 1,50,000 people, of whom the RSS estimates some 1,00,000 were its own members and sympathizers.[9] When Prime Minister Gandhi unexpectedly called for fresh elections on 18 January 1977, the RSS leadership went all out to defeat her. The Janata Party prevailed over the Congress in those elections, and its cabinet included three Jana Sangh members, all of them swayamsevaks. The Congress won only 154 of 542 contested seats, its poorest showing until then.[10]

In the second instance in 2014, the RSS feared that another Congress victory, the third in a row, would severely undermine any hope of implementing a Hindutva agenda. Modi, the three-time chief minister of Gujarat and a former RSS pracharak, seemed to possess what the swayamsevaks were seeking in a prospective prime minister: a forceful and decisive leader with Hindutva credentials to inspire and unify a fractious BJP, while also appealing to undecided and moderate voters. Modi had by then portrayed himself skilfully in the national consciousness as a strong decision maker who, based on his long tenure at the head of one of India's fastest-growing states, could be relied upon to stimulate economic growth and jobs. Modi's image as a strong leader appealed to those who were disenchanted with the perceived undermining of the authority of the prime minister. Many swayamsevaks also sympathetically viewed him as a victim of a witch-hunt at home and abroad regarding the 2002 Gujarat anti-Muslim riots, for which he was pulled up on charges that India's Supreme Court eventually rejected for lack of evidence.[11] Alarmed by the prospect of the Congress government imposing restrictions on their activities due to charges of Hindu terrorism, the RSS leadership, in the aftermath of the BJP's loss in the 2009 elections, decided to fully invest in defeating the ruling party in 2014. In an effort to maintain its apolitical reputation in the process, the RSS established a parallel national booth-level agency to encourage voter turnout.[12]

The tale of how the RSS leadership came to support Modi as the potential prime minister is more complex than it may seem, especially given the lukewarm attitude towards him within the Gujarat RSS. The RSS leaders, in their tour of the nation following the disappointing 2009 elections, found that there was overwhelming support from the local cadres for Modi to become the next prime minister if the BJP received a parliamentary majority. Reflecting this support, the BJP Parliamentary Board on 10 September 2013 unanimously selected Modi to head the campaign; two days later

Rajnath Singh, then president of the BJP, announced that Modi would be the prime minister if the BJP won. Despite this vote of confidence, there were some reservations in both the BJP and the RSS about Modi's candidacy. In a unique move, the RSS chief informed BJP leader L.K. Advani—who had resigned from all party posts in protest over Modi's selection—of the cadres' opinions, and further told him that the RSS leadership agreed with them. Advani withdrew his resignation and went on to contest a seat in Gujarat. We were informed that the RSS does not anticipate repeating this level of support for the BJP in the years to come; the RSS expects its affiliates, including the BJP, to train its own workers, and the BJP has already begun training booth-level workers.[13]

Our earlier book came out in the late 1980s, just as the RSS was beginning to transition to a more politically active orientation, addressing a far wider range of issues than before, with a more inclusive definition of Hindutva. Its second chief executive (*sarsanghchalak*), Golwalkar, during his thirty-three-year term had kept the organization largely aloof from the political process, and had been criticized widely within the RSS for his apolitical agenda.[14] He also kept the organization tied to an elitist high-caste perception of Hindutva, especially with his focus on individual perfection through the 'character-building' process. Yet, despite dissension regarding his philosophies, there was never a serious internal challenge to Golwalkar and his leadership. We have been told by senior RSS figures that mounting either an internal rebellion or establishing a breakaway group would mean separating from those remaining in the mainstream RSS, and thus isolation from any kind of nationalist support network. There nonetheless have been some minor dissident groups, mainly in Maharashtra, which tried to form parallel organizations, but their short-lived efforts failed to build a support base.[15]

Among those most critical of Golwalkar's hands-off approach to the political process was his hand-picked successor, Madhukar D. Deoras (generally referred to as Balasaheb Deoras), RSS chief for over two decades, and his brother Muralidhar D. Deoras (generally referred to as Bhaurao Deoras). Both were early recruits of RSS founder Hedgewar, and were among the first full-time workers.[16]

Bhaurao Deoras was as politically inclined as his more accomplished brother, and recused himself from RSS activities in the 1950s as a protest against Golwalkar. The most senior figures of the BJS (Atal Behari Vajpayee, Advani, Deendayal Upadhyaya and others), were initiated into politics by Bhaurao, and Balasaheb relied on his brother to push a more activist agenda, appointing him assistant general secretary with special responsibility for the political, student, public service and labour affiliates, especially in the field of education. Anticipating the expansion and mobilization that would characterize his tenure, Balasaheb supported the formation of the Vidya Bharati, the national coordination body of RSS-affiliated schools that teach from the elementary level to college. Vidya Bharati now claims that it is the largest non-government scholastic system in India.[17]

Deoras was in some ways an unusual choice to head the RSS.[18] Unlike Golwalkar, he was neither spiritually nor philosophically inclined. He was foremost an organizer, with a keen interest in making the RSS more relevant in an India undergoing rapid social and economic change. Yet Golwalkar appointed him *sarkaryavah* (general secretary) in 1965, just as the RSS began to pivot towards a more activist orientation. Senior RSS figures in Nagpur have told us that Golwalkar recognized that Deoras's policy activism was suited to the times and so, after consulting with other senior figures, chose him to be the next sarsanghchalak. There was no open resistance to this choice, even from the more conservative elements within the RSS leadership. This may be due in part to the pervasive view within the organization that the incumbent sarsanghchalak has sole discretion regarding his succession.

Two occasions offered Deoras a chance to lend the RSS a more activist outlook. The first was in May 1974 (a year after he took over); he made waves by publicly criticizing the caste system—especially the concept of untouchability—as one of the significant factors that had kept Hindus divided since the arrival of the Islamic rule.[19] He argued that religious texts which appear to justify institutional caste hierarchies had to be re-evaluated with the goal of Hindu consolidation in mind, a view that is included in Upadhyaya's *Integral Humanism* (considered by the RSS to be a central catechism of its ideology). It was in this speech that Deoras famously argued, 'If untouchability is not a sin, then there is no sin in the world,'[20] and it is regarded by insiders as the most important speech in the sangh's history. Deoras's 1974 speech was effectively an exhortation that the RSS take a more activist stand on significant social problems. The current sarsanghchalak, Bhagwat, reinforced the point, stating:

> Special efforts were made to establish contact with different social groups and bring them to RSS Shakha activity; especially the social groups that were psychologically uncomfortable in calling themselves as Hindus due to discriminatory practices were focussed on.[21]

The current RSS general secretary, Suresh 'Bhaiyyaji' Joshi, told us that this speech was a turning point in the RSS, and was directly responsible for the activism that was to gain momentum in the 1990s.[22]

The second occasion was Indira Gandhi's Emergency (1975–77). One of the prime minister's first acts during this period was to ban the RSS (for the second time since Independence) and to arrest most of its senior leadership, including Deoras.[23] This act inadvertently gave the RSS and the sangh parivar a chance to regain the sympathy (and support) it had lost in the wake of Mahatma Gandhi's assassination in early 1948. During the ban, the RSS established a communications network that enabled underground cadres to stay in contact with each other; it also liaised with overseas RSS chapters and distributed anti-Emergency literature.

Despite this renewed popularity, the newly formed Janata Party (and the government it led) collapsed within a few years of its 1977 victory because of internal factionalism. The exit of the Jana Sangh element came in 1980, when the Janata Party leadership demanded that members drop their association with the RSS, fearing that the sangh could exert considerable influence on the ruling party and might even come to dominate it.[24]

Jana Sangh members withdrew from the Janata Party in short order, forming a new party, the BJP, with a far more activist orientation. This new party incorporated elements of its parent Janata Party, such as a commitment to Gandhian socialism and a statement of principles that included nationalism, national integration, democracy, positive secularism and value-based politics. Many swayamsevaks were displeased with this new non-Hindutva orientation, and were quick to inform the RSS leadership of their dissatisfaction.[25] Some of these dissatisfied swayamsevaks were even attracted to the soft Hindutva actions made by Prime Minister Indira Gandhi after she returned to power in 1980. This dissatisfaction may have contributed to the party's dismal performance in the 1984 parliamentary elections, when it won only two of 542 seats. The BJP, having thus failed to gain significant public support at the national or state levels in its initial years, moved away from such platforms as 'Gandhian socialism' and 'positive secularism', and instead turned towards its earlier ideological roots; this shift seemed to pay off in the 1989 parliamentary elections. While there were other factors aiding this political comeback—such as the charges of corruption against Rajiv Gandhi and declining support for the Congress through much of the country's Hindi-speaking heartland—the BJP's electoral success brought the wayward swayamsevaks back into the fold. The party in 1985 had accepted Upadhyaya's *Integral Humanism* as its official ideological gospel, thus sidelining the concept of Gandhian socialism that had upset many traditionalists.[26] Advani, considered to be more committed to Hindutva than Vajpayee, took over the party presidency in 1985. The VHP had by then become a potential resource for the BJP due to its success in mobilizing popular support across the Hindu caste spectrum for its temple marches in the 1980s. The BJP's parliamentary strength grew from the two seats (of 542) won in 1984 to eighty-five seats in the 1989 elections and 120 in 1991.[27] By 1989, the party's national executive, pursuing the pan-Hindu agenda of the larger parivar, passed a resolution supporting a Hindu temple dedicated to Lord Ram at a site in Ayodhya, then in the possession of a Muslim trust.[28] This site, acclaimed by some Hindus as the Ram Janmabhoomi—the location at which the god Vishnu was incarnated in human form as the mythological hero Ram—was to become a central actor in the RSS's fortunes. In the wake of the BJP resolution, Advani launched a Ram Rath Yatra (a Ram chariot procession) on 25 September 1990, from the ancient temple town of Somnath in Gujarat to Ayodhya in Uttar Pradesh. The RSS supported this march by providing volunteers and logistical assistance, a commitment that gave many swayamsevaks their first taste of political activism.[29] Advani's Ram Rath Yatra never made it to Ayodhya, however, as he was arrested on the orders of the Janata Dal chief minister of Bihar, Lalu Prasad Yadav, on the grounds that the march would trigger communal violence. Simultaneously, the Uttar Pradesh chief minister, Mulayam Singh Yadav, prohibited Ram Janmabhoomi volunteers from demonstrating at the disputed site, and resulting confrontations with the marchers led to several deaths. These deaths in turn led the RSS to adopt an unusually confrontational role with the authorities while it reached out to the caste spectrum in rural Uttar Pradesh, thus advancing its larger goals of building up a support base among rural Indians and the Other Backward Classes (OBC). The next year, the BJP won the Uttar Pradesh state elections with the assistance of RSS volunteers and thus began building a brand of RSS–BJP cooperation.

The success of this new strategy of pan-Hindu cooperation was made manifest by the BJP's string of electoral victories beginning in 1989. Corruption and economic hardships combined to bring various Opposition parties—led by the Janata Dal under V.P. Singh— together in the wake of the 1989 elections; the BJP, remembering the dual membership controversy that had plagued the Janata Party, supported this new coalition from without. Its relationship with the ruling coalition quickly soured, however, as Prime Minister Singh resurrected as a key public policy platform a report advocating a 27 per cent reservation of jobs for the so-called OBC. This attempt at class mobilization was a direct challenge to the efforts of the BJP (and the parivar generally) to build a pan-Hindu identity and, more specifically, to garner support among the backward classes that constituted some 40 per cent of the Hindu population. It was at this point that the BJP and the RSS came out in support of a Ram Temple in Ayodhya, and took a prominent role in organizing the Ram yatras. The BJP campaign manifesto in the 1991 parliamentary election campaign (in which the Congress defeated the incumbent Janata Dal coalition) was even entitled *Towards Ram Rajya*.[30] Again, the tack towards Hindutva paid electoral dividends, with the BJP increasing its parliamentary seats from eighty-five (with 11.36 per cent of the vote) in 1989 to 120 in 1991 (with some 20.11 per cent); just as importantly, it established a lucrative support base in the south for the first time.

The end of 1992 brought yet another ban (the third in forty years), as the BJP and VHP were indicted by the new Congress government under Narasimha Rao for their alleged roles in the 6 December destruction of the Babri Masjid in Ayodhya by a Hindu mob. Several prominent leaders of both parties, including Advani and VHP President Ashok Singhal, were arrested but, unlike the two earlier bans, no RSS leaders were actually imprisoned and no orders were given to close the shakhas. Indeed, the ban was never practically enforced, and was officially lifted by court action in June 1993.[31] Prime Minister Rao's critics alleged that this leniency was due to his long association with RSS leaders.[32] Vinay Sitapati, the author of an authoritative biography of Rao,[33] contests this assertion, arguing that his error was that of misjudgement and not, as has been alleged, of complicity.[34] Sitapati argues that Rao erred by assuming that the 'troublemakers' of the Bajrang Dal and Shiv Sena could be controlled by the BJP and the RSS.[35]

The late 1990s to the present saw a decline in the RSS's use of traditional Hindutva themes (such as the Ram Temple in Ayodhya) in favour of economic arguments; indeed, their earlier pan-Hindu strategies were virtually dropped, leading up to the new millennium.[36] The parivar projected Vajpayee, perhaps its most liberal face, as national spokesperson for the BJP and then as prime minister of the National Democratic Alliance (NDA) coalition government of 1998–2004. The BJP leadership, calculating that the era of one-party dominance might have ended, worked out new arrangements with several regional parties—arrangements motivated by tactical, rather than ideological, considerations. These tactics had the additional advantage of mobilizing support from low-caste Hindu voters to supplement the largely high-caste orientation of the parivar.

The surging popularity of the parivar across the socio-economic spectrum, however, brought out major differences within both the BJP and, to a lesser extent, the RSS. Divisions arose between those favouring, on the one hand, economic liberalization to grow the economy and reduce India's high poverty rate and, on the other, ideological conservatives who saw foreign investment as a threat to India's independence and culture. During the long tenure of Golwalkar, the RSS had adopted a very critical attitude towards what it called 'consumerism', viewing multinational corporations as cultural threats that would undermine national sovereignty and advance western-style hedonism contrary to traditional Indian mores.[37] The economic reforms of Rao's Congress regime in 1991—which reduced government intervention in the economy and again permitted foreign multinational corporations entry in some areas—led the RSS and most of its labour-oriented affiliates (such as the BMS) to take public stands against the government; the BJP, however, did not follow suit. In fact, the BJP, under the brief National Front government in 1990 had already supported economic liberalization, though it remained highly critical of foreign multinationals doing business on Indian soil. On balance, it remained generally supportive of the reforms of the Rao government. This dichotomy of opinion between the BJP and the RSS actually became somewhat embarrassing when the BJP-led NDA took control of the government in 1998.[38]

The divisions on economic policy within the parivar came to a head with the formation in the early 1990s of the SJM (Front for the Mass Awakening of Economic Nationalism) by groups within the parivar—especially the labour affiliate—in response to Rao's reforms. Its focus was and remains opposition to the entry of foreign multinational companies, though the SJM has also opposed privatization measures it perceives as anti-labour.[39] The SJM was prominently involved in demonstrations calling for the cancellation of an agreement between the Congress government and the American company Enron for the construction of a huge power plant in Dabhol, Maharashtra, a state which was then ruled by a coalition government including the BJP and a local Hindu nationalist party, the Shiv Sena.

Deoras retired from office in 1994 due to a severe illness, selecting the RSS's general secretary, Rajendra Singh, to succeed him.[40] India was in the early stages of an economic growth surge, and the RSS was similarly growing; the BJP was optimistic that it would build on its 1991 record in the 1996 national elections. The RSS for its part needed someone who could guide it through these changing times, and Singh—a physics graduate who had written his dissertation under a Nobel laureate—had demonstrated both organizational and diplomatic skills as general secretary under Deoras. The sangh was now expanding rapidly from its home base in Maharashtra, and its new outlook was reflected in the choice of Singh. He was the first non-Brahmin[41] and non-Maharashtrian to occupy the office of sarsanghchalak. He was from India's most populous state, Uttar Pradesh, a state that was central to the RSS's pan-Hindu initiatives. Moreover, he had already been baptized by fire, having presided over the general secretariat during the height of the Ram Temple controversy. He was no stranger to politics either: as assistant general secretary in early 1991, Singh and the then general secretary, H.V. Seshadri, had quietly mobilized RSS support for the BJP in the 1991 parliamentary elections, reflecting even then the increased importance of politics in the growing parivar network. While Singh had a relatively short six-year tenure (1994–2000), he would set the tone for the current RSS–BJP relationship, as it was during his primacy that the BJP-led NDA—with active support from the RSS—came to power in 1998.

The BJP did a better job than the Congress in working out electoral agreements with regional parties in the campaign for the 12th Lok Sabha elections in 1998; these successes continued in the 13th elections a year later. In the latter, it put together a workable majority with the thirteen parties in the NDA, grouped around the 182 seats won by the BJP (tying the record number won in the previous year).[42] Several other factors worked in their favour, especially the Kargil War between India and Pakistan in the summer of 1999, which aroused a tidal wave of Indian nationalism that played to the parivar's strengths. More impressive than forging this alliance, however, was maintaining it, which the BJP accomplished by de-emphasizing its traditional Hindutva elements and increasingly touting policies that would produce economic growth, and thus jobs. The BJP and its allies agreed on a 'National Agenda for Government' that dropped such fundamental Hindutva issues as the Ram Temple in Ayodhya and the abolition of Article 370 granting autonomy to Kashmir. Vajpayee's new government pledged its adherence to this agenda, a necessity to retain the loyalty of many regional allies who felt threatened by Hindu nationalism and, in some cases, depended on local Muslim support in their respective states. Building on this 'National Agenda for Government', the NDA's 1999 election manifesto promised a 'moratorium on contentious issues'.[43] The party's new economic orientation may also have been a factor in its ability to expand beyond the traditional Hindu upper-caste urban voter base.[44] Moreover, the BJP had come out in support of expanding job reservations allocated for the OBCs, putting itself on the opposite side of the RSS leadership on this issue—the RSS has consistently condemned such quotas as socially divisive. Despite these differences, Singh, who had a very good personal relationship with Prime Minister Vajpayee, was able to keep RSS–BJP ties at an amicable level—indeed, we were informed by senior RSS figures that the organization during this period generally deferred to Vajpayee on political issues. For his part, Singh often downplayed the sangh's differences with the government so as not to embarrass the prime minister.[45] He also supported the volunteer political work of swayamsevaks during the BJP's electoral campaigns.

Two years into the new BJP-led government, Singh stepped down owing to illness. His place was taken by Kuppalli Sitaramayya Sudarshan, a Brahmin and the first south Indian to lead the sangh.[46] The choice of Sudarshan underscored the rapid expansion of the RSS in the four southern Dravidian-speaking states of India, suggesting that the RSS's Brahmanical Hindutva orientation was no longer as great a liability in the south as it had been in the past. Sudarshan, however, was far more outspoken than the diplomatic Singh, and his personal relationship with Vajpayee was, according to some of our interlocutors, far more fraught than that between Vajpayee and Singh. Vajpayee, elder to Sudarshan by seven years, was not only more senior than him, but also had a longer membership in the RSS. Sudarshan was an outspoken proponent of economic swadeshi and, to the embarrassment of the Vajpayee government, vocally pushed for Hindutva issues; the 'iniquity' of Article 370, which grants the state of Jammu and Kashmir special autonomy, was one of his favourite talking points. He also criticized Prime Minister Vajpayee for an inadequate response to the festering Ayodhya issue. Following the NDA's loss in 2004 to a Congress coalition government, their relationship reached its breaking point after Sudarshan suggested that the senior leadership of the BJP, including Vajpayee, resign to make way for new blood. In the wake of BJP President Advani's June 2005 visit to Karachi in Pakistan (where he was born), the RSS strongly criticized his labelling Mohammed Ali Jinnah, the father of Pakistan, as 'secular'. The RSS's press spokesman denounced this statement, saying, 'What Advaniji said in Karachi and earlier was not in line with RSS thinking. The cadre is unhappy and confused and the people are angry.'[47] Advani promptly stepped down as BJP president and walked back his remarks on Jinnah. On announcing his exit, Advani reportedly stated that the RSS should leave politics to the BJP, lamenting 'the impression that has gained ground that no political or organizational decision can be taken [by the BJP] without the consent of RSS functionaries'.[48] Sudarshan, for his part, would outlast both Vajpayee and Advani, finally relinquishing control of the sangh in 2009 to Bhagwat, its present sarsanghchalak.

In our earlier study, the interview data suggested that the common 'character-building' training shared by the leadership of the RSS and the BJP (as well as leaders of affiliated groups) inculcated a sense of common purpose and loyalty within the collective parivar. The question is whether the RSS will be able to mediate the increasingly wide policy disagreements among its affiliates in ways that keep the 'family' harmonious and stable. The RSS leadership, always mindful of the importance of solidarity within the parivar, is likely to seek unprecedented compromises, and our case studies underscore the primacy of this objective in resolving internal differences. Soon after the BJP's selection of Modi as putative prime minister, Bhagwat, in his annual Vijayadashami speech in October 2013, focused on the economy as an element in Hindutva, thus placing himself on the same developmental plane as Modi, despite key differences between the two on several economic issues.

This brings us to the rise of Prime Minister Modi, who has emerged as arguably the most influential figure in the parivar's history, despite his often-tense relationship with senior figures within the RSS and the VHP in his home state of Gujarat during his long tenure there as chief minister (2001–14). Modi began to participate in RSS daily meetings at the age of eight in 1958, an experience that lent a sense of purpose and discipline to his life.[49] It certainly imbued him with an idea of Hindu nationalism that was to characterize his life and career. After graduating from high school, he renounced the notions of family and marriage and, at the age of seventeen, set off on a two-year pilgrimage across India to visit ashrams and other holy places. On his return to Gujarat, he re-established contact with the RSS and attached himself to Lakshmanrao Inamdar, a Maharashtrian Brahmin lawyer in Ahmedabad who had founded the city's first RSS shakhas in the early 1950s. Modi, on becoming a pracharak, began living at the RSS headquarters in Ahmedabad—one of his associates from those days says that the shift 'gave Narendra an identity and a sense of purpose in life. Now for the first time he was not alone, he was part of a bigger family.'[50]

As a pracharak on loan to the Gujarat unit of the ABVP, Modi quickly developed a reputation as a tireless and superb organizer, a reputation bolstered by his underground opposition efforts during the Emergency. He worked directly for the RSS for the next decade, and was deputed to the Gujarat BJP in 1987. He continued to build on his reputation during several yatras, or public marches, that addressed grievances either in the state (for example, the liquor mafia in Ahmedabad) or at the national level (the Gujarat leg of Advani's 1989 Ram Rath Yatra). He helped organize Advani's successful 1991 Lok Sabha victory in Gujarat (i.e., the Gandhinagar seat). Through his close association with Advani, Modi was soon introduced to the national-level politics of the BJP. Advani brought him to Delhi in 1995 as a party secretary and, just three years later, Modi was promoted to general secretary, thanks mainly to his successful supervision of several state Assembly elections, including the 1998 contest that brought the BJP to power in Gujarat. His assertive—perhaps even aggressive—leadership in Gujarat and Delhi soon aroused complaints; Modi, according to some of his colleagues, did not often evince the collegial style expected of a full-time RSS worker.[51] One BJP colleague from his time in Delhi reportedly noted that, 'He did not function the way a full-time RSS pracharak should. He was seen as projecting himself and seeking the limelight.'[52] Still another source, according to Kingshuk Nag, stated that even 'Sudarshanji [the RSS head] was annoyed with Modi's ways and even stopped talking to him.'[53] Modi nonetheless remained the party's general secretary for the 1996 elections, during which the BJP emerged as the nation's single largest party. He would repeat this role for the 1998 and 1999 polls, which saw the BJP remain the largest party, but now at the head of the NDA coalition government, with Vajpayee as prime minister.

The inept handling of the relief and rehabilitation operations after the 2001 Gujarat earthquake led the BJP to lose confidence in the leadership of its incumbent chief minister, Keshubhai Patel. The ground was laid for Modi's elevation as chief minister of Gujarat after losses in several key by-elections undermined the BJP's faith in Patel's ability to keep the party in power through the Assembly elections of 2002. Patel was pressured to resign, and the Centre selected Modi to succeed him. He was sworn in as chief minister on 6 October 2001, and immediately faced a number of hurdles, including several powerful BJP state figures not happy to see such an ambitious overachiever back in Gujarat.[54] Internecine squabbles would soon be the least of his problems, however. Four months after taking office there was an incident in the small town of Godhra that was to have a profound impact on Modi and on Indian politics. Following some sort of altercation at a railway station, a sleeper car was set alight, killing fifty-nine passengers, including VHP *kar sevak*s (pilgrims) returning from Ayodhya. While a special court convicted thirty-one Muslims for the arson, the decision was highly controversial, and the exact circumstances of the day are cloaked in ambiguity.[55] The day after the incident, mobs were roaming the streets of the state capital of Ahmedabad, calling for revenge against Muslims. Horrific violence soon followed. The VHP in Gujarat, for its part, called for a bandh in the state, followed the next day by its national leadership calling for a bandh across the nation. One of the most striking features of that day of destruction, according to observers, was the virtual absence of police in Ahmedabad. The Congress party minister of state for home, Sriprakash Jaiswal, reported to the Rajya Sabha that of the 1044 people killed in the riots, 790 were Muslim and 254 were Hindu; over 2500 more—of various denominations—were injured.[56]

The scale of the atrocities aroused national and international attention and, on 4 April 2002, Prime Minister Vajpayee visited Gujarat personally to express his dismay. The prime minister reportedly wanted Modi to resign for his sluggish response to the violence, but this was thwarted by Modi's widespread support within the party and the relative apathy of the BJP's major allies in the NDA coalition.[57] Modi, for his part, sensed that Gujarat's Hindu population supported him, and called for fresh Assembly elections ahead of schedule. These elections of December 2002 proved him right; the BJP returned to power with an even larger majority than before.[58] Indeed, the BJP led by Modi went on to win comfortable majorities in the next three Assembly elections. He focused his agenda throughout the rest of his term on economic development, and showed a flair for salesmanship and marketing in the annual 'Vibrant Gujarat' events aimed at attracting investment to the state.[59] He argued that investment was the most effective long-term means of reducing poverty and creating jobs, a line that was to be the centrepiece of his 2014 national campaign. His carefully cultivated public image in Gujarat—coupled with the economic booms he presided over—helped to change his international and national perception from a tough Hindutva leader to a modernizer who was personally responsible for his state's rapid growth. His critics, meanwhile, argued that this economic surge was not matched by improved social indicators in areas like health and education.[60] According to journalist Sheela Bhatt—one of the most astute observers of Modi's political career—Modi replaced the 'old-style,

20th century Gujarat-based Rashtriya Swayamsevak Sangh (RSS) chapter that brought him into public life' with a new strategy that was instead oriented towards development.[61]

At the national level, the BJP and the RSS (and the parivar in general) were looking for a change, and Chief Minister Modi saw a dual opportunity to gain the support of both the party and the electorate,[62] a task made easier by the intense factionalism within the BJP. The BJP had fought the losing 2009 parliamentary elections under the guidance of its remaining senior national figure, Advani; following its disappointing defeat, there seemed to be no one left to assume his national role, as there was no primus inter pares in the second rung of the party.[63] The elevation of Nitin Gadkari, a wealthy businessman from Nagpur, to the party presidency in 2010 was predictably controversial in this stratified atmosphere. Moreover, Gadkari lacked the charisma and reputation for good governance that Modi had already achieved on the national stage. Gadkari had one major advantage, however: his closeness to Bhagwat, the new head of the RSS, who succeeded Sudarshan in 2009. Even this was insufficient to make him the party's standard-bearer in 2014.[64] Gadkari's chances were further undermined by allegations of cronyism and conflict of interest in his business, which could have weakened the anti-graft plank of the BJP's campaign against the UPA government.[65]

In fact, Bhagwat quickly became a Modi supporter as the campaign for 2014 began to take shape. Bhagwat, a Maharashtrian Brahmin whose family had been involved in the RSS since its inception in 1925, was born the same year as Modi, and became a full-time worker at the same time as him in the mid-1970s. He developed during this time a reputation as a superb organizer. He was initially assigned as a full-time worker to the strategically important city of Nagpur. From 1991 to 1999, he held a set of national positions that culminated in his being named sarkaryavah (general secretary), which is widely considered the training ground for the next head of the RSS. Bhagwat clearly performed well, as he was elected to three subsequent three-year terms and served collegially under Sudarshan until the latter's retirement in 2009.

Bhagwat, however, was considerably more cautious in his public stands than was his predecessor—and expended his efforts instead towards developing a working relationship with the various parts of the parivar, especially with the BJP and Modi. One of his first major tasks, in fact, was to repair the frayed relationship between the BJP and RSS. Bhagwat soon involved himself in reducing the factionalism that had been festering within the BJP since the 2009 parliamentary defeat.[66] He used the *samanvay* coordinating mechanism to meet regularly with BJP leadership, providing an opportunity to iron out differences within the parivar—we will address some of the results of these mediatory mechanisms in our case studies.[67] Both Modi and Bhagwat seem to understand that they need each other—hence the frequent meetings and periodic official consultations described in the Introduction. Pursuant to this, BJP President Amit Shah brought together top BJP and RSS officials in mid-July 2014, about two months after the formation of the Modi government, to set up a top-level coordination group to supervise the interactions between the two organizations. On the RSS side, that first meeting included General Secretary Suresh 'Bhaiyyaji' Joshi and two assistant general secretaries, Suresh Soni and Dattatreya Hosabale. On the BJP side, the representatives included Shah and two former party presidents, Home Minister Rajnath Singh and Transportation Minister Nitin Gadkari.[68]

The RSS leadership, initially hesitant to openly express its support for Modi, came around following a canvassing of opinion within the ranks. Given the overwhelming support for Modi among the cadre, the RSS decided that it was time to use the organization more systematically on behalf of the BJP.[69] Moreover, calculating that they were locked in an ideological stalemate with the Congress party under Sonia Gandhi and her son, Rahul, the sangh looked at the 2014 polls as critical for its future.[70] For many rank-and-file RSS members, this was a 'do or die' election—and they looked to Modi to finally lead the party to victory.[71] The extreme adulation heaped upon Modi from the ranks of ordinary RSS workers, however, prompted Bhagwat to remonstrate with his subordinates that their primary loyalty was to the RSS, and not any individual.[72] For the

RSS, the BJP is but one of several elements of the sangh parivar, and not necessarily the most important at that. While recognizing the importance of politics and public policy, the sangh's core leadership still views lasting change as the product of society rather than government; moreover, they fear the authoritarian potential of a personality cult coupled with growing state power.

TWO

Affiliates

The Public Face of the Parivar

The ever-increasing public policy orientation of the sangh parivar is due in large part to the growth of its affiliate organizations (see Appendix II), which interact much more directly with the public than does the RSS proper. These affiliated groups now play a major role in the BJP's electoral strategies, supplying workers and sponsoring a large network of service projects to build support for the party.[1] RSS affiliates, which have an extensive presence in India's associational life, canvas their membership to gauge public perception on a wide range of topics, including the BJP government and voters' issue preferences. While the RSS after 1947 was hesitant to expand into areas other than its traditional 'character-building' training, these new activities are now a central element of the 'family'. This greater diversity has also led to multiple definitions of Hindutva, from a narrowly religious context for those affiliates that focus on cultural issues to a primarily nationalist and even secular orientation for organizations that work with labour, farmers and small-scale entrepreneurs; the sangh's political affiliate seems to shift directions on various elements of Hindutva ideology depending on its current electoral considerations.

After the ban of 1948–49 was lifted, the RSS leadership was forced by its younger members to consider new ways of achieving its nationalist goals. This shift was motivated partly to protect the

RSS from further restrictions and partly to provide an outlet for the growing number of activists within the ranks who wanted to be actively engaged in nation-building. From the beginning, the work of affiliates was seen as another means to advance Hindutva, in a way tailored to fit the needs of a given segment of society. With the ensuing surge in membership, particularly since the early 1990s, many of these groups have become influential players in their respective fields. At the same time, policy differences have arisen among them, as these groups represent different constituencies whose interests often are quite different from one another. Some of the affiliates (especially the Bajrang Dal, the youth wing of the VHP) have displayed a level of intolerance towards non-Hindu minorities that threatens to outflank the Modi government from the radical right and undermine its message of inclusive economic development. Prime Minister Modi, in his first Independence Day speech from the ramparts of Delhi's Red Fort, appealed for a moratorium on divisive issues, such as caste or religion.[2] Prime Minister Modi and RSS chief Bhagwat have both spoken out against this intolerance, but such incidents continue. Ending the bigotry may, in fact, require public cooperation between the leadership in the Modi government and in the RSS, but both would likely proceed with great caution for fear of alienating a large part of their core support base.

These affiliated organizations, despite their policy differences, have as a group demonstrated remarkable cohesiveness over the past seventy years, and the RSS has continued to serve as their ideological mentor without involving itself directly in their decision-making process. Their organizational cohesion, we maintain, is largely due to two factors: the *sangathan mantri* (organizational secretary) system practised by all affiliates and the autonomy granted them by their parent body. Under the sangathan mantri model, first adopted by the political affiliate, the BJS, key organizational positions— almost always including the role of general secretary—are held by full-time pracharaks.[3] The RSS assigns these pracharaks to the affiliates—usually on a long-term basis—and occasionally mediates disputes when the internal consensus system does not work; it also organizes formal and informal intra-parivar discussions of common issues, often focusing on how government policy will affect them. Decision-making within the various affiliated organizations, as in the RSS proper, proceeds only by consensus.

A 2015 catechetical primer on the RSS notes that there are thirty-six organizations affiliated to the RSS[4] (see Appendix II for the list). Among them are India's largest labour union, the BMS; its largest student group, the ABVP; and the country's ruling political party, the BJP.[5] These thirty-six groups span a broad spectrum of interests, including politics, agriculture, public health, education, veterans' affairs, religion, entrepreneurship and tribal welfare. Moreover, new groups continue to form to address fresh challenges, including a new affiliate that focuses on strengthening family bonds (the Kutumb Prabodhan) and another for female empowerment (the Stree Shakti). There are also numerous groups with links to the RSS, but which are not counted as full affiliates because the organization expects them to first demonstrate the administrative capability to operate autonomously. Both the Kutumb Prabodhan and the Stree Shakti started outreach work years ago (in 2010 and the late 1990s respectively) and only became full affiliates in 2017. Still another group not counted as an affiliate is the MRM formed in 2002; it is left out of this reckoning due to the widely held view within the RSS that the MRM will fail in its efforts to make Muslims culturally Hindu—indeed, many believe that its links with an organization like the RSS will only antagonize Muslims.[6] There is no similar group working with Christians, because the RSS leadership is even less confident of a positive response from them.[7] Regardless, the broad range of activities carried out by the affiliates provides the RSS with many alternative ways to carry out its Hindutva mission. In the process, the sangh is now compelled to address issues that were not on its agenda earlier.

Prior to Independence, the RSS limited itself to its traditional training programme and had only one affiliate. That affiliate, the Rashtra Sevika Samiti, was established as a female counterpart to the all-male RSS. It was established in 1936 through the lobbying efforts of Lakshmi Bai Kelkar, a widowed mother of four who argued that women would play an important role in India's liberation and thus they needed both intellectual Hindutva training and martial arts skills to empower themselves in society.[8] Explaining why the RSS itself did not open its doors to women, the organization's leadership at the time argued that the larger society would not accept men and women practising martial arts together, and moreover that a training programme for women would by necessity be different from one for men.[9] Kelkar laid the groundwork for the Rashtra Sevika Samiti by closely consulting with RSS chief Hedgewar—she also served as its head (*pramukh sanchalika*) until 1978.[10] The discipline and organization of the samiti parallels that of the RSS: it has the same swallow-tailed saffron flag as its forebear, it runs a large number of service projects and it sends representatives to the RSS's annual deliberative body, the Akhil Bharatiya Pratinidhi Sabha (ABPS).[11] However, it is different from other affiliates in that it does not employ RSS pracharaks, instead training its own full-time workers (*pracharika*s), many of whom are widows or choose not to marry.

The RSS's view of the role of women in advancing the cause of Hindutva has also changed over time. Golwalkar wrote some fifty years ago that the ideal role of a woman was as a mother and wife, upholding traditional cultural norms.[12] These days, the sangh advocates more assertive social roles for women outside the family. Reflecting a change in perspective, RSS delegates at the March 2016 ABPS meeting passed a resolution supporting the general secretary's report calling for the elimination of restrictions on female entry into Hindu temples, adding that in religious matters 'both men and women are naturally considered to be equal partners'. But the report goes far beyond this, noting favourably that women are now officiating as priests.[13] While the report advises that the parivar's default strategy should be negotiation rather than agitation, affiliates have not hesitated to engage in agitation, sometimes violent, to protest actions considered detrimental to their membership. In the samiti's narrative of Hindutva, heroic figures are mainly women engaged in activities that took them out of the home, such as the warrior queen Lakshmibai, the Rani of Jhansi, who organized and led the resistance to British rule during the Mutiny of 1857, or Sister

Nivedita (Margaret Noble), an Irish devotee of Swami Vivekananda. The married samiti members that we met tended to describe themselves and their husbands (almost always RSS members) as equal partners, both in terms of managing family matters and in their respective civic lives. These women typically had a network of relatives in the RSS or its affiliates. The Rashtra Sevika Samiti, while increasingly popular across India and overseas, has lagged far behind the growth of the RSS over the past two decades, perhaps because there are now many more opportunities for women to engage in public service, such as the thousands of service projects and campaigns run by virtually every RSS affiliate. The samiti website reports that in 2016 it sponsored some 600 service projects and held 875 daily shakhas, as well as 4340 weekly shakhas—about a tenth of the number held by the RSS that year.[14]

On the eve of Partition, activists in the RSS began pressing the leadership to establish media outlets so that the Hindu nationalist perspective on such issues as Partition (against it) and the governance of the new India (centralized) could be expressed on the national stage. Accordingly, the RSS launched its English-language weekly, *Organiser*, in July 1947; the Hindi-language *Panchjanya* followed in January 1948. These two publications, considered the dual voices of the RSS, are still operating. The early editors of the two national weeklies were drawn from a pool of young, talented RSS activists who were to play major roles in the sangh parivar, especially for its political affiliate. Long-time Jana Sangh/BJP leader Advani, for example, was an assistant editor of *Organiser*; Vajpayee, later prime minister, was the editor of *Panchjanya*. Pracharak Shivram Shankar 'Dadasaheb' Apte established in 1949 the Hindustan Samachar, a news service in indigenous languages.[15] The RSS in the 1980s, prompted by the Ram Janmabhoomi movement, established a newsletter (*Sanskrutik Varta*) aimed at keeping rural Indians informed of national developments. Another publication, this one available online, is the *Samvad*, aimed at RSS members overseas. Recognizing the growing power of social media, Manmohan Vaidya, the then RSS *prachar* pramukh (chief spokesperson), started a training programme in 2015 to teach RSS workers how to utilize social media more effectively, how to answer interview questions coherently and argue persuasively in televised debates.[16] In 2016, the RSS added a course on debate techniques to its third-year training camp in Nagpur, considered the final phase of training for prospective full-time workers.

The 1947 Partition of British India, the 1948–49 ban, and the virtual exclusion of RSS members from the ruling Congress party and its affiliates came as major shocks to the RSS membership, and prompted intense internal debate about whether something more than 'character-building' programmes was required to fulfil its Hindu revivalist mission. In addition, embittered members debated the role of the RSS in an independent India. As we noted in our previous book, many in the RSS leadership, including Golwalkar himself, were wary of deviating too far from their established practices.[17] However, there were many younger members who had joined the RSS during World War II, who supported a more activist orientation. The failure of the Quit India movement, called by the Congress party in 1942 to bring India closer to independence, was the motivation for many of these young men to join the RSS.[18] The communists, who supported the British war effort at that time, were not a viable alternative for these nationalist students.

The government's ban on the RSS in 1948 provided a powerful argument for RSS involvement in politics. RSS activists such as K.R. Malkani, the then editor of *Organiser*, used that publication to campaign vehemently for a political affiliate. Many of these activists supported the efforts of India's most respected Hindu nationalist politician at the time, Syama Prasad Mookerjee—ex-cabinet minister, former president of the Hindu Mahasabha and scion of one of the most prominent Hindu families in Bengal—to establish a nationalist alternative to the Congress.[19] Mookerjee negotiated with an initially hesitant Golwalkar to gain the RSS's cooperation in this endeavour. According to one authoritative account of those negotiations, Golwalkar agreed with Mookerjee that the new party must be open to people of all religions[20]—as a result, the name of this new party, the 'Bharatiya Jana Sangh', would not include the word 'Hindu'.[21] As a compromise between the traditionalists, who wanted to continue prioritizing the training programmes, and the activists, who pushed for entry into the political arena, Golwalkar assigned Upadhyaya, one of his most capable pracharaks, to help establish an organizational base for the new party.[22]

Tensions were bound to surface in the new party, as the politicians and the RSS activists involved had starkly different visions of its mission.[23] The politicians who followed Mookerjee wanted to focus on defeating the Congress, and as such formed alliances with some groups whose agendas the RSS itself refused to support (like large landholders who opposed distributing land to actual farmers). These politicians preferred a loosely organized and democratic decision-making system, somewhat similar to the Congress. RSS activists, on the other hand, wanted a highly disciplined party that aimed to create a culturally unified and 'Hindu' India. Unlike the politicians, they were in no hurry to show success. With this time-consuming rejuvenation in mind, they used the party's local units to focus on social and economic regeneration, an approach that was to be adopted by many of the affiliates later established by the RSS. Despite optimistic estimates for the new BJS, it won only three of 489 seats in the first parliamentary elections of 1951 and 1952,[24] but this setback did not seem to dampen the activists' enthusiasm. With the death of Mookerjee in 1953, the pracharaks, who already controlled the key organizational posts, soon assumed full control of the party under the leadership of Upadhyaya, who was now the party's general secretary and would later become its president and chief ideologue.[25]

The 1948–49 ban on the RSS also provided the activists the justification to get involved with enlisting college students. They started in 1948 at universities in Delhi and Punjab and, a year later, formed the ABVP, an all-India umbrella organization (though it was not until 1958 that the student front began to function nationally).[26] The next significant affiliate that took shape was the BMS, the labour group, which was formed in 1955. The sangathan mantri model of the BJS was adopted by both the student and labour fronts, and provided a template for affiliates established later on. The ideological mission of both the labour and student affiliates was to provide a nationalist counterbalance to the communist agenda of class conflict.[27] During the consolidation phase of the RSS under Golwalkar (roughly the decade after the 1949 lifting of the ban), most pracharaks were assigned to work within the RSS itself. It was not until after 1962 that the more activist Deoras began to assign pracharaks to the affiliates en masse.

The spiritually inclined Golwalkar himself played a role in organizing and unifying the deeply splintered Hindu ecclesiastical community to make it more relevant to a modernizing India.[28] He laid the groundwork for this approach by collecting signatures on a 1953 petition demanding a national ban on cow slaughter, thus demonstrating that the RSS had a significant voice within the Hindu community and winning respect within the Hindu religious establishment in the process. He invited a select group of religious leaders to Bombay in August 1964 to consider ways to work more closely with one another to advance Hindu religious interests at home and abroad; from this meeting grew the VHP. Apte, a Bombay lawyer by training, was designated its first general secretary. As the founder of the Hindustan Samachar news agency, he had developed close relations with several prominent political and business figures, who could provide funds and political support to the new organization. He was also close to several prominent moderate religious figures, whose support attracted attention from the growing urban middle class. Apte was assisted in this effort by an Advisory Council composed of prominent Hindu ecclesiastical leaders from a variety of sects, thus giving the RSS access to the influential Hindu sadhus. Among the new supporters were the Kanchi Shankaracharya, the most socially active of the four Shankaracharyas;[29] Swami Vishweshwar, perhaps the most prominent advocate of the dualist Dvaita Vedanta tradition; and Swami Chinmayananda, founder of the international Chinmaya Mission, who underscored his modern approach to religion by preaching in English and reinterpreting Hinduism to make it relevant to twentieth-century lifestyles.[30] The lingering respect for Chinmayananda's pan-Hindu message within the sangh parivar can be seen, for example, in the Modi government's release of a commemorative coin on his birth centenary on 8 May 2016, or in an effusive 2016 article celebrating Chinmayananda's birth centenary in *Organiser*.[31]

Initially, the VHP's focus fell squarely on programmes that would promote pan-Hindu unity, such as an international conference on Hinduism at Allahabad that ran from 22 to 24 January 1966, featuring a broad spectrum of Indian religious leaders. In that same year, it launched a movement to ban cow slaughter—this may even have helped the Jana Sangh electorally, as the latter reached power in non-Congress coalition governments in Madhya Pradesh, Bihar and Uttar Pradesh, as well as in Delhi the next year. Yet another VHP-sponsored international conference was held in January 1979, with a much larger number of delegates and with the added participation of the Dalai Lama (representing Tibetan Buddhism), but missing were two of the four Shankaracharyas (Badrinath and Sringeri).[32] A Hindu Solidarity Conference would follow in July 1982 in the southern state of Tamil Nadu, convened to protest the conversion of several hundred low-caste Hindus to Islam in Meenakshipuram village in the state the previous year.

After the second ban was lifted in 1977, the RSS leadership pressed the VHP to take a more activist role, and consequently assigned workers to it. These included two of its best pracharaks, Moreshwar Nilkant (aka Moropant) Pingle and Ashok Singhal (later to become VHP president). The VHP reoriented itself into a populist organization to advance pan-Hindu objectives. In late 1982, it organized its first *ekatmata* yatra (unity pilgrimage) in response to the Meenakshipuram conversions. That same year, it also organized its first parliament of Hindu religious leaders (referred to as a dharma *sansad*), during which Dau Dayal Khanna, a senior Congress state legislator from Uttar Pradesh, introduced a resolution to construct a Ram Temple in Ayodhya, on a site occupied since the sixteenth century by the Islamic Babri Masjid complex.[33] The VHP, with RSS support,[34] soon launched a populist protest movement utilizing yatras (religious marches) to mobilize mass support for such a temple. These marches lasted through the 1980s and into the early 1990s, with the most notable ones occurring in late 1991 and early 1992.[35] The BJP passed a resolution on 11 July 1989, committing the party to this Ram Janmabhoomi movement.[36] In line with this resolution, BJP President Advani launched his controversial Ram Rath Yatra on 25 September 1990. The 'D-Day of Karseva' on 30 October 1990—when Uttar Pradesh security personnel fired on marchers for violating the chief minister's order to halt their march—aroused populist fury and may have laid the groundwork for the destruction of the Babri Masjid by a militant Hindu mob on 6 December 1992.[37] But the destruction did nothing to advance the issue of rightful possession of the disputed property. Following a complicated legal battle, the Allahabad High Court on 30 September 2010 accepted the existence of a Hindu temple on the site where the Islamic religious structure had been constructed, though both sides were dissatisfied with the division of the property and the case was taken to the Supreme Court.[38] As of late 2017, the issue of rightful possession of the disputed site was still being settled by the Supreme Court (see our case-study chapter on Ram Janmabhoomi for more details).

The VHP, since the late 1980s, has increasingly broadened its activities from its original purview of pan-Hindu unity; it sponsored 59,121 service programmes in such areas as education, health and social services in 2015, constituting almost a third of all service projects in the sangh parivar.[39] One of the VHP's more successful efforts has been its Ekal Vidyalaya Foundation, established in 1986, which is devoted to educational and infrastructural development in rural areas and tribal villages across the nation. Perhaps reflecting a somewhat less confrontational orientation of the VHP, there is no mention of marches or other such agitational strategies in its current mission statement. The construction of a Ram Temple at the site of the former Babri Masjid nevertheless remains part of its agenda, as does the return of other properties where Hindu temples were once located.[40] The sidelining of the firebrand ideologue Pravin Togadia and his close associate Raghava Reddy at the VHP election on 14 April 2018—the first such election in fifty-two years—suggests an RSS effort to restrain the radical elements within the VHP.[41] The new VHP leaders—International President Justice V.S. Kokje, former chief justice of the Rajasthan High Court, and Working President Alok Kumar, the Delhi sanghchalak—are more moderate than their predecessors.[42]

By contrast, the all-male youth branch of the VHP, the Bajrang Dal, continues to cite such contentious issues as Ram Janmabhoomi as its highest priorities. The Bajrang Dal was launched in 1985 to mobilize support for and provide protection to the various agitations and marches in Ayodhya. Its formation enabled the VHP to transform itself from a small, quietist entity working exclusively with Hindu religious figures into a populist organization with a much broader activist agenda.[43] The Bajrang Dal is specifically sworn to oppose activities that denigrate the country, the Hindu faith and Indian cultural norms. The Dal's current website says that the organization stepped up its activities after December 1992, when the Babri Masjid was torn down and the VHP was consequently banned, albeit only briefly. It moreover asserts (in a rather threatening tone) that the Dal's membership now is 'in no mood to compromise in any way with the issue of security of the country, Dharma and Society'.[44] It also lists the issues that the Dal continues to vehemently support, including: renovation of religious sites, cow protection, protection against 'vulgar' media programming and such decadent events as beauty contests and Valentine's Day parties, protection against 'insults' directed at Hindu traditions, conventions and beliefs, and opposition to illegal migration.[45] An example of its more current agitations would be the protests it staged at the entrance to New Delhi's Jawaharlal Nehru University (JNU) campus, which were directed against the allegedly seditious rallies held there in early 2016. The VHP has also established a young women's affiliate, the Durga Vahini, that recruits from the same demographic (fifteen to thirty-five years) as the all-male Dal—its organizational model and activist objectives are also nearly identical to its parent group.[46] It was established by one of the most public firebrands of the parivar, Sadhvi Rithambara, in 1991. Its weekly meetings, like those of the Bajrang Dal, provide opportunities for its members to discuss current issues, take the RSS's nationalist narrative to outsiders and new members, and conduct exercises, with a special emphasis on self-defence and firearms training. It also manages a number of educational and health service projects for disadvantaged groups. As with the Bajrang Dal, one of the main justifications given by the

Durga Vahini for these service activities is to block efforts to convert socially disadvantaged Hindus to other religions.

The RSS, since its formation in 1925, has used college students as one of its main support bases, and during the 1948–49 ban it relied heavily on college-going swayamsevaks to continue its undertakings under the guise of extracurricular activities. These meetings served as the impetus for the creation of a separate student group reflecting the Hindutva ideology of the RSS. The ABVP was thus formed in July 1948 by a group of student activists.[47] The ABVP differs significantly from other student groups in that it recruits from all sections of the university community, including faculty and staff. It also claims to be independent of any partisan political affiliations. While this may technically be true, the ABVP has actively worked for the BJP during political campaigns, and sends representatives to the RSS's national deliberative body, the ABPS.[48] The ABVP was initially hesitant to take part in student politics, but this began to change quickly in the 1970s, when the group came out in support of Jayaprakash Narayan's national movement against corruption.[49] This politically charged assertiveness was challenged by several senior figures in the RSS as contrary to the sangh's ethos. Eknath Ranade, an iconic national RSS leader, argued at the time that the ABVP should not dilute its educational focus by playing politics;[50] this advice was ignored. The ABVP's rise and increasing activism have often brought it into conflict with leftist student groups, as was the case in early 2016 at JNU, where it took up rhetorical arms against the three communist student groups on campus for alleged anti-nationalism. Nonetheless, the tensions associated with such activism are, as Ranade noted, contrary to the RSS's emphasis on social harmony. Reflecting this dilemma, the ABVP website asserts, 'We are "above student politics" but we also accept that social activity cannot be non-political in a strict sense.'[51] Translated, this statement essentially says that the ABVP only dabbles in politics when the needs of the Hindu nationalist movement require it to.

The ABVP's student activism has been a training ground for politically inclined students and, not surprisingly, such training as they receive in India's rough-and-tumble world of student politics tends to equip them with the organizational, analytical and rhetorical skills necessary for a career in politics. ABVP alumni are represented throughout the BJP—several of the most important and capable members of the Modi government came into politics through the ABVP. These include Finance Minister Arun Jaitley, Law and Justice Minister Ravi Shankar Prasad, Road Transport and Highways Minister Nitin Gadkari, Vice President Venkaiah Naidu and several second-rank ministers of state. BJP state governments have a similarly heavy representation of ABVP alumni. Several of the BJP's general secretaries (Kailash Vijayvargiya, Bhupender Yadav and Murlidhar Rao) also emerged from the ABVP. The ABVP, already India's largest student group, has seen its membership surge alongside the recent expansion of the BJP. Between 2003 and 2013, its membership doubled from 1.1 million to 2.2 million, adding approximately 1,00,000 members a year. In 2014, the year that the BJP took control of the central government and several states, membership expanded at its fastest rate ever, resulting in an additional million members over eighteen months, with a total of 3.2 million members in 2016.[52]

The RSS has taken an even more direct interest in shaping education at the primary and secondary levels. This was an especially urgent priority in the first years after Independence, prompted both by the growing demand for education on the part of the RSS's largely urban, middle-class base and by the sangh's conviction that national values were inadequately represented in the curriculum, both in public schools and in private Christian schools. In 1946 Golwalkar laid the foundation stone of the Gita Mandir, the first affiliated elementary school at Kurukshetra in the state of Haryana.[53] Following this up, Nanaji Deshmukh—a pracharak in Uttar Pradesh—established the Saraswati Shishu Mandir at Gorakhpur. It provided a model for similar schools within the large state of Uttar Pradesh. This scholastic network grew so rapidly that the RSS established an agency to coordinate its development. In the decade after the ban, when the RSS was still operating under a cloud of suspicion, these schools provided an alternative way to spread the

RSS's message of national unity and pan-Hinduism. Teachers at these schools often insert nationalist narratives into the social science and history books prescribed by national authorities, as these texts are held by some RSS circles to be devoid of respect for the country's distinct civilization.[54] The schools also celebrate Hindu festivals, and their facilities are typically adorned with Hindu religious symbols. It was our impression that these schools, like the shakhas, play a major role in engendering a sense of communal solidarity among their participants, and we were told that this is an important objective.[55] The rapid spread of these schools beyond Uttar Pradesh led to the formation of a national coordinating body, the Vidya Bharati Akhil Bharatiya Shiksha Sansthan (or simply the Vidya Bharati), in 1977. The current website of the Vidya Bharati notes that its prime objective is 'To develop a National System of Education which would help to build a generation of youngmen [sic] and women that is committed to Hindutva and infused with patriotic fervor.'[56] Other objectives include 'building up a harmonious, prosperous and culturally rich Nation', as well as 'service of our those [sic] brothers and sisters who live in villages, forests, caves, and slums and are deprived and destitute, so that they are liberated from the shackles of social evils and injustice'. Describing the 'Indian national Ethos' taught at these schools, the Vidya Bharati places primary importance on an 'integral approach to life', with other facets of the curriculum including 'recognition of divinity in every form of life' and 'blending of materialism and spirituality'.[57] These objectives are virtually identical to those used by other affiliates and even the RSS itself; predictably, their end goal is social harmony and Hindu unity.

These affiliated elementary and high schools—numbering 5241 and 2635 respectively, with a total of over 3 million students enrolled in the 2012–13 academic year—now represent by far the largest private school system in India. The Vidya Bharati also now includes such institutions as colleges and teacher-training schools (some forty-four nationally), as well as what it refers to as 'Informal Education' units (9806), according to statistics collected by it for 2012–13.[58] In a sense, this RSS-affiliated school system has turned the tables on the concerns the sangh once had regarding Christian missionary schools educating Hindus, as it now enrols a considerable number of Muslims and Christians—a recent report estimates that some 47,000 Muslim students are enrolled in such RSS-affiliated schools.[59]

In addition to these schools, yet another affiliate, the ABVKA has a significant educational programme, including separate hostels, libraries and sports academies that work among India's 110 million tribals. The RSS, since the 1950s, has made tribal outreach a key part of its pan-Hindu agenda. A major motivation for these initiatives—launched in December 1952 in the small town of Jashpur in Bastar, a tribal region of Chhattisgarh, with the support of the local ruler—was to counter the activities of Christian missionaries, who prioritized tribals over rural and urban Indians as potential converts.[60] The ABVKA's 2015–16 Annual Report states that it has 4460 schools—mostly single-teacher establishments— and 1,25,415 students.[61] This report also notes that the group has 820 full-time male workers and 650 part-time male workers, though it is not clear how many of them are RSS pracharaks; it additionally notes that there are 192 full-time and 416 part-time female workers. The ABVKA, like other affiliates, has developed close collaborative relations with BJP state governments and the national government. Gujarat's minister of tribal development, for example, attended the 8 May 2016 release of the ABVKA 'Vision Statement' in the state, which called for increased government assistance to tribals in order to reduce incidents of conversion. The minister, Mangubhai Patel, told the gathering that his government was responding to these concerns, and added that government efforts to reduce poverty among tribals had already blocked Christian missionary efforts. He ended by noting, 'We led a revolution and today we can say for sure that conversion has stopped because of government's intervention.'[62]

The ABVKA, like many RSS affiliates, has spoken out against public policies it judges not to be in the interest of its goals, even criticizing the Modi government for those policies it considers 'anti-people'. For example, it (along with the labour and farm affiliates of the RSS) opposed a land acquisition bill that the Modi government was pushing during a 2015 parliamentary session to stimulate investment and thus create jobs, one of the BJP's major objectives.

The ABVKA was reportedly vehemently opposed to provisions such as lowering the percentage of landowners who needed to approve before the government could seize a given piece of property.[63]

The initial motivation for establishing the labour affiliate, the BMS, was to counter the national influence of communists in the workforce and their ideology of class struggle. Golwalkar in the late 1940s asked Dattopant Thengadi, a pracharak with labour union experience, to draft a feasible plan for a nationalist labour union.[64] The BMS was subsequently established in July 1955, and its website notes that its 'base sheet-anchors would be Nationalism', and that it would be unique among Indian trade unions by remaining separate from political parties.[65] Its robust criticism of the past two BJP-led governments for their support of the market reforms of the early 1990s underscores this independence. Thengadi publicly characterized Vajpayee's finance minister as a 'criminal', and his policies as 'anti-national'.[66] He even described fellow pracharak Vajpayee at one point as a 'petty politician playing into the hands of his policy advisers with doubtful credentials'.[67] The BMS has been equally critical of the Modi government's support of reforms that would give greater power to businesses to hire and fire workers. The class dilemma faced by the parivar thus centres on the tensions between the economic liberalism supported by much of the rapidly growing urban middle-class base and the labour rights promoted by the urban working class and rural labourers, a tension reflected in Modi's cautious approach to further reforms.

The BMS has advanced a swadeshi (self-sufficiency) model that is wary of private enterprise, capitalism, foreign direct investment and the globalization of trade—all of which are at the heart of Modi's economic agenda. This socialistic model envisages workers managing their own work units (referred to as the 'Labourisation of Industry') and sharing profits among themselves. The BMS website spells out a new industrial policy that envisages the 'Replacement of profit motive by service motive and establishment of economic democracy resulting in equitable distribution of wealth'.[68] The BMS strongly opposes the privatization of public-sector enterprises, a process that started on a significant scale during Rao's administration and was enthusiastically continued under Vajpayee. In contrast to the latter, however, Modi has not created a cabinet position overseeing privatization. The BMS has similarly opposed the globalization of trade, arguing that the Rao government's policy of easing tariff rates would threaten Indian industry and thus result in widespread joblessness. In a letter to Prime Minister Manmohan Singh in 2013, the then BMS President C.K. Saji Narayanan argued against a free trade agreement with the European Union, on the grounds that free trade agreements with developed countries would hinder the development of industry in India and undermine the national goal of economic self-sufficiency.[69]

While the BMS claims that its methods and philosophy are different from those of other labour unions (such as its opposition to the notion of class struggle), the affiliate is in fact very similar to them (in terms of its tactics, opposition to market reforms and privatization, and support for economic self-sufficiency). While the student branch of the RSS incorporates all members of the academic community and claims to speak on their collective behalf, the BMS, like other labour unions, does not allow managers or executives—private or public—in its ranks. Also like other labour unions, it has a very poor record mobilizing or representing the so-called unorganized sector, which comprises the vast majority of the Indian workforce. Pragmatic issues regarding the well-being of its working-class members virtually monopolize the BMS agenda, and the significance of such civilizational issues as religion and a common Hindu consciousness are consequently diminished. Prime Minister Modi, committed to economic growth in order to fulfil his campaign pledge to create jobs, seems to view private enterprise (with minimal government interference) as the prime vehicle of that growth. For this, the BMS has openly (and frequently) criticized the Modi government. However, the BMS often meets government ministers and departmental secretaries to discuss such controversial issues, including the proposed land acquisition bill.[70] This is in line with the RSS's overarching cooperative philosophy, as the sangh encourages the various parts of the parivar to discuss differences and occasionally mediates those discussions to work out compromises.[71]

The growth of the BMS was slow at first; it was not until 1967 that the first national conference was held and the first national executive selected. Following the sangathan mantri organizational model used in all RSS affiliates, founding pracharak Thengadi was named general secretary, and other pracharaks were appointed to key organizational positions. Its growth rate afterwards was rapid, exploding from some 2,40,000 members registered in 1967 to 1.2 million in 1984; by 1996 it had become the nation's largest labour association with over 3.1 million members and it continued to balloon, reaching 11 million in 2010.[72] The rapid growth of both the BMS and the BJP has created a dilemma for the RSS as it seeks to maintain a measure of harmony among its various affiliates. The BJP appeals to a surging urban middle class that increasingly privileges consumerism over the more austere traditional RSS message which resonates with the lower middle class and the poor.[73] The RSS's encouragement of the SJM—intellectuals opposed to foreign economic penetration in India[74]—in the mid-1990s underscored the still-strong undercurrent of economic nationalism within the RSS. The first campaign of the SJM was against the entry of an American power company, Enron, into the state of Maharashtra. It later expanded its programme to oppose a broad span of economic liberalization efforts.

The RSS also encouraged the formation of a farmers' affiliate, the Bharatiya Kisan Sangh (BKS). Here again, it was Thengadi, one of the RSS's most trusted pracharaks, who laid the foundation of the new organization in 1979. Despite its theoretical commitment to a harmonious society and, as such, its opposition to class struggle—a stance common to virtually every affiliate—the BKS, like the BMS, engages in protests and strikes, sometimes even against BJP state and national governments. Its causes célèbres include such issues as opposition to genetically modified crops, pressing for minimum support prices for a range of goods and opposition to the Modi government's proposals for labour and land reforms.[75] While its website claims that it is the nation's largest farmers' union,[76] we have been told by some of its workers that the deep social divisions in rural India have complicated collective action there. Nevertheless, the organization's access to the Modi government is reflected in the fact that six amendments to the national land ordinance, later presented as legislation to Parliament, were reportedly suggested by the BKS.[77]

We close our discussion of the affiliates with a brief reference to one of the more recent entrants, the Laghu Udyog Bharati (which works among small- and medium-scale industries), because it demonstrates not only the growing diversity within the sangh parivar, but also the conflicting interests that can arise among affiliates. The Laghu Udyog Bharati, formed in 1994, represents small entrepreneurs with interests and goals often quite different from those of the farmer and labour affiliates analysed above. The first two objectives in its website relate to reducing the role of government: 'Relief from Inspector Raj . . . [and] simplification of registration process.'[78] It claims to have 1000 registered members across 400 districts of India, and carries out programmes aimed at helping entrepreneurs navigate the labyrinthine regulations of the Indian bureaucracy; it also organizes classes in such matters as management skills.[79] But, like many of the other affiliates, it also engages in public protests to protect its membership, and it has a running campaign against the BJP government in Madhya Pradesh for what it considers to be unfair increases in maintenance charges for industrial plots.[80]

India's rapid economic development since the adoption of market reforms in the early 1990s has made Indian society more complex than ever before, and this complexity is reflected in the diversity of affiliates within the parivar. The expansion of affiliates was a way for the sangh parivar to reach out to various constituencies that were not traditional supporters of the RSS. Spreading its tentacles into various branches of national associational life was a way for the sangh to fulfil its founder's vision of 'uniting the Hindu society from Kashmir to Kanyakumari'. Our discussion of the various affiliates underscores not only their rapid growth, but also the widening policy differences among them—and the increasing challenges the RSS faces in mediating those differences. Senior RSS leaders in Nagpur, well aware of this challenge, told us that one solution to this dilemma could be national coordination meetings—perhaps with government ministers and senior bureaucrats in attendance— to establish consensus when possible and to put issues on the back-burner when impossible. The differences over the land acquisition bill, for example, have as much to do with opposition from within the parivar as criticism from the BJP's political competitors. An additional consequence of India's rapid economic development is the steady move away from traditional social values, many of which are rooted in Hindu religious views and practices. Such a shift is clearly evident in the more neutral attitude towards homosexuality recently expressed by some senior leaders of the parivar. Still another example is the changing notion of the ideal Hindu woman, from the caring mother and loyal wife so poetically described by Golwalkar half a century ago to the increasingly prevalent image of Indian women as activists and leaders, as exemplified by two very capable current female cabinet ministers, Defence Minister Nirmala Sitharaman and External Affairs Minister Sushma Swaraj.

So what keeps the sangh parivar from disintegrating altogether, given the wide range of often-competing interests that it hosts? The key element, in our view, is the sangathan mantri system: the 6000 trained RSS pracharaks who occupy top management positions (organizing secretary, general secretary and joint general secretary)[81] in the RSS proper as well as in virtually all the affiliates. These pracharaks have all gone through the same training and internship experience as *vistaraks*. Their permanent roles are initially assigned by the sangh's pracharak pramukh (head of pracharak affairs) in consultation with senior *kshetra* (regional) and *prant* (state) pracharaks. Lacking (at least ostensibly) family obligations, caste commitments, or material assets, they have few distractions from their service to the RSS and its Hindutva goal of pan-Hindu unity, which endows them with an aura of legitimacy for leadership roles in the parivar. Adding to their legitimacy in the RSS system is that most of them are well educated and hold college degrees. On graduating into the full-time ranks of the RSS, they are expected to serve for life and, we are told, the attrition rate is quite low among those who make this commitment. Service in the affiliates tends to be long-term as specialized and experiential knowledge is often required, especially for those affiliates that address economic and labour issues. While RSS-trained pracharaks continue to occupy the top ranks of such affiliates, they have had to turn increasingly to non-pracharak specialists to handle technical issues and coordination with other affiliates or the government. The long-term service of pracharaks in the various affiliates has made them sympathetic to the interests of the organizations they serve. Those assigned to the RSS itself usually start at the local level and move up through the ranks, perhaps to another prant or to an affiliate. The RSS training system has been able to prepare enough workers to staff the organizational steel frame of the 'family', and these trainees—while still largely high caste and hailing from the north and west of India—are becoming ever more diverse, both in terms of origin and caste, and even include a few Muslims.[82]

Besides the ideology binding the office-bearers of the 'family' together, there are several structural elements that also serve to unite these often-disparate factions. All the affiliates, including those overseas, are represented at the RSS's yearly ABPS, the central deliberative body that discusses major issues and passes resolutions on those considered most pressing. Beyond this, there are the *samanvay* samitis (coordination meetings) which bring representatives of the various affiliates together to discuss substantive policy issues; when the BJP is in power, members of the government usually join these discussions. The 'family' also publishes journals, some restricted to specific affiliates, and some with a larger audience at the state and national levels. In addition, the core leadership of the RSS is constantly on the road, attending some of the hundreds of conferences and meetings held annually by the various elements of the parivar. The core RSS leadership uses these opportunities to gauge the opinions of the rank and file on issues and personnel choices (such as the swayamsevaks' opinion of Modi before the RSS leadership came out for him prior to the 2014 parliamentary elections). There remain unresolved differences within and among the affiliates, several of which will be discussed in the case studies, but while individuals have left, so far no affiliate has separated itself from the parivar, and we are unaware of any serious past effort to do so. Finally, and importantly, each of the affiliates operates autonomously, and the RSS usually asserts itself only when there is a power vacuum (as in the BJP after the 2009 parliamentary losses) or to mediate differences within or among the affiliates. Even this is a relatively rare occurrence—the parivar operates by consensus precisely to avoid the kind of destructive factionalism that has ruined so many of its non-RSS peers and competitors.

THREE

The RSS Overseas

Unifying the Hindu Diaspora

It was the afternoon of 28 September 2014, and in downtown Manhattan's iconic Madison Square Garden, a capacity crowd of some 20,000 sent up a thunderous cheer for Narendra Modi. The event, and the roar of the crowd, marked the inauguration of Modi's first official visit to the United States after the Indian elections that year. As the attendees anxiously awaited the new prime minister's imminent speech, the stage was crowded with Indian musicians and dancers; behind the speaker's platform, a huge screen chronicled Modi's circuitous journey from his father's tea stall at Vadnagar railway station to the seat of power at 7, Lok Kalyan Marg in New Delhi. The narrative was that here was a leader who came from among the people and understood their aspirations. Ushering the audience into the huge hall were volunteers from the Hindu Swayamsevak Sangh (HSS), the overseas counterpart of the RSS in the US. The event had the freewheeling atmosphere of a campaign rally—and in many ways, it was. The crowd had come for a rousing populist speech from a spellbinding orator and, by all accounts, they were not disappointed.[1]

Prime Minister Modi in his initial years in office addressed dozens of similarly mammoth overseas rallies. Alongside these speeches, he often built into his diplomatic schedule visits to the common workplaces and religious sanctuaries of the Indian diaspora.[2] No previous Indian prime minister had demonstrated a comparable interest in connecting with overseas Indians. These speeches consistently reiterated two primary objectives: to encourage overseas Indians to work together to advance their community interests and to use their skills and money to help India's own development efforts. He had often touted these same goals overseas during his long tenure as chief minister of Gujarat. The 2014 BJP Manifesto, reflecting these central themes, stated that, 'The NRIs [Non-Resident Indians], PIOs [Persons of Indian Origin][3] and professionals settled abroad are a vast reservoir to articulate the national interests and affairs globally. This resource will be harnessed for strengthening Brand India.'[4] He has continued to court the diaspora after ascending to the position of India's prime minister. At the 9 October 2014 Global Development Summit in Indore, for example, he encouraged India's state governments to identify the most useful talents evinced by overseas Indians from their state, and to encourage the use of those skills on behalf of Indian infrastructure efforts.[5] At the 2015 Pravasi Bharatiya Divas—an annual event that honours the contributions of overseas Indians to the motherland—Modi called on the diaspora to take pride in their common heritage and to use this pride to work collectively in ways that benefit both themselves and the Indian nation.[6]

The diaspora in several countries (perhaps most prominently in the US) has a rich history of lobbying on behalf of Indian national interests. Perhaps the best example of this is the significant role the Indian American community played in lobbying the US Congress to secure passage in 2008 of the landmark United States–India Nuclear Cooperation Approval and Non-Proliferation Enhancement Act.[7] This legislation was a long-term effort that faced fierce opposition in the US and India since its proposal in 2005—despite a joint statement of support that year by Indian Prime Minister Manmohan Singh and US President George W. Bush. The proposal had to go through a complicated process that included amending US domestic law regarding nuclear issues and the approval of all the members of the Nuclear Suppliers Group before the US Senate gave final passage. What made this bit of legislation a particularly hard sell was India's status as a nuclear power which had not signed the 1970 Non-Proliferation Treaty. Non-proliferationists in the US (and elsewhere) saw the bill as a dangerous precedent that could severely weaken the cause of global nuclear disarmament. The long and uphill battle to pass this bill thus represented the Indian American community's coming of age as a unified political force. However, the American HSS—consistent with the apolitical orientation of HSS national units in other countries—was not directly involved in the cause, though individual members did lend their support. This neutrality would not be a recurring theme for the organization—two subsequent events quickly triggered a politicization of the American HSS. The first was a 2005 controversy over the way Hinduism was portrayed in certain Californian public-school textbooks. The second was the organized opposition to Modi's first US visit by some (predominantly on the ideological left) American groups, who alleged that he supported intolerant and anti-minority policies (we shall analyse both events below).

The HSS is very much politically active now—indeed, the drawing power of Modi's overseas rallies owes much to the efforts of HSS activists in the three dozen countries where it has a presence.[8] All national HSS units are administratively and legally independent from one another and from the RSS proper, though full-time RSS pracharaks from India are often assigned to them. Working closely with the HSS to organize Modi's rallies is the Overseas Friends of the BJP (OFBJP), an administrative wing of the BJP operating from the party office in New Delhi. Current OFBJP coordinator, Vijay Chauthaiwale, a former non-resident Indian in the US, said his critical first task in orchestrating these rallies is to identify what he described to us as 'talented, energetic, pro-Indian and selfless team players' to work as volunteers with the local HSS.[9] Chauthaiwale himself brings to these endeavours a legitimacy among overseas RSS members born of generations of RSS involvement by his family. His father was an RSS activist, his uncle a pracharak close to Golwalkar and Deoras; his wife is heavily engaged in the India Foundation in New Delhi (a think tank with close ties to the Modi government), while his daughter is involved in an affiliated organization. Another family with both deep RSS roots and a spirit of overseas volunteerism is the Vaidya family; the sangh's joint general secretary (formerly its prachar pramukh) is Manmohan Vaidya, whose father Prof. M.G. Vaidya was the first prachar pramukh of the RSS, and whose brother Ram Vaidya, a pracharak, heads the HSS in Europe. This growing network of deeply committed RSS families—linked both to the sangh and with each other—is becoming a significant recruitment pool for RSS workers and sangh parivar activists.

The RSS's interest in the overseas Indian community is rooted in its overriding goal of pan-Hindu unification. The first overseas shakhas were started in Kenya and Myanmar in 1947 by emigrant swayamsevaks from India, who were also the catalysts for the further spread of the organization overseas.[10] As early as 1953, Golwalkar, in a lecture to state pracharaks, put the RSS's interest in overseas Hindus in a philosophical context, saying that the RSS had a 'world mission' to propagate the Hindu notion of the world as a single family.[11] This 'long distance nationalism', to use a phrase of Benedict Anderson,[12] is aimed at mobilizing a unified Hindu community to assist the cause at home, with its primary focus on financial and volunteer support for the many service projects run by the sangh parivar in India and elsewhere. Our own research suggests several motivating factors for this long-distance nationalism besides Anderson's hypothesis that it serves to assuage the guilt diasporic Indians harbour for having abandoned the motherland. These factors include: the nationalist message of the RSS; nostalgia and homesickness; identifying with family members remaining in India; and, for many, a justification for social interaction with other members of the Indian community— thus providing an opportunity to enhance one's social status through contributions to communal activities.

These efforts to help the home country can take many forms, such as the substantial assistance to victims of natural disasters provided by overseas contributors—the 1978 Andhra cyclone,[13] the January 2001 earthquake in Gujarat, the December 2004 tsunami off the south-eastern coast of India, and the 2015 floods in the Himalayan foothills are just a few. They can also take on a political orientation, such as the organization (and financing) of the aforementioned mass rallies that Prime Minister Modi has addressed during his overseas trips (some seventy, as of late 2017). Some efforts even extend to directly abetting the political ambitions of the BJP: several dozen overseas Indian professionals, for example, went back to India to provide IT expertise to the 2013–14 Modi parliamentary campaign. Ullekh N.P., in his splendidly researched book on the mechanics of that campaign, has a chapter analysing the specific (and substantial) contributions of the overseas Indian community.[14] Among the several Indian American professionals he mentions is Amitabh Sharma—CEO and founder of Asterix Solutions—who utilized various media platforms in his native Uttar Pradesh to sell lower-class voters (especially Dalits and Muslims) on Modi's infrastructure and skill-based education models which promised to improve their living standards far more than conventional social welfare measures.[15] Another such example is Narain Kataria—founder of the Indian American Intellectuals Forum—who mobilized support for Modi across various Indian American communities, communities that in turn lobbied for the BJP among their friends and relatives living in India.

The overseas presence of RSS-inspired groups is, outside of neighbouring Nepal, strongest in three English-speaking countries: the US, the United Kingdom and Australia (though there are reports of such organizations in at least thirty-nine countries worldwide).[16] The basic unit in all these overseas organizations is called a shakha, though the practical format varies widely depending on local circumstances. While Nepal has the largest number of shakhas outside of India itself, the US comes in second with 172 (in 2016), a number that reportedly is growing rapidly.[17] The Indian American community, totalling over 3 million people, is the largest and wealthiest stratum of the Indian diaspora. According to the Pew Research Center's 2014 study of religion in the US, Hindus constitute only .07 per cent of the total population;[18] however, they also comprise the country's leading ethnic group in terms of education—77 per cent of Indian American adults have a college or postgraduate degree[19]—and income—70 per cent earn $50,000 per capita or more.[20] The American Hindu community is relatively religious, with 79 per cent of those polled reporting that religion is 'very important' or 'somewhat important' in their lives.[21] This would seem like a promising recruitment pool for the RSS, though the regular attendance for US HSS shakhas as of 2017 is only between 5000 and 7000 (that number would increase several times if one counted occasional attendance or participation in HSS programmes and parivar-supported projects).[22]

Each national HSS, like all RSS affiliates, is autonomous, though there are global coordinators.[23] Most national HSS units, like the RSS in India, have a women's branch, referred to as the Hindu Sevika Samiti (this branch is not present in the US, Australia or New Zealand, where shakhas are organized on a family basis). The HSS in the US, moreover, trains its own vistaraks and *vistarika*s (male and female part-time workers), and is unique in having female full-time workers and a female regional director.[24] The HSS in the US runs its own week-long training camps on the proper organization of shakhas. Those who successfully complete three of these training camps (referred to as *Sangha Shiksha Varg*) can either attend the RSS's second-year training programme in India or newly launched second-year training camps in Trinidad and Kenya, two countries with a large Indian minority. Those who complete the second-year camp can attend the longer third-year camp at the RSS headquarters in Nagpur. A senior HSS official told us that several American HSS members have participated in these programmes.[25] The anticipated growth of these overseas training centres will create an international pool of potential RSS workers to be assigned anywhere in the world to spread the message of Hindutva.

We spent an evening in July 2016 attending an HSS shakha in a Virginian suburb of Washington DC in order to compare it with those held in India. Our host was a practising engineer[26] and the *karyavah* (director) of shakhas for the DC area. His weekly shakha lasts for about an hour and a half. He told us that after migrating from India (where he was an RSS member), he decided to join the HSS because he believed it was important to instil proper Indian values in his children. Moreover, echoing Anderson's 'long-distance nationalism', he said that participation in the HSS evokes a sense of collective Hindu pride among Indian emigrants. Those fifty-odd emigrants—men and women both—attending this particular shakha were almost all college-educated professionals fluent in English. He told us that this night's attendance was less than half the average because many participants were on vacation. He also noted that the number of regular participants had doubled in the past few years, partly a reflection of the growth of the Indian American community in the DC area and partly because more Indian Americans are becoming aware of the HSS's activities. The administration of the American HSS is divided into five regions, and these DC area shakhas form part of the East Coast region. While each shakha is an autonomous unit, the national HSS general secretary—in consultation with other central, regional and local officers—selects the local shakha leaders. Each region has also rented facilities for residential camps (which usually last a week); these camps are critically important in engendering loyalty to the HSS and support for its Hindutva ideology among new volunteers and young people.[27]

We were told that all shakhas in the US are family-oriented, and we noticed that most of the attendees at our meeting came as families. Our host told us that the format of his shakha is common to those across the US—and in India, for that matter, except that in the US both men and women attend. The shakha began with the participants seated in rows based on their age, as in India, and proceeded as follows: first the saffron-coloured *Bhagwa Dhwaj* (similar to the flag used at shakhas in India) was hoisted and saluted;[28] then an opening prayer for Hindu unity was recited, with specific reference to the religion's diversity, mentioning Vedic Hinduism, Buddhism, Jainism and Sikhism as legitimate forms of worship; yoga, *surya namaskar* (a traditional exercise) and callisthenics followed for the adults, while the children engaged in more vigorous exercises, including traditional Indian games like *kho kho*; thence followed the *bouddhik*, a group-wide discussion of social or political issues; and finally a concluding prayer in Sanskrit which refers to 'Mother Earth' and humanity, a divergence from the closing prayers in India, which refer to Bharat Mata ('Mother India'). The opening prayer was recited by a teenage boy and the concluding one by a teenage girl. At this particular meeting, the bouddhik was delivered (in Sanskrit) by a visiting America-based RSS pracharak[29] representing an organization aiming to popularize Sanskrit as a spoken language.[30] Also attending was a local representative of Sewa International USA, which operates a wide range of service activities in the US and is managed mainly by HSS activists. Sewa International operates various national units across the globe, and has experienced a surge in activities (and volunteers) since the 1990s. The US national unit, formed in 2002, provides opportunities for American swayamsevaks to strengthen bonds to the sangh parivar in India and in other countries. The Sewa service activities of this particular shakha include donating food to the indigent and food banks, as well as tutoring sessions led by high school students. The American unit was heavily involved in relief efforts in 2017—such as providing volunteer doctors and other medical specialists—after several hurricanes swept across the US.

The VHP became the first RSS affiliate to enter the US in 1970, just six years after its formation in India. Changes to US immigration laws in 1965 led to a substantial migration of Indians, including some swayamsevaks, to the States, and this presented a wealth of opportunities for the VHP to engage in its traditional 'mission work'. Mahesh Mehta, a former pracharak, established the first VHP chapters and focused on youth work (*bal vihar*) to build a cadre for the group's future expansion into the US.[31] He worked initially with the few Hindu temples that then existed, but they offered little in terms of real assistance in organization-building. Recognizing that he had to establish his own support networks, he organized the Coalition of Hindu Youth to encourage young people to stay active in their local mandirs.[32]

The American branch of the VHP launched in a major way on 4 July 1984, with a mass rally at Madison Square Garden, announcing its intentions to aggressively propagate Hindutva as a spiritually based universal ideology.[33] Mehta told us that the rally avoided any reference to Hindu nationalism, as the VHP in the US is a purely American organization.[34] The VHP soon after became much more activist in character, starting or expanding a number of projects, including the

India Relief and Development Fund, the Hindu Student Council, Support a Child and Ekal Vidyalaya (which funds education projects in India). The American Ekal Vidyalaya has developed into a major source of funds for its parent group's projects in India, and claims to have received donations of some $6 million in 2016.[35] In 2002, the American VHP held the first Hindu temple conference, aimed at promoting coordination among the 800-odd Hindu temples in the US.[36] Eight years later, it held the first conference of Hindu priests, a conclave aimed at prodding the Hindu ecclesiastical establishment to be more active in social welfare initiatives (and, of course, more sympathetic to the VHP).[37] The VHP of America defines 'Hindus' as

> all those who believe, practice, or respect the spiritual and religious principles having roots in Bharat. Thus Hindu includes Jains, Buddhas [sic], Sikhs and Dharmic people, and the many different sects within the Hindu ethos.[38]

The VHP, like the RSS and other members of the sangh parivar, has always faced a definitional dilemma when distinguishing Hinduism as a cultural concept from Hinduism as a religion. The US VHP website makes that distinction in the following manner:

> The word Hindu is a *civilizational* [sic] term expressed as Hindu culture or 'Sanskriti.' And the word Dharma includes religious practices *only* [sic] as a subset [of this culture].[39]

The VHP at home and abroad openly proclaims itself a Hindu religious organization—quite different from the RSS and parivar generally, which claim to be cultural organizations open to people of any faith. This explicit identification of Hinduism as a religious characteristic has probably proved an asset in mobilizing local support for the VHP and its many projects.

In recognition of the overseas VHP's contribution to India, Mehta received the 2017 appreciation award from the Pravasi Bharatiya Divas (PBD), an initiative established in 2003 specifically to forge links between overseas Indians and the motherland. The

PBD was launched by the BJP-led Vajpayee government in 2003 as an annual event sponsored by the ministry of overseas Indian affairs and supported by the country's apex business organizations: the Federation of Indian Chambers of Commerce and Industry (FICCI), and the Confederation of Indian Industry (CII).[40] The first gathering, held under the present Modi government in early 2015, was unsurprisingly the largest to date, drawing a reported 4000 delegates from forty-four countries to an exhibition area of over 1 million square feet.[41] Among the most significant results of these PBD conclaves were the changes to Indian immigration policy. The Indian government, taking into consideration the constitutional ban on dual citizenship, passed legislation in 2005 creating the Overseas Citizens of India (OCI) category, which provides multiple-entry and lifetime visas, granting OCIs a range of privileges similar to those of Indian citizens.[42]

The American VHP and HSS have worked with other Hindu organizations in the US to take up controversial issues, a tactic that has set both on a politicizing track that mirrors the sangh parivar in India. We analyse two prominent examples that demonstrate this trend in the US. The first relates to a public-school history textbook in the state of California that allegedly presented the Hindu religion in a negative fashion. The second was a reaction to those American groups protesting Prime Minister Modi's visits to the US, charging that he was responsible for the 2002 riots in Gujarat and that he allegedly undermined the free expression of ideas after becoming prime minister.

On the textbook issue, the VHP and HSS—and other Hindu groups across several countries—have demanded what they consider a respectful portrayal of Hinduism in public-school textbooks. In some cases, this has involved adding descriptions of Hinduism to school textbooks where there had previously been none (as in the UK and Kenya); in others, the moderation of what they considered biased and uninformed accounts of Hinduism (as was the case in California). The UK VHP representatives in the mid-1990s sat on a national board that was mandated to prepare content that would serve as a guide to teaching Hinduism in public schools.[43] Similarly, the government of Kenya accepted the references to Hinduism suggested by the Hindu Council of Kenya, an umbrella organization of over 150 Hindu groups in the country.[44] Those efforts, however, did not involve any controversy over the actual portrayal of Hinduism, which characterized the textbook issue in California.

The California textbook controversy was triggered by a review of the state's public-school curriculum as pertaining to the portrayal of non-Christian religions. The issue quickly escalated into a debate over how Hinduism should be portrayed in the popular consciousness. On the one side was the South Asia Histories For All (SAHFA)—a coalition of various ethnic and religious groups claiming to represent the interests of Muslims, Sikhs and Dalits—as well as some academic Indologists, who argued that the revisions to the curriculum proposed by several Hindu groups, including the Hindu Education Foundation, the Vedic Foundation and the Hindu American Foundation (HAF), as well some American academics, offered an inaccurate and ahistorical portrayal of Hinduism.[45] This latter group of revisionists argued that the existing language of the textbooks was offensive to Hindus and violated the California regulation that public schools not ridicule any religion. They claimed further that the existing school texts portrayed Hinduism in negative ways that undermined Hindu students' pride in themselves and their culture. These Hindu groups used this argument to mobilize support from the large and rapidly growing Hindu population in California, estimated to be about 1 million in 2016. Protests were quickly organized and petitions drawn up against this perceived effort to denigrate Hinduism. Demonstrating a growing political sophistication, the revisionists approached several prominent politicians for support, and Congresswoman Tulsi Gabbard (D-HI) wrote a letter to California state authorities labelling some of the changes proposed by SAHFA as inaccurate and confusing.[46]

The HAF, probably the best-organized Hindu advocacy group in the US, then brought legal heft to the textbook issue by arguing that the proceedings lacked fairness, as the state's deliberative process was not transparent.[47] The controversy persisted for several years, and broke out fully again in 2016, when some academics (again largely Indologists) referring to themselves as the South Asia Faculty Group proposed three textual changes that were anathema to the VHP and their allies. Those three proposed changes were: that any reference to India prior to independence in 1947 be altered to 'South Asia', that the Vedic texts be delinked from Hinduism[48] and that any reference to the authors of the two classic Sanskrit sagas as 'non-Brahmins' be dropped on grounds that they were in fact Brahmins. The California Department of Education's Instructional Quality Commission came out against the first and third of these proposed changes.[49]

Both sides claimed victory when the California State Board of Education adopted a new 'History-Social Science Framework'.[50] The Hindu Education Foundation, one of the litigants, issued a statement saying that,

> While we believe that a lot more needs to be done to correct biases and stereotypes, we made significant progress in improving the content [of the school textbooks] and in resisting Hinduphobic content from being added to the textbook framework. The attempts to erase India and Hinduism from textbooks by a few Hinduphobic academicians were firmly thwarted, as the whole community united and stood up against the move.

A spokesman for the HAF stated that they were generally satisfied with the outcome, telling the publication *India Abroad* that his group was, however, 'disappointed that the state board failed to reinsert two important references to "Hinduism" that were previously removed as a result of pressure from the South Asia Faculty Group'.[51] He specifically complained about the inclusion of the phrase 'religions of Ancient India, but not limited to early Hinduism' in the textbooks, a complaint that was echoed in the letter from Congresswoman Gabbard.[52] The Department of Education's proposals still have to be vetted twice more before entering textbooks, which guarantees that the controversy in California will continue.

This textbook activism has proved to be a useful mobilizing tool for the VHP and its allies, which tend to portray their opponents as anti-Hindu and thus disrespectful of the Indian community. Such groups' concerns for how Hinduism is portrayed to students go far beyond the issue of textbooks, however. One senior figure in the HAF told us that his group, recognizing that tools other than textbooks are growing increasingly important to education, launched a programme for teachers, entitled 'Hinduism 101', to present a 'balanced and nuanced' picture of Hinduism through various educational methods.[53]

The HSS website suggests a special focus on building social solidarity and appreciation of Hindu culture among the children of the diaspora.[54] As in the RSS, the various overseas branches believe that long-term commitment to the cause stems from early association with Hindutva groups, even though the activities they sponsor might not always be explicitly cultural. These include sports contests, a children's programme called Balagokulam (with an accompanying magazine), Hindu Heritage camps, Guru Vandana (teacher appreciation events), and involvement in service projects like providing food and health services in the aftermath of natural disasters.[55]

The Hindu Educational Foundation, listed on the HSS website as an affiliate, is an example of the American HSS's assertiveness in removing 'misconceptions that prevail in academic settings about Hindu culture',[56] a reference to the multiple legal and lobbying battles it has waged over the textbook issues. But the Hindu Educational Foundation, backed by the HSS, can claim many more platforms than that. In cooperation with the HAF, it holds seminars on Hinduism for public-school teachers, facilitates classroom presentations on Hindu religious customs and provides multimedia resources to teachers. The HSS also actively honours teachers during special ceremonies at its shakhas.[57]

The HSS has also placed vistaraks in sensitive identity-building activities; Ram Madhav, when still a press spokesperson for the RSS, introduced us in 2012 to Darshan Soni, a vistarak who spent a year in Ohio working among Hindu Nepali refugees from Bhutan. He was assigned to organize some of the 80,000 Nepali Hindu refugees in the nation, who he said were subject to intense Christian evangelism. Under the guise of humanitarian assistance, the ultimate goal of these Christian groups, he claimed, was conversion. He was a young and enthusiastic engineering graduate, spoke fluent and American-accented English, and told us that he had decided to give a few years of his life to the 'cause' of Hindutva before starting a family. Following the usual pattern, this vistarak later married a vistarika.

HSS swayamsevaks, in the wake of the California controversy, have become increasingly vigilant regarding public criticism of the sangh parivar. After the 2014 elections and Modi's five subsequent visits (as of 2017) to the US, this criticism often took the form of letters signed by activists—primarily academics in the social sciences and humanities—critical of his past human rights record and the alleged growing intolerance for non-Hindus in India since he assumed office. One senior HSS figure told us that these letters critical of Modi and the sangh parivar have, in fact, proved to be among the HSS's most useful mobilization tools. He claimed that the academic opposition to Modi is disadvantaged by its lack of structural links to the Indian American community, and thus these petitions have had little influence in either the Indian American community or the larger political arena. One faculty letter that aroused especially significant resentment within the HSS was issued on 27 August 2015, just prior to Modi's visit to Silicon Valley that September. That letter was entitled 'Faculty Statement of Narendra Modi's Visit to Silicon Valley',[58] and was signed initially by 125 academics (with ten more signing later). The letter drew attention to the denial of his visa applications between 2005 and 2014, and asserted that there is still 'an active case' in Indian courts regarding his role in the riots of 2002. The letter further stated that:

> Modi's first year in office as the Prime Minister of India includes well publicized episodes of censorship and harassment of those critical of his policies, bans and restrictions on NGOs leading to a constriction of the space of civic engagement, ongoing violations of religious freedom . . . These alarming trends require that we, as educators, remain vigilant not only about modes of e-governance in India but also about the political future of the county.[59]

This letter immediately triggered a barrage of responses on social media, with many Indian Americans highly critical of its content. A counter-petition with over 1100 supporters was quickly put up on the website change.org, accusing the anti-Modi letter writers of lacking 'academic integrity' and alleging that the real object of censorship and distortion was Modi himself.[60] The counter-petition exhorted those who had signed the letter 'to introspect, change, and for once seek to earn the trust and respect of the community in whose name they have been making a living all these years'.[61] This last point is a rather sardonic reference to the widely held view among Hindu advocates in the US that these academics live in a bubble and speak almost exclusively to each other, rather than to the larger Indian American community, and that the academics purport to be the representatives of the Indian American community. Hindutva activists point to Modi's enthusiastic reception by the digital community in Silicon Valley and the passionate response to his 2016 address to a joint sitting of the US Congress as examples of the failure of his critics to understand his relevance to the diaspora in America.

The furore directed at those opposed to Modi's visits reached such a fever pitch, in fact, that it triggered another faculty letter, this one entitled 'Faculty Response to Harassment by Hindu Nationalist Organizations' and issued on 15 September 2015.[62] This letter asserted that, 'We find it no accident that attacks on us come from members of U.S. Hindu nationalist organizations.' It then identified as Hindu nationalist organizations the Hindu Vivek Kendra—a self-described intellectual resource centre for Hindutva headquartered in Mumbai[63]—and the aforementioned HAF which, despite its past advocacy alongside the HSS, is not itself formally linked to the sangh parivar. The HAF was probably picked out because two of the individuals, both medical doctors, who were involved in its establishment in 2003,[64] Dr Mihir Meghani and Dr Aseem Shukla, both board members of the HAF, were among the most active critics of the original faculty letter. Responding to claims that the original critical faculty letter reflected an underlying bias against Hinduism, its writers took pains to emphasize that

[W]e are not anti-Hindu or against Hinduism. We are, however, extremely concerned by the growth of Hindu nationalism which has resulted in well-documented discrimination and attacks against Indian minority communities.

This disclaimer of genuine respect for Hinduism as a religion was widely rejected by Hindu groups. The problem with this assertion, we believe, lies in these academics' failure to define with any sense of precision what 'Hinduism' is, let alone what 'Hindu nationalism' is. We attempt to demonstrate in our chapter on Hinduism that the sangh parivar itself has several (often contradictory) definitions of Hinduism, and that those definitions, moreover, seem to change with the times. Critics of the Modi visit are correct that Hindu nationalism is not really about religion, much as Zionism is not really about religion. While Hindu nationalism claims to be apolitical and cultural, many of its leaders see religion as a subset of culture. In the US, and other countries with a Hindu minority, Hindu nationalists consider it their duty to guarantee the religious freedom of Hindus to worship as they please—and to provide Hindus a sense of pride in being Hindu and being Indian. This Indian pride often shows up in their lobbying for Indian interests, for example, in their support for making India an exception to the provisions of the 1970 Nuclear Non-Proliferation Treaty following its nuclear tests in May 1998—and in the enthusiastic welcome Modi receives when he visits the US.

The inclusion of the HAF as a Hindu nationalist organization in the second anti-Modi letter reflects the difficulty in distinguishing Hindu activism from Hindu nationalism, a dilemma HAF leaders tell us they face constantly. Hindu nationalism is closely linked to the sangh parivar, and the HAF sometimes cooperates with parivar affiliates such as the HSS and VHP. The HAF website, in describing the organization, refers to this dilemma as follows:

> The Hindu American Foundation is not affiliated with any religious or political organizations or entities. HAF seeks to serve Hindu Americans across all *sampradayas* [Hindu religious schools of thought] regardless of race, color, national origin, citizenship, caste, gender, sexual orientation, age and/or disability.[65]

A pamphlet issued by the HAF, 'The Coalition against Genocide: A Nexus of Hinduphobia Unveiled' argues that its critics seek 'to essentialize HAF as but one manifestation of several India based socio-religious organizations with existential links to the "Sangh Parivar."[66] The HAF's six stated goals, however, would not raise objections among parivar affiliates: (1) promoting pluralism; (2) establishing an accurate understanding of Hinduism as a 'living tradition'; (3) highlighting and securing the human rights of Hindus across the globe; (4) representing the Hindu American community's needs to legislators; (5) solving contemporary problems by applying Hindu philosophies; and (6) building a sustainable institution that will remain a permanent advocate for 'dharma communities'.[67]

The HAF was established in 2003 as the first group explicitly focused on advocacy for Hindu rights. Prior to its formation, various Hindu groups, some within the sangh parivar and some without, engaged in advocacy in a rather hit-or-miss fashion. The HAF was different; it was professionally run with a full-time staff (its central office in Washington DC employs nine as of 2017), it cultivated ties to policymakers and their staffs, and it served as a bridge between the many Hindu-oriented groups in the US and the political arena. Gabbard, for many years the only Hindu in the US House of Representatives, was a frequent participant in HAF programmes, as are members of the Congressional Caucus on India and Indian Americans, one of the largest country-specific caucuses in Congress.

A review of just a few of the HAF's activities underscores its broad agenda: on 1 May 2015, it testified before a Congressional committee on the plight of religious minorities in Bangladesh and strongly supported H.Res.396, which calls on the government of Bangladesh to protect the human rights of all its citizens; on 19 November 2014, it organized an event on Capitol Hill with a delegation of Bhutanese Hindu expatriates to address the circumstances of the 80,000 such refugees in the US; on 6 June 2015, it celebrated International Yoga Day on Capitol Hill; on 17 March 2006, it filed its aforementioned suit against the California State Board of Education in the California Supreme Court in Sacramento regarding the textbook drafting process— and related to this, conducted a survey of middle school students to demonstrate that a significant percentage of Hindu students were harassed and bullied because of their identification as Hindus, harassment at least partly attributed to the way Hinduism was presented to students; and in 2010, it organized a yearly senior internship programme for six Indian American youths to work on Capitol Hill.[68] On 20–21 June 2016, it organized its first Policy Conference in Washington DC aimed at explaining its legislative priorities. Its director of government relations, Jay Kansara, explained to us that—while his organization had become an active voice for Hindu-Americans over the past fifteen years— the diasporic community generally has not focused on advocacy relating to its own interests, perhaps because the community is relatively new to the US and still uncertain about its role in the American political system.[69] However, issues like the California controversy have demonstrated the value of using the political system to advance group interests—and the passage of the United States–India Nuclear Cooperation Approval and Non-Proliferation Enhancement Act in 2008 provides a model of what an organized Indian American community can achieve.

Overseas HSS shakhas are now also beginning to syncretize elements of the various cultural settings in which they operate. For example, HSS shakhas in the US permit both men and women to attend, though it continues to segregate its training camps by gender.[70] As such, the HSS leadership decided specifically that there is no need to establish an American equivalent of the Rashtra Sevika Samiti, the RSS's dedicated female branch.[71] The HSS (and VHP) prayer has replaced the word 'Motherland' used in India with 'Mother Earth', and the phrase 'Bharat Mata ki Jai' (victory to Mother India) was replaced by 'Vishwa Dharma ki Jai' (victory to universal moral principles); it has renamed the shakha exercises from 'surya namaskar' to 'health for humanity'; it has shifted the concept of the *raksha bandhan* celebration (a symbol of a brother's protectiveness towards his sister, signified by the sister tying a thread around her brother's wrist) to a ritual, referred to as 'universal oneness day', where a thread is tied around the wrist of a respected community member to show appreciation for their work (for example, teachers, first responders, legislators and so on). Some shakhas in the US have organized baseball teams, and in the UK, there have even been inter-shakha soccer matches—the idea of hosting scouting units is now being considered in the US.

A more self-confident RSS is now beginning to command an assertive presence on the world stage, justifying this new stance on the notion that all people are children of the same 'mother earth', and thus should live cooperatively as a family—with the RSS as the unique evangelist of this good news. Reflecting this confidence, RSS chief Bhagwat asserted that a major goal of the RSS is social transformation at home to make India a 'vishwa guru' (a global exemplar).[72] The RSS's conception of social transformation, as we have noted elsewhere in the book, includes reduced emphasis on materialism and hedonistic consumption as well as the strengthening of family bonds. Taking a page out of Modi's book, senior RSS officials made a high-profile trip to the UK in late July 2016 to deliver what they considered a unique message of peace and cooperation.[73] Bhagwat and the all-India joint general secretary, Hosabale, celebrated the golden jubilee of the HSS in the UK, and thus demonstrated the importance of the overseas counterparts of the RSS within the larger cause of Hindutva. They met with several senior politicians and such pre-eminent religious authorities as the Archbishop of Canterbury. In addition, senior RSS figures have for some time now regularly visited countries with large Hindu populations (such as Fiji, Mauritius, Bangladesh, Sri Lanka, Nepal, Burma, Suriname and Jamaica) to strengthen the self-confidence of those elements of the diaspora by stressing the pan-Hindu links among co-religionists worldwide, from Delhi to Dubai and from Bengaluru to Berlin.[74] Yogi Adityanath, a Hindu monk who was appointed as the chief minister of Uttar Pradesh, told us in an interview that even overseas Hindus regard India as their holy land.[75] Yet another new initiative, reflecting again a more self-confident RSS, is the International Centre for Cultural Studies (ICCS), a non-profit group founded in India by senior swayamsevaks with the support of the RSS to advocate for indigenous peoples by holding conferences and providing grants for study. It has established contact with groups whose traditions and customs are threatened by external cultural forces, such as the

Roma and Sami peoples in Europe and other indigenous groups in Africa and South America.[76] Our conversations with its staff in Nagpur suggest that the ICCS wants to revitalize indigenous cultures away from the aegis of what some referred to as destructive Western cultural imperialism, bringing them instead closer to that which Upadhyaya defined as their 'national soul' (*chiti*), the cultural essence of what makes them a distinct people. This would include reviving threatened indigenous languages, religious concepts, arts and music—and, most importantly, renewing their pride in their own cultures.

The various HSS units across the globe are likely to multiply and become more activist as the Indian diaspora continues to grow and as its social and political capital likewise expands. But the major long-term challenge facing the overseas RSS in most countries lies in justifying its presence as a unique organization while its membership continues to be assimilated culturally into the host country's society. The RSS at home and abroad tries to present itself as a purely cultural group, but the assimilation process may drive its overseas counterparts into a definitively religious orientation.

FOUR

'Indianizing Education'

The RSS has always viewed education as its core mission and virtually all its affiliates engage in some form of it, some with the specific mission of managing schools at the primary, secondary and tertiary levels—and on a mass scale. From the 1980s, the RSS has encouraged its affiliates to engage in educational experiments in order to package its Hindutva message in ways that make it more relevant and thus more appealing to Indians. This has included the introduction of sports meets, music, art, skill-oriented instruction and coaching classes. Its educational affiliate, the Vidya Bharati, announced on 2 January 2015 a plan to establish model schools in all of India's 9000-odd administrative blocks to serve as an example of excellence to be emulated by government schools.[1]

The RSS's decision to set up its own school system, starting in the late 1940s, was motivated by what it viewed as the deliberate attempt of India's post-Independence Congress government to deny RSS members and their Hindu message any place in the educational system. While the educational role of the shakha (referred to as 'character-building') is viewed by the RSS as an effective technique to train a future nationalist leadership, this message was, in its view, often drowned out by the anti-Hindu messages coming from the universities, the press, the Congress government and much of the intellectual class. With a commitment to restore (or 'Indianize', to use its term) Hindu values in the schools of India, the RSS first forayed into formal education by supporting a private school at Kurukshetra in Haryana soon before independence, in 1946, with RSS chief Golwalkar taking part in the groundbreaking ceremony.[2] Prior to this, during the colonial period, RSS leaders did not seriously address setting up a separate school system in large part due to the existence of alternative national schools run by individuals and groups with a nationalist outlook acceptable to the RSS.[3] Prominent among such groups was the Arya Samaj, a Hindu reform organization, whose schools incorporated its message of the unity of a Hinduism found in early Vedic literature.[4]

Following the 1948–49 ban on the RSS, an activist pracharak, Nanaji Deshmukh, established at Gorakhpur in eastern Uttar Pradesh the first RSS-affiliated school whose goal was to provide a Hindu orientation to the educational experience.[5] As we noted in our previous book on the RSS, its activists in the post-ban period lobbied their own leadership to establish a broad array of affiliated groups to keep the Hindu nationalist message alive as the state penetrated such areas as education.[6] A further incentive to setting up even more schools was their effectiveness as a recruitment tool for shakhas at a time when RSS membership was declining. These schools also provided jobs to RSS members who were sometimes blocked from government employment. The Hindu orientation of these RSS-affiliated schools, according to a study of them by Tanika Sarkar, includes observance of Hindu rituals and festivals, the practice of yoga, the teaching of Sanskrit, classes on 'Indian civilization' from a Hindu perspective and a profusion of Hindu symbols.[7] While these schools are required to follow a mandated state curriculum, they have an element of discretion in the choice of textbooks and extracurricular activities that directly address issues of importance to them.

Following a rapid expansion in the number of schools in the 1960s and 1970s, the RSS in 1978 established a separate affiliate, the Vidya Bharati, to manage its burgeoning school network, which at that time included some 700 schools.[8] The Vidya Bharati's 2016 statistical report shows the very quick growth in the number of affiliated schools since 1978, noting that there are over 13,000 schools with some 32,00,000 students and 1,46,000 teachers, making it the largest private school system in India.[9] In addition to these Vidya Bharati schools, another RSS-affiliated educational group, the Ekal Vidyalaya, established in 1986, has about 15,00,000 students in some 54,000 one-teacher, one-school facilities located mainly in remote rural and tribal areas.[10] With such a large potential market for textbooks, RSS-affiliated groups have commissioned books on history and ethics for use in the Shishu Mandirs and other RSS-affiliated schools.[11] Some of these groups, such as the RSS-affiliated Shiksha Sanskriti Utthan Nyas, lobby the ministry of human resource development (HRD) to ensure that textbooks recommended to the states include some with a value orientation they consider appropriate.[12]

Controversy over the content of textbooks, especially on subjects related to culture and history, have existed from the time of India's independence when the Congress party was in power. A parliamentary committee appointed in 1966, for example, reported that textbooks in some states 'were overweighted with Hindu mythology' and 'Hindu beliefs are presented in a manner as if they are universally held by all Indians'.[13] The federal Education Commission in 1964, in reference to this issue, stated, 'It is necessary for a multireligious democratic State to promote a tolerant study of all religions so that its citizens can understand each other better and live amicably together.'[14] The establishment in 1972 of the Indian Council of Historical Research (ICHR) in the federal bureaucracy triggered a reaction from the right of a growing Marxist bias in the history texts that it commissioned. Debates often centred on issues regarding the level of religious tolerance in states with Muslim rulers, the level of social harmony between Muslims and Hindus, the degree of social and religious unity among Hindus as well as larger philosophical questions regarding the influence of culture and economics on human behaviour. Historians on the right, Dinesh Raza writes in an analysis of the debate on the teaching of history, argue that historians on the left undervalue the culture and civilization and focus instead on class and economic factors.[15] He notes, citing the controversy over the interpretation of Indian history in textbooks following the Congress's return to power in 2004, that an agency of the HRD ministry withdrew an earlier recommendation for a book on medieval Indian history by historian Meenakshi Jain, as part of its effort to 'de-saffronize' textbooks, presumably because she argued that Islam entered India with a cultural world view very different from the indigenous Indian civilization.[16] This ideological battle over how to interpret history has deeply divided Indian historians and triggered political tensions that are almost unique to India. Two professional history associations differ on ideological lines, the Indian History Congress on the left of centre and the Indian History and Culture Society on the right. The sangh parivar even has its own association of historians, the Akhil Bharatiya Itihas Sankalan Yojana (ABISY), which claims to have published over 350 books since it was formed in 1984. Its website says that the organization is pledged to present 'Bharatheeya Itihasa [history] from a national perspective'. It argues that this is necessary because

> The British distorted Bharatheeya history, destroyed/perverted the traditional heroes, cultures, literature. Hence ABISY coordinates patriotic, bold, and incorruptible scholars and historians to write history truthfully on the basis of facts and evidences [sic].[17]

The RSS and its educational affiliates usually review their performance four times a year where new initiatives are proposed to make their schools more relevant to India's changing needs. A case in point was the discussion in the 1980s to set up study centres for students in slum areas to address the poor quality of instruction, especially in mathematics, science and English. In 2000, coaching classes for college students sitting for competitive examinations were added.[18] These groups are now planning model schools for India's 9000 blocks that will lay emphasis on improving vocational training instruction to provide the skills needed in India's growing economy. This goal fits the job-creation objective of Prime Minister Modi's government. With this educational objective in mind, Modi addressed leaders of the Vidya Bharati school system (on 12 February

2016) and the Ekal Vidyalaya (on 12 October 2015, 8 February 2016 and 18 May 2017) advising them to come up with ways to provide job-oriented skills that would make Indians more competitive in Indian and foreign job markets.[19]

As the RSS and sangh parivar have expanded, especially in rural India and among lower-caste Hindus, debates have emerged over the appropriate focus of their educational efforts. Among those debates is how to address the different needs of rural and urban students. On the urban side is a largely middle-class population advocating merit and specialized education in an increasingly technical world. On the rural side is a need for skill-based education that would address the demand for jobs among the huge number of students from farming families who cannot make a living as farmers because of the tiny size of most Indian farms. The demand for education in vernacular languages is also stronger in the rural areas, though the ABPS in 2008 issued two language-related resolutions, one arguing that the 'Medium of education must be Bharatiya Languages' and the other, 'Excessive importance given to English in all spheres of governmental activity must be ended.'[20]

A dilemma confronting the RSS is that, despite all the effort and finances lavished on education by the organization itself and by its affiliates, comparatively few intellectual advocates of Hindutva have emerged in the top ranks of the country's prestigious cultural and academic institutions.[21] This scarcity has resulted in a shallow pool of people from which to draw, a situation that has been criticized by its ideological opponents. The lack of credentialled intellectuals may be partly due to the policies of the Congress party which, during its long tenure in power, often used ideological criteria in dispensing favours and appointments.[22] The RSS, tarred with the involvement of a former member (Nathuram Godse) in the assassination of Mahatma Gandhi and held at least partly responsible for the communal riots during the Independence period, was maligned, often with official backing, as fascist, authoritarian and obscurantist. Many in the RSS wanted to respond publicly to counter the widely held negative view of the organization among Indian intellectuals, but Golwalkar strongly opposed the RSS engaging in public debates. Nonetheless, the RSS published three works still considered the ideological foundation of Hindutva: Golwalkar's own major philosophical work *Bunch of Thoughts* (1966), BJS President Upadhyaya's *Integral Humanism* (1968) and labour leader Thengadi's *Labour Policy* in English and *Shramneeti* in Hindi (1969). Following Golwalkar's death in 1973, the earlier RSS reluctance to defend itself publicly was altered by his successor Deoras, who encouraged the publication of a seven-volume collection of the writings of Golwalkar and a set of essays analysing Upadhyaya's concept of integral humanism.[23] A justification for this effort to disseminate these basic statements of the RSS philosophy as widely as possible was that it would provide its membership with arguments to respond to or challenge its critics.

When the first BJP-led government came to power under Vajpayee (1996 and 1998–2004), the new prime minister selected one of the party's most outspoken ideologues, Murli Manohar Joshi, to head the HRD ministry, the ministry responsible for education. Joshi, an academic physicist and a former activist RSS pracharak, responded to complaints of excessive Marxist influence in scholarly research bodies under his control by removing left-leaning scholars from their positions. He triggered a political firestorm by selecting non-Marxist scholars, many sympathetic to the BJP and the RSS, and to a range of institutions, including the ICHR, the Indian Council of Social Science Research (ICSSR) and the National Council for Educational Research and Training (NCERT) that recommends textbooks to states. His opponents charged that he was 'communalizing' these institutions and so distorting historical and social science research in addition to undermining the secular foundations of the Indian state.[24] In response, Dina Nath Mishra, a journalist and author sympathetic to the RSS, wrote a stinging rebuttal reflecting the raw emotions unleashed by these changes. He began his response by charging that, 'The octopus-like grip of the card-holding Communists and fellow travellers over the Indian Council of Historical Research (ICHR) for over a quarter century has distorted and gave ideological colouring to the history of India.'[25] The new orientation of the NCERT was especially controversial as this body is responsible for publishing textbooks in various fields, including, most prominently for our purpose, history. A common RSS complaint is that textbooks written during periods of Congress rule lacked a 'value orientation' and gave insufficient attention to the unique contributions of the Hindu civilization. The controversy over the Hindu nationalist orientation of its history texts came to a head in 2002 when the NCERT recommended four books that its critics argued created an inaccurate historical image of a united Hindu society and culture. As education is a state subject in India's federal system, several non-BJP state governments declined to use these textbooks.[26]

When the BJP returned to power in 2014 after a ten-year hiatus during which the intervening Congress government sought to 'de-saffronize' the lists of recommended textbooks, the RSS resumed the earlier dialogue with the HRD minister to undo what its leaders saw as a deliberate attempt to denigrate Hinduism. Within months of the BJP's victory, then HRD Minister Smriti Irani met with senior RSS figures who called for a revamping of the Indian education system so that the essentials of Indian culture are reflected in the curriculum of schools across the country.[27] Attending that meeting was the influential RSS sah sarkaryavah Hosabale, who has taken the lead in the RSS on educational matters. A year later, on 6–7 September 2015, the education and culture ministers of the BJP-controlled states met with Irani and RSS participants to talk about a uniform educational policy in the states.[28] Given the importance of the HRD ministry in implementing the RSS goal of 'Indianizing' education, the party on 5 July 2016 selected one of its rising stars, Prakash Javadekar, to replace the controversial Irani[29] as the HRD cabinet minister. He brought to his HRD responsibilities the prestige (at least within sangh parivar circles) of active participation in the RSS since childhood, followed by a set of leadership positions in the ABVP, a training ground for BJP politicians. In 1981, he became a full-time worker for the BJP, focusing his efforts on the party's youth wing, and through that came to know senior figures in the BJP and the RSS. Javadekar was elected to the Rajya Sabha in 2008 and, after the BJP's 2014 victory, was named by Modi as both minister of state (independent charge) for environment, forest and climate change as well as

minister of state for parliamentary affairs and briefly as minister
of state for information and broadcasting. At the December 2015
Paris Climate Conference, he skilfully used the forum to give a
Hindu rationale for environmental reform, which won him high
praise in RSS circles. Just a month after assuming his new post,
on 27 July 2016, Javadekar called a meeting that included senior
RSS and BJP officials[30] and other constituents of the sangh parivar
engaged in education to discuss the draft education policy earlier
initiated by Irani as well as suggestions to 'instill nationalism, pride
and ancient Indian values in modern education'.[31] To underscore
his evolving close relation with other elements of the sangh parivar,
the HRD minister in May 2017 released the prospectus for a new
nine-month course for future political leaders, headed by Vinay
Sahasrabuddhe, also a vice president of the BJP, to be held at the
spacious 150-acre Rambhau Mhalgi Prabodhini academy on the
outskirts of Mumbai.[32]

The HRD minister's appointments to sensitive cultural and
academic bodies under his jurisdiction aroused a chorus of criticism
similar to the reaction to appointments made earlier by Murli
Manohar Joshi during Prime Minister Vajpayee's BJP-led coalition.
Among the first steps taken was the removal of Parvin Sinclair,
director of NCERT during the previous Congress government,
and criticized in RSS circles for overseeing what one critic of
the RSS—and supporter of Sinclair—has called a 'process of
"de-saffronisation", which led to widely acclaimed, secular-liberal
pedagogically vastly superior, school textbooks'.[33] Another early
controversy in the Modi government was the naming of Gajendra
Chauhan as chair of the Film and Television Institute of India
(FTII). Chauhan, while an actor, was criticized for a mediocre
career and thus was believed to lack the prestige for such a post.
One press analysis of this appointment argues that the explanation
for Chauhan's somewhat surprising appointment is the thin talent
pool the BJP has to draw upon in this area.[34] The RSS for its part
has complained about what it argues is the growing influence of
Western and non-Hindu themes in the Indian film industry and,
a year after the Chauhan controversy, it formed a film-oriented

affiliate (Chitra Sadhana) with the cooperation of several well-known film directors and actors.[35] Also triggering controversy is the militancy of the far right of the sangh parivar, whose sometimes violent actions in a number of areas (for example, cow protection) have periodically embarrassed the BJP and even the RSS leadership, in part due to complaints that the leadership of both were either slow to criticize these actions or remained silent. One example of silence in the area of literature occurred when Penguin withdrew *The Hindus: An Alternative History*, a book by American academic Wendy Doniger.[36]

A direct strategy to create a competitive Hindutva intellectual narrative is reflected in the proliferation of RSS think tanks, eight of them in the Delhi region alone, that sprang up following the surprise BJP loss in the 2004 parliamentary elections. These have emerged as major players in the think-tank world of Delhi in the wake of the BJP victory of 2014. Ram Madhav, the RSS pracharak turned BJP general secretary, has taken a leading role in making them a venue for policy debates involving a range of policy experts, both Indian and foreign. The oldest of these RSS-affiliated think tanks in Delhi is the Vivekananda International Foundation, whose head, Ajit Doval, was selected as Modi's national security adviser. The influential and the most recent is the India Foundation established in 2014. On its board are Union Minister for Railway, Commerce, Industry and Civil Aviation Suresh Prabhu, Minister of Defence Nirmala Sitharaman, Minister of State for Civil Aviation Jayant Sinha, BJP Minister of State for External Affairs M.J. Akbar, BJP General Secretary Ram Madhav and Doval's son, Shaurya. The India Foundation hosts two international conferences each year, one in India that focuses on broad philosophical questions and the other overseas, addressing strategic issues.[37] Associated with these Delhi-based think tanks are the who's who of the BJP and the Modi government, such as the principal secretary to the prime minister, Nripendra Misra, NITI Aayog members Bibek Debroy and V.K. Saraswat, BJP national executive member Bal Desai, prominent BJP member of Parliament and former editor of both *Organiser*

and *Panchjanya* Tarun Vijay, BJP National General Secretaries
Arun Singh and Ram Lal, National BJP Vice Presidents Shyam
Jaju, Prabhat Jha and Vinay Sahasrabuddhe. There are still older
RSS-affiliated think tanks such as the Deendayal Research
Institute that centres on economic development, the Rambhau
Mhalgi Prabodhini that conducts training classes for politicians
and their staff, the Jammu Kashmir Study Centre that focuses on
the integration of Kashmir into the Indian Union, and the Shiksha
Sanskriti Utthan Nyas that monitors books published in India,
especially those recommended as texts by the NCERT. The first
RSS-affiliated think tank was the Prajna Pravah established in the
early 1980s with the encouragement of the then sarsanghchalak
(chief) Deoras, who selected. Sudarshan, the then bouddhik
karyavah (intellectual secretary) and Thengadi, the founder of
several RSS-related affiliates and, after the deaths of Golwalkar
and Upadhyaya, considered the most authentic RSS ideologue, to
lay the foundation for this new venture in public outreach. As the
RSS has historically been averse to publicity, asserting that the
organization's work speaks for itself, these respected figures had
the legitimacy to get RSS members to consider the value of taking
their case to the larger public. The major purpose of these think
tanks was to provide a forum for RSS swayamsevaks to discuss the
relevance of Hindutva in the modern era. As the RSS affiliates'
policy activism has become more complex, several of them have
established think tanks to support their policy positions. C.K.
Saji Narayanan, the president of the BMS, noted in an interview
that the affiliates' focus on research is a recent phenomenon.[38]
The affiliates use this research to lobby policymakers.[39] The RSS's
labour affiliate (BMS), famers' union (BKS) and the SJM, three
of the more policy-oriented affiliates, have established research
units. The RSS currently publishes a vast amount of literature
on what they do and there are several publishing houses which
the RSS and its affiliates use to publish authorized books and
pamphlets in English and most Indian languages, such as Suruchi
Prakashan in Delhi, Rashtrotthana Sahitya in Bangalore and the
Bharatiya Vichar Sadhana in Pune and Nagpur.

Commitment to Reservations in Education

Written into the Indian Constitution is the notion of affirmative action applicable to elective bodies, public-sector employment and educational institutions of higher learning for groups identified as historically disadvantaged Dalits and tribals, now calculated at about 22.5 per cent of the population. At the federal level and in most states, the beneficiaries are restricted to Hindus, Sikhs and Buddhists, religions whose roots are in India. Christians and Muslims are not included as beneficiaries at the federal level, though some states offer affirmative action benefits to them if they can convince the relevant authorities that they belong to a historically disadvantaged group. Some forty years after the adoption of the Constitution, the employment and education benefits were expanded to include Hindu castes referred to as OBC that added another 27 per cent to the permitted category of beneficiaries.[40] There has always been a debate on the appropriate criteria to use for identifying which castes would qualify as OBC beneficiaries, and there have been periodic protests by castes which felt they were unfairly excluded. While the RSS at least since the 1970s has actively pushed for the removal of restrictions applied to those at the bottom of the Hindu caste hierarchy (such as temple entry),[41] the use of caste categories to identify state affirmative action beneficiaries is contrary to its goal of unifying Hindus into a single ethnic category. The RSS in its own operations ignores caste, and its major ideologues, such as Golwalkar, argue that the classic practice of Hinduism rejects the notion of hierarchy in society as a perversion of the faith.[42]

Despite this philosophical aversion to caste as a basis for state benefits, the sangh parivar has remained largely neutral on the reservation issue even though the policy of affirmative action almost certainly strengthens caste identity and legitimizes caste as a basis for provision of state benefits. Hindu solidarity is compatible with the BJP's goal of 'development for all' ('Sabka Saath Sabka Vikas') and the RSS's goal of social unity and stability. Nonetheless, the political arm of the sangh parivar, the BJP, has for largely political reasons defended reservations as a legitimate tool for social reform and has rejected a review of how it is implemented. The BJP, after some hesitation about the extension of the benefits to include OBCs in the early 1990s, did express public support for its expansion and has remained committed to that view. With over 45 per cent of the population in castes eligible for OBC status, the BJP has little room to manoeuvre on this issue if it wants to stay competitive politically. The most explicit RSS resolutions on the reservation question, 'Tactics of Internal Disruption' and 'Issue of Reservation', were passed by the ABPS in 1981 and reflect the RSS's dilemma in shaping policy on this issue. The major recommendation in these resolutions is the formation of a special committee of 'non-partisan social thinkers' to evaluate who should be included and for how long,[43] a stand that allowed it to avoid a specific statement on the merits of reservation. The first of the two resolutions asserts that, 'The A.B.P.S. affirms the basic truth of our national life being one and indivisible and endowed with rich diversity.' But that same resolution also states that, 'The R.S.S. considers it necessary that reservations be continued for the present with a view to bringing all these brethren of ours who have remained backward in educational, social and economic fields over the centuries at par with the rest of society.'[44] These resolutions try to satisfy the conflicting stands on this issue, stating:

> The A.B.P.S. agrees with the Prime Minister's viewpoint [Indira Gandhi at that time] that reservations cannot be a permanent arrangement, that these crutches will have to be done away with as soon as possible and that because of this arrangement merit and efficiency should not be allowed to be adversely affected.[45]

It says nothing, however, on the criteria for a timeline on ending reservations or how to measure the effectiveness of the benefits, or how to keep merit from being adversely affected by the reservation policy.

The RSS in 2015 found itself on the defensive regarding its stand on reservations after a twenty-five-year hiatus when it avoided the issue. The public debate over the RSS's stance was triggered by a

20 September 2015 interview RSS chief Bhagwat had with the editors of *Organiser* and *Panchjanya*, two RSS-affiliated weeklies, where he used almost exactly the same words as the ambiguous 1981 ABPS resolutions on reservations, asserting that reservations have been used for political ends, and suggested setting up an apolitical committee to examine who needs reservation benefits and for how long.[46] The context for these remarks was the violence that grew out of the protests by some members of the Patel community in Gujarat demanding they be included as a disadvantaged group eligible for OBC reservations. This was a sensitive time politically, as Bhagwat's remarks were made on the eve of elections to the Bihar legislative assembly, and the RSS, and by implication the BJP, was attacked by the Opposition which sought to use those remarks to show that the BJP and RSS were seeking to end the policy of reservations. Within weeks, the RSS sarkaryavah Suresh 'Bhaiyyaji' Joshi issued a statement on behalf of the RSS stating that, 'Reservation can continue as long as it is needed in society. That's our stand . . . Whatever was said [by Bhagwat] was not presented in proper words. Nowhere was it said that there should be a review of the reservation policy.'[47] The issue resurfaced when Vaidya, then the RSS prachar pramukh and now its joint general secretary, made a statement at the prestigious Jaipur Literature Festival in January 2017 suggesting that reservation for OBCs encourages separatism.[48] Almost immediately the sah sarkaryavah, Hosabale, who was present at the festival, issued a statement that, 'The Sangh's opinion is very clear that the constitutionally provided reservations for the Scheduled Castes, Tribes, and Other Backward Castes should continue. It is still needed and it should be implemented entirely. This is the authorized view of the RSS.'[49] Vaidya also issued a clarification using very similar language. Finance Minister Jaitley in a 15 March 2016 statement in the Rajya Sabha on behalf of the Modi government assured the members that, 'The government policy is clear: reservation will continue.'[50] The RSS has committed itself to the continuation of the Modi government and, despite private concerns about the reservation policy by some members, it will try to avoid doing anything publicly that could embarrass the BJP government or complicate its electoral prospects. RSS swayamsevaks are still relatively inexperienced in making

public appearances, but are increasingly doing so and, in the process, learning the art of avoiding statements on politically sensitive topics. To underscore this commitment to the Modi government from the collective sangh parivar, Nitin Gadkari, minister for road, transport, highways and shipping, who is reputed to be close to the RSS's senior leadership, said that the Modi government needs ten years to implement his programme.[51] Bhagwat has lavished praise on Prime Minister Modi as the ideal swayamsevak whose *ujjwal* (brightness) comes from his *aprasiddhi* (unheralded) stint of service within the RSS.[52] The BJP's control of the government provides the RSS and its affiliates unparalleled opportunities to influence policy, particularly important for the educational affiliates like the Vidya Bharati and the Ekal Vidyalaya.

The debate over educational goals has intensified within the sangh parivar, a development linked to the very rapid growth of the RSS and its affiliates over the past two decades and the accommodation of groups with differing interests (for example, rural vs urban on what skills to emphasize, and high and low castes regarding reservation). Influencing the debate is the growing support for the BJP among low-caste voters in rural areas. The party already gets about half of the parliamentary seats reserved for Dalits and tribals, far more than any other party.[53] It is very likely that the demographic composition of the RSS and its other affiliates is also shifting in this direction. These developments make it highly unlikely that the BJP or the RSS would seriously tinker with reservations. The RSS, initially supportive of its own educational system primarily to preserve cultural values, has, like Prime Minister Modi, added the promotion of economic development as a reason for continued investment in RSS-affiliated schools. With this increased focus on job creation, the areas of collaboration with the government are also expanding. The dilemma for the RSS is that these collaborative arrangements between the government and the growing RSS-affiliated school system opens the door to a substantial government voice in the affairs of these institutions, a development that could result in the politicization of education that the RSS fears and has historically opposed.[54]

FIVE

What Does Hindutva Mean?

The mission statement on the RSS website refers to the unity of Hindus as the organization's guiding principle, though there is no formal RSS definition of what Hindutva is.[1] It states that the goal of the RSS is 'reorganizing the Hindu society on the lines of its unique national genius' and that the 'ideal of the Sangh is to carry the nation to the pinnacle of glory through organizing the entire society and ensuring the protection of Hindu Dharma'. Analysing what RSS members mean by Hindu-ness (or Hindutva), however, is complicated by the fact that the term has meant different things to different individuals and groups in the parivar. Perhaps this is to be expected of a religious tradition with no unifying structure and no universally accepted set of religious texts. This meaning has also altered over time in response to social, economic and political changes. As Pratap Bhanu Mehta has written, the amorphous nature of Hinduism has produced a series of movements to create the notion of a single Hindu community, partly as a result of actions by state authorities to define who is (or is not) a Hindu.[2] In lieu of a paramount ecumenical or cultural authority in organized Hinduism, the government has played a major role in both defining Hindu identity and reforming Hindu personal law. The development of the census by the British colonial authorities in the nineteenth century involved producing definitions of who a Hindu was (or was not), as does the determination of Hindu caste-dependent state benefits in independent India. Likewise, the legislatures and courts of a democratic India have themselves significantly modified the various statements of Hindu personal law.[3] These practices worked to homogenize the deeply fractured Hindu community as did Mahatma Gandhi in his use of such religiously endowed terms as 'Ram rajya', 'ahimsa', 'satyagraha' and 'swarajya'.

That said, the RSS leadership has never referred to Hinduism in the narrow religious sense. Manmohan Vaidya said in an email interview that India is a civilizational nation state. He noted that all inhabitants of the land share a common value system about individual and collective life.[4] It has never talked of making Hinduism a state religion, as that would be complicated both by the accepted narrative of India as a secular state and by the deep sectarian and philosophic divisions among those who identify as religiously Hindu. RSS literature, in fact, speaks approvingly of the religious and cultural diversity of Hinduism. Hindu religious iconography was virtually absent within the RSS until the Ram Janmabhoomi movement of the late 1980s. After that movement lost much of its emotional attraction in the late 1990s, the RSS and most of its affiliates, with the prominent exception of the VHP, have only rarely used Hindu religious symbolism in their programmes.[5] The current RSS mission statement, for example, emphasizes culture and patriotism rather than metaphysical issues or religious doctrine. At least at the leadership level, the RSS has never shown favouritism to any particular sect of Hinduism (probably a necessity given the diverse forms of Hindu worship). As Vaidya noted in the email interview, the RSS recognizes that there are multiple paths to the divine, all of which are equally valid, a more inclusive definition of Hindutva that seeks to accommodate the non-indigenous faiths.[6] To underscore the non-metaphysical definition of Hinduism in the RSS, Golwalkar, the most religiously inclined of the RSS heads, wrote that,

> People go to temples and try to concentrate on the idols, taking them as emblems of the Almighty. But all this does not satisfy us who are full of activity . . . We want a 'living' God.[7]

He identifies the 'Hindu nation' as that 'living God'.[8] The present head of the RSS told us that when he refers to the term 'Hindu', he also uses a cultural rather than religious definition, one applicable to all people in India, not just those who practise Hinduism.[9] More recently, probably to escape the negative connotation associated with the term Hindutva, the RSS chief has used 'Hindu-ness' to signal inclusiveness when he asserted that it is free of the dogmas associated with Hindu religion.[10] The changes in the social composition of the RSS, especially with the entry of members of upwardly mobile social groups, and the imperatives of its political affiliate have prompted the RSS to be more inclusive. Notice that the RSS mission statement mentioned above also refers to the organization of 'the entire society' and not just of those who consider themselves religiously Hindu. In the sixth and seventh chapters, we will explore this broadened vision of what constitutes a 'Hindu' in the context of the formation of RSS-affiliated groups for Muslims, as well as the BJP alliance with the People's Democratic Party (PDP), a political party in the Muslim-majority state of Jammu and Kashmir that draws its support from Muslims. This effort to be more inclusive is, however, relatively new, and not all parts of the parivar subscribe to it. Perhaps the most relevant term to use for this study is Hindutva (or perhaps Hindu nationalism), as it focuses on how the RSS aims to operationalize its ideology in such fields as social welfare, labour, education, politics and so on.

The term 'Hindutva' was popularized and defined by Vinayak Damodar Savarkar (1888–1966) in his 1923 book *Hindutva—Who Is Hindu?*[11] Savarkar builds on the early use of the term employed in the late nineteenth century by a Bengali writer, Chandranath Basu, in his book *Old Hindu's Hope: Proposal for Establishment of a Hindu National Congress.*[12] This book had a significant influence on the founder of the RSS, and its ideas have been repeated frequently in RSS publications.[13] Savarkar essentially says that a Hindu is a person who equates 'fatherland' (*pitrbhoomi*) with 'holy land' (*punyabhoomi*). A closer reading of Savarkar clearly shows that his term punyabhoomi refers to culture and not religion in the conventional sense. For Savarkar, what was essential to Hindu-ness was the subjective perception of identity with and loyalty towards the Hindu nation. He included groups whose religions had originated in India (Buddhists, Jains, Sikhs and so on), as they presumably did not have extraterritorial loyalties, but he remained sceptical about whether Muslims or Christians, whose religions originated outside the subcontinent, could be culturally Hindu and owe loyalty to the Hindu state. Savarkar, however, did not apply this argument to India's small Parsi and Jewish communities, perhaps because both are non-evangelizing faiths. The RSS itself moved away from the exclusionary view in the 1970s by accepting Muslims and Christians. Regarding the territorial and cultural aspects of Hinduism, Savarkar always placed more emphasis on the cultural side. This emphasis has also been the RSS's position from the time of Hedgewar. In fact, Savarkar—an atheist and advocate of an economically, militarily and scientifically developed India—was personally contemptuous of religious Hinduism. Contrary to what some critics of Hindutva have argued, Savarkar actively worked to eliminate caste hierarchies within Indian society.[14] Almost all advocates of Hindutva after Savarkar have considered caste—especially the practice of untouchability—an impediment to the goal of Hindu unity. Savarkar's most authentic biographer, Dhananjay Keer, reports that he organized pan-Hindu festivals that focused on granting temple entry to the so-called untouchables.[15] In a public speech, Savarkar, deliberately challenging Hindu orthodoxy, stated that, 'From today I shall not believe in highness or lowness of caste. I shall not oppose the intermarriage between the highest and lowest castes. I shall eat with any Hindu irrespective of caste. I shall not believe in caste by birth or by profession and henceforth I shall call myself a Hindu only—not Brahmin, Vaishya, etc.'[16]

Hedgewar, the founder of the RSS, who very much admired Savarkar,[17] viewed Hindus as 'the people of the land'; anyone else living in India did so at the sufferance of the Hindu majority and consequently should be expected to adopt Hindu culture. He wrote that, 'We [Hindus of India] do not say that others should not live here. But they should be aware that they are living in Hindusthan of Hindus.'[18] Savarkar never abandoned his scepticism of whether Muslims or Christians could ever become culturally Hindu. Golwalkar,

Hedgewar's successor, subscribed to this scepticism as well. In his major work on ideology, he said that the 'territorial concept' proposing that all people living in what is territorially classified as India are Hindu undermines what he referred to as the 'real Hindu nationhood'.[19] He further explains that, 'Hindu society, whole and integrated, should therefore be the single point of devotion for all of us.' 'Even today,' he writes, 'Muslims, whether in high positions of the Government or outside, participate openly in rabidly anti-national conferences. Their speeches too carry the ring of open defiance and rebellion.'[20] His description of the so-called Christian threat is less harsh, though he says that Christian activities are primarily concerned with conversion, with the end result being that the Hindu convert's 'hereditary religion, philosophy, culture and way of life should become absorbed in a world federation of Christianity'.[21]

Hedgewar followed the example of Savarkar by advocating a Hinduism in which hierarchies were of marginal significance. In a collection of his sayings, he notes that, 'We must behave with equal affection to all Hindu brothers, without any feeling of inferiority or superiority. To be contemptuous to anyone considering him as inferior will amount to sin.'[22] Deoras, Golwalkar's successor, launched a more activist phase of the RSS in the late 1970s by publicly attacking caste hierarchies. Jaffrelot argues that the RSS's recruitment of pracharaks from the broad spectrum of Hinduism—whatever their caste or religious origins (and now including Muslims)—and the demand that they live a life of ascetic renunciation bears remarkable resemblance to a casteless Hindu monastic sect; it provides a career of renunciation for full-time workers outside the everyday social world of hierarchies.[23] RSS camps, as we explained in our previous book, have a set of activities—such as requiring all participants to alternate between serving food to others and cleaning latrines— that aim to undermine notions of purity and pollution associated with various kinds of work in the many layers of the Hindu caste hierarchy.[24] At a breakfast at the RSS headquarters in Nagpur on 8 July 2015, we, as guests, were served food by a young man who said he was a tribal from a nearby area; he told us that his goal was to study engineering and contribute to the nation's well-being. He also told us that his co-workers at the RSS headquarters treated everyone (by which he probably meant himself) as equals. These comments bring to mind Hedgewar's last speech, made in 1940, comparing the RSS to the 'Hindu Rashtra in miniature', as he regarded it as an egalitarian 'family'.[25] While some RSS members have reservations about a casteless society, most of the senior RSS officials we met (primarily Brahmins) view social and civic equality as a legitimate goal for Indian society, and thus, a goal for the RSS as well. As we note elsewhere, this notion of equality is a central idea in Upadhyaya's exposition of what he called 'integral humanism'. If there is any book that is recognized as the ideological statement of the sangh parivar, it is Upadhyaya's book on that subject. He and others have argued that without this equality, the goal of a unified society—the guiding principle of the RSS—would be problematic. This emphasis on unity lies behind the misinterpretation of why current RSS leaders question the quota system adopted during Independence for the most disadvantaged castes. The editor of *Organiser* told us (as have others) that what they question is not the quota system itself, but the benefits that the 'creamy layer' within such groups reaps from the quota, at the expense of the lower strata of such groups.[26]

As the various affiliates of the RSS, especially the political members of the parivar, began to operate in their respective fields, it soon became obvious to some of their leaders that there was an advantage in keeping the door open to Muslims (comprising over a tenth of the population) and others who did not identify themselves as Hindu religiously. Manmohan Vaidya told us in an email interview that the RSS's dialogue with Muslims and Christians is active and ongoing. More recently, the RSS and its service affiliates have organized several activities in a bid to reach out to the Christian communities in the Northeast.[27] The narrow view of what constituted a 'Hindu' became less and less viable, and even the RSS opened itself up to non-Hindu (mostly Muslim) participation in shakhas in 1979. Its core national leadership gradually began to refer to all people in India as part of a broad Hindu culture that accommodated the country's significant diversity.[28] The RSS even formed a group in 2002, the MRM, to work among Muslims.

RSS-affiliated schools have thousands of Muslim students. While this group and its agenda of cultural assimilation are unlikely to gain substantial Muslim backing, the very fact that the RSS and its affiliates are mobilizing Muslims indicates a shift from the older perception that Muslims could not join the Hindu nation. The MRM's national convener, Indresh Kumar, told us that the MRM has passed resolutions advising Muslims to support a ban on cow slaughter, honour the Hindu demands on Ram Janmabhoomi and remove Article 370 of the Indian Constitution (which grants autonomous status to the Muslim-majority state of Jammu and Kashmir)—and that none of these cultural/political issues undermined Islam as a faith. He was confident that increasing numbers of Muslims would join what he referred to as the 'national cultural mainstream', similar to the accommodation of the indigenous Hindu culture by Indonesian Muslims.[29] While the broader cultural scope of what it means to be a Hindu seems to have been adopted by most of the senior leadership of the RSS, there are still many at all levels—and in other affiliates—who do not support this definition; in part, as we explain in the chapter on the MRM, they doubt whether Muslims will identify with the indigenous culture. This difference is particularly the case in the VHP, the affiliate that works among the Hindu ecclesiastical establishment. The VHP is opposed to conversion from Hinduism—and consequently engages in evangelism on behalf of Hinduism—on the assumption that organized Islam and Christianity represent a danger to Indian unity and the security of India.

We encountered a mix of definitions among RSS contacts regarding the meaning of Hinduism. For some, it relates mainly to respecting specific cultural inheritances (such as the Ram Temple at Ayodhya and such classics as the Mahabharata); for others, it is the fulfilment of social duties linked to the notion of dharma; still others contend it is the worship of traditional deities and adherence to traditional rules of behaviour. However, there is a common theme running through these disparate responses—nationalist patriotism. Golwalkar, for example, explained, 'Every particle of dust, every thing living or non-living, every stock and stone, tree and rivulet of this land is holy to us.'[30] As a corollary, he advocates the virtue of serving Hindu society: 'No other consideration, whether caste, sect, language, province or party should be allowed to come in the way of that devotion to society.'[31] Central to this idea of public service is the act of making India a strong country, one respected on the world stage. Golwalkar writes that

> the foremost duty laid upon every Hindu is to build up such a holy, benevolent and unconquerable might of the Hindu people in support of the age-old truth of our Hindu nationhood.[32]

But very little in his writing describes precisely how to bring about this Hindu identity, except the 'character-building' training programmes of the RSS. The expansion of affiliated groups, especially under the activist leadership of Deoras in the 1970s and 1980s, provided agency to the goal of building Hindu unity. Relying on tactics beyond just that of shakha-associated 'character-building', this expansion included labour strikes, lobbying and participation in various social welfare activities (for example, flood relief, education in job-related skills for the poor, food distribution in areas affected by droughts and so on) and of course politics. Yogi Adityanath, who has never been an RSS member but has had links with the VHP, told us in an interview that even those who do not want to self-identify as Hindu because of its religious overtones can identify as Bharatiya.[33]

The centrality of the state is imperative to the RSS's conception of who a Hindu is, both in its narrow and broader definition. For Hindu nationalists, loyalty to the nation is the core value and fundamental patriotic duty of all citizens. Bhagwat, the current RSS head, broadened the notion of loyalty to the nation to include concern for environmental problems—such as deforestation, and air and river pollution—as well as sensitivity to poverty, illiteracy, poor health and social discrimination.[34] The issue of patriotism burst into the public arena when students associated with left-of-centre political groups at New Delhi's prestigious university JNU organized a march on 9 February 2016, protesting the 2013 execution of Afzal Guru,[35] a Kashmiri separatist charged with complicity in the December

2001 terror attack on the Indian Parliament. In the process, these students raised slogans that RSS-affiliated student groups at JNU (the ABVP and the Bajrang Dal) argued were in violation of India's subversion laws, laws that are in fact rooted in legislation passed during the colonial period.[36] The president of the JNU Students Union, Kanhaiya Kumar—a member of the Communist Party of India's All India Students' Federation—was arrested on 12 February 2016 along with two other JNU students; they were charged with organizing a march on campus in which anti-national slogans were raised. Kumar was given a six-month conditional bail on 2 March by the Delhi High Court, on condition that he not engage in any anti-national activities.[37] He and his supporters argued that they had not engaged in seditious speech, and that the issue at hand was one of free speech rather than sedition, claiming further that they did not know those who had shouted the anti-national slogans.[38] Meanwhile, a JNU administrative committee found on 16 March 2016 that the march had been held without permission and indeed involved people shouting anti-national slogans. Regarding the issue of free speech, the 2 March judgment of the Delhi High Court, while providing a six-month interim bail to the president of the JNU Students Union, stated among other points that seditious rhetoric against the nation does not qualify as protected speech.[39]

The events at JNU, and other campuses across India, galvanized the ABVP (and other RSS-affiliated groups) as they concerned the group's central issue of patriotism. The furore unleashed by the demonstration sparked competing 'teach-ins' on nationalism at JNU (and other campuses), with the various leftist student groups on one side and the ABVP and Bajrang Dal on the other. This debate revolved around what kind of society India should aspire to be. Kumar returned to give a speech at JNU in which he claimed that he was seeking, not freedom from India, but freedom *within* India, and labelled the RSS as 'the opposition'.[40] *Organiser* published a series of articles focusing on the nationalist case in this controversy. A guest editorial by Prabhu Chawla, editor-in-chief of the *New Indian Express*, argued that the marches at JNU were actually aimed at 'destroying the idea of India', and that

India's borders are a 'non-negotiable pillar of nationalism'.[41] The 6 March column argued that the students' calls for free speech and educational autonomy were in reality a smokescreen for conflating both opposition to the Modi government with defence of anti-national activities and the protection of disadvantaged groups with support for Afzal Guru.[42] Other articles in that issue called for a tightening of academic standards at JNU, questioning why the twenty-nine-year-old Kumar was still on the student rolls. The Modi government approached the JNU issue carefully, as it was at that time seeking to renew a BJP alliance with the largely Muslim PDP following the death of PDP Chief Minister Mufti Mohammad Sayeed; the PDP in turn depends heavily on Muslim support in the Valley of Kashmir, where there is considerable sympathy for Afzal Guru. (PDP leaders in the past had even expressed scepticism about the evidence against him.) Following Sayeed's death, the PDP and the BJP renegotiated the alliance with the support of the RSS, and Sayeed's daughter, Mehbooba Mufti, was sworn in as chief minister of Jammu and Kashmir on 4 April 2016. This political alliance in Jammu and Kashmir—the only Muslim-majority state in India—had been important to the RSS because it was seen as a move that would both strengthen national unity and prove that the sangh is not anti-Muslim.[43] A similar rationale was given for the almost half-century-old alliance between the BJP and the Akali Dal, a party representing Sikh interests in Punjab, another border state with a non-Hindu majority.[44] The nationalist justification for these alliances fit the RSS's core goal of ensuring the territorial integrity of independent India as well as the cultural assimilation of the country's various religious groups.

The controversy at JNU that was prompted by the 9 February 2016 march quickly took on national proportions, with considerable media commentary from all sides. The RSS and several of the affiliates—including the BJP and the ABVP—jumped enthusiastically into the fray as it addressed the core issue of nationalism, seeing the furore as an opportunity to gain popular support by appealing to patriotism. Then came the controversy over whether those elected officials who refused to use the slogan

'Bharat Mata ki Jai' were disrespecting the Constitution, as the
BJP national executive argued they were in its March 2016 political
resolution.[45] That part of the resolution on 'Bharat Mata ki Jai'
starts out with the assertion that:

> Nationalism, national unity and integrity are an article of faith
> with the BJP. A very tiny microscopic minority in this country is
> today indulging in a kind of demagogy that goes against the essence
> of our Constitution. Our Constitution guarantees Freedom of
> Expression to every citizen, but that freedom is enjoyable only
> within its framework. Talking of destruction of Bharat can't be
> supported in the name of freedom of expression.[46]

The BJP in this legalistic statement drew a marker in the sand
as to speech that was not covered by constitutional protection,
a proposition that echoes the Delhi High Court's 2 March 2016
decision regarding events at JNU.

Soon afterwards, the national decision-making bodies of the
RSS—the ABPS and the Akhil Bharatiya Karyakari Mandal
(ABKM)—met at their annual 7–15 March 2016 conclave,
assembling at Nagaur in Rajasthan;[47] one of the three resolutions
made there indirectly referred to the nationalism debate under the
title of 'Social Harmony among Hindus'.[48] That resolution notes
that India is an 'ancient nation' with its own unique customs and
philosophies, the core philosophic underpinning being the 'oneness'
of all existence, including the 'oneness' of all human beings. It
further states that the decline of India was rooted in growing social
inequalities and such 'inhuman customs' as 'untouchability'. It also
emphasized the importance of social harmony, which is a long-
standing RSS view that was perhaps best analysed by Upadhyaya
in *Integral Humanism* and is close to what he referred to as the
'national soul'. The resolution, however, does not go into particulars
about how these noble virtues are to be achieved.

The RSS general secretary's Annual Report to the March 2016
national assembly[49] is more specific in its criticism of the JNU march
and the slogans raised there. The Annual Report notes that,

> We expect the central and state governments to deal strictly with
> such anti-national and anti-social forces to ensure the sanctity and
> cultural atmosphere by not allowing our educational institutions
> to become centres of political activities.

It further states that,

> In the name of freedom of expression how can the slogans calling
> for the breaking up and destruction of the nation be tolerated and
> how can the guilty who had hatched the conspiracy to blow up
> Parliament be honoured as martyr?

In this affirmation of nationalism, however, neither the resolutions
nor the general secretary's report refer to such staple Hindutva
issues as the Ram Temple at Ayodhya,[50] the abolition of Article
370 of the Constitution and the institution of a uniform national
civil code (perhaps because that would detract from Prime Minister
Modi's insistence that the BJP, and by implication the sangh
parivar, focus on economic development).[51] By portraying economic
development as at least equal in importance to these usual Hindutva
issues, the prime minister seems to be making development a key
element that shapes his views regarding Hindu nationalism,[52] a
principle that is far less controversial and far more inclusive than the
traditional Hindutva platform. Adding support to this notion was
Bhagwat's statement in a speech to entrepreneurs that business—
and by extension prosperity—should be thought of as part of one's
dharma.[53] In his email interview, Manmohan Vaidya added that
while Hindutva permits the accumulation of material wealth, it is
an individual's duty (dharma) to share wealth with disadvantaged
co-citizens. The dilemma remains, however, that many activists in
the sangh parivar—especially within the VHP—look at Hindutva
in traditional terms and now feel empowered to speak out about it,
often in ways that embarrass the prime minister and his government.
The prime minister has been criticized, including by some in the
sangh parivar, for not speaking out more promptly and forcefully
against those on the hard-line fringes that make militant statements

or engage in violence against Muslims and Christians, as he did during the 2014 parliamentary campaign.[54]

Demonstrating the importance of nationalism as a mobilization tool, officers of various RSS-affiliated organizations and invited experts met in New Delhi on 22–23 March 2016, soon after the ABPS conclave in Rajasthan, to discuss tactics that would address the topic of nationalism, among other issues. Those members we spoke to following that conclave seemed confident that this issue was, as a participant put it, 'one that was made for us'.[55] Others added that the 'left-leaning JNU' was a bubble, and the 'anti-national sentiments expressed there' did not represent the views of the vast majority of Indians, nor even the majority of Indian students. But soon after these meetings, Bhagwat said in a 28 March 2016 meeting that forcing others to chant 'Bharat Mata ki Jai' is wrong, stating that, 'All people living in the country are our own and we can't force our ideology and thinking on them.'[56] To give further evidence of the acceptance of this view at the high levels of the RSS, Manmohan Vaidya, the then all-India prachar pramukh, stated, 'There is nothing new about what the RSS chief has said. We are a democratic country and we can't force anybody to chant slogans.'[57] Despite the apparent contradiction between Bhagwat's statement and the BJP resolution, a party spokesman asserted there was no difference between the RSS's and the BJP's views, but also emphasized that the party 'has repeatedly said that debate on "Bharat Mata ki Jai" is non-negotiable, and the party sticks to that'.[58]

The other issue discussed at the 22–23 March meeting was a strategy to prevent the loss of support from Dalits. This issue was of particular importance given the controversy over the RSS's suggestions during the 2015 Bihar Assembly elections that caste-based reservations be re-evaluated, as well as the January 2016 suicide of a Dalit activist at Hyderabad University, blamed by the parivar's critics on alleged harassment by the ABVP. These events could impact the BJP negatively in the forthcoming elections unless handled with care. This is especially important politically as the BJP has recently done very well in parliamentary constituencies reserved for Scheduled Castes (i.e., Dalits) and tribals, and it does not want to lose support from that numerically large part of the Indian electorate. RSS critics have sought to use the two issues to demonstrate that the parivar is fundamentally controlled by high-caste Hindus unconcerned about the social and economic well-being of Dalits. At the ground level, the RSS has worked hard—and studies show it has had some success—to implement a wide range of social welfare activities among Dalits and tribals.[59] At the political level, the BJP president, Amit Shah, in an announcement coinciding with the March 2016 ABPS meetings, issued an order to party members to celebrate annually the birthday of Bhimrao Ramji Ambedkar, the Dalit scholar who chaired the drafting of the Indian Constitution and remains an iconic figure for Dalits today.[60] Prime Minister Modi, according to a March 2016 press report, has had ten occasions to celebrate Ambedkar, including an appearance at his birthplace on 14 April 2016, the 125th anniversary of Ambedkar's birth.[61] At the 2016 ABPS meeting, the RSS passed a resolution calling for war against all forms of untouchability and did so at a venue named after Ambedkar.[62]

Bhagwat, aware of the advantages of keeping the BJP in power, is wary about the RSS taking steps that would undermine the popular standing of either the prime minister or the party. To walk back Bhagwat's and the RSS's traditional criticism of caste-based benefits,[63] which created problems for the BJP in the 2015 Bihar Assembly elections, for example, Vaidya told a reporter (almost certainly with Bhagwat's approval) that, 'As long as there is social discrimination in our society, reservations should continue.'[64] This acceptance of reservations, at least for now, seemed to be the consensus of the delegates we met at the conclusion of the sangh parivar strategy session.

The internal ideological stirring within the sangh parivar can be witnessed in the questioning by senior figures of long-held conservative social views in early 2016. Manmohan Vaidya reportedly said that the RSS does not dictate food habits and that RSS members in the Northeast eat beef,[65] a point that was reiterated by one of the most influential cabinet ministers, Gadkari, when he said that the government should not interfere in dietary habits.[66] Hosabale tweeted that 'homosexuality is not a crime, but a socially immoral act in our society'.[67] Regarding 'Bharat Mata ki Jai', Bhagwat said, 'We don't want to force it on anyone.'[68] Prafulla Ketkar, editor of *Organiser*, told us that these stands are an evolution of existing ideas and do not represent a new policy direction, which seems to be the standard RSS explanation.[69] At least part of the caution regarding what appears to be a more liberal stand may be a sort of testing of the waters to see how RSS members and the larger society responds. We also believe that this cautious liberalization is possibly due to the much greater social diversity of the RSS sangh parivar, whose active membership includes a significant part of the newly emerging urban middle class. We cannot imagine that senior figures of the parivar would have openly expressed such unconventional views even in the recent past.

The essential element of Hindutva seems to be a relatively straightforward patriotism, something bordering on an adoration of the motherland/fatherland and visually represented by the iconography of Bharat Mata. There exists a corpus of writings (most prominently Upadhyaya's *Integral Humanism*) that provides a coherent set of statements with basic explanation of the ideology. But most members of the RSS, or the BJP or the other affiliates, very likely do not think in these ideological terms and, when they use them, they lack the coherence and consistency of the ideologues and senior leaders. Most of the members, for example, almost certainly accept caste as a social construct as well as a caste hierarchy, though RSS ideologues reject both as contrary to the social unity they seek. Mass support often responds to non-ideological cues that people believe are important in their lives,[70] such as social stability and economic development and maybe even 'Hinduism in danger' or 'illegal migration from Bangladesh'. The rapid growth of the RSS and other affiliates since the early 1990s probably is due to their appeal to a similar yearning for social stability in a time of rapid change. Their continued success in attracting popular support depends on providing a narrative more relevant to the Indian people than competitive groups.

SIX

The Muslim Rashtriya Manch

An Experiment in Accommodating Muslims

On the afternoon of 2 July 2015, a simple press announcement for a unique Iftar party in New Delhi soon escalated into a media firestorm. Such parties—evening celebrations in which devout Muslims break their ordained day-long fasts—are a fixture of the Indian political calendar during the holy month of Ramzan. In New Delhi, the most political of Indian cities, an Iftar dinner is an occasion for politicians, bureaucrats, diplomats and journalists to exchange political gossip and enjoy sumptuous Mughlai delicacies. But this proposed Iftar dinner was unusual in many respects, perhaps the most notable being that it was organized by the MRM which describes itself as an organization established with the support of the RSS 'to bridge the widening gap between Hindu and Muslim communities in India'.[1] The furore over this Iftar party was because of the inclusion of a particular invitee, Abdul Basit, the then Pakistani high commissioner to India, one of several diplomatic leaders from Muslim-majority countries invited to the dinner. What made this invitation so controversial was that a few days earlier, an attack allegedly sponsored by the Pakistani terrorist group Lashkar-e-Taiba in Pampore, Jammu and Kashmir, had claimed the lives of eight Indian paramilitary personnel. When Basit was asked about the attack during an unrelated Iftar at the Pakistani High Commission, he reportedly (and indifferently) urged the assembled journalists to 'have the Iftar party and enjoy'.[2]

The controversy stirred up by Basit's perceived insensitivity prompted the MRM to disinvite him from their Iftar party. Because of grumbling from within the ranks of the RSS over this invitation, several RSS leaders believed it necessary to clarify the sangh's relationship with the MRM. RSS publicity chief Vaidya, seeking to delineate the two groups, told reporters that media accounts of the RSS sponsoring the Iftar party were 'factually incorrect', and that the MRM—which he described as an independent Muslim organization 'working to create national awareness'—was the sole organizer.[3] The ambiguity over the MRM's links to the RSS stems from the fact that it was established with RSS assistance in 2002, and has been guided ever since by an RSS pracharak, Indresh Kumar,[4] formerly a provincial RSS organizer in Jammu and Kashmir—and, paradoxically, a Hindu. His formal title in the MRM is *margdarshak* (guide). Kumar has also served as a member of the very influential ABKM, the central executive committee of the RSS. During our 25 March 2016 visit to his office in New Delhi, we noticed photographs of the first two sarsanghchalaks, Hedgewar and Golwalkar, as well as a large lithograph of Mother India on the wall above his desk. While the ambience there was culturally Hindu, his large office complex was filled with Muslims seeking assistance of various kinds.

Despite the RSS's links to the MRM, the latter has never been included on any official list of RSS affiliates.[5] Nonetheless, the RSS's senior leadership was the catalyst for its formation, and they have supported it since its inception in 2002.[6] The then sarsanghchalak Sudarshan participated in its official launch on 24 December of that year, and he attended every national MRM convention until his death in 2012. Yet the RSS has faced a recurring dilemma regarding how far it should go in supporting the MRM, and how openly it should acknowledge its association. On the one hand, the sangh does not want to offend those of its many Hindu members who have negative views of Indian Muslims and Islam. On the other hand, it genuinely wants to bring Muslims closer to what it considers the national mainstream, both for reasons of political stability and to help the BJP garner political support among Muslims, some 14 per cent of the population. At least for now, it has fixed on a course of supporting the MRM while also keeping it at arm's length by emphasizing the MRM's independence.

What, then, is the true relationship between the RSS and the MRM? The answer to this is rooted in the evolving debate within the RSS over the Muslim community's place in India. The RSS's perception of Indian Muslims and Islam is not static. Golwalkar in the 1960s sought to resume the pre-war RSS–Muslim overtures made by Hedgewar towards certain Islamic religious leaders, but these efforts, like Hedgewar's, found virtually no success. Golwalkar publicly blamed Muslim political leaders for his lack of progress, and concluded that the only effective approach was for the RSS and its affiliates to work directly among Muslims.[7] The first step, taken by the political (BJS) and labour (BMS) affiliates, was to open membership to people from all religious backgrounds, including Muslims. These two affiliates went even further, establishing units tailored to address issues of interest to Muslims, though their results were rather meagre.[8] The more influential of these units is the Minority Cell (later called the Minority Morcha) of the BJS (later to reorganize as the modern BJP). The Minority Morcha's overriding goal is to mobilize electoral support from Muslims for the BJP's candidates—the MRM, by contrast, engages in a much broader range of outreach activities. The MRM did, however, work for the BJP in the 2014 parliamentary elections, and there are reports that it also worked for the party in the Bihar and Gujarat Assembly elections in 2015 and 2017 respectively.[9] The Minority Morcha also differs from the MRM in that its office-bearers are all from the minority communities and include Christians. Given the separate organizational links of the two groups, they work apart from each other even where they share overlapping goals, such as the mobilization of Muslim voters. The fact that only seven of the 427 BJP parliamentary candidates in 2014 were Muslim suggests that these two groups had limited influence in pushing Muslim representation within the party. As it was, all seven candidates lost anyway.[10] The criterion for nomination that seems to have been set by the party president, Amit Shah, is the ability to win elections, regardless of religious affiliation. The message of the MRM and the Minority Morcha to Muslims thus seems to be that they can trust Hindu candidates from the BJP to represent their interests more effectively than Muslim candidates from another party. The BJP's leadership has long argued that—unlike the Congress and the leftist parties—it does not 'pander' to the Muslim community to get votes, but rather has adopted the RSS's strategy of changing Muslim perceptions about the sangh parivar by creating jobs and providing good governance. This message was underlined by M.K. Chisti, convener of the Gujarat Minority Morcha and the BJP's (Hindu) candidate in a Muslim-dominated constituency in the 2017 Gujarat Assembly elections. Chisti reportedly told his largely Muslim audiences that, 'You are my family, not my voters'—the implication being that the BJP had thus committed itself to looking after their interests as if they were family members.[11]

Besides these groups which were set up by the parivar specifically for Muslim outreach, there is also the Union ministry of minority affairs, which, since the BJP came to power, has been headed by prominent BJP Muslims: Najma Heptulla,[12] the initial minister after the BJP's 2014 victory, was replaced two years later by Mukhtar Abbas Naqvi, the party's senior Muslim leader in the Rajya Sabha. The ministry's website asserts that it is tasked with improving the lives of minorities through educational and health programmes, that 15 per cent of all government schemes are earmarked for minorities, and the ministry is 'to give special consideration to minorities' for civil service recruitment at both the state and federal levels.[13]

Following the lead of its affiliates, the RSS itself formally opened its membership to Muslims (and Christians) in 1979. Muslims are now in the RSS as well as virtually all its affiliates, Muslim students attend RSS-affiliated schools, and there are many Muslim beneficiaries of RSS-sponsored health and skill-training service projects. There are even a few Muslims in the RSS who have gone through the three-year training programme that produces the full-time corps of pracharaks. But there remains an undercurrent of suspicion throughout the sangh regarding Muslims (and, to a lesser extent, Christians), as we shall show below.

The historical narrative the RSS portrays is that the 1000 years of Muslim domination in the subcontinent were the result of external invasions; likewise, the Muslim ruling classes are always portrayed as foreign imperialists, though not the Muslim masses, who are acknowledged to be converts. That distinction enables the RSS to claim that Muslims are in fact 'sons of the soil', a definition that eventually justified opening membership to them. The very existence of Pakistan, however, was considered illegitimate, and the notion of undoing Partition and reunifying India (referred to as Akhand Bharat) was widely accepted in RSS circles for decades after the schism in 1947. Muslims remaining in India at the time were typically portrayed as a fifth column, sympathetic to the state of Pakistan. Golwalkar, in his book *Bunch of Thoughts*, wrote:

> It would be suicidal to delude ourselves into believing that they [Muslims] have turned patriots overnight after the creation of Pakistan. On the contrary, the Muslim menace has increased a hundredfold since the creation of Pakistan which has become a springboard for all their future aggressive designs on our country.[14]

This was hardly the first expression of such a sentiment: Golwalkar in 1939 wrote that, 'The non-Hindu peoples in Hindustan must either adopt the Hindu culture and language, must learn to respect and hold in reverence Hindu religion' if they were to 'stay in this country'.[15]

This scepticism regarding the loyalty of Muslims to India traces back to the very formation of the RSS. The organization was founded in 1925, in part as a response to Hindu–Muslim rioting in central India.[16] The goal at its inception was to unite the fractured Hindu community to defend Hindus, with Hindu solidarity additionally being perceived as a necessary precondition for independence—Muslims were seen as an obstacle to that larger national goal. Partition and the subsequent Hindu–Muslim communal violence that ravaged India deepened this popular perception of Muslim disloyalty. A.G. Noorani, in his study of

Indian Muslims, writes, 'the Muslims of India found themselves facing the same traumatic change which confronted their forbears ninety years ago at the time of the Mutiny in 1857'. He further notes that, 'As in 1857, their loyalty to the new state was suspect.'[17] The RSS, which played a significant role in organizing Hindu migration from Pakistan and in settling those Hindu refugees in India, was always foremost among those questioning the loyalty of Muslims—there was never any serious consideration by the RSS at that time about accepting Muslims at RSS shakhas. Golwalkar, in the wake of the 1948–49 ban, responded to those demanding that the RSS open itself to Muslims by arguing that the RSS had no problem with Islam as a religion or with Indian Muslims (who he claimed were ethnically the same as Indian Hindus), but that he doubted any Muslims would join a nationalist organization like the sangh.[18] What is unstated here is that RSS members were also adamantly opposed to accepting Muslims—and many oppose doing so even now.

It took a quarter of a century after Independence for the memories of Partition to fade to the point that the RSS could consider allowing Muslims to join. Golwalkar's choice of Deoras as the third sarsanghchalak in 1973 signalled a significant shift from the introverted reconstruction phase following the devastating 1948–49 ban to a more extroverted activist phase as advocated by Deoras. Clearly, Golwalkar before his death questioned how much the RSS would and should change under a successor. His two leading candidates were, according to our sources, on opposite sides of this issue.[19] The reconstruction phase was primarily consumed with rebuilding the Hindu membership base, and one part of that strategy was to add a Hindu spiritual element to the militant focus of Hindutva.[20] There were several senior RSS figures who would have been a better fit with Golwalkar's introverted Hindu consolidation efforts,[21] but he likely chose the activist Deoras as the most effective leader should the sangh be banned again.[22] Just two years after the elevation of Deoras, Prime Minister Indira Gandhi declared a state of Emergency that inadvertently prompted the RSS under his leadership to move well beyond the reconstruction phase, adopting a far more activist social programme and, consequently, a far more inclusive membership policy, one that accommodated Muslim and Christian participation. Many organizations involved in the protest against Prime Minister Gandhi, including the RSS, were banned during the Emergency, and many of their senior leaders, including Deoras, were arrested. While in prison, Deoras and other RSS leaders interacted with prominent figures of the banned Jamaat-i-Islami, an influential Muslim organization that was also critical of Indira Gandhi's increasingly authoritarian regime;[23] this is how the new Janata Party government in 1977 improbably came to be supported by both the RSS and the Jamaat-i-Islami. To reduce, if not eliminate, the stigma of Hindu communalism in the new united party, several prominent Janata Party figures[24] pressed the RSS to open its membership to Muslims and Christians, thus providing the context for RSS leaders to finally move on opening their ranks to Muslims.[25] Deoras, to justify this about-turn, asserted that Hedgewar himself had stated that he 'would be happy to live with Muslims and Christians with spirit of brotherhood as children of mother India'.[26] He also quoted Golwalkar as saying that any group in India not demanding special minority rights, such as Jews and Parsis, should be considered part of Hindu culture.[27] Malkani, long-time editor of *Organiser*, further quoted Golwalkar as saying, 'The main reason why there is Hindu–Muslim tension in India is that the Indian Muslim is yet to identify fully with India, its people and its culture. Let the Indian Muslim feel and say that this is his country and all these are his people and the problem [of Hindu–Muslim tensions] will cease to exist. It is a matter of changing his [Muslim] psychology.'[28] Deoras felt sufficiently confident, two years after the end of the Emergency in 1977, to officially open RSS shakhas to Muslims (as well as other non-Hindus) in order to enact this aforementioned change on the 'psychology' of Muslims, a sentiment used by his successor, Sudarshan, twenty-five years later to justify the RSS's support for the MRM. However, there was fierce resistance from the more conservative elements of the sangh. One reputable source, for example, notes that K.B. Limaye, a former sanghchalak in Maharashtra appointed by Hedgewar, wrote to Deoras:

> You have been the position [sic] of the chief of the RSS of Dr. Hedgewar. Kindly run that Sangh and try to foster its growth. Do not try to change it. If you think a change is necessary, start a new RSS. Leave the RSS of Dr. Hedgewar for the Hindu consolidation to us. If you change this RSS . . . I will not be able to have any relationship with that Sangh.[29]

This demand for the supremacy of the status quo reflected Golwalkar's own desire not to use his position to alter the organization he had inherited from Hedgewar.

Given the limited success in attracting Muslims to the RSS or its affiliates, the RSS leadership turned its focus to the creation of an independent Muslim activist organization, one that would interact directly with Indian Muslims. This was the genesis of the MRM as an organization tailored to propagate Hindutva ideology directly among Muslims. The first convention of the MRM in 2003 passed a resolution demanding a total ban on cow slaughter.[30] The second national convention in 2004 added a demand that Article 370 of the Indian Constitution (making the Muslim-majority state of Jammu and Kashmir autonomous) be abolished to further the cause of national integration, in addition to proclamations denouncing terrorism and demanding equal rights for Muslim women. At its tenth convention in 2012, national convener Mohammed Afzal—after reporting that MRM activists had unfurled the Indian national flag in Srinagar—submitted a memorandum to the President of India, replete with the signatures of a million Muslims, demanding an end to cow slaughter.[31] The MRM contributed workers to the BJP's 2014 parliamentary campaign, and lent similar aid to BJP candidates in subsequent state Assembly contests in Jammu and Kashmir and in Bihar.[32]

The RSS's approach to Muslims, as noted above, started much before the formation of the MRM in 2002, and even before the

RSS formally opened its doors to Muslims in 1979. Golwalkar, in 1951, supported the policy of Mookerjee, founder of the BJS, to open his all-India party to people of all faiths. He also advised Mookerjee to avoid the use of 'Hindu' in the new party's name, so as to distinguish itself from the explicitly sectarian Hindu Mahasabha.[33] A small number of Muslims became parliamentary candidates in Mookerjee's new party, but none of them won under the BJS label; a few were successful in state Assembly and metropolitan council contests, one even becoming mayor of Delhi.[34] The successor, BJP, formed in 1980, also had a few Muslim candidates at the state and central levels, and several served in the cabinets of Vajpayee and Modi. Among these ministers were Najma Heptulla, Arif Beg, Sikander Bakht, Mukhtar Abbas Naqvi, Syed Shahnawaz Hussain, and M.J. Akbar, all six members of the Rajya Sabha. The BJP's 2014 campaign manifesto stands out for its concessions to Muslims, such as improving the quality of education in Muslim communities, greater power to Muslim charitable boards, and the institution of state-sponsored interfaith dialogues. The part of that document addressing Muslim issues states,

> It is unfortunate that even after several decades of independence, a large section of the minority, and especially Muslim community, continues to be stymied in poverty. Modern India must be a nation of equal opportunity.[35]

The Muslim vote share for the BJP and its allies in the 2014 parliamentary elections, by one estimate, doubled from 4 per cent in 2009 to 8 per cent in 2014.[36] However, only a handful of Muslim BJP candidates were nominated for the Lok Sabha which selects the prime minister. None of them won. Neither was any Muslim nominated for the subsequent state Assembly elections in the two large states of Bihar and Uttar Pradesh, though each has a substantial Muslim minority, and though Muslims have been nominated for elective posts in other states. Perhaps the most interesting case is in Gujarat, where Modi as chief minister had developed a close relationship with business-oriented Shia sub-sects such as Bohras and Ismailis. While there have been no Muslim candidates at the parliamentary and Assembly levels in recent elections, the BJP nominated Muslims to some 450 seats (of a total of 4778 seats—or about 10 per cent, about the same as the Muslim percentage in Gujarat) in the state's 2015 local body elections. Several of these nominations were in Muslim-dominated areas where the BJP support for job growth initiatives seems to have been a motivating factor.[37]

The RSS's focus on reaching out to Muslims directly deepened during the religious tensions of the Ram Janmabhoomi movement of the 1980s.[38] Sudarshan, when he served as head of the intellectual wing of the RSS, took the initiative to start a dialogue on the subject with Muslim religious figures, bypassing Muslim political leaders and academics entirely; he had probably concluded that these religious leaders had much more influence with the Muslim masses and had a better sense of their concerns. Among the Muslim leaders he met were Maulana Jameel Iliyasi, the president of All India Imam Council, Maulana Wahiduddin Khan, the Shahi Imam of Fatehpuri Masjid, and Mufti Mukarram Ahmed.[39] These religious figures were all present at the birth of the MRM in late 2002.

Why, then, has the RSS remained reluctant to accept the MRM as an affiliate? The RSS's ambivalence reflects a continued difference of opinion within the sangh about how to approach the Indian Muslim community. The sceptical view is perhaps best captured by Dr Shreerang Godbole, a Pune-based endocrinologist and a former city-level RSS sanghchalak.[40] In his view, the notion that Indian Muslims can be Indianized is, at best, quixotic. He acknowledges that some sangh intellectuals, including Balraj Madhok and Upadhyaya, were the proponents of the Indianization (or *Bharateeyakaran*) of Indian Muslims. But, he argues, the long history of Islam shows that communal and religious identity will always take precedence over national identity.

The alternative, according to Dr Godbole, is for Indian Muslims to be Hinduized, not Indianized. The path should be conversion (ghar wapsi) rather than assimilation[41] and, he writes, it is his personal view that participation in the MRM discourages and impedes ghar wapsi. In fact, he writes that the MRM has a vested interest in keeping Muslims Muslim, and 'I shall have no regrets if MRM fails; indeed if it were to succeed, I would get concerned as that may actually damage *gharvapsi*.'[42] Most Muslims (and Christians) in India retain their Hindu caste identity and ancestral customs, Godbole maintains. The MRM's outreach to these communities could dissuade them from becoming Hindus and thus abandoning their identity as minorities. He fears, moreover, that the favourable publicity given to the MRM by the RSS press machine can lead the largely Hindu RSS readership to the conclusion that "good Muslims" are in significant numbers. This is simply not the truth.'[43] This negative view of the MRM, however, is not the current RSS policy, as explained below.

The arguments for the RSS's social expansion through the agency of the MRM are articulated by Virag Pachpore, MRM co-convener, in the 26 June 2016 edition of *Organiser*. He argues that the MRM represents an effective middle-ground approach to bring Muslims into the nationalist mainstream, the two unsatisfactory alternatives being appeasement and rejection. On appeasement, he writes that,

> While Congress' policy of appeasement resulted in vivisection of our [India's] 'Madar-e-Vatan,' the 'Hate Muslim' policy further expanded the already existing gap between the two [communal] 'brothers.'[44]

During the freedom movement, he argues, the Congress 'pampered' Muslims as a means of achieving Hindu–Muslim unity. The MRM provided, he says, a third way, since:

> Indian Muslims share the same ancestors, culture, traditions, language and customs with their Hindu brothers. Only they have changed their way of worship some time ago due to certain historical and social compulsions. But changing way of worship did not make them give up their past and detach them completely from their ancestral history and heritage.[45]

In an article published on the MRM's website, Pachpore states that,

Muslims in India are [an] integral part of the Indian society and share ancestors, culture and motherland with the Hindus. The need is to make them realise this underlying current of unity in diversity . . .[46]

Writing approvingly of Muslims and Hindus attending a meeting at a Hindu temple in Gujarat, where they commemorated cow protection, he mentions local Muslim leaders who reportedly urged their fellow Muslims to abstain from eating beef, presumably to demonstrate a common cultural affinity with their Hindu neighbours.[47]

The MRM website reports an extensive list of programmes, including a beef-free Iftar party in Ayodhya to promote cow protection, flag hoisting on 26 January (Republic Day) at mosques and madrasas nationwide, periodic meetings between RSS leaders and Muslim intellectuals, and a campaign for a uniform civil code. On a larger scale, the MRM organized celebrations in 2007–08 to commemorate the 150th anniversary of the 1857 Rebellion (referred to as the First War of Independence in nationalist circles). In 2009, the MRM organized a dialogue between Hindu and Muslim clergy on the Ram Temple controversy in Ayodhya.[48] In line with the RSS's increasing involvement in service activities, the MRM has started a campaign to promote education in Muslim communities under the slogan 'Aadhi Roti Khaayenge, Bachchon ko Padhayenge' (which roughly translates to 'We will eat half a roti, but educate our children'). It founded the Amar Shahid Ashfaqullah National Memorial School in 2016 to carry out this educational goal. It has in addition organized seminars for Kashmiri students about government scholarships for which they may qualify.[49] The co-convener of the MRM told the press in 2017 that the organization had 10,000 regular members, was present in twenty-two states, and was overseen by a twenty-four-member national executive that holds monthly strategy meetings and is in regular contact with the RSS office in Delhi.[50]

The MRM has been engaged not only in reaching out to Muslims, but also in clearing up presumed misconceptions about Indian Muslims within the RSS itself. To address the widespread belief among RSS members that all Muslims eat beef, for example, the MRM published a pamphlet arguing that neither the Prophet nor the Holy Quran directs Muslims to engage in cow slaughter or beef consumption. The pamphlet, which further states that there are over 100 cow shelters managed by Muslims,[51] was a compilation of articles by several Muslim clerics highlighting the importance of the cow in Islam. The MRM organized its first cow-shelter meeting in Haryana on 13 September 2015, which was attended by Haryana Chief Minister Manohar Lal Khattar and All India Imams Council leader Umer Ahmed Ilyasi; it has plans to open other such shelters in the future. In keeping with the RSS's increasing support for the BJP, the MRM, ahead of the 2017 Assembly elections in Uttar Pradesh, reached out to local Islamic clerics to correct misconceptions about the RSS in a state where Muslims form almost a fifth of the population.[52] However, the BJP did not nominate a single Muslim candidate either for the 2014 parliamentary election or the subsequent state Assembly election in this state, India's most populous.

The formation of the MRM underscores just how much the RSS's perception of Islam and Indian Muslims has changed since Partition, during which the sangh's familiar stereotype of the 'disloyal Muslim' was truly codified. Mushirul Hasan in his analysis of India's Muslims writes that

> [T]he unprecedented scale of violence [during Partition] was accompanied by one of the greatest mass migrations [in] this century. Hindus and Sikhs in Pakistan were mercilessly displaced or brutally slaughtered. Between August 1947 and March 1948, about 4.5 million Hindus migrated from West Pakistan to India and about 6 million Muslims moved in the reverse direction.[53]

More were to move between the two countries over the next several years. The progressive fusion of Hindu and Muslim cultures over some 1100 years of interaction was now replaced by an effort to clearly dichotomize the two communities. Many Hindus (certainly those in the RSS) viewed Muslims after Partition as part of the great 'other', a people defined by either foreign loyalties or secessionist demands— while, of course, downplaying or ignoring their cultural similarities. Yet, the RSS faced a dilemma with this new dichotomy. On the one hand, the RSS had never questioned that Hindus and Muslims were both basically 'sons of the soil'. Yet Muslims were also perceived as inherently un-Indian, because of their religion and because of Pakistan. A number of factors have eroded, though by no means eliminated, this jaundiced view of Muslims. Among these factors were the gradual fading of Partition into the hazy annals of history and the political importance of India's large Muslim population.

The changes in the RSS's policy on India's Muslims have been evolutionary rather than revolutionary. As an organization that emphasizes cohesion and consensus, the RSS evolves slowly in response to changing social norms and economic circumstances. Nonetheless, one sign of its slowly shifting stance was the invitation of a prominent Muslim to speak at a 2017 Dussehra celebration at the RSS headquarters in Nagpur, one of the major events on the RSS ceremonial calendar. Dr Munawar Yusuf, a prominent Bohra Muslim homoeopath, was the chief guest of the *shastra pujan* (worship of tools), a function for younger swayamsevaks—this marked the first time a Muslim has been given such an honour at any major RSS gathering.[54] Earlier in 2017, Bhagwat visited Syedna Mufaddal Saifuddin—the fifty-third Dai-al-Mutlaq (spiritual head) of the wealthy Dawoodi Bohra Muslim community—at his Mumbai residence. The Syedna's father, the fifty-second Dai, had developed a close relationship with Modi when he was chief minister of Gujarat, the ancestral home of most Bohras. Syedna himself supported several of Prime Minister Modi's major initiatives, such as his anti-corruption campaigns and the 'Make in India' and 'Swachh Bharat' (Clean India) initiatives.[55] At the first mass gathering of the Bohra community in Surat after his ascension, the fifty-third Dai invoked God's blessing on the newly inaugurated Modi: 'May Almighty bless him in all the initiatives undertaken by him and give him great success and sound health.'[56] A large contingent of Dawoodi Bohras attended Modi's 28 September 2014 events in New York City and, at the dinner that evening, Modi probably spent more time talking with them than with any other group.[57] The Bohras are a sub-sect of Shia Muslims with an estimated 30 million members in India (Shias themselves comprise somewhat more than 20 per cent of India's

Muslim population).[58] One study of 2014 parliamentary voting patterns maintains that the BJP's growing support among Muslims (from 4 to 8 per cent) was mainly due to the increased backing of Shia Muslims.[59] Another indication of the growing Shia support for the BJP was the establishment in May 2018 of the Indian Shia Awami League—an organization sympathetic to the BJP. Maulana Yasoob Abbas, spokesperson for the All India Shia Personal Law Board, had said, 'The Shia community will continue to support the BJP if it ensures better education and job opportunities for Muslim women.'[60]

But even these Muslim outreach efforts have to be carried out with caution, given the fears among some RSS figures that such activities could undermine the organizational solidarity of an increasingly diverse membership. In response to the mixed reviews this outreach elicits, the RSS leadership has taken the middle ground: the sangh patronizes the MRM, but will not accord it formal affiliate status. Bhagwat, who attended the MRM's annual national conclave for the first time during his tenure in December 2016, made statements afterwards underscoring the continuing ambivalence of many swayamsevaks towards Indian Muslims. In a thinly veiled criticism of RSS hardliners, Bhagwat remarked, 'No one has the right to measure another person's patriotism.'[61] Soon after, however, he repeated his controversial contention that 'Muslims are Hindus by nationality.'[62] The goal of the MRM is to narrow the gap between Muslims and the RSS's brand of patriotism, an objective strongly supported by the RSS national leadership, thus reaffirming that the RSS is prepared to accommodate Muslims—but only on its own terms. Despite some success in laying an organizational groundwork, this goal is still a work in progress. The MRM has yet to demonstrate that it will make a considerable impact on India's Muslim community, or even that it has significant influence within the RSS.

SEVEN

Jammu and Kashmir Quandary

Tactics vs Strategy

Ram Madhav, the BJP's general secretary and the person who in 2015 negotiated the party's alliance with the People's Democratic Party (PDP), a party that drew its support almost exclusively from Jammu and Kashmir's Muslim population, also announced the termination of the alliance on 19 June 2018.[1] The announcement caught many, including the PDP chief minister at the time, Mehbooba Mufti, by surprise. The Governor of the state, M.N. Vohra, reportedly called the chief minister to inform her of the BJP's decision to withdraw support only minutes before Ram Madhav addressed a press conference to publicly announce the move.[2] The official justification noted by Madhav was the Kashmir government's inability to curtail militant violence and to provide for equitable progress in all areas of the state, developments which challenged the BJP's and the RSS's purported larger strategic goal of national integration. The RSS, which had agreed—somewhat reluctantly—with the original decision to form the alliance, was reportedly consulted and backed the decision to pull out, even though many within it always considered the alliance as improbable and likely to be short-lived.[3] A sceptical RSS had gone along with the proposed alliance in 2015 for larger strategic reasons such as strengthening national integration (i.e., drawing India's only Muslim-majority state more closely into the Indian Union) and making Hindutva more inclusive (i.e., including the state's Muslim majority—and, by extension, Muslims everywhere in India). The RSS also wanted to project a more inclusive image—one that would make the organization appealing to members of upwardly mobile social groups. In 2015, a fractured state Assembly seemed to present the right circumstance to push the tactic of an alliance to achieve the larger strategic objectives noted above. However, Madhav and other BJP figures in June 2018 said that changing circumstances had made the alliance tactic in Kashmir unviable, though the larger strategic object of national integration remained.[4] The Kashmir experiment in inclusiveness is rooted in the efforts of the then RSS head Deoras and BJS leader Vajpayee in the mid-1970s to link up with other groups opposed to Prime Minister Indira Gandhi's 1975–77 Emergency, to support merging with those parties to form the Janata Party and then to join the Janata government that won the parliamentary elections which took place when the Emergency was lifted.[5] While the BJS pulled out of the Janata coalition, this experiment provided an ideological basis for the BJP's subsequent tactical alliances with other parties and, ultimately, the alliance in Kashmir.

What were the favourable circumstances that permitted the 2015 tactical experiment in Kashmir? The BJP, which had recently come to power with a majority after the 2014 national elections, was optimistic about its ability to bring about Prime Minister Modi's promise of *achhe din* (good times). In addition, the November–December 2014 elections in Jammu and Kashmir resulted in a hung Assembly that triggered a scramble among several political parties to assemble a majority. The BJP, whose support was in the Hindu-majority Jammu region of the state, moved with tacit RSS backing to create a governing alliance with a party that had traditionally represented Kashmiri Muslim interests in the state. Modi seemed to be fond of Mufti Mohammad Sayeed, the head of the PDP who had earlier served as cabinet minister in the Congress and Janata Dal governments in New Delhi, including as the first Muslim Union home minister (1989–90).[6] In supporting the coalition in 2015, the RSS in Jammu and Kashmir was forced to balance the narrow interests of the state's Hindu minority with its strategic imperative of integrating Kashmir into the Indian Union. That strategic goal implicitly included an effort to reduce the Kashmiri Muslim alienation. What was once sacrosanct Hindu nationalist doctrine— such as the abolition of Article 370 (which grants autonomous rights to the state of Jammu and Kashmir)—was set aside and the Common Minimum Programme (CMP) agreed to the continued inclusion of Article 370 in the Indian Constitution.[7]

The RSS's decision to support the coalition thus required an expansion of the definition of the word 'Hindu' to mean something more than a community that identified as religiously Hindu. Expanding the conception required melding the older restrictive notion of Hindu cultural nationalism with the more inclusive one of territorial nationalism applicable to all people living in India[8]— thus justifying the use of 'Hindu' as a synonym for 'citizen of India', regardless of religious affiliation. The wide social and cultural diversity among Hindus had already forced Hindu nationalists to propose that, however different they are culturally from each other, Indian Hindus are in fact a distinct ethnic group linked somehow by kinship and culture.[9] While Savarkar, an ideologue who popularized the term 'Hindutva', basically accepted this kinship argument, he contended that Muslims and Christians—though largely of common blood with other Indians—do not identify with their fellow countrymen because of their different cultural traditions.[10] Golwalkar, RSS head for over three decades from 1940–73, had held similar views. Many swayamsevaks, especially those in the VHP, still do. The RSS, particularly since the late 1970s, has begun to modify its stance on this issue, engaging in programmes aimed at the cultural assimilation of Muslims, Christians and others who do not practise Hinduism as a religion. Non-Hindus are accepted into shakhas; there have been Muslim pracharaks; and RSS-affiliated schools enrol a large number of non-Hindus. The MRM, mentored by a Kashmiri pracharak, has a broad array of programmes aimed at convincing Muslims to abstain from eating beef, to practise yoga,[11] accept the great epics (the Mahabharata and the Ramayana) as part of their own cultural legacy and respect Ram as a cultural icon.[12] In addition to encouraging efforts at cultural assimilation in Kashmir (and elsewhere), the RSS also backed Prime Minister Modi's policy of using the connectivity that comes from infrastructure development to enhance the sense of a common Indian citizenship.[13]

Following the alliance with the BJP, Sayeed took oath as chief minister of Jammu and Kashmir on 1 March 2015. While willing to give this experiment a chance, many in the RSS considered the alliance as unnatural and thus likely to be short-lived, given the two parties' wide policy differences on such core issues as Kashmir's autonomy and the revocation of the Armed Forces Special Powers Act (AFSPA), which grants wide-ranging powers to the Indian armed forces in the state. The BJP (and the RSS), drawing its support almost entirely from the Hindu-majority Jammu region of the state, had in the past adamantly opposed autonomy for the state, and favoured retaining the AFSPA. The PDP, its support base mainly in the Muslim-majority Valley of Kashmir, took an opposite stand on both. Yet, senior RSS office-bearers—while having reservations about the viability of the alliance and highly critical of some of the initial actions of the new PDP chief minister—were willing to remain relatively silent on these and other traditional issues (such as alleged discrimination against the Jammu region) as part of a larger national effort to support the BJP and advance the nationalist agenda. Extended negotiations were required to form this new coalition government, as the state Assembly election results (announced 23 December 2014) produced a hung Assembly, leading to the imposition of Governor's rule as an interim measure. The two largest parties in the eighty-seven-seat Assembly were the PDP, with twenty-eight seats, and the BJP, with twenty-five—the two-month-long secretive talks that would lead to the CMP were basically between these two parties. The core element of that programme was a pledge to review the AFSPA and maintain Article 370, a stand which the RSS has long opposed.[14] This deal survived the death of Chief Minister Sayeed on 7 January 2016, and the selection of his daughter, Mehbooba Mufti, as his replacement. The absence of Sayeed, however, made a difference. His daughter neither had the stature or admiration of prominent figures in the RSS 'family' nor possessed the political astuteness of her deceased father. Ram Madhav, in a press interview following the fall of the coalition, went so far as to say, 'had he [Mufti Mohammad Sayeed] lived longer, probably we would have succeeded in taking it [the coalition] forward'.[15]

Representing the BJP in the coalition negotiations was Ram Madhav,[16] an RSS pracharak and its national sah sampark pramukh (media spokesman) before being deputed to the BJP as its national general secretary shortly after the 2014 elections. He was personally selected by Prime Minister Modi to negotiate the coalition. While in the RSS, Madhav developed a reputation as an astute negotiator who frequently engaged with often-antagonistic individuals and groups in India and abroad to explain the RSS's views on issues, a role somewhat at odds with the sangh's traditional aversion to publicity.[17] With his reputation as a detail-oriented and patient troubleshooter, willing to listen to others, the affable Madhav was a wise choice to represent the Modi government in what everyone knew would be difficult negotiations. Kashmir posed an especially difficult challenge as Madhav had to win approval from three quarters, all with different objectives: the RSS (representing the Hindus of Jammu who long believed they were sidelined by governments representing the interests of the majority in the overwhelmingly Muslim Kashmir Valley), the PDP, and senior figures in the Modi government which had just come to power several months before and was anxious for a policy victory, especially in a fractious battleground like Kashmir. Complicating Madhav's effort was the possibility that the PDP and other 'secular' parties in the state would align together against the BJP to form a government.[18] But within the often-sceptical sangh parivar, his effort to negotiate a deal with the PDP had on its side growing support at the national leadership level for accommodating territorial nationalism as a part of Hindutva. This amalgamation of territorial and cultural India even has its own quasi-religious icon: Bharat Mata (Mother India), often placed in RSS facilities, usually pictured as a woman clad in saffron and framed by a map of India.[19]

The RSS leadership needed to vet the deal to reach a consensus and reduce the chance of open opposition from the more sceptical elements of the sangh parivar. Almost immediately after the new government was sworn in, on the eve of the 13–15 March 2015 meeting of the RSS's national policymaking body, the ABPS, the BJP party president, Amit Shah, met with RSS chief Mohan Bhagwat and several other senior figures to review a slate of national issues, primary among them being the PDP–BJP coalition government in Kashmir. Though Shah clearly received the support of the RSS central leadership on the Kashmir deal, the 2015 Annual Report of the ABPS reflected RSS concerns about the coalition government by harshly criticizing the PDP chief minister's statement upon taking office that seemed to give credit for the peaceful elections to the militant Hurriyat Conference and Pakistan. This statement, the report noted,

> [Is] undesirable in all aspects. The credit of peaceful elections in Jammu-Kashmir should be given only to the peace-loving citizens of the state, political parties, the defence [sic] and security forces, administrative officers and the election commission.[20]

On the first day of this national conclave, RSS sah sarkaryavah Hosabale felt it necessary to assert that the 'RSS's stand on Article 370 has not changed, we will never compromise on it',[21] even though the CMP agreed to the inclusion of Article 370 in the Constitution. While he admitted that there were 'teething problems' in the new coalition government, and that the 'country is angry' about some of the PDP stands, he nonetheless added that for strategic reasons, 'it is good if the alliance succeeds. It is necessary for a nationalist party to endeavour to set things right in a state like Jammu and Kashmir while being in power. A message should go out in the country and abroad to our neighbours that such an effort is being made.'[22] He further underscored the importance of BJP participation—and its willingness to compromise for the sake of national integration by asserting that 'The issue of Jammu and Kashmir is not between two parties in an alliance . . . It is attached to national sentiment.'[23] The decision of the RSS to back the alliance was another demonstration of its support for the BJP's ambitions to represent all parts of the country, including India's only Muslim-majority state and to draw the state's Muslims more closely into the national mainstream. According to the 2011 census, more than two-thirds of Jammu and Kashmir's approximately 1.25 million residents are Muslim, with the remaining population almost exclusively Hindu or Buddhist. These ethnic boundaries are territorial as well as cultural, with some two-thirds of the Jammu region's citizens being Hindu while 96 per cent of the Valley's residents are Muslim. Ladakh's relatively small population is evenly divided between Muslims and Buddhists.[24]

Despite his hopes for the coalition's survival, Hosabale warned during the national conclave that, 'If the situation does not improve, then we will decide [whether to continue supporting the coalition].'[25] The coalition, not surprisingly, faced several subsequent crises that tested the RSS's resolve to continue backing it. Chief Minister Sayeed in his first week in office directed the state's police chief to consider the release of political prisoners not facing criminal charges; the first such prisoner to be released was Masarat Alam Bhat, chief of the Jammu Kashmir Muslim League and general secretary of the All Parties Hurriyat Conference. He had been in protective custody for leading protests that were judged a violation of the state's Public Safety Act. This triggered a barrage of criticism from the BJP at both the federal and state levels, as well as second thoughts about the alliance from elements within the RSS and the Hindus of Jammu. Bhat's release had not been cleared either with the state BJP or the Union home ministry. A furious BJP, both in the state and at the Centre, demanded an explanation, and were not satisfied by the chief minister's justifications that he was following an order of the state's high court, that it had been done to facilitate talks with dissident groups and that no other separatist leader would be released without consultation.[26] Yet, despite the strains mainly related to the issue of crackdown on separatists, the coalition survived as long as it did because the leaders in both the BJP and the RSS wanted it to continue.[27]

Following the death of Chief Minister Sayeed on 7 January 2016, his daughter and political heir, Mehbooba Mufti, held out for three months before agreeing to assume her father's position; her delay was probably intended to determine if she could extract concessions from the Modi government. The BJP conceded nothing beyond the earlier CMP and, rather than risk fresh elections that might result in a loss of seats, she finally took the oath of office as the head of a coalition with the BJP on 4 April 2016. Just a few months later, in July, her government faced an outbreak of mass public protests in the Valley following the death of a twenty-three-year-old militant, Burhan Wani, commander of the Hizb-ul-Mujahideen, a group that the Government of India has characterized as terrorist. This prolonged violence raised questions about the ability of the Mehbooba Mufti government to handle militant protests and repeated armed attacks by anti-Indian terrorist groups. These concerns were voiced again, a year later, when separatist leaders called for a week of mass protests on the first anniversary of Wani's death.[28] The protests coincided with the 10 July 2017 attack on Hindu pilgrims trekking to the holy cave shrine of Amarnath in the Himalayas, some 80 miles north of the capital of Srinagar (the site draws several hundred thousand Hindus from all over India during the pilgrimage period of late June to early August).[29] This attack, resulting in seven deaths, was only the latest such incident over the past two and a half decades: Union Minister of State for Home Hansraj Ahir reported that there have been thirty-six terrorist attacks on the pilgrimage since 1990.[30]

The PDP leadership called for an end to such attacks, but with little success, because the militants viewed the PDP alliance with a Hindu nationalist party like the BJP as a betrayal of Kashmiri Muslim interests. Reacting to these attacks on Hindu pilgrims, the VHP issued a circular that, on the surface, called for a tough law-and-order approach to the violence, but was in fact also a criticism of the expansive concept of Hindutva. The circular included several striking hard-line demands: 'stop recruiting Kashmiri Muslim youth in any security forces of Bharat and in J & K'; 'all state Govts should close down shops/businesses by Kashmiri Muslims in tourist destinations/pilgrimage places/markets/hotels/stations etc.'; 'the Central Govt [should] repeal article 370 from [sic] Kashmir & also get POK [Pakistan-occupied Kashmir] and not waste time in dialogue with Pakistan and China on this'; 'Govt must give complete freedom to the Army to handle the situation their way & not be cowed down by publicity blitz and by anti-national activism'.[31] Neither the RSS nor the BJP leadership backed these hard-line demands, though many swayamsevaks undoubtedly did. There are several issues on which the sangh parivar and the PDP, despite the CMP, have deep differences—differences that defy compromise as they arise from either side's core ideological principles. The most contentious of these issues are Constitutional Articles 370 and 35A (the latter sustains the state's uniquely Muslim demographic orientation). Article 35A addresses the unique sectarian character of Jammu and Kashmir by permitting the state to decide which residents could vote, hold public office and possess property. After the adoption of Article 35A in 1954, the BJS and the RSS have criticized it for empowering the state of Jammu and Kashmir to define who qualifies as a 'permanent resident'—and what privileges 'permanent residents' can enjoy, in ways that seem to discriminate against Hindus, undermine the national scope of what it is to be an Indian and seem to support the controversial two-nation theory which Jinnah had proposed to justify the creation of Pakistan. The Constitution of Jammu and Kashmir—adopted on 17 November 1956—defined a 'permanent resident' as a person who was a state subject on 14 May 1954, or had been a resident of the state for at least ten years.[32] The Jammu and Kashmir Legislative Assembly later stipulated that the rights to vote, hold public office and own property were limited to 'permanent residents', thus guaranteeing that the state would maintain its Muslim majority. In mid-2015, the Jammu and Kashmir Study Centre, a Delhi-based think tank sympathetic to the sangh parivar, was instrumental in generating support for a challenge to the constitutionality of Article 35A in the Delhi High Court. Subsequently, the issue was taken up in India's Supreme Court.[33] A petition filed in the Supreme Court claimed that the President of India had in 1956–57 improperly bypassed Parliament in the inclusion of Article 35A as a part of the Indian Constitution, and that it also violated the principle of 'equality before the law' mandated by Article 14.[34]

With the RSS strongly opposed to both Articles 370 and 35A, the BJP found itself in a difficult position when the state's law minister, Syed Basharat Ahmed Bukhari, reportedly assured the Jammu and Kashmir Legislative Assembly on 6 October 2015 that 'We are here to safeguard and protect Article 370 and Article 35A.'[35] In a warning to the BJP (and, by extension, the RSS), Chief Minister Mehbooba Mufti in a 28 July 2017 speech in Delhi argued that the political fallout of removing Article 35A would reduce the political space in Kashmir for politicians like her who owed allegiance to the Indian Union.[36] The chief minister's message seemed to have registered with the BJP-led government in New Delhi, as well as with the BJP party in Kashmir, which remained relatively silent on the coalition government's opposition to any change in Article 35A. Attorney General of India K.K. Venugopal told a Supreme Court bench that the Modi government was not keen to file its own affidavit in the existing petition challenging the constitutionality of Article 35A before the court. Admitting that the petition was a 'very sensitive' matter requiring a 'larger debate', he said that the Modi government favoured referring the matter to a larger bench, as significant constitutional issues were involved.[37] This prudent move for continued legal discussion would delay a decision, and thus keep the issue out of the political arena and within the confines of legal analysis. Resorting to the legal system on this and other controversial issues has proved a convenient tactic to delay a decision.

The Modi government was prepared to compromise in order to buy time both to allow the coalition to coalesce and to give the government's infrastructure projects time to provide substantial employment to the state's restive youth, thereby drawing them closer to an Indian identity. Union minister Gadkari announced on 2 April 2017 at the dedication of the Chenani–Nashri tunnel that connects Jammu to Srinagar that seventy-two new projects had been sanctioned in the state. These included another tunnel to provide connectivity to Leh (the major city in the north-eastern Ladakh region), as well as a bridge over the Chenab River (nearly 360 metres tall, which would make it the highest in the world on completion) in order to improve connectivity within the state and with other parts of India.[38] While dedicating the tunnel connecting Jammu and Srinagar, Prime Minister Modi focused on a major political objective of these infrastructure projects: 'The Kashmiri youth have a choice to select one of the two paths—one of tourism and the other of terrorism. The path of bloodshed has not helped anyone and will never help anyone.'[39] It is probably no coincidence that the BJP controlled all the infrastructure-related ministries of the Jammu and Kashmir coalition government. An important political advantage of controlling these ministries is that they provided BJP state ministers the discretionary power to determine subcontractors, giving the party an opportunity to strengthen its support base among Muslim businessmen in the Valley of Kashmir.[40] Infrastructure development addresses the major long-term problem of the high rate of unemployment among the state's youth and the comparative lack of job opportunities. The state's Economic Survey 2016 attributes this largely to a quarter century of unrest, which is a disincentive to private and public investment and an impediment to education and to the potentially lucrative tourist trade. Some 24.6 per cent of the population in the age group of eighteen to twenty-nine is unemployed, which is nearly twice the national average, with the proportion of unemployed women and men in this age group pegged at 45.1 per cent and 17.8 per cent respectively.[41] One of the consequences of the lack of opportunities is the migration of ever larger numbers of young people seeking jobs outside the state. Their remittances provide a substantial boost to its economy.

Amid the furore over the July 2017 attack on the Amarnath pilgrims, the RSS held its annual national Pracharak Baithak, a conclave of some 200 senior pracharaks and sanghchalaks from both the RSS and affiliates, in Jammu. Its purpose was threefold: to discuss the challenges facing the sangh parivar, to evaluate the attendance at the recently concluded third-year training camp for prospective pracharaks[42] and to formulate the upcoming schedule of tours for national RSS leaders. While such meetings are a regular annual feature of the RSS calendar,[43] what was unique about this meeting was its locale—the Jammu region of Kashmir. It was the first time that a senior RSS body had met in the state since the founding of the organization in 1925. To underscore the assembly's importance, several national leaders were in attendance, including RSS chief Mohan Bhagwat, its general secretary, Suresh (aka Bhaiyyaji) Joshi, and four joint general secretaries, Dattatreya Hosabale, Krishna Gopal, Suresh Soni and V. Bhagaiah. These leaders arrived early to participate in the core group discussions that would determine the agenda on particularly critical issues such as the deteriorating security situation in Kashmir, made manifest by the attack on the Amarnath pilgrims. The key roles of Indresh Kumar, formerly the Kashmir prant pracharak and the ideological guide of the RSS-backed MRM, and the then Kashmir prant pracharak, Arun Kumar (now the RSS prachar pramukh), in organizing the conclave pointed to its deliberate Kashmir focus. The importance given to the Amarnath pilgrimage by the sangh parivar suggests, according to journalist and scholar Raksha Kumar, an effort to turn the site into a kind of Indian Jerusalem, 'mixing religious and national sentiment to turn the disputed territory into sacred ground that can never be surrendered'.[44] Kumar persuasively argues that religious tourism has been employed to strengthen the claim of India over Jammu and Kashmir.[45] Reflecting the linkage of religious tourism and patriotism, India's government-run Press Information Bureau in 1999—shortly after the Kargil War between India and Pakistan—published an article that asserted:

> The eternal pilgrimage centre of Amarnath has been threatened from across the Line of Control [dividing Indian and Pakistani Kashmir] this year. Hence, it is a special occasion for the devotees to show their abiding faith in Lord Shiva . . . by paying a visit to the Holy Cave in the higher reaches of Kashmir . . .[46]

The VHP, which played a role in mobilizing support for the Amarnath Yatra in the 1990s, continues to organize its own pilgrimages in the state, and often refers to Amarnath in terms of national integration.[47] The VHP was largely responsible for transforming what was a local shrine into a national pilgrimage centre. Reflecting the success of the VHP in garnering official support for the pilgrimage, the

Governor of Jammu and Kashmir is designated the ex officio chair of the Shri Amarnathji Shrine Board, and both the state and central governments provide accommodation and medical facilities at the site, as well as security for the pilgrims. Estimated to number around 2,60,000 in 2017, the pilgrims receive free food and medical care.[48]

At the senior pracharak conclave in Jammu, one of the major topics discussed was the expansion of the RSS's presence in the state's Muslim-majority Kashmir region, where there are currently no shakhas. The Jammu and Ladakh regions, by contrast, have about 300.[49] This goal of mobilizing Muslim support in the state was showcased in a 7 January 2017 Delhi meeting of the MRM, which is mentored by Indresh Kumar, reportedly held to counter the efforts of militants to convince the Muslim youth of Kashmir that violence is the solution to their problems.[50] This meeting sought to draw Muslim youth away from militancy by addressing their frustrations with allegedly rampant corruption and the poor implementation of state programmes meant to provide education and jobs. This effort, with the apparent support of the RSS, is another example of the shift of Hindutva away from the traditional goal of defending Hindu group interests in Kashmir and towards cultural assimilation instead, a stark about-turn from the RSS's original motive for establishing a presence in the state.

In 1942, RSS chief Golwalkar had sent one of the organization's most dynamic young pracharaks, Balraj Madhok, to the princely state[51] to establish shakhas among Hindus in the Jammu area; the goal was to organize Hindus and thus enable them collectively to defend their interests from the Muslim majority.[52] The sanghchalak of the Jammu and Kashmir region after 1947 was Pandit Prem Nath Dogra, an influential Hindu leader in Jammu, who, after Independence, worked with Madhok to establish the Praja Parishad party, lobbying for the full integration of the state within the Indian Union—and, by extension, opposing any constitutional provision of autonomy to the state.[53] India, however, provided special status to Jammu and Kashmir under Article 370, which, among other things, allowed the Indian Parliament to legislate only the state's defence, foreign affairs and communications, and permitted Kashmir its own symbols of power, such as a flag and a state constitution.[54] The Praja Parishad built its structure on the existing RSS network in Kashmir, and became the state affiliate of Mookerjee's new BJS. The nationalist fervour of the RSS and the Parishad was primarily stoked by two factors: the recurrent Pakistani demand that Kashmir, as a Muslim-majority state, should be incorporated into Pakistan, and the first Indo-Pakistan War in 1947–48 which ended in a UN-administered ceasefire.[55] Muslim-majority Kashmir's incorporation into the Indian Union is important, as it underscores the country's secularism, and the Indian Parliament has passed legislation asserting that all of Jammu and Kashmir, including PoK, are legitimately Indian.

The Praja Parishad addressed the frustrations of the Hindus of Jammu, who baulked at the political dominance of the mostly Muslim ethnic Kashmiris concentrated in the Valley after India's Independence. The Parishad, moreover, opposed any form of autonomy for Kashmir, backing instead either full integration into India and/or autonomy for the Jammu region. The Parishad also represented the grievances of the ethnic Dogras who had previously dominated the region under the Hindu maharaja whom the nascent republic had forced to turn over power to Sheikh Abdullah and his National Conference, a long-time opponent of the princely order and the feudal land system dominated by a largely Hindu landholding class.[56] According to Behera, some 8,00,000 acres of land were transferred to 2,47,000 tillers without compensation, a move many Hindus feared would dramatically alter the social order of the state.[57] The Parishad, with the full support of the RSS and other Hindu organizations, launched an agitation in late 1952 whose primary goal was the abolition of Article 370 and the full integration of the state into the Indian Union. It also demanded the separation of Hindu-majority Jammu from Kashmir. This demand for self-determination rested on the reality that ethnic Kashmiri Muslims, as the majority, would dominate the politics of the state. The protest received the full support of the new BJS and its president, Mookerjee, and Kashmir was placed at the top of the sangh parivar's agenda.[58] Mookerjee focused on the Kashmir government's requirement that people coming to the state from India were required to get a permit from Kashmiri authorities before crossing the border. Determined to draw public attention to the issue, he crossed over to Kashmir without a permit on 11 May 1953, and was promptly arrested. Just over a month later, on 23 June, the government announced that he had died of a heart attack while in custody. The BJS thus had a martyr for the cause of nationalism (the RSS continues to celebrate the memory of Mookerjee as a martyr). Behera argues that Mookerjee's death 'sharpened political differences between Indian Prime Minister Nehru and Abdullah, triggering his dismissal and arrest in 1953'.[59] The process of integrating Kashmir into the Indian Union became federal policy, so that its relationship with the national government resembles that of other Indian states. This erosion of autonomy, however, came with considerable central interference in the state's politics, not to mention a perception among many ethnic Muslim Kashmiris that they were losing control over the affairs of their own state—even though the Valley continued to dominate the state politically and received the bulk of state resources and public sector jobs. This perceived favouritism stoked sustained popular support for the BJS and its successor party, the BJP, among the Hindus in Jammu. Still another factor in the BJP's success among the Hindus of Jammu was the increasing violence by Islamic secessionist groups, which took a serious turn in the late 1980s and has continued into the new century. This violence in the Valley contributed to the flight of almost all of the 1,50,000-odd Kashmiri Pandits, a remnant of the once prevalent Kashmiri Hindu population. Most Pandits fled initially to the Jammu region, where many still live, some in refugee camps. A spate of militant violence about two decades later—some of it supported from across the LoC—led to armed confrontations with Indian security forces, further antagonizing large parts of the Muslim population of the Valley. This violence also led to even stauncher RSS support for a tough response to militancy in the state. However, and perhaps more importantly, it also made the RSS sensitive to the need for a more inclusive view of Hindutva nationalism, rather than the traditional support of specific interests of the Hindu religious minority in the state.

The goal of greater inclusiveness makes the Kashmir political experiment something of a test case of the RSS's willingness to accommodate identity concerns of the religious minorities. The BJP, probably for electoral reasons, has done so in Goa for Christians, on the issue of state financial support for English-language Christian schools. While the RSS supports education in the mother tongue, it has gone along with the language policy of the ruling BJP in Goa. In Kashmir, the periodic outbursts of violence by Muslims underscores a deeply held insecurity about their future that must be addressed if there is to be a restoration of stability. Hence the insistence of the PDP in the 2015 CMP that the autonomy provisions of Article 370 must continue.[60] The heavy arm of the state represented by the presence of Indian security forces under authority of AFSPA contributes to the Kashmiri Muslim view that they are second-class citizens in their own state. The CMP recognized this problem by pledging the coalition government to re-examine the need for the continuation of AFSPA in areas defined as 'disturbed'.[61] The CMP also had a provision calling for the government to initiate a dialogue among all stakeholders regardless of their ideological views, which offered an opportunity to get the federal government on board for significant moves to address Muslim discontent. Prime Minister Modi suggested moving on this issue in his Independence Day speech in 2017, a tacit admission that military force was a blunt instrument to restore stability to the state.[62] Perhaps with this in mind, the Modi government followed the precedent set in 2001 by former Prime Minister Vajpayee by selecting a person of stature, in this case Dineshwar Sharma, former head of India's Intelligence Bureau, to start a dialogue with all stakeholders in the state.[63] The home minister, who made the announcement on 24 October 2017, said that Sharma would decide which individuals or groups to involve in his discussions.[64] Sharma wasted little time to get started and began his interactions almost immediately, including discussions with people who have a secessionist agenda. A set of challenging circumstances in 2018, however, convinced the BJP (and an already sceptical RSS) that such gestures were futile. The continued communal cleavages in the state were evident in the mass protests and counter-protests following the tragic rape and murder in early 2018 of a young Muslim girl in Kathua in Hindu-majority Jammu. This was followed by disagreement between the coalition partners over the question of extending the Indian government's Ramzan ceasefire, announced on 16 May 2018, and the broad-daylight murder on 14 June 2018 of a prominent Kashmiri journalist, Shujaat Bukhari, in Srinagar. Ram Madhav asserted that the continuing violence, including attacks on army convoys, led the Modi government to conclude that 'it was time for us [the government] to hand over the administration to the governor for some time'.[65]

Any discussion of Kashmir must address the international dimensions as well, because Kashmir is both a domestic issue and an international one. It is on the border with Pakistan which claims that the state is legitimately theirs and two wars (three, if one counts the 1971 war where the theatre of warfare was East Pakistan, now Bangladesh) and several near-wars have been fought over it. The key to any possibility of long-term stability in Kashmir depends, in our view, on two developments: providing greater autonomy to Kashmir (and that might require autonomy of Hindu-majority Jammu within Kashmir) and ensuring robust economic growth that creates jobs in a state where unemployment is high. The latter is almost certainly not possible without the former. But movement on the first also depends on an improvement in relations between the two countries as the current bilateral malaise prompts Pakistan to encourage armed resistance to the Indian presence in Kashmir, often employing the services of anti-India militant groups.[66]

Therefore, a win–win–win solution for Pakistan, India and the Kashmiris is required. Several back-channel discussions were attempted in the wake of the 1999 Kargil War between India and Pakistan that focused on how to arrive at a solution acceptable to all the major actors.[67] One possibility, roughly summarizing the nature of the back-channel talks, was openly suggested in a 2006 proposal that recommended no change in legal sovereignty of the two sides of Kashmir, while India and Pakistan pull back their security troops and work out an imaginative way to provide for a Kashmiri voice on such governance issues as law and order and energy.[68] Deep suspicions on both sides have blocked these efforts so far.

Our central thesis here is that the RSS approach to Kashmir includes a balancing of strategic goals and tactics. The strategic goals (national integration and a definition of Hindutva that includes Muslims) are firm while the tactics to achieve them will vary depending on circumstances. A key consideration on whether to modify or change tactics depends heavily on the reaction of the state's Hindu population. Escalating violence in Kashmir and a perceived favouritism towards the Muslim-majority Kashmir Valley were eroding the confidence of Hindus in the Mehbooba Mufti government. The RSS's information-gathering apparatus would have picked up on the growing restiveness of the Hindu community, which likely prompted its steady stream of criticism of the Kashmir government. With the general elections fast approaching, the national leadership, in consultation with the RSS and others, decided to withdraw from the alliance and impose Governor's rule. This gives the central government room to manoeuvre to restore stability and rebuild Hindu confidence as well as burnish the party's nationalist credentials among Hindu voters in the rest of India. The BJP, with support limited to the Jammu region, can only come back to power by working out another alliance with a party that draws much, if not all, of its support from the state's Muslim majority. Ram Madhav, who announced the BJP withdrawal, phrased his comments to suggest that the BJP–PDP alliance was the right tactical thing to do at the time and that the coalition had attained some significant achievements. He left the door open for negotiations with all stakeholders in the state, indicating that political dialogue would supplement security measures. While the RSS's strategic imperatives have not changed, tactics may change or be modified, as happened in this case.

EIGHT

A Debate on Economic Self-Sufficiency

Mediating Conflicting Views within the Parivar

Prime Minister Modi's BJP government, in line with its 'Make in India' campaign, announced on 20 June 2016 what it called a 'radical liberalization' of India's Foreign Direct Investment (FDI) regime by easing rules to encourage investment in a range of fields, including defence, civil aviation, multi-brand retail trading and pharmaceuticals. In his plenary speech at the 2018 World Economic Forum in Davos, Modi highlighted the steps his government had taken to liberalize FDI norms and improve the business environment. Addressing the global business elite, Modi exhorted them to invest in India, calling it an 'investment in the future'.[1] The progressive liberalization of FDI norms seems to have paid off as the FDI inflows nearly doubled from $36 billion in 2013–14 to $60 billion in 2016–17, higher than that of any other country in 2016–17.[2] However, not all sangh parivar constituents shared Modi's enthusiasm for this surge in FDI. The BMS, an RSS-affiliated labour group, and the SJM, a national lobby group advocating economic self-sufficiency and set up in the early 1990s with the support of RSS leaders, blasted the 2016 FDI liberalization as a 'betrayal of trust' and an 'anti-national' act.[3] Ashwani Mahajan, the all-India co-convener of the SJM, issued a statement saying that the 'SJM contests the government's argument that FDI would bring growth and create employment in the country' and further asserted that, 'Experience of Indian economy in the last 25 years of globalisation has been very distressing whereby rate of growth of employment has slowed down, rate of reduction of poverty has come down, inequalities have widened and there is no reprieve for the common man.'[4] He exhorted Indian consumers to shun foreign goods, clarifying later that this boycott should extend beyond trade to commerce, and thus include Indian companies set up with Chinese investment, such as Paytm, an Indian company with investment from Chinese e-commerce giant Alibaba. In direct opposition to this criticism of economic globalization within the sangh parivar, Prime Minister Modi in his speech at the 2018 World Economic Forum at Davos put India on the side of globalization, criticizing what he called 'a growing trade protectionism'. In an emulation of the previous year's inaugural speech at the forum by Chinese President Xi Jinping, Modi suggested that India could provide leadership for global trade liberalization.[5]

Prime Minister Modi's praise of economic globalization and his rhetorical commitment to liberalization, however, run somewhat counter to his government's policies. The 2018 budget increased duties on a range of imports, including mobile phones, automobile parts, electronics, edible oils and television components.[6] In the budget speech, Finance Minister Jaitley announced a 'calibrated departure from the underlying policy [of reducing customs duty] of the last two decades'.[7] Arvind Panagariya, the former head of NITI Aayog, criticized the decision to increase customs duty as a return to the days of the licence permit raj.[8]

Bhagwat's 2017 Vijayadashami address—to the RSS faithful, somewhat akin to the State of the Union speech by the US President—catalysed a populist turn in the Modi government's economic policies. Just four days after Bhagwat's speech, the government cut levies on petrol and diesel to buffer the impact on consumers of rising crude oil prices.[9] On the same day, three BJP-ruled states—Gujarat, Maharashtra and Madhya Pradesh—cut state taxes on fuel.[10] The Goods and Services Tax Council—a statutory body of state and Union finance ministers set up to decide tax rate and the structure of the controversial GST—announced changes that significantly eased the compliance burden of small businesses, such as by allowing them to file taxes quarterly instead of monthly. The GST Council also reduced tax rates for several items that are commonly used by low- and middle-income households, such as chappals (Indian footwear), chapattis (flatbread), plastic, rubber and yarn. Chastened by the outcome of the Gujarat state elections, where analysts counted farm distress[11] among the reasons for the BJP's worse than expected performance, the 2018 budget announced several sops for farmers. The government announced a policy of higher farm-support prices—it declared its intent to set the Minimum Support Price (MSP) for all crops at one and a half times the production cost.[12]

Perhaps because of feedback from the sangh network of public discontent over the economic record of the Modi government, especially on the issue of job creation, Bhagwat has repeatedly exhorted the government to continue its populist policy orientation. In a speech delivered on 16 April 2018 at the Bombay Stock Exchange (BSE) to an audience of business elites from India's financial capital, Bhagwat argued that economic policymakers should pay special attention to the needs of farmers and small enterprises.[13] His BSE speech was perhaps the clearest enunciation of the RSS economic philosophy. He reiterated that the RSS is not wedded to any economic 'isms'. Arguing that debates over ideological labels are counterproductive, he said the yardstick to judge an economic policy should be whether its benefits have reached those at the bottom rung of the social hierarchy—similar to Gandhi's famous economic talisman. Because of its belief in the efficacy of bottom-up social change, the RSS has placed a great deal of emphasis on the individual. The preoccupation of the RSS is to train individuals by inculcating discipline and socializing them in the sangh ideology. As such, Bhagwat argued that while Hinduism is not an ascetic faith that precludes wealth creation, an individual's economic conduct should be mediated by dharma (righteousness). An individual's major goal in life should not therefore be wealth accumulation or hedonistic consumption.

A string of RSS resolutions dating back to the 1950s and issued by its chief policymaking bodies strongly reflected its support for swadeshi over the next five decades. Such resolutions became more frequent in the 1990s when the Congress government of Prime Minister Rao introduced a set of far-reaching policies aimed at reducing state controls over the economy and opened the markets to outside investment, a step that triggered the formation of the SJM. The first public campaign of the SJM was to organize protests against the involvement of Enron, an American company brought in for the construction of a power-generating facility south of Mumbai, which was charged with bribing public officials and politicians. Criticism of the government's liberal reform policies also continued during the BJP-led coalitions of Vajpayee (1998–2004), which accepted many of the market reforms as necessary to spur economic growth. Among those most outspoken in favour of swadeshi was the RSS sarsanghchalak. Sudarshan (2000–09), who had an often-strained relationship with Vajpayee and who served as a critical monitor of the government's approach to FDI. His openly critical views on this issue also played well with an ideologically hard-line element in the party such as ideologues Murli Manohar Joshi and General Secretary K.N. Govindacharya,[14] who were especially apprehensive about the cultural and social impact of opening the country to foreign investment. Just months after Vajpayee assumed office in March 1998, the SJM organized a rally in early September 1998 protesting the new government's economic policies. Pralay Kanungo reports that Sudarshan, who was then the RSS joint secretary and its designated liaison with the BJP, attended the steering committee planning that protest march, and characterized the SJM agitation itself as 'almost a revolt against the government'.[15] The RSS's top policymaking body, the ABKM, issued in 1998 a resolution on self-reliance that verges on a lecture to the Vajpayee government, stating:

It is well known that the R.S.S. has always been in favour of Swadeshi, which connotes self-reliance and economic independence. Therefore, the ABKM regards as improper the

Central Govt's decision to open the Insurance Sector for direct foreign investment.[16]

The same year the ABPS, the RSS's 'parliament', passed a resolution expressing its 'grave apprehensions' that the policies of the World Trade Organization (WTO) have 'started adversely affecting local agriculture and industry, particularly small, medium and agro-industries . . .'[17] It appealed to the government to implement a six-point programme that included organizing developing countries 'to stand up and fight the economic imperialism of WTO, G-7 countries, MNCs, World Bank and IMF', amending the Indian Patent Act 1970 to ensure that 'farmers should not be deprived of the traditional knowledge, crops, flora and fauna . . .' and reviewing tariffs reduced to an average level of 'only 30%', which allegedly had adversely affected several Indian industries.[18] The next year, the ABPS passed a resolution arguing that India propose amendments to the WTO, suggesting that there was a 'conspiracy of developed nations' to establish a monopoly on hybrid plants and seeds to 'make the agriculture of developing countries wholly subservient to them' and that they are using information technology 'to create a mindset attuned to their commercial interests, through high profile propaganda'.[19] Despite this open opposition to liberalizing India's trade and investment policies by some influential elements of the sangh parivar, Vajpayee's choice of non-RSS member Yashwant Sinha as the finance minister, a decision opposed by the RSS, signalled that the new government intended to continue the economic reform goals set by Rao.[20] But the critical response to this commitment to liberalization by many within the party and within the larger sangh parivar required a cautious review of its impact on important support groups. When Sinha announced a continuation of the policies that permitted foreign investment in the power and telecommunications sectors, for example, he also clarified that he would not permit FDI in consumer non-durables, a sector in which a powerful element of the BJP coalition (small-scale traders) has a direct interest.

The person most responsible for establishing the SJM and the BMS and for shaping their left-of-centre economic orientation was Thengadi (1920–2004), a pracharak viewed within the RSS as one of its three most influential ideological figures, the other two being Upadhyaya and Golwalkar. Thengadi firmly believed that a truly independent India must avoid dependence on and influence of the capitalist West and countries in the communist bloc and was thus committed to swadeshi as a central element in his views on economics. Both he and Golwalkar were consequently alarmed by the strong presence of the communists in India's trade union movement, a concern that led him to lay the groundwork for a labour union with a competing Hindutva ideology. With the support of Golwalkar, Thengadi established the BMS in 1955 and, employing the RSS's organizational methods, relying on the support of local RSS networks and building a union base initially with independent local unions formed by RSS members, he launched the national BMS in 1967.[21] What distinguished this labour union from more conventional ones was its commitment to the well-being of workers as well as to India's cultural and social heritage, at least that part of the heritage compatible with the social unity message of Hindutva. Part of that uniquely Indian heritage in the labour field was his rejection of class as a notion that undermines the sense of community and social solidarity that is the core tenet of RSS ideology. In its place, he called for uniting the various parts of the economic process so that this corporate body owns/runs the industrial unit, and explained this goal with the slogan 'nationalise the labour, labourise the industry, industrialise the nation'.[22] The adoption of market reforms, starting on a modest basis under Prime Minister Rajiv Gandhi (1984–99) and pursued more aggressively by Prime Minister Rao (1991–96), included foreign investment as a major goal. The BMS responded to these initiatives by declaring at its tenth National Conference in 1994 'A War of Economic Independence against Western Imperialism'.[23] The BMS website further notes, 'After 1990s when developed countries spread their economic empire, SJM was formed and BMS participated in many of its agitational programmes.'[24] The website points out that even with the BJP in government, the independent BMS 'During the tenure of the NDA Government [the BJP-led coalition] also . . . had "friends" of BMS in it. BMS had to oppose the anti-labour policies.'[25] One sign of that opposition in action was a mass rally in New Delhi on 16 April 2001, during the tenure of Prime Minister Vajpayee, in which one of the messages was a demand that the government push for the establishment of an alternative WTO composed of the 'so-called third world countries'.[26]

The RSS leadership, despite the harsh criticism of the Modi government's globalization policy by some of its affiliates such as the SJM and the BMS, has remained relatively silent on FDI and swadeshi since the BJP returned to power in mid-2014. The RSS under Bhagwat differs from its predecessor in that it has largely avoided harsh public criticism of a BJP government's economic policies, even though the RSS tends to take a more populist stand on economic issues than does the Modi government. Economic growth and the creation of jobs seems increasingly to be the Modi government's standard by which to measure policy. The cautious, more diplomatic, approach gives critics of the BJP within the sangh parivar space to make their case and serve as a watchdog on the government's policies. It also protects Bhagwat's working relationship with the Modi government and thus enables the intra-parivar coordination committees (samanvay samitis)[27] to serve as a forum where the participants can air differences behind closed doors and work out compromises rather than take their disagreements to the press and to the streets. Modi also enters his dealings with the RSS on a much stronger political base than did the previous BJP prime minister, Vajpayee. Modi's BJP won an absolute majority in the 2014 parliamentary elections with a campaign promising economic growth and jobs. Vajpayee had to rely on coalition partners to stay in power and faced a debate within the NDA government and within his own party on the merits of economic reform. Modi, with his winning populist nationalist slogan of 'Sabka Saath Sabka Vikas' (development of all, with participation of all) and unchallenged leadership within his party, has faced considerably less internal party debate and came to the prime ministership with years of governing experience at the state level. He had served for twelve years as chief minister of Gujarat where he launched a successful effort to attract foreign investment. Modi's investment showcase in the state was the

Vibrant Gujarat Global Summit held every other year since 2003, providing him the opportunity to network with Indian and foreign investors that worked to his benefit when he later became prime minister. The BJP's enthusiasm for FDI underscores how far the party has come since its reincarnation in 1980, when it aligned itself to Gandhian socialism which was viewed as a commitment to self-sufficiency and appealed to many in the RSS as it was considered compatible with Upadhyaya's doctrine of 'Integral Humanism'. Ironically, the RSS leadership has always implicitly accepted the self-reliance policies adopted by India's first prime minister, Nehru (1947–64).

Capitalism and socialism, in Upadhyaya's view, were flawed as socially destabilizing and thus at variance with the core Hindutva goal of social solidarity. In their place, he proposed an 'integral' approach aimed at creating a harmonious society that is conscious of protecting the environment. He argued that Indian tradition obligates its statesmen to design institutions that both build and sustain social solidarity. The Hindu notion of Advaita Vedanta (recognition of ourselves in all life) provided a philosophic foundation for this view. To put this integral philosophy into practice, Upadhyaya further argued that social solidarity requires popular involvement in the decision-making process. On the economic side, he proposed worker control of the means of production with larger units run as cooperatives. While he accepted democracy as a legitimate form of government, he thought the democratic process would be a sham unless the citizens were relatively equal both socially and economically.[28] The website of the SJM in its statement of 'goals and objectives' attempts to spell out what such equality would look like in practical terms. It proposes a narrowing of the wealth gap so that the income of the top 20 per cent and the bottom 20 per cent should not exceed the ratio of ten to one.[29] It further proposes that the state guarantee to everyone as a basic right food, clothing, housing, education, health, drinking water, energy, transport and employment.[30] This sort of approach should have appealed to the left, but the Hindutva programme was anathema and they kept their distance from the SJM.

By the time the Rao government introduced market reforms in the early 1990s, the BJP had replaced Gandhian socialism[31] with Upadhyaya's 'Integral Humanism' as a statement of party ideology—and a debate had emerged within the party on the merits of FDI, at least in high-tech areas, with the catchy slogan of 'computer chips and not potato chips'. On FDI, the party seemed to be shifting to the right at this time, with a declaration of support for robust economic development accompanied by gradual reforms initially directed at making the domestic manufacturing and retail sectors more competitive, and then moving to permit measured competition from abroad as well as FDI.[32] This internal debate shows up in a BJP policy statement released in 1992 in which the party tries to make the case that the notions of swadeshi and liberal reforms are not necessarily contradictory. That document asserts, 'There can be no real Swaraj [independence] without Swadeshi. But not the Swadeshi of an inward-looking nation afraid to face an increasingly complex and aggressive world . . . on terms of equality.'[33] That document then provides a justification for modifying its views on swadeshi by adding, 'The role of foreign capital will naturally be limited, though it can be crucial at certain stages and for specified national goals.'[34] The BJP's 1999 parliamentary campaign manifesto in its discussion of swadeshi argues that the adoption of FDI must be gradual and with government support for Indian industry in this transition to a more globalized economy, both to protect it and to make it more competitive. The first sentence of the section dealing with swadeshi states, 'We will continue with the reform process, give it a strong Swadeshi thrust to ensure that the national economy grows on the principle that "India shall be built by Indians",' further explaining, 'It [swadeshi] means that we will facilitate the domestic industry to gain enough muscles to compete with the multinationals in the local and global market.'[35] At the same time, the manifesto underscores the rationale for continued use of FDI, stating that 'the country cannot do without FDI because besides capital stock, it brings with it technology, new market practices and most importantly employment'.[36]

The relative lack of debate on the dangers of economic self-sufficiency within the RSS is linked to its lingering suspicions that large-scale business is somehow the greedy agent of foreign companies and by extension neglects the welfare of workers to maximize profits and perpetuate a culture of hedonism. Large-scale business is contrasted with the accepted RSS business model of small-scale enterprise, viewed as an extension of the family, where concern for the well-being of the individual worker is at least on a par with the profit motive. On a more philosophical level, RSS resolutions on swadeshi warned of the dangers of Western consumerism and its impact on Indian culture (for example, pre-eminently, the weakening of family bonds and the pursuit of self-centred hedonism) as well as the threat to national sovereignty by economic domination of outside interests, sometimes alluding to the fact that British colonial power came to India through a British multinational company, the British East India Company. The SJM website has posted a letter by economist Bharat Jhunjhunwala that reflects the deep suspicion of the alleged corrupting influence of consumerism inherent in modern business:

> The businessman promotes a culture of consumption in order to fulfill his heart's desire of making money. He converts the rest of society into a consumption machine. He makes advertisements and TV programs that ensure that the heart's desire of the clerk to walk on the banks of the river is suppressed and he develops the desire to go to the disco.[37]

To represent and lobby to protect the small-scale family-oriented business and the more austere spiritual lifestyle assumed to be associated with it, the RSS even established an affiliate, the Laghu Udyog Bharati.

With the selection of Bhagwat as sarsanghchalak in 2009, the RSS muted its comments on controversial economic issues like FDI and focused instead on building up the BJP following the party's two successive defeats in the national parliamentary elections. While addressing a gathering of Indian business and intellectual elites in

Delhi on 2 November 2013, Bhagwat suggested that the sangh had moderated its once implacable opposition to liberalization, privatization and foreign investment.[38] The sangh, Bhagwat noted, was 'not bound by dogma'.[39] Allaying apprehensions over the sangh's alleged antediluvian views, Bhagwat noted that the RSS understood that changes in the global economy meant that its views would need to 'evolve over time'.[40] Bhagwat's comments, coming as they did in the run-up to the 2014 Lok Sabha elections where the RSS had decided to use its network to aid the BJP's election campaign, were an indication of a closer alignment between the RSS's economic orientation and Modi's policy agenda. Prior to this, the RSS was consistently an outspoken supporter of economic self-sufficiency. Indeed, the SJM was established on 22 November 1991 at Nagpur, the headquarters of the RSS, with the blessings of the RSS core leadership and the support of RSS-affiliated groups representing workers, farmers, cooperatives and students who worried that their jobs would be threatened by the opening up of the Indian economy.[41] Swadeshi would also serve the interests of what had been the RSS's core support group—urban small-scale entrepreneurs opposed to the competition of foreign goods and to the foreign values they feared would accompany significant foreign business involvement in India.

The robust debate within the BJP on swadeshi had no counterpart in the RSS or in most of the affiliates, and certainly not the SJM. There will be continuing differences between the BJP and the RSS on a range of key political and economic issues, such as the role of the state in economic activity, on merits of globalization and FDI, on labour and land laws, and on federalism, to name just a few, but the intensity of the differences is likely to diminish as the RSS adopts a more assertive mediatory role in handling internal parivar debates. The shift of the RSS's urban membership core from the lower middle class (including small-scale traders) to educated professionals has moderated its once implacable opposition to globalization as well as encouraged its greater openness on a wide range of social and economic issues. The rapid growth of the parivar, especially the BJP, has created a broader range of often-differing interests which

has generated a closer analysis of policy minutiae rather than the
earlier generalized bromides against privatization, FDI and foreign
conspiracies. Moreover, the younger leadership of the RSS seems
more prepared to compromise than the older generation. For the
former, nationalist goals are achieved by looking outward, while
the latter group sees them achieved by looking inward and to the
past. Moreover, the power balance between the party and the RSS
seems to be gradually shifting in favour of the party. One factor in
this shift is almost certainly the RSS fear that the charge of Hindu
terrorism against it, stemming from a series of bomb explosions
in 2006–07, could result in another ban, and thus it must rely on
the BJP to shield it from this action.[42] Particularly disturbing to
the RSS and the BJP are charges of involvement in incidents of
'saffron terrorism' levelled at it on the eve of the 2013–14 campaign
by the then home minister Sushilkumar Shinde, who is quoted
telling a Congress party conclave that, 'Reports have come during
investigation that BJP and RSS conduct terror training camps to
spread terrorism . . .', further adding that, 'We will have to think
about it seriously and will have to be alert.'[43] The BJP spokesperson,
Syed Shahnawaz Hussain, responded by terming the comments
irresponsible and socially divisive.[44] While Shinde backed away from
this statement, such public charges underscored the importance
of a BJP victory to the RSS to protect itself from another set of
restrictions on its programmes by an unfriendly government. Yet
another factor driving this shift is the popularity of Prime Minister
Modi, who is highly regarded among the RSS cadre. The India
Today 'Mood of the Nation' poll, including one in May 2018, shows
a decline in Modi's popularity but suggests that his approval still
exceeds that of his political rivals.[45] At a March 2014 meeting of
the ABPS, the RSS leadership effectively endorsed Modi, and the
sah karyavah, Hosabale, told reporters that, 'Modi is a strong leader.
He is a swayamsevak [RSS member] and we are proud of it. The
country wants a change. He has proved his worth in Gujarat. We
are proud of him as our karyakarta [worker].'[46] Yet just days after
this pledge of support, Bhagwat also felt it necessary to caution the
thousands of RSS members working in the campaign that while it

was in the 'national interest' to bring the BJP to power, 'We are not in politics. Our work is not to chant "NaMo NaMo" [abbreviation for Narendra Modi]. We must work towards our own target.'[47] The RSS has typically been critical of a personality cult in government and that clearly also applies to Modi as prime minister, a concern that is suggested in the RSS chief's 2017 Vijayadashami speech at a time when Modi and the BJP appeared politically ascendant.[48] The RSS aims to plan for the long run, while prime ministers and their governments are transitory.

The selection of the business-friendly Modi by the BJP to lead its 2013–14 parliamentary campaign signalled the decline of swadeshi support in the party, and its follow-up parliamentary victory was attributed in large part to the promise of job creation that appealed to a growing aspirational group that crossed caste and even sectarian lines.[49] The BJP's 2014 campaign manifesto has a section devoted specifically to FDI in contrast to the 2009 manifesto where it is not mentioned except for one reference prohibiting foreign investment in the retail sector. The 2014 manifesto states:

> Barring the multi-brand retail sector, FDI will be allowed in sectors wherever needed for job and asset creation, infrastructure and acquisition of niche technology and specialized expertise. BJP is committed to protecting the interest of small and medium retailers. The FIPBs (Foreign Investment Promotion Board) functioning shall be made more efficient and investor-friendly.

Nonetheless, the selective opposition to the government's economic policies by the BMS, the SJM and other labour-oriented affiliates[50] continued under the Modi government, though the intra-sangh consultations led by the RSS have moderated the differences among them and toned down the public rhetoric, if not necessarily facilitating a consensus. A good example of the attempt to work out a consensus is the BMS's response to the pending set of labour demands originally presented to the Congress government of Manmohan Singh (2004–14). Almost immediately after the BJP's parliamentary victory in May 2014, the BMS joined other labour unions, including groups affiliated with the communists and the Congress, in pressing the government to address the charter of labour demands. A year later, it reached out to other unions (including those affiliated to the Congress and to India's two major communist parties) to plan a joint union protest against the Modi government's alleged inaction regarding these demands. What is interesting about this event are the reported efforts of the RSS to play a mediating role to dissuade the BMS from taking part in protests that would embarrass the Modi government on its first anniversary in office, relying on behind-the-scenes consultations within the 'family' that would produce an acceptable compromise. Drawing attention to this effort to get the BMS to withdraw from the national strike on 2 September 2015, BMS chief B.N. Rai reportedly stated, 'The Sangh [the RSS] is trying to keep up its efforts as head of the "parivar" to ensure there is no confrontation within the family and we want to keep it that way. But there are issues of ideology, and we cannot go against the labour laws and the interests of workers.'[51] The BMS, however, ultimately decided to opt out of the 2 September Bharat Bandh (all-India strike) in the wake of discussions with Finance Minister Jaitley; BMS General Secretary Virjesh Upadhyay announced that it would give the government more time to respond to the union's demands.[52] The intra-sangh consultations that usually take place on contentious matters like this managed to prevent a fallout between the BMS and the BJP government. But the general record of this mediation is mixed. There have been advances on domestic labour issues such as minimum wages and a social security net. But the consultative mechanisms have been less successful on differences regarding the Modi government's support for FDI to achieve its core goals of economic growth and job creation.

The Modi government's decision to create a more liberal FDI regime to include multi-brand retail trade thus ignored the one specific FDI prohibition in the 2014 election manifesto. This continuous incremental liberalization of FDI demonstrates that the RSS's mediating efforts have yet to create a consensus on many of the differences over economic issues within the sangh parivar, in part because many of the positions are in fact so far apart. This fundamental difference is perhaps best demonstrated in the area of labour and land legislation proposed by the Modi government, both aimed at growing the economy but opposed by worker affiliates like the BMS (labour) and the BKS (farmers) because of their potential to harm the interests of their core support groups. The labour legislation would make it easier to fire workers and the land legislation would make it easier for the government to use eminent domain to acquire land for development purposes.

The cases of coal denationalization, labour legislation and royalty of genetically modified (GM) seeds illustrate the differences in the degree of the parivar's influence on the BJP government's policies. Contrary to the assertions popular in sections of Indian media, the sangh parivar does not shape the key elements of government policy on issues of high importance, such as economic development. The issue of coal denationalization illustrates the limits of the RSS affiliates' influence. The coal sector was nationalized by Prime Minister Indira Gandhi in 1973. The sector was partially liberalized (i.e., allowing private companies to mine coal for their own use) in the 1990s. But the process of allocating coal mines to private companies was non-transparent and, according to the Comptroller and Auditor General of India, the country's national auditor, led to a 'windfall gain' of Rs 1.86 trillion (approximately US$30 billion) to private companies.[53] In 2014, the Indian Supreme Court cancelled the allocation of coal mines on grounds of arbitrariness and directed the central government to frame a policy for auctioning of coal mines.[54] In 2014, the government issued an ordinance denationalizing the coal sector, ending Coal India Limited's monopoly on coal mining in India. The BMS joined other trade unions in opposing the legislation, terming it 'anti-national'.[55] Y.N. Singh, then deputy general secretary of Akhil Bharatiya Khadan Mazdoor Sangh, a major trade union in the coal sector, said that Piyush Goyal, the then coal minister, 'doesn't understand the issues related to the coal sector'.[56] Through the mediation of the RSS leadership, a backchannel was established for the BMS to negotiate with the government.[57] The initial negotiations between the coal sector unions, including the RSS-affiliated BMS and the government, failed to achieve a breakthrough, which led the unions to collectively call for a five-day strike starting 6 January 2015.[58] The strike was called off after the government assured the parties concerned that it had no intention of privatizing Coal India, but it did not budge on the policy of opening up coal mining to the private sector.[59] Subsequently, the government announced that it would auction coal mines for 'merchant mining' of coal (without end-use restrictions).[60]

The RSS leadership's role in mediating policy disagreements between its affiliates is also evident in the BJP government's efforts to amend land acquisition legislation. The cost as well as the difficulty of acquiring land were a hurdle for industrialization, which is the key to fulfilling the Modi government's promise of job creation. The RSS was also sensitive to a fair land acquisition policy as part of its efforts to mobilize support in rural India. These two purposes were sometimes contradictory, which is why it has been difficult to arrive at a consensus on the issue within the sangh parivar. Prior to 2013, the eminent domain powers of the government were regulated by colonial-era laws. Politicians and bureaucrats had the discretion to determine both the location of land acquisition and compensation for involuntary land acquisition. These discretionary powers were often abused, especially when farmers' land was acquired for private purposes. Because of antiquated regulations, much of rural India was designated as farmland. The market value of land was artificially depressed because zoning regulations prevented the land from being used for more productive purposes, such as the construction of factories or housing. Politically well-connected speculators worked with local politicians to purchase farm land at artificially depressed values. The land was then rezoned, multiplying its value. The backlash against such speculation and cronyism prompted the Congress government of Prime Minister Manmohan Singh to pass a new land law proscribing the government's ability to use eminent domain to acquire land for private purposes.

By 2014, it was clear that the safeguards introduced in the land acquisition bill created cumbersome procedures that increased the time and cost of acquiring land for infrastructure and industry. In late 2014, the government issued an ordinance to speed up the acquisition of land for five categories of projects: defence, rural infrastructure, low-cost housing, industrial corridors, infrastructure.[61] The amendment sped up the acquisition of land by exempting the projects from detailed social impact assessment and by easing the requirement that the government obtain the consent of 80 per cent of the landowners prior to acquisition.[62] The BKS threatened to take its protest to the streets to register its disapproval of the legislation which it termed as antithetical to farmers' interests. Other labour-oriented RSS affiliates—the BMS and the SJM—also opposed the legislation which they perceived as tilting the scales in favour of industry. Hosabale said that the RSS affiliates should bridge their differences 'in a spirit of coordination and not confrontation'.[63] Recognizing the Modi government's imperative to ensure growth and rapid job creation, an RSS leader said, 'BJP's whole development promise hinges on land acquisition. If the party is unable to push it, it will end up cutting a sorry figure. More so, if the problem is posed by the parivar's own organisations.'[64] Representatives of the BKS met Amit Shah (BJP president), Ram Lal (RSS pracharak who is a general secretary of the BJP and the link between the BJP and RSS) and Ram Madhav (an RSS pracharak who was brought in by Prime Minister Modi as a BJP general secretary) to determine if a compromise could be worked out.[65] The government subsequently included nine amendments to its land acquisition legislation, many of which incorporated suggestions from the BKS and other RSS affiliates.[66] After its suggestions were incorporated, the BKS diluted its opposition to the land acquisition legislation.[67] However, in the face of implacable resistance from the Congress party and the Opposition, the government lacked a numerical majority in the upper house of the Parliament and had to abandon its efforts to pass a national legislation to expedite land acquisition. But the Modi government found a way to get around this problem to achieve what it believed was necessary for economic growth and the creation of jobs. A provision in the Indian Constitution permits the states, if they have central approval, to pass legislation in areas where both the states and the Centre have responsibility (as with land). Four states, Tamil Nadu, Gujarat, Rajasthan and Telangana, have passed legislation to speed up acquisition of land for industrial use. While the Modi government did not get its desired federal law on the subject, the RSS leadership had successfully mediated between the BJP and the various labour-oriented affiliates to arrive at a compromise that each of the major actors in the sangh parivar could accept.

SJM, the most openly critical of the affiliates towards the Modi government's economic policies, has had more success in getting the government to impose regulatory restrictions on GM seeds through price controls. As chief minister of Gujarat, Modi was enthusiastic about GM technology. As prime minister, he asserted that, 'India has the potential to become a major producer of transgenic rice and several genetically modified or engineered vegetables.'[68] The SJM's co-convener, Mahajan, advised the government not to follow 'MNC-promoted GM crop science blindly'.[69] The SJM and BKS joined Nuziveedu Seeds, an Indian seed company, to oppose the pricing policy of Monsanto, the patent holder for GM crops. Prabhakar Kelkar, the vice president of BKS, said, 'It is important for all of us to unite to wage a war against Monsanto . . . for greater good.'[70] The BKS lobbied Radha Mohan Singh, India's minister for agriculture, to act against Monsanto as it 'was a threat to seed sovereignty'.[71] The Modi government slashed the royalty on GM cotton seeds by 74 per cent, disregarding the threat by Monsanto to re-evaluate its India business.[72] After the intervention by Penny Pritzker, the then US commerce secretary, and Richard Verma, the then US ambassador to India, the Modi government suspended the order.[73] Its decision to cap royalty rates for GM seeds despite Monsanto's threat to review its India operations demonstrates the influence of the RSS and its affiliates in areas where their support base has a direct interest.

The SJM's nationalist aversion to a reliance on foreign assistance and advice extends beyond economic policy to foreign NGOs, a stance that has widespread support within the sangh parivar. The philanthropic activities of the Bill and Melinda Gates Foundation, for example, came under criticism from the SJM because of its alleged ties to pharmaceutical companies. Mahajan even called the Gates Foundation's philanthropic work in India the modern-day version of the 'white man's burden'.[74] In response to complaints from the SJM, the government cut the financial ties between India's apex immunization advisory body, the National Technical Advisory Group on Immunisation, and the Gates Foundation.[75] The SJM went even further by suggesting that the government ban the Gates Foundation in 'the larger interests of society'.[76] The SJM has also criticized those who look to foreign expertise for policy advice, arguing that India 'shouldn't look to Harvard and Columbia to formulate policy'.[77] This suspicion of foreign input into the decision-making process was echoed in Bhagwat's 2017 Vijayadashami speech. This stance is similar to the Indian left's insistence during the previous Manmohan Singh government that experts from the World Bank and the International Monetary Fund (IMF) should not be consulted on policy issues.

As we will explain in Chapter Nine, China's involvement in the Indian economy is fast expanding from the earlier focus on trade in commercial goods to include investment and technology transfers. While the core RSS leadership seems to recognize that the capital and technological know-how of Chinese companies gives them an important—perhaps indispensable—role in the development of renewable energy and various forms of e-commerce in India, the key economic affiliates are adamantly opposed to most Chinese investment. The Modi government's renewable energy and electric vehicle goals, to name just two, would be difficult to fulfil without Chinese imports, and Indian players in these areas have investments from Chinese companies such as Alibaba, Tencent, Ctrip, Fosun and Hillhouse Capital Group. Chinese companies have the experience of operating on a large scale and in a geography with the variable infrastructure quality of India. While the RSS has mediated differences between the BKS and the BJP on land acquisition, the BMS and the BJP over coal denationalization and labour law, and the SJM and the BJP over GM seeds, it has not backed the SJM's demand that the government stop Chinese investments or put regulatory hurdles in the operations of Indian companies with significant—and growing—Chinese investment (for example, Paytm, Flipkart). Even while the Modi government defended the country's security interest against China during the standoff in the autumn of 2017, it tried hard not to let this disrupt the China–India bilateral economic relationship, much of it carried out by Chinese and Indian private enterprise which plays an important role in India's development.

These cases illustrate the limits of the influence of the RSS and its affiliates on the Modi government when core elements of the government's economic policy are at odds. The parivar organizations, however strong their views, do not determine the contours of government policy, but can make a difference on policy issues that do not undermine the government's core objectives, such as the royalty rates of GM seeds and Chinese high-technology investment. When disagreements have arisen between the BJP government and various parivar organizations, the RSS leadership under Bhagwat has tried to mediate the differences and work out a consensus. One senior RSS official told us that when a consensus is impossible, the government will either address the issue later or, as in the case of land and labour legislation, pass the issue to the states. What is different from the earlier Vajpayee government is that the RSS under Bhagwat's leadership is more committed to working out the differences behind closed doors, out of the public gaze. But there are cases, as with FDI, where the issue is so important to the government's goal of economic development and job creation, that it bypasses opposition even in the face of public criticism from elements of the sangh parivar. This policy split has not fractured the parivar and is unlikely to do so, though the internal tensions have grown greater in a much more socially complex network of organizations than was the case two decades ago when the RSS and its affiliates began to expand rapidly. Years of inculcation of the RSS-trained leadership in all the affiliates have sustained a belief that going off on your own undermines national unity, and that this unity outweighs all less consequential economic concerns, even though the Modi government takes a far more globalist approach to trade and investment than the RSS has historically accepted, and many within it and among some of the affiliates remain critical of the government's commitment to globalism.

NINE

China

Balancing Security and Economics

At the time of India's independence in 1947, the RSS was a critic of Chinese expansionism into territories it considered important strategically and culturally to India, especially Tibet, Nepal and Bhutan, that stretch across the Himalayan frontier between India and China. This fear was deepened by the Chinese incursion into Kashmir in the late 1950s and into India's north-east in 1962, both resulting in the loss of territory. When construction of a road across Kashmir's Aksai Chin plateau became public knowledge in 1959, the ABKM, the highest-level decision-making body of the RSS, issued a resolution that year blaming Chinese aggression on the 'weak and unrealistic policy of appeasement followed by the government for the last ten years'.[1] Following the October 1962 incursion of Chinese troops into India's Northeast and in the Ladakh area of Kashmir, the ABKM issued a resolution arguing, 'It is unbecoming and illogical to talk or negotiate with her [China] so long as we do not completely liberate our lost territory.'[2] Beyond liberating Indian territory, the resolution proposed that, 'Tibet's freedom is also a must if China's expansionism is to be contained and the right of all nations to a free existence is to be upheld and permanent security of India's borders is to be assured.' The ABPS came out strongly the next year against the Colombo Conference's offer to mediate the border differences between India and China, arguing instead that

'We should also sever our diplomatic ties with Communist China, support Tibet's freedom movement by recognizing and helping the émigré Government of Dalai Lama and forge a united front of all powers willing to combat Communist China's expansionism.'[3] While these hard-line proposals were not adopted by Nehru, the RSS benefited from the upsurge of patriotism that accompanied this war and the Nehru government even permitted it to participate as a separate contingent in the 1963 Republic Day parade in New Delhi.[4] On the eve of the fiftieth anniversary of the 1962 war, the ABPS, echoing Golwalkar's earlier call for a free Tibet, passed a resolution again, demanding that the government commit itself to taking back all territory occupied by the Chinese in the Ladakh area of Kashmir and adhere to the unanimous November 1962 parliamentary resolution pledging the country to take back all territory occupied by China. Several RSS affiliates, most notably the VHP (focused on the Hindu religious establishment) and the ABVP (focused on the academic world), took the lead in building support for the Tibetan cause. The VHP's support for Tibet involves more than geostrategic considerations, but is also motivated by a long-held contention in the sangh parivar that Buddhism and Hinduism, both with their roots in India, are linked to each other. The VHP's acceptance of Buddhism as a part of the Hindu mosaic of religions was reflected in its decision to include both the Dalai Lama and RSS chief Bhagwat in the inauguration ceremony of the World Hindu Congress, New Delhi, one of its major international activities, on 21–23 November 2014.[5] Building on this outreach to Tibetans, the RSS, in line with its strategy of forming single-interest groups seeking to gain support among target ethnic groups, assisted in the formation of the Bharat-Tibbat Sahyog Manch (BTSM) in 1999 to push for the political and cultural rights of Tibetans both in India and abroad. Assuming a prominent role in this effort was Indresh Kumar, an RSS pracharak who was later to take the lead in organizing the MRM, the RSS-supported group that seeks to draw Indian Muslims into the country's cultural mainstream as defined by the RSS.[6]

Further, on border tensions with China, the Modi government's decision in late June 2017 to send troops to the Bhutan-China-India tri-junction to counter Chinese construction of a road in a strip of territory (the Doklam Plateau) was applauded by the RSS and seen as a sign that the policy of appeasement towards China was at an end, particularly in defence of vital real estate. The Doklam area claimed by Bhutan is just north of a critical passage of land connecting the main body of India to its resource-rich Northeast, part of which is claimed by China. Following a two-month standoff that many feared could lead to a shooting conflict, the two sides, on 28 August 2017, reached an 'understanding', ending the confrontation by the mutual withdrawal of troops and the apparent termination of China's road-building activities. The next day, India announced that Prime Minister Modi would attend the BRICS Summit at Xiamen, China, on 3–5 September 2017. Bhagwat interpreted the 'understanding' as an Indian victory, claiming, 'It has been demonstrated clearly that the nation will no longer be cowed down on matters like defence and security.'[7]

The Modi government had effectively decoupled the strategic and commercial relationship that reflected a recognition that the success of many of its flagship projects, especially 'Make in India', 'Digital India' and the solar mission, depends critically on Chinese investment, material and technical know-how. There is also an expanding cultural interaction between the two countries. A growing number of Chinese Buddhist pilgrims visit religious sites in India associated with the life of the Buddha. The Shanghai Museum has almost a whole floor dedicated to 1000-year-old bronze artefacts heavily influenced by Indian art and philosophy. Yoga has become a popular form of exercise and meditation in a country that is increasingly looking back on its traditional culture for answers to the problems of modern life.[8]

The RSS, however, has a less nuanced perspective on the bilateral India–China relationship, reflecting the fact that it does not have to make the difficult foreign policy choices that confront the Modi government as it seeks a set of policies that satisfy India's security and economic interests. At the outset of the Doklam confrontation, the RSS and its affiliates quickly condemned what they claimed was Chinese 'aggression' and launched a move to boycott Chinese

products. At a meeting on 8–9 July 2017, representatives of
RSS-affiliated groups convened by the BTSM called on Indian
shopkeepers to stop selling Chinese products and exhorted Hindus
not to use religious items made in China.[9] It is not surprising that
the RSS chose this Tibetan group to sound the alarm against China
as Tibet rouses both strategic and cultural issues for the RSS. The
SJM launched a boycott of Chinese goods in the state of Gujarat,
coupled with a 25 August–4 September 2017 'awareness drive'
to draw attention to a wide range of China's alleged anti-India
policies, such as its border aggression, its dumping of products in
India, and the floods in India allegedly caused by China's upstream
river activities.[10] Local units of the VHP and its youth affiliate,
the Bajrang Dal, launched a campaign on 1 September in the
south-western coastal state of Karnataka to burn Chinese goods
to register their opposition to what a senior Bajrang Dal official
said was China's encouragement of Pakistan's terrorist activities in
India.[11] Responding to the Chinese blocking the transit of Hindu
pilgrims to the holy site of Kailash Mansarovar in Tibet during this
confrontation, the VHP called for a national boycott of Chinese
goods.[12]

Even so, India and China have not allowed elevated strategic
tensions to undermine their relationship in other spheres, most
prominently in economic relations. Notwithstanding the RSS's
hostility to China both on a strategic and cultural basis, Prime Minister
Modi has taken a pragmatic view of the bilateral relationship—and
the RSS leadership seems to recognize the bifurcated strategic and
economic character of the Indian approach to China. Shivshankar
Menon, a former Indian ambassador to China and former foreign
secretary, notes that India's Line of Control (LoC) and international
border with Pakistan is fully demarcated, with an agreement between
both militaries on the border. Nonetheless, there is regular cross-
border firing on the LoC. The India–Pakistan ceasefire has stopped
neither cross-border firing nor infiltration.[13] However, despite the
lack of demarcation, no bullet has been fired across India's border
with China in the last twenty-five years. The Deng Xiaoping–Rajiv
Gandhi agreement in the late 1980s has been maintained for almost

three decades, and Prime Minister Modi seems to appreciate that his core goals of economic development and job creation will be more difficult without Chinese cooperation. His government has not allowed border disputes to disrupt a deepening of Sino–Indian economic relations.

Seeking cooperation with China in other spheres, especially economic, even during times of strategic tensions, captures the essence of the Modi government's China policy—a policy that, with some notable exceptions, seems to have been accepted by the wider sangh parivar as a prudent exercise of foreign policy and a reflection of India's strategic limitations. Modi has decoupled the security aspect of the India–China relationship from its commercial one. His government has forcefully defended India's strategic interests vis-à-vis China. India was the only major country to boycott the Belt and Road Forum held in Beijing on 14–15 May 2017.[14] Both Japan and the United States, China's strategic adversaries, sent low-level representatives to the Belt and Road Forum. India's objections to the forum centre on the violation of its sovereignty—part of the Belt and Road Initiative (BRI) passes through a portion of Kashmir that is currently in the possession of Pakistan but is claimed by India.[15] The Indian government also argues that many of the BRI projects are commercially unviable. Hambantota port in Sri Lanka is a case in point. Sri Lanka's inability to service the debt taken for the construction of the port led China Merchants Port Holdings, a Chinese state-owned company, to take an 85 per cent stake in Hambantota.[16] To assuage India's security concerns, the deal stipulated that a Sri Lankan government–owned company would be entrusted with the security operations at the Hambantota port. Even so, India fears that many of the ports envisaged in the BRI road map are commercially unviable, which could lead to Chinese government–owned companies possessing strategically critical assets in the Indian Ocean littoral, posing potential risks to India's security.

Even while Indian and Chinese troops were engaged in eyeball-to-eyeball confrontation at the Doklam Plateau, India did not suspend official interactions. India, in addition, did not back down on security considerations in the face of Chinese propaganda taunts, some of it likely triggered by expressions of outrage by the RSS press and RSS-affiliated organizations. *Global Times*, the hyper-nationalist Communist Party–aligned tabloid, republished the front page of its 22 September 1962 edition—threatening India if it continued to probe the disputed boundary prior to the Sino–Indian war that ended so disastrously for India—to underscore China's ability to again inflict a 'bitter lesson' on India.[17] The tabloid further warned that China would inflict 'greater losses than 1962'.[18] The Chinese press went so far as to assert that 'Hindu nationalism risks pushing India into war with China', according to *Global Times*.[19] The article further argued that Prime Minister Modi's election 'fueled the country's nationalist sentiments' and 'it [the government] can do nothing if religious nationalism becomes extreme, as shown in its failure to curb violent incidents against Muslims since he came to power in 2014'. Ignoring the provocative commentary from Chinese state-run media,[20] three Indian cabinet ministers—Prakash Javadekar (human resources), J.P. Nadda (health and family welfare) and Mahesh Sharma (culture and tourism)—visited Beijing as part of an official Government of India delegation to meet their BRICS counterparts.[21] In his keynote address to the BRICS cultural ministers' conference, Sharma noted that the Indian government wanted to move ahead on 'cultural cooperation among BRICS countries'.[22]

US and Indian positions on China's BRI have increasingly converged. India's concerns about the BRI were echoed in the US–India joint statement released after Prime Minister Modi's first meeting with President Donald Trump:

> . . . the leaders: reiterate the importance of respecting freedom of navigation, overflight, and commerce throughout the region; call upon all nations to resolve territorial and maritime disputes peacefully and in accordance with international law; support bolstering regional economic connectivity through the transparent development of infrastructure and *the use of responsible debt financing practices, while ensuring respect for sovereignty and territorial integrity, the rule of law, and the environment.* [emphasis added][23]

The then Secretary of State Rex Tillerson's 18 October 2017 speech at the Center for Strategic and International Studies, Washington DC, his first country-specific policy address, echoed India's concerns about China-financed infrastructure projects. He noted that, 'China, while rising alongside India, has done so less responsibly, at times undermining the international, rules-based order . . .'[24] He called China's financing mechanisms for infrastructure projects 'predatory economy' because it saddles countries with 'enormous levels of debt' and is 'structured in a way that makes it very difficult for them to obtain future financing, and oftentimes has very subtle triggers in the financing that results in financing default and the conversion of debt to equity'.[25]

More significantly, the Modi government has shed the trappings of India's traditional non-alignment in the face of Chinese assertiveness to form a closer security partnership with the US and Japan. The annual Indo–US Malabar naval exercise in the Indian Ocean has expanded in size and scope after Japan, despite Chinese protests, was made a permanent participant in 2015. The US, moreover, conducts more joint security exercises with India than with any other country. Japan's foreign minister has publicly mooted the revival of 'the quad'—a multilateral security dialogue between India, the US, Japan and Australia—with an objective of securing 'a peaceful maritime zone from Asia to Africa'.[26] 'The quad' would cross an important rubicon because it is perceived by the Chinese as an explicit alliance to 'contain' China. In the past, India has been hesitant to become part of a grouping explicitly perceived as 'anti-China'. But the recent upsurge in Sino-India tensions has led the Modi government to re-evaluate India's 'multi-alignment' policy to pursue a closer strategic relationship with the US and Japan. To be sure, the driver of India's policy shift has been China's assertiveness in the Indian subcontinent and the increased frequency of perceived Chinese violation of Indian sovereignty through border incursions.

Despite the security challenges, Modi has not allowed these incidents to undermine the economic links with China, which play an important role in his government's plans for an economically robust India. China is India's largest trading partner (the US is the largest if services are included). Chinese investment and technical know-how, much of it from such private Chinese companies as Alibaba and Tencent, are crucial for India's development goals. Indian firms have joint ventures with Chinese companies in a broad range of areas, including renewable energy, electric vehicles, e-commerce and digital payments. Notwithstanding strategic differences, the two countries have continued to cooperate on multilateral forums on issues of common interest, such as reform of global governance and climate change. India is the second largest shareholder of the Asian Infrastructure Investment Bank, which was set up in part because of the inability of developed countries to give China and India a greater voice in the governance of multilateral financial institutions.[27] Prime Minister Modi and the chief ministers of various states have visited China to solicit investments, as Modi himself did several times when he was the chief minister of Gujarat. India continues to welcome Chinese investment; Tencent and Alibaba, the Chinese e-commerce giants, continue to engage with Indian companies for potential investment opportunities.[28] Given the large untapped consumer Internet market and its fecund demographics, India has been described as the next battleground for Chinese Internet companies.[29]

Chinese investment activity in India is not dominated just by 'new economy' enterprises. Invest India, a public-private partnership which was set up to handhold foreign companies investing in India and to promote India as an investment destination, notes that 42 per cent of the investment proposals (which total $100 billion) have come from Chinese companies.[30] The list of Chinese companies is dominated by old-economy enterprises—Sany Heavy, Pacific Construction, China Fortune Land Development and Dalian Wanda. While all these proposals may not materialize, it does underscore the fact that both Chinese old-economy and new-economy companies are interested in investing in India. More than half a dozen Chinese handset companies—Huawei, Xiaomi, Gionee, LeEco, Oppo and Vivo—have opened manufacturing operations in India.[31]

The RSS applauded the Modi government for standing up to China's assertiveness by including Japan as a regular participant in its annual Malabar naval exercises, by sending troops to stop

China's border road construction and by boycotting the One Belt One Road (OBOR) conference in Beijing. For them, as for the Indian government, this is a matter of sovereignty. The tensions with China gave the RSS another opportunity to highlight the core of what it means by Hindutva—to assert nationalism. It was especially pleased that Modi had raised the issue of Pakistan-based terrorism at the BRICS Xiamen summit and had managed to get China to accept the naming of the Pakistan-based Haqqani network, the Lashkar-e-Taiba and the Jaish-e-Mohammed as terrorist groups in the summit's formal declaration which referred to terrorism seventeen times.[32] In the wake of the 'understanding' over the Doklam standoff, *Organiser* wrote,

> We are near a goalpost to reformulate the rules of dealing with China. If China does not accord a One Bharat Policy, we may do the same of challenging the One China Policy.[33]

A major theme that runs through RSS commentary of the standoff is that Modi's firm response demonstrates India will not concede to China's terms when its own interests are involved, and India will forcefully defend its interests during the contention. The Modi government had sent a signal that India considers itself a part of a multipolar Asia rather than one that is centred on China. At the start of its tenure, the Modi government had signalled its determination to assert Indian interests by inviting two senior figures in the Tibetan exile government, Prime Minister Lobsang Sangay and Home Minister Dolma Gyari, to attend the prime minister's inauguration on 26 May 2014.

While there is a prevalent view within the RSS ranks that China will again challenge India along the long-disputed border once the October 2017 Chinese Communist Party Congress concludes, the sangh has faith in Modi's ability to protect the country's interests. This view was confirmed when China pulled out of the disputed area, and reaffirmed again when the BRICS summit declaration named several Pakistan-based militant groups as terrorist organizations. Despite massive anti-India protest marches in the Muslim-majority Valley of Kashmir at the time, China publicly dismissed calls by

the Organisation of Islamic Cooperation to get India to implement
past UN resolutions regarding a plebiscite in Kashmir. The Chinese
foreign ministry spokesperson, Lu Kang, reiterated China's stand
on Kashmir since the mid-1990s, saying China's position is 'clear-
cut' for a Pakistan–India resolution of the Kashmir issue, further
explaining that, 'The Kashmir issue is left over from history. China
hopes India and Pakistan can increase dialogue and communication
and properly handle relevant issues and jointly safeguard regional
peace and stability.'[34]

The border tensions are only one of several Chinese actions
in which the RSS saw a pattern of anti-India behaviour. Other
issues noted are China's use of a veto to prevent the UN Sanctions
Committee from designating Masood Azhar, Pakistani chief of the
Jaish-e-Mohammed, as a terrorist; its veto of India's request to join
the Nuclear Suppliers Group and the lack of Chinese support for
India's goal of becoming a permanent member of the UN Security
Council. While the government-controlled Chinese press engaged in
emotional and sometimes threatening diatribes against India during
the standoff, the BJP government avoided the hyper-nationalist
tone of the Chinese—and of the RSS.

The RSS leadership is not unaware of Modi's pragmatic
approach to China to gain the country's capital for infrastructure
investment and technology. Modi visited China several times seeking
investment funds when he was chief minister of Gujarat and has on
more than one occasion expressed his admiration for China's rapid
economic development. One of the better biographical studies of
Modi notes that, as the Gujarat chief minister, he was aware of the
importance of China to the state's economic growth.[35] He reports,
for example, that China imported about 75 per cent of the cotton
produced in Gujarat.[36] During a 2011 visit to China, he reportedly
said that his development goal was to compete with China and not
with other Indian states.[37] China, unlike the US and other Western
nations which, after the state's communal rioting in 2002, banned
him from visiting, expressed a keen interest in working with him.
Despite the month-long standoff at Doklam, he and Chinese leader
Xi Jinping did not let that get in the way of larger strategic and

economic objectives and they seemed to get along well at the ninth BRICS summit in 2017. The cultural affiliates of the RSS, like the VHP, and the economic nationalists, like the SJM, may have winced at this close economic interaction, but they did not publicly oppose a chief minister—and later prime minister—who used this economic relationship to make Gujarat one of India's fastest growing states, a factor that the BJP used in the 2014 parliamentary campaign to demonstrate why Modi should become prime minister.

As long as Modi and the BJP do not back away from asserting India's strategic interests and continue to work for a militarily strong country (which includes a growing security relationship with the US and Japan), the RSS and its affiliates will continue to support Modi's right to shape Indian foreign policy. For this reason, it applauded Modi's firm response to the Chinese road-building effort, his boycott of the OBOR conference and his provision of additional funds for Indian infrastructure at the border with China. The RSS leadership thus seems prepared to go along with the Modi government's policy of distinguishing India's geostrategic imperatives, as at Doklam, from the valued economic dimensions of the India–China relationship. The RSS has not backed the SJM's demand that the Modi government stop Chinese investments and put regulatory hurdles in the operations of Indian companies with significant Chinese investment. The challenge is to make sure that one part of this equation does not overwhelm the other. In short, that the rest of the parivar does not buy into the SJM's policy prescription that incidents like the Doklam incursion justify a prohibition of all Chinese investments in India. Also that such incidents do not necessarily mean that China is an imminent threat as long as India makes clear that it has the will and the means to defend its strategic interests.

The RSS's lashing out at China's attempt to build a road in what the Indians say is contested territory is consistent with the long-held Hindu nationalist suspicion of China as a security threat and its conviction that Nehru's efforts to build a close security relationship with China were based on an unrealistic romantic vision that was to have disastrous consequences for India. The historical background of Hindu nationalist wariness of China is perhaps best analysed by Ram Madhav in his book on India–China relations.[38] It is instructive that Madhav's analysis is based almost entirely on the strategic challenges. He points out that Indian suspicion of China's hostile intentions is not new, and starts his analysis with the views of the early-twentieth-century nationalist intellectual Bipin Chandra Pal who warned that India's real long-term threat 'came not from pan-Europeanism but from Pan-Islamism and Pan-Mongolianism [a reference to China] . . .'[39] Pal saw next-door China, with its huge population, as the only nearby country that could challenge India and so its awakening represented a dire threat. Madhav writes about anti-Chinese nationalist Aurobindo Ghose (1872–1950) who, at the time of India's independence, wrote of the dangerous security consequences of an alliance between a communist Russia and a communist China, quoting him as saying that, 'The basic significance of Mao's Tibetan adventure is to advance China's frontiers right down to India and stand poised to strike at the right moment and with the right strategy . . .'[40] He then quotes a detailed letter in late 1950 to Prime Minister Nehru from Home Minister Sardar Vallabhbhai Patel, who is perceived in the parivar as a tough-minded nationalist leader in contrast to the romantic idealist Nehru. The letter repeats Ghose's warning about China, but in even stronger terms, stating:

> Chinese irredentism and communist imperialism are different from the expansionism or imperialism of the western powers. The former has a cloak of ideology which makes it ten times more dangerous. In the guise of ideological expansion lie concealed racial, national or historical claims. The danger from the north and north-east, therefore, becomes both communist and imperialist.[41]

Madhav argues that India under Prime Minister Nehru's guidance virtually ignored Patel's warnings and reacted to China's absorption of Tibet by a policy of appeasement in the false hope of forging a Sino–Indian leadership in Asia as a counter to a reassertion of Western power.[42] The end result, according to Madhav, was the

Chinese incursion into the Northeast Frontier Agency (today's Arunachal Pradesh) on 20 October 1962 against a poorly equipped Indian Army that suffered a humiliating loss, before the Chinese, a month later, made a unilateral withdrawal to the Line of Actual Control as it existed in the western border area when the war began. The Chinese, however, occupied and annexed a sliver of territory in the east. In the wake of that war, then RSS chief Golwalkar wrote that India needed to build itself up militarily, including universal military service and the development of nuclear weapons capability, to counter what he characterized as an 'expansionist' China. Elaborating on this, he argued:

> Napoleon had forewarned over one hundred and fifty years ago not to rouse that yellow giant lest he should prove a grave peril to humanity. Seventy years ago, Swami Vivekananda had specifically warned that China would invade Bharat soon after the Britishers quit. For the past eight years we of the Sangh, too, had been unambiguously warning that China had aggressed into our territory at various strategic points.[43]

Arguing that the country's northern frontiers are vulnerable as long as the Chinese remain in Tibet, Golwalkar proposed that India must work for a 'free Tibet' and, 'For that, if it becomes necessary to cross our frontiers let us do it without the least hesitation.'[44]

The long diplomatic India–China deep freeze following the 1962 war began to thaw with Prime Minister Rajiv Gandhi's 1988 visit to China to work for closer economic and cultural ties even if the border issues remained unresolved. Despite a significant growth in bilateral trade since Gandhi's visit, Madhav describes a China that aims to encircle India and is using its considerable financial holdings to make investments that advance both its economic and strategic interests, a scenario that requires a countering Indian strategy, which, as of 2013 when he wrote the book, he found generally wanting.[45] In a chapter entitled 'A New Strategic Outlook', Madhav summarizes his argument of the future long-term Chinese threat by writing that,

Both China and India aspire for the same goals in the same geographical region; hence they will, at any given time, be more of competitors than friends.[46]

One key element of India's strategy vis-à-vis China is the 'Look East' policy of Prime Minister Rao and its refinement to the 'Act East' policy of Prime Minister Vajpayee, while Prime Minister Modi has made it an essential component of his foreign policy.

Madhav argues that the 'Act East' strategy must expand from its security focus to include cultural objectives, a policy perspective that seems to be guiding Prime Minister Modi's Asia policy. In a 2017 interview, Madhav argued that the cultural objectives of foreign policy included connecting with cultural leaders in foreign countries and engaging with the scattered Indian diaspora to bring them together, something similar to the 'long-distance nationalism' we analysed in Chapter Three. He argued that, 'It [the diaspora] was a divided entity and not very effective. But now we have been able to unite them. Once they have been united and organized, they have emerged as a politically influential and strong political constituency.'[47] This state policy is compatible with the RSS's own active efforts to unite the Hindu diaspora, and the overseas affiliates of the RSS have provided volunteers for the prime minister's speeches that are a regular element of his overseas trips. The volunteers work together on a wide range of service projects—cooperation that demonstrates the importance of the diaspora for the BJP and its affiliates. Madhav in his interview also elaborated on the 'Act East' policy by explaining that it involves building up the country's naval capacity to protect Indian interests and looking at the continuing importance of the US through the prism of the South East Asian states, an apparent suggestion that India must itself take a more proactive role in Asia to counter an assertive China.[48] He made this point more explicitly in a talk to the Indian community in the Washington DC area on the occasion of Prime Minister Modi's June 2017 visit to the US, where he said that India, along with its neighbours, must assume responsibility for establishing peace and 'law and order' in the Indo–Asia Pacific region, though he added that he expected the US to maintain a pivotal role in the region.[49]

In the turbulent seventy-five years before India's independence in 1947, Hindu nationalism represented by individuals from such groups as the Arya Samaj, the Brahmo Samaj, the Hindu Mahasabha, the RSS and a substantial part of the Congress had a pre-independence 'Look East' perspective that was fuelled by the perceived dangers that came from the West: colonialism, Islam and Christianity, and such Western ideas as communism and capitalism. They applauded Japan's defeat of Czarist Russia in 1905 as a victory for Asia. They looked favourably on anti-colonial movements elsewhere in East and South East Asia. Many engaged in terrorist acts against the agents of British colonial rule, especially in Bengal, the eastern state that was the seat of the capital of British India until 1926 (though the announced transfer of capitals was in 1912), with a rapidly growing Indian urban middle class in Calcutta.[50] Many identified with the radical rhetoric of Indian nationalists who might otherwise have been wary of referring to themselves as Hindu nationalists. What these militant Indian nationalists seemed to have in common—and what attracted the support of the radical Hindu nationalists—was their determination to overthrow British rule, to use a pan-Asian strategy to achieve this goal and to reject Gandhi's strategy of non-violence. Many in addition supported such goals as a centralized state, socialism and adoption of modern technology, often linked to a Hindu reformist discourse, aimed at modernizing the country and its society and thus preparing them for self-government and eventually independence.[51]

Perhaps the best known of those who actively utilized pan-Asian solidarity to rid India of British rule were Rash Behari Bose (1886–1945) and Netaji Subhas Chandra Bose (1897–1945), both high-caste Hindu Bengalis who cooperated with the Japanese and the Germans during the Second World War to achieve their objective of an independent India. Subhas Chandra, who had a fallout with Gandhi over his doctrine of non-violence, resigned from the Congress where he had served as party president. With the outbreak of the Second World War, he led demonstrations against Britain's unilateral decision to declare war on behalf of India and, one step ahead of the British authorities, he made a dramatic escape to Germany in early 1941. Once in Germany, he helped organize a Free India Legion to fight alongside the Germans; with German backing, he moved in an equally dramatic fashion to Japanese-held South East Asia in May 1943 where he took charge of the Indian National Army (INA). Rash Behari, a resident of Japan since 1915, had helped form the INA and handed over its command to Subhas Chandra. Rash Behari's strategy was even more radical than Subhas's. He had participated in a failed assassination attempt of the British Viceroy in 1912 and was involved in a bid to trigger a mutiny in early 1915 among Indian soldiers in India (referred to as the Gadar Revolution). He fled to Japan in 1915 where he almost immediately associated himself with Japanese pan-Asian groups and established the Indian Independence League in 1924. Perhaps his major achievements in Japan were to convince the Japanese government in the early years of the Second World War to support the overseas struggle for Indian independence and to permit the formation of an Indian fighting force (the INA) following the capture of many Indian soldiers during the Japanese campaign through Malaysia and the fall of Singapore in 1942.

Both Boses (unrelated) grew up at a time when religion shaped the identity of high-caste Hindu Bengalis. Subhas Chandra, in his autobiography, *An Indian Pilgrim*, notes with pride his family's participation in the Hindu reformist agenda of the Brahmo Samaj.[52] The Bengali author Nirad C. Chaudhuri wrote of the impact of the Hindu religion on Subhas Chandra:

> He was in no sense a bigoted or even orthodox Hindu. But he had grown up in the first two decades of the twentieth century in Bengal, where owing to the influence of Bankim Chandra Chatterjee and Swami Vivekananda there was a fusion of religion and nationalism so that the nationalist feeling has a pronounced Hindu complexion and Hinduism a pronounced political character.[53]

The same Hindu religious influence would have applied to fellow Bengali Rash Behari as well. While in Japan, Rash Behari wrote on the epic Ramayana and the Bhagavad Gita (a philosophical dialogue on duty that is part of the other great epic of Indian antiquity, the Mahabharata). Rash Behari, in a biographical sketch of Savarkar to commemorate his release from a British prison in 1937, presented his own positive views of Hindu nationalism, writing:

> He [Savarkar] is the one who always kept the fire of India's freedom burning; he is a patriot who risked his life for the freedom of India in the early 20th century and is a founder exponent of the doctrine of cultural independence in the current times.

More specifically relating to Savarkar's views on Hindutva, he further writes:

> It does not make sense to take all Indians as one. In Turkey, Turkish are nationals. In India Hindus are nationals and [those] who believe in other religions are minorities. He defined Hindus as those who have faith in the area around the Indus River.[54]

Rash Behari, who retained contact with Savarkar, had established a branch of the Hindu Mahasabha in Japan.

The RSS and the sangh parivar generally have appropriated both Subhas Chandra and Rash Behari as nationalist heroes. Underscoring that sentiment, Prime Minister Modi on 23 January 2016 (the 119th birth anniversary of Subhas Chandra) made public 100 formerly secret files of Netaji, fulfilling a long-standing demand of some members of the Bose family and many Bengalis.[55] He and members of his cabinet attended the release ceremony at the National Archives of India in New Delhi. Days later, Chandra Bose, a grand-nephew of Subhas Chandra, joined the BJP.[56]

The RSS's decision to follow Modi's lead in his policy towards China is yet another example of its recognition that the political affiliate, and now the governing party, should receive the benefit of the doubt that what it does is in the interest of a stronger India. The RSS, for instance, had no comments on the 'informal' Modi–Xi summit at Wuhan, China, in May 2018, which was aimed at 'resetting' India–China ties. On such matters, the RSS leadership is under less pressure at home as few significant interests are directly affected by foreign policy issues. The RSS does not propagate an isolationist 'India First' outlook, though there are affiliates—and many in the RSS itself—whose professed views on economic autarky, statism and strategic autonomy are at some degree of variance from the Modi government's globalism. The RSS, for example, did not forcefully back the demand of some of its affiliates that the Modi government impose regulatory restrictions on Chinese investment in India. The Doklam Plateau standoff ended well from the Indian perspective, and the RSS did not need to engage in behind-the-scenes mediation and diplomacy to calm differences of view. Had things progressed in a less favourable manner, however, it would likely have backed an even more assertive stance towards China regarding such issues as Tibet or the OBOR projects in parts of Kashmir controlled by Pakistan but claimed by India. But China is also part of the East that the RSS finds culturally and strategically appealing against a domineering and threatening West. Xi Jinping has, more than any recent Chinese leader, stressed the importance of tradition and some of that tradition has common roots in India. A Chinese effort to resolve the border dispute and show greater sensitivity regarding its help to Pakistan (similar to what it displayed at the BRICS summit) would help the bilateral relationship. Perhaps most important, it needs to accord pre-eminence to India's security interests in the Indian Ocean. Otherwise, India is likely to gradually drift closer to Japan and the US in ways that draw those three together against what they now see as an assertive China.

TEN

Ghar Wapsi (Homecoming)

Politics vs Ideology

Rajeshwar Singh, an RSS pracharak in charge of a highly publicized movement to convert Muslims and Christians to Hinduism in western Uttar Pradesh, was removed from his position at the end of 2014.[1] He was told by RSS leaders in Uttar Pradesh to go on an indefinite sick leave, as his efforts were undermining the larger goal of ghar wapsi (conversion of non-Hindus to Hinduism) by focusing critical media attention on it. Singh was a functionary in the Dharma Jagran Samiti (DJS), a group established to convert non-Hindus in a process referred to as ghar wapsi (literally translated as homecoming); the term emphasizes the return of non-Hindus in India to their indigenous cultural roots.[2] The Opposition had labelled Singh's activities a threat to a secular India, and used them as justification to stall important parts of Prime Minister Modi's legislative programme. The political fallout of Singh's activities is another example of actions from the far right that can threaten both the mobilization efforts of the BJP and its legislative agenda. It also reflects the internal divisions within the sangh parivar as the RSS seeks to reconcile sometimes conflicting ideological and political objectives.

Part of the controversy surrounding Singh was his related campaign in western Uttar Pradesh to end what he referred to as 'love jihad', the alleged practice of Muslim men converting young

Hindu girls through marriage. He is quoted as remarking that, 'Such a campaign is the need of the hour because the population of a particular community [Muslims] is growing in the country as compared to the Hindus because of "love jihad" that is frequent in western UP.'[3] Conversion, ghar wapsi and battling 'love jihad' are seen as tactics to limit the spread of Islam in India; Muslims are estimated by the 2011 census to make up 14.23 per cent of the total population and 19.26 per cent of the population of Uttar Pradesh—this compared to 11.7 per cent in 1991, a growth at the national level of about 2.5 per cent over the past three censuses, while the Hindu percentage over the same period dropped from 82.4 per cent to 79.8 per cent.[4] However, the average Muslim yearly population growth rate dropped from 3 per cent in 1991–2001 to 2.2 per cent in the 2001–11 period, while the Hindu yearly rate dropped only from 1.8 per cent to 1.6 per cent in the same period.[5] Prior to his removal, Singh reportedly told the press that, 'Our target is to make a Hindu Rashtra by 2021. The Muslims and Christians don't have any right to stay here. So they would either be converted to Hinduism or forced to run away from here.'[6] He claimed to have conducted ghar wapsi for tens of thousands of people,[7] though it was a ceremony regarding the conversion of fewer than 100 Muslims on 8 December 2014 in the city of Agra that made headlines and triggered his removal later that month.

Ghar wapsi efforts have been going on for a long time, and remain a major activity of the VHP. Former hard-line VHP leader Togadia, who was replaced as the international working president of the VHP in 2018 by someone less strident,[8] told the press in early 2016 that the average 'return' had climbed from 15,000 converts a year to 40,000 in 2015.[9] Indian history is replete with instances of communal reconversion, such as that of many formerly Hindu Sindhis after the establishment of Muslim rule in the eighth century, using a set of rituals referred to as the *devalsmriti*. Another more recent example is the reconversion of several thousand Catholic Gaudas—low-caste Marathas living on the coast of Portuguese Goa—in the 1920s.[10] So it was not ghar wapsi itself that was held against Singh, but rather the highly publicized and provocative nature of his activities, which were especially embarrassing to the BJP and the RSS. We found a similar situation in the RSS reaction to a rebellious faction protesting the language policy of the BJP government of Goa. (See Chapter Thirteen for a discussion of the Goa crisis.)

Singh's highly publicized reconversion activities not only presented a political challenge to the BJP, but also revealed a divergence of views on the issue of reconversion to Hinduism between the cultural affiliates (like the VHP) and those with a political orientation (like the BJP). The former are far more willing to accept publicity from reconversion, as happened in this case, than is the RSS—or the BJP. In contrast, we were told by the guide of the RSS's reconversion efforts that the organization considers such publicity to be both unnecessarily provocative and against the interests of the convert in question.[11] Besides the problem of tactics, issues of religion are of much greater importance to the VHP than to the BJP. The BJP needs to mobilize vast numbers from India's diverse society to vote for their candidates, and is much more sensitive to the secular foundations of the Indian state and the need to recruit across a broad social spectrum. The VHP has no such compulsions, as they appeal almost exclusively to Hindus.[12] One important function of the RSS within the sangh parivar is to arbitrate such differences either within or between its member organizations. This issue emerged when the RSS's publicity chief, Manmohan Vaidya, responded to Singh's activities at a press conference by rejecting the notion that ghar wapsi is about conversion, and emphasizing that it is instead a 'homecoming for those who have a natural urge to reconnect with their roots'.[13] Perhaps realizing the weakness in a distinction that seems to claim that Muslims and Christians who do not convert do not consider themselves Indians, he added that the RSS does not seek to convert Muslims and Christians who attend RSS shakhas, as 'Our ancestors were also the same [ethnically]. So we believe all are Hindus.'[14] Vaidya's comments assume that most Muslims and Christians are descendants of converts from an indigenous South Asian religion. Hence the use of the term ghar wapsi to denote the return to an original state that is often defined with the composite term 'Hindu' and described as a golden age of bliss—albeit one that masks the deep social and cultural divisions of India and includes a hierarchical order that justifies social stagnation. (Though a common counterargument is that this rigidity set in after the Muslim and British invasions as a way of protecting the Hindu population from outside assaults).[15]

The fusion of ethnicity with Hinduism conforms to the repeated statements of RSS chief Bhagwat that all Indians loyal to the country, whatever their religion, are Hindus. This broad definition of Hinduism, however, is at variance with the notion of ghar wapsi. It is also at variance with the more exclusive use of the term Hindu in the Indian Constitution, which includes Jains, Sikhs, Buddhists and tribals but not Muslims, Christians, Parsis and Jews. In addition, the Hindu Code Bill of 1952 defines a civil code applicable only to Hindus as a religious group, and the Indian Parliament has not passed a civil code bill applicable to all Indians, though the sangh parivar has demanded a Uniform Civil Code. Any convert to Hinduism with long-term family ties in India is defined as having once been Hindu, and so the term ghar wapsi would apply to them. Given the vast doctrinal differences within Hinduism as a religion, the current RSS leadership's view of Hinduism as a broad ethnic category keeps the RSS out of both the deep sectarian controversies within Hinduism and the contentious debate over which groups should be called 'Hindu'.

The prominent pre-independence Hindu nationalist Savarkar—an avowed anti-caste atheist—defined Hindus in the narrow sense of those who consider India both their fatherland (territorial) and holy land (religious), a definition which excluded Christians and Muslims. This narrow definition was the predominant view of most Hindu nationalists up to the time of Golwalkar, and is still a view held by many Hindu nationalists. Golwalkar laid the groundwork for a broader definition of what it is to be Hindu by separating 'Hindus' as an ethnic group/nation from 'Hinduism' as a religion. Hinduism conceived as a religion would not include Muslims and Christians, but Hindu nationalism surely would include Indian Muslims and Christians as part of the Indian state. What Golwalkar and Savarkar did agree upon, however, is that unifying the fractured Hindu community was a prerequisite for a stable political order, as it would create a sense of oneness and common identity as Indians.[16] In a speech directed against Hindu orthodoxy on caste issues, Savarkar stated:

> [F]rom today I shall not believe in highness and/or lowness of caste. I shall not oppose intermarriage between the highest and lowest castes. I shall eat with any Hindu irrespective of caste. I shall not believe in caste birth and henceforth I shall call myself a Hindu only—not Brahmin, Vaishya, etc.[17]

For the RSS founder, Hedgewar (1889–1940), the guiding principle of the organization was to train men who would work among Hindus to bring about the social unity that many Hindu reformers considered a prerequisite for India's revival. While Hedgewar and his successors sought a society where caste and sect barriers would crumble, they were not very specific on practical ways to bring about the desired unification of society or how to fit the non-Hindu convert into India's pervasive caste system. This ambiguity is at least partly due to their recognition that caste had been a critical element of Indian identity for so long that it would be difficult to remove. Former RSS head Deoras told us that while it would take a long time for a caste-less society to become a reality, the RSS would in the meantime take steps to remove the notion of high and low caste and, with it, the social discrimination faced by low-caste Hindus.[18] Another senior RSS source told us that caste identity among low-caste Hindus and tribals in fact makes some positive contributions to the pride of the individuals in these groups, often providing them with a strong social, cultural and economic foundation to better face the harsh realities of everyday life. Moreover, this source added that caste pride may be a major factor standing in the way of conversion to Christianity and Islam. He suggested that the most practical approach to achieving Hindu unity would be to ensure that people in these low-caste categories are provided educational and economic opportunities, while also condemning the caste consciousness among high-caste Hindus that encourages social discrimination and stands in the way of Hindu solidarity.[19]

Golwalkar, the first post-Independence head of the RSS, basically agreed with Savarkar that Hindu caste distinctions get in the way of Hindu unification. In Golwalkar's book *Bunch of Thoughts*—which compiles his lectures—he argues that sectarian and cultural diversity among Hindus is not an insurmountable obstacle to Hindu unity. Rather, Golwalkar asserts that there is a common dharma (ethical principles of life) which has held India's diverse society together for millennia—in an indirect way of explaining the social problems facing both converts and those seeking to move up the caste hierarchy, though he argues that the practice of dharma has deteriorated and needs to be revived in a proper form, presumably one that would lead to a more egalitarian social system.[20]

While there remains a certain ambiguity on what specific policy steps are required to bring about this desired Hindu unity, Golwalkar is very clear about the dangers to national harmony. *Bunch of Thoughts* has separate chapters analysing Islam, Christianity and communism as the three most serious dangers to Indian society, and, by extension, to India's unique cultural attribute, dharma.[21] On the first point, he warns of the continuing secessionist aspirations of those Muslims who remained in India following Partition.[22] Of Christians, he notes that some are inclined to use their vast array of social-service institutions to convert Hindus and advance the goal of making India a Christian nation.[23] Finally, he argues that communists stress a materialism that is foreign to India's historic culture.[24] The cure to all of these alleged dangers, Golwalkar states, is nationalism, and a critical agency for this revival of national greatness comprises the 'character-building' activities of the RSS.[25] He does not call, however, for denying non-Hindus citizenship, or deporting them or reconverting them en masse to Hinduism. One indication of Golwalkar's thinking on the assimilation of minorities into India's national life as full participants was his insistence that the new political BJS, formed with RSS support in the early 1950s, be open to people of all religions, and that its name use the more religiously neutral term 'Bharatiya' instead of 'Hindu'.[26] The RSS followed suit in the late 1970s by opening its membership to Christians and Muslims, and in the early years of the new millennium established a specific organization, the MRM, to disseminate its nationalist message to the Muslim community. A similar organization for Christians is under consideration.[27]

In its own activities, the RSS operates as if there are no caste or religious distinctions. It discourages the use of caste names. Its camps mix work assignments that cross caste barriers to demonstrate the equal value of all work. It rejects the notion of purity and pollution while denouncing the materialism of socialism and communism; the writings of Golwalkar and his successors as well as the RSS training system support an egalitarian society.[28] On India's caste system, Golwalkar, for example, makes the dubious claim in *Bunch of Thoughts* that caste in its original form was a kind of division of labour based on merit and devoid of any notions of purity and pollution. He writes:

> The feeling of inequality, of high and low, which has crept into the Varna system is comparatively of recent origin . . . But in its original form, distinctions in the social order did not imply any discrimination of big and small, high or low, among its constituents. On the other hand, the Gita tells us that the individual who does his assigned duties in life in a spirit of selfless service only worships God through such performance.[29]

Pursuing this line of thought, Golwalkar further writes that:

> [T]he work of social consolidation which is truly the realization of Nation-God can be carried on only on the basis of . . . a spirit of identity as will render us capable of seeing a beggar on the street and a great scholar with an equal eye of love and brotherhood.[30]

While the RSS and its affiliates recognize the dangers that caste poses to the social unity it seeks, caste is still a major factor in the lives of most Hindus, especially for the two-thirds who live in rural India. A practical problem posed by conversion/reconversion, therefore, is where the non-Hindu convert will fit into the pervasive Hindu caste system. A number of strategies have been adopted to ease this social transition. Gene Thursby, for example, notes the creation of a Rajput Shuddhi Sabha, aimed at establishing commensal and marriage relationships between Hindu Rajputs and reconverted Malkanas (Muslim Rajputs) in the 1920s.[31] Conversion may pose less of a problem in urban India where the possibility of reinventing yourself is easier than in the countryside, but caste still retains a residual importance in these spaces in terms of marriage partners, food, names, religious customs and so on. But there also remains the problem of where the convert from the bottom rungs of the social ladder would fit. Such a person would surely not want to be treated as the bottom rung of the Hindu social hierarchy. For this reason, some RSS activists working among Dalits and tribals have suggested that converts might turn to Buddhism, where there is—at least philosophically—no caste system, as a way out of this dilemma.[32] This proposal is the subject of a robust debate within the RSS. Seeking to remove one significant barrier to low-caste Hindus and thus affirm the basic equality of all Hindus, the RSS, at least since the 1970s, has consistently advocated efforts to remove prohibitions on low-caste entry into temples and pilgrimage centres. This affirmation of inclusiveness in places of worship was made when a Dalit was selected to lay the foundation stone of the proposed Ram Janmabhoomi temple in 1989. The RSS has also supported inter-caste marriages and inter-caste dining as a means of breaking down caste barriers and advancing the goal of Hindu consolidation.[33] It has in addition sought to incorporate cultural elements of low-caste Hindus (what some refer to as the 'little tradition' of Hinduism) into the broad mosaic of what it is to be a Hindu.

The conversion debate among Hindu nationalists has two sides: Hindus converting to other religions and others converting/ reconverting to Hinduism (referred to originally by nineteenth-century Hindu renaissance advocates as *shuddhi* or purification). The first aspect of conversion, not surprisingly, has been bitterly opposed by Hindu nationalists like the RSS,[34] whereas the second tends to be viewed favourably as another step towards buttressing national unity. Conversion arouses very strong emotions as it speaks to basic issues of identity.

Several groups emerged in the late nineteenth century to reform Hinduism, with one of their major objectives being the consolidation of Hindu society. Among the more influential of those reform movements was the Arya Samaj, which viewed conversion, either by choice or coercion, as an important part of its mission (shuddhi);[35] its philosophy was guided by the ancient text *Deval Smriti*, which provided rules of admission to Hinduism.[36] The disciples of its founder, Dayanand Saraswati, spread the message of social reform and Hindu consolidation throughout the country and abroad, including all the aforementioned aspects of conversion to full Hindu status. It also vigorously fought against the conversion of Hindus to other faiths. The founding leadership of the RSS took its inspiration from the reformist philosophic tradition of Dayanand—conversion to Hinduism was always seen as a valid activity, partly as a counter to the proselytizing activities of Christians and Muslims and partly to consolidate the Hindu community. Prior to independence, the RSS had worked closely with the Arya Samaj on issues relating to Hindu consolidation, the geographic unity of India (Akhand Bharat) and the security of Hindus. After Independence, the RSS grew somewhat distant from the largely urban Arya Samaj, and directed greater attention to traditional rural Hindus less interested in the Samaj's social reform agenda and its position on the use of idols. In line with this new approach, the RSS under Golwalkar's leadership began to focus on such traditional cultural issues as cow protection and the restoration of historic temples (specifically those at Ayodhya, Kashi/ Benares and Mathura), thus establishing a rapport with Hindu religious leaders.

Conversely, the RSS views the conversion of Hindus to Islam and Christianity as a potential threat to the cultural pre-eminence of Hinduism in India and, by extension, a threat to national unity. Regarding Muslim efforts to convert Hindus, the RSS tends to interpret such actions as an effort to increase the Muslim population in India to strengthen Islamic influence and even create movements aimed at carving out independent Muslim states. Such efforts have triggered periodic calls to make all forms of conversion illegal, taking as a precedent colonial laws limiting conversion, which existed in several princely states.[37] Perhaps the best-known early case of a state limiting conversion in independent India is that of Madhya Pradesh which, in 1968, enacted the Madhya Pradesh Dharma Swatantrya Adhiniyam, prohibiting 'conversion from one religion to another by use of force or allurement or by fraudulent means'.[38] It also required that the subject of the attempted conversion report it to the district magistrate within a set period of time or risk imprisonment. India's Supreme Court upheld the Madhya Pradesh law and a similar one in the state of Odisha on the grounds of public order, and made a distinction between the legal right to preach and the right to convert, on which there are permissible limitations.[39] Other states, such as Gujarat, have enacted increased fines and jail terms for those involved in the illegal conversion of women, Dalits and tribals; the legislation in Gujarat requires advance notice to a district magistrate of the conversion and the magistrate's judgment that the conversion did not involve force or allurement.[40] So far, such laws have been passed only at the state level, though the RSS has called for legislation at the national level as well. A legal disincentive to conversion among low-caste Hindus is that low-caste converts to Christianity or Islam lose the economic and political benefits granted to them as Hindus by the Constitution of India. This legal record has provided a narrative in which the state seeks to protect the convert who is viewed as a victim.

The conversion to Islam in February 1981 of some 180 Hindu Dalit families in the village of Meenakshipuram in the Tirunelveli district of Tamil Nadu was interpreted by the RSS and others as another sign not only of the growing vulnerability of low-caste Hindus, but also that of Hinduism generally.[41] Sikh separatists in the northern state of Punjab were at that time targeting the Hindu minority in that state, killing some and driving others out. There were simultaneous reports of a surge of Muslims from densely populated Bangladesh into the north-eastern region of India, and the forced exodus of Hindus from the Kashmir Valley. This sense of Hinduism in peril was the context for a national campaign by the RSS and many other groups to strengthen Hindu solidarity, part of which was to address the complaints of the Dalit communities. Seshadri, the then RSS general secretary, wrote at the time that a Muslim Action Committee had a plan to convert millions of Dalits nationally to ensure that 'the Muslim percentage becomes sufficiently high to enable them to carve out, in the first instance, independent, Islamic States in Bharat [India], and finally to islamise the entire Bharat'.[42] BJP leader Vajpayee stated during a visit to Meenakshipuram that the conversion was part of a 'sinister conspiracy . . . to undermine the demographic and secular complexion of the country and turn it to a theocratic state like Pakistan and Iran'.[43] An anthropological study by Frank Fanselow, however, claims that the conversions were 'less of [a] protest against the existing social order, than an opportunistic move by an underprivileged community seeking to improve its position within the existing order by allying with powerful groups formally outside the caste structure'.[44] Questioning why these conversions created such a national sense of crisis among Hindus, he adds that, 'Rather than being the vanguard of a strategic Muslim resurgence aimed at subverting Hindu society, they [the conversions] were at the tailend [sic] of a long established pattern of tactical conversion.'[45] The sense of urgency created by Meenakshipuram was one of the major factors that led the RSS to support the revival of the VHP in the early 1980s with its convocation of the first Dharma Sansad (religious parliament) in April 1984; this parliament focused on the twin goals of uplifting the social status of low-caste Hindus and protecting them from the conversion efforts of 'alien' faiths. That gathering proposed twelve activities 'to make Hindu society strong, faith-propelled and Dharma-oriented'.[46] Those activities included:

[1] To prescribe the Dharmic guidelines for the growth of integration amid Hindu society in the perspective of the modern era . . . [2] To give an experience of equality and integrity to our neglected and backward brethren by awakening a sense of dignity of labour in the society . . . [3] To prescribe guidelines for welcoming those of our brethren who got converted to alien faiths

due to some reason, if they are willing to return to Hindu Dharma, assimilating them in Hindu society . . . [4] To foil by every means the conspiratorial attempts by the adherents of alien faiths to reduce the Hindu population and by forcing the administration to have commitment to the Hindu interests.[47]

This first Dharma Sansad was attended by over 500 leaders of seventy-six Hindu *panth*s (orders) from all over India. The inaugural function was presided over by one of the major figures in Hinduism, the Shankaracharya of Jyotish Peeth, one of the four monastic centres established in the eighth century in various parts of India to propagate a more systematic study of the Hindu faith. This religious parliament was a successor of several unity conferences held first in south India soon after the Meenakshipuram conversion, and then all over the country.[48] Alongside these unity conferences, the VHP organized deliberative groups called Margdarshak Mandals representing different Hindu sects, whose goal was to provide advice on key problems facing Hinduism; major topics included how to bring an end to 'untouchability' and how to integrate 'untouchables' and tribals into Indian society.[49] Much of the VHP's organizational success was due to the emergence of a brilliant coordinator, Ashok Singhal, an RSS pracharak who joined the VHP in 1982 as joint general secretary and then became its general secretary in 1986. Under his leadership, the VHP launched a range of activities that helped to attract a considerable part of the fractious Hindu ecclesiastical leadership and thus succeeded in providing the VHP and the sangh parivar a large measure of legitimacy as the defender of Hinduism and the catalyst for Hindu unity.

Ghar wapsi remains a controversial political issue thanks to the wide publicity by members of the VHP-supported DJS, such as Rajeshwar Singh. The RSS, which itself opposes publicizing its own reconversion efforts, used its role as arbitrator on this issue between the BJP, which seeks the support of India's religious minorities, and the VHP. The RSS walks a fine line, and is likely to act as it did here only when publicity undermines its own activities and those of other members of the sangh parivar. Its preferred approach to these differences is holding quiet, behind-the-scenes negotiations among leaders of the affected groups and creating compromises that are not incompatible with the basic objectives of the member organizations. In this case, the removal of Singh (and the termination of his highly publicized activities which created problems for the BJP and the RSS) and the continuation of the practice of ghar wapsi seems to have been the negotiated solution.

ELEVEN

Protecting the Cow

Between the Pious and the Profane

The RSS in 1952 collected about 17 million signatures on a petition demanding a national ban on cow slaughter, its first mass public action after Independence.[1] This programme was carefully selected as part of an effort to rehabilitate itself after the devastating 1948–49 ban imposed following charges of its involvement in civil violence.[2] Cow protection has remained a core issue of the RSS, though it has subsequently advocated a more nuanced approach to a policy which threatens the lucrative multibillion-dollar beef and leather industries employing several million workers, creates economic problems for many farmers and is unpopular among many Indians, especially in the Northeast and the south. We will also look into the dilemma it faces when handling the issue of vigilante outbursts from the right without appearing to take the side of those who engage in violence against people suspected of consuming beef and/or transporting cows to the market for the purpose of slaughter.

Cow protection as a tactic to assert Hindu identity has deep roots, especially among Hindu reform groups like the Arya Samaj in the latter half of the nineteenth century.[3] It enjoyed widespread support in the ruling Congress party and several Congress-ruled states after Independence passed laws restricting or banning the slaughter of cattle. The decision of the RSS to focus on cow protection after the humiliating ban brought several advantages to Golwalkar and itself:

it strengthened Golwalkar's position within the RSS, established a rapport with the Hindu religious establishment and gave the RSS popular appeal among parts of the population that revere the cow. Reflecting the political potential of the cow protection issue, the BJS—a political affiliate of the RSS—made cow protection one of its core issues in the wake of its poor performance in both the 1951–52 parliamentary elections and the simultaneous state Assembly contests.[4] It pursued this objective separate from two Hindu-oriented parties that also supported a national ban on cow slaughter, the Ram Rajya Parishad and the Hindu Mahasabha. The leadership of the young BJS considered both of them overly sectarian, unlike the BJP, and representative of high-caste interests, but most importantly both had poor relations with the RSS and its leader.[5] The RSS was disappointed that its efforts towards cow protection did not mobilize the Hindu ecclesiastical establishment to come together towards the cause. Hindu establishment clerics, unaccustomed to political activism and fearful of antagonizing the dominant Congress party, did not on their own form a lobby to advocate banning cow slaughter. Eventually, in 1964, the RSS would seek to organize the clerics for cow protection and for other cultural issues through one of its own affiliates, the VHP.

The cow protection issue today, while still drawing the support of the RSS, is handled with greater caution than in the past, perhaps because the matter has unleashed violence from the radical right that undermines the efforts of the RSS (and the BJP) to convey a moderate image of Hindu nationalism.[6] No serious effort has been made either by the national BJP governments of Vajpayee or Modi to change the Indian Constitution to shift this matter from the states to the federal government, a constitutional action that would be needed to legislate a national ban, though the Modi government made a controversial regulatory move in May 2017 to hinder transportation of bovines for slaughter. India is thus left with a patchwork of state laws on cow protection ranging from no bans to total prohibition. On how to proceed politically, there is a mixed response from many RSS interlocutors. Some argue that action at the national level must wait until the BJP controls both houses of Parliament and

most state governments so that the stringent legal requirements of
a constitutional amendment will be met. However, there is also a
contending view that the political energy required for an amendment
could undermine the party's economic development strategy, and so
it continues to leave the issue to the states. In what some conservative
Hindutva advocates termed an inadequate approach to the issue, the
Union ministry of environment, forest and climate change on 23 May
2017, issued an order[7] banning the sale of cattle for the purpose of
slaughter in open markets on a national basis, including mandating
a complex set of rules requiring record of sales as well as a broad
definition of cattle to include bulls, bullocks, cows, buffaloes, steers,
heifers, calves and camels.[8] Togadia, the then working president of
the VHP, quickly issued a statement asserting that the new order only
partially addressed the issue of cow slaughter, arguing that it in fact
only applied to the prohibition of the sale of cattle for the purpose
of slaughter and was not the national prohibition ban that the VHP
advocates.[9] This order provoked outrage in the Northeast and the
south, and the Tamil Nadu High Court stayed the execution of the
regulation in that state. On 11 July 2017, the Supreme Court ordered
the Union environment ministry to revise its order; it extended
the Tamil Nadu High Court ruling to the whole country until the
ministry came back with something that would pass constitutional
requirements and also removed buffaloes and camels from the list
that could be regulated.[10] The then Supreme Court Chief Justice
Jagdish Singh Khehar moreover stated that the transportation ban
struck a ruinous blow to the livelihood of many people.[11]

Given this reaction, the RSS has avoided repeating the VHP's
characterization of the new regulation as insufficient and rather has
taken a low-key approach, reflecting an evolving attitude in the RSS
towards cow protection that is less confrontational. This shift is
evident in the most recent 'objectives' section of the website of the
Go-Vigyan Anusandhan Kendra, an RSS-affiliated cow protection
group that focuses its attention on using science to improve Indian
cattle and their economic usefulness as well as providing shelter to
cattle.[12] That same document also argues against the use of violence
by quoting from a talk by Golwalkar where he had stated:

As patriotic and sober citizens we cannot indulge in acts of lawlessness and violence, the only language which unfortunately our Government seems to understand and bows down before. We can not stoop to bully the Government to surrender for it will detract from the necessary prestige of the Government which we feel to be our very own. What then can we do? Under the present set up, agitations, demonstrations are apparently well-recognised means to achieve any objective . . . But there is one more very respectable and universally accepted means, that of demonstrating our approbation or disappropriation . . . . [and it is] through the ballot box.[13]

But the reality remains that many are not willing to rely on the ballot box, choosing instead to pursue cow protection vigilante activity either as a sacred duty or for personal gain—or both. Vigilante activity existed before Independence, but the associated violence has become much more of a political issue in this era of social media and digital networks.[14] More people are now aware of what is a serious law-and-order question. What seems to have set off the current debate on vigilante activity was the highly publicized lynching of a Muslim for allegedly storing and eating beef, in a village in Dadri some 50 miles east of Delhi on 28 September 2015. There are also dozens of examples of vigilante seizure of cows being transported to markets for sale. The public attention on the violence associated with cow vigilante activity presented the RSS (and the BJP) with a dilemma—how to support cow protection while distancing itself from the associated violence. Soon after the lynching of a Muslim dairy farmer in BJP-ruled Rajasthan by cow vigilantes on 1 April 2017, RSS chief Bhagwat condemned such violence, stating, 'Nothing should be done while protecting cows that hurts the beliefs of some people. Nothing should be done that is violent. It only defames the efforts of cow protection.'[15] At the same time, he reiterated the long-standing RSS proposal for all states to ban cow slaughter.[16] Several months earlier, in the wake of another incident related to cow vigilante violence, Prime Minister Modi, who also favours a national ban on cow slaughter, stated that most of these vigilante groups are not legitimate—many of them are 'antisocial' groups masquerading as protectors of the cow—though he was widely criticized for having waited so long to condemn the violence.[17] A newly appointed police chief in Uttar Pradesh, Sulkhan Singh, said on 28 April 2017 that he had strict orders from his BJP Chief Minister Yogi Adityanath to crack down on anyone indulging in criminal activities, including those who engage in 'moral policing' in the name of cow protection.[18] Sulkhan Singh's directions included instructions to register an FIR (First Information Report), a report that initiates a police investigation, against such vigilantes and to prepare dossiers on them.[19]

What has triggered these responses critical of cow vigilantism has almost certainly been a surge in public awareness of such attacks, and the news that the motive behind such violence is often theft and extortion rather than the protection of cows. *India Today*, for example, reported on 7 April 2017 the activities of two large organized cow vigilante groups in the states of Haryana and Uttar Pradesh, noting that a common model of operation was to blockade a road, use intimidation and sometimes engage in violence to seize the cattle from the trucks, and to then distribute the cows among themselves—all in the name of protecting the sacred cow.[20] In the wake of such continuing incidents, India's Supreme Court entered the discussion in late 2017; it recommended that all states take stern steps to stop violence in the name of cow protection by appointing a senior police officer in every district, and further directed chief secretaries to file a status report noting what action had been taken to prevent cow vigilantism.[21]

In the context of increasingly publicized cow vigilante violence, a few senior BJP and RSS leaders have even questioned whether the government should involve itself in the issue of beef consumption at all, other than to crack down on offenders. Union minister Gadkari, who is very close to the RSS leadership, in a statement criticizing the Dadri lynching, reportedly stated, 'I personally believe that the government should not have any role in deciding what people should eat.'[22] This remark was almost identical to the Supreme Court's July 2017 ruling that the Union government did not have the constitutional mandate in its May 2017 regulatory action to determine what people can eat, even though some Indian states have had laws against cow slaughter since Independence. The then RSS all-India prachar pramukh, Manmohan Vaidya, responding on 9 December 2015 to press questions on the RSS policy towards beef-eating, said, 'We [the RSS] don't tell society what to eat,' adding that even people who eat beef could join the RSS.[23] He made the statement on a visit to the north-eastern state of Arunachal Pradesh where consumption of beef is widespread and cow slaughter is permitted (and where, reportedly, some RSS members eat beef).[24] The finance minister of the newly elected BJP coalition government of the north-eastern state of Assam, Himanta Biswa Sarma, told the press that, 'Our party is very sensitive about the north-eastern states. We know that it has a different culture and customs. So specifically our idea is to develop [the] Northeast, promote its economy, so we do not want to [get] bogged down by an issue [beef consumption] which has no economic, political and cultural consequence here.'[25] Assam has a law banning cow slaughter, though it is permitted if there is a 'fit-for slaughter' certificate issued by the government. When asked about the cow slaughter issue in Muslim-majority Kashmir, the general secretary of the BKS, the farmer affiliate of the RSS, stated that while 'organic farming based on cow dung and cow urine produced bumper crops', he was unwilling to comment on a ban on cow slaughter. 'You better ask this question to the BJP and PDP [then coalition partners],' he said, and reportedly added that the beef ban issue was not the concern of his organization.[26]

The dilemma for the RSS (and the BJP) on the issue of cow slaughter is that while the cow has a special spiritual or emotional significance for many Hindus, a number of potential supporters in India's north-eastern and southern states and among low-caste Hindus nationally do eat beef, as do of course many Christians and Muslims as well as some urban middle-class Hindus. Moreover, the regulatory ban on transportation for slaughter was a blow to a lucrative multibillion-dollar meat and leather industry. A Reuters report notes that India's meat and leather exports alone in 2016 were worth more than $16 billion in sales.[27] The Supreme Court's

removal of buffalo, not considered sacred, from the list is a major
boon to the leather and meat industries as a large part of such exports
are from buffalo. The sangh parivar's reaction to this criticism of
tougher federal measures and to the issue of cow protection in the
states is (1) to emphasize the value of research that would make live
cattle even more important and (2) to encourage placing stray cows
at gaushalas (cow protection centres), many of which get funding
from the state governments. But there are hundreds of thousands
of stray cattle released by farmers because of the fear of transporting
non-productive animals to sell for their meat and leather. This is
a financial loss of some significance to small farmers.[28] Moreover,
the stray cattle are a threat to crops, forestry and grazing land for
productive cattle. The situation is especially acute in the BJP-ruled
state of Madhya Pradesh, and the chairman of the executive council
of the state's Cow Protection Board, Swami Akhileshwaranand,
reportedly stated that, 'We want to introduce a penalty for owners
who abandon their cows.'[29]

The issue of cow protection in the Northeast is a case study
of the RSS adjusting to a culture that is on the frontier of Indic
Asia. With a mix of ethnicities and cultures, Hindu nationalism is
faced with the challenge of accommodating itself to diverse regional
cultures on a range of core Hindu nationalist issues, like the
veneration of the cow. The RSS, from at least the immediate post–
Second World War period, has prioritized establishing a presence
in the Northeast, in large part to counter both Christian missionary
activity among the region's substantial tribal population and the
possible demand that large parts of the region be incorporated into
the eastern part of what was then a united Pakistan.[30] In an effort to
build a common Hindu-oriented identity in the Northeast, the RSS
has sought both to create a narrative of the region linking classic
Hindu traditions with local religious practices and consolidate
support through a range of welfare activities.[31] An example of this
appropriation of traditional heroic figures in Christian-majority
Nagaland is the sangh parivar's publicizing Naga spiritual leader
Gaidinliu (1915–93) for her opposition to British rule and conversion
to Christianity.[32] Especially important in this effort have been the

RSS-affiliated schools which teach in local languages and link local traditions to those of classic Hinduism.[33] The RSS penetration of the Northeast, which was initiated soon after the Second World War, has recently begun to pay dividends for the organization and its affiliates, especially the BJP.[34]

Starting in 2016, the BJP (aligned with regional allies) made significant electoral advances in the north-eastern states of Arunachal Pradesh, Assam, Manipur and Tripura, forming governments on its own in all four; the BJP is also part of the governing alliance in Nagaland and Meghalaya. All but Manipur allow slaughter of cows under some circumstances and the state BJP leadership in these states has remained virtually mute on the issue; the local RSS has been equally discreet. Yet, the first reported instance of cow vigilante activity in Assam occurred on 30 April 2017, when a mob killed two men for stealing cows.[35]

The RSS first entered the Northeast in Assam and, among the states of the region, that is where it remains the strongest.[36] The state's organizing secretary told the press that in 2016 there were 903 shakhas, 423 service projects of various kinds and 500 Vidya Bharati schools with 1,40,000 students; twenty-one of the RSS's three dozen affiliates operate in the state.[37] The BJP has also surged as a political force in the state: it won seven of Assam's fourteen parliamentary seats in the 2014 elections, and then sixty (eighty-six including regional allies) of 129 seats in the 2016 Assam Assembly elections, paving the way for its expansion elsewhere in the Northeast.

In the three Christian-majority states of the Northeast— Meghalaya, Mizoram and Nagaland—the BJP is also seeking to make further electoral gains. In those three states, there are no restrictions on cow slaughter or the consumption of beef. While Meghalaya is almost two-thirds Christian, the RSS has been operating in the state since it attained full statehood in 1972 and it has laid a service foundation for an expansion of the sangh parivar, including the BJP. The RSS (and affiliated organizations), according to one report, had in 2016 over 6000 swayamsevaks in Meghalaya, ran fifty schools located in all eleven districts of the state and managed medical camps in about 1000 villages.[38] Responding to Christian suspicions of Hindu nationalists, it conducted the 'Know RSS' campaign for teachers in 2016, some of whom some were reportedly Christian clergy.[39] The RSS's state prant pracharak (organizing secretary), employing ecumenical terms, stated that, 'We are Indians outside no matter whatever religion we follow at home,' and further that, 'People from different religions, different age groups and different income levels are gradually joining the organization [the RSS].'[40] Nagaland and Mizoram, both almost 90 per cent Christian, have a much weaker RSS presence than Meghalaya. The ABVKA, the RSS affiliate working on the cultural and economic uplift of tribals, has a presence in these states, as it has throughout the Northeast.[41] The RSS (and the BJP), seeking to avoid letting the cow slaughter issue give it an anti-Christian image or even the impression that it was against local food habits, has largely stayed on the sidelines of this sensitive topic in the region. This was rather dramatically demonstrated at the 1967 VHP conference in Guwahati, Assam, when RSS chief Golwalkar said that the tribals, who comprise a large part of the population in the Northeast, are in fact Hindu and that their consumption of beef is based on isolation from mainstream Hinduism and on economic necessity.[42] While proposing that efforts should be made to bring the tribals more in line with traditional Hindu practice, he did not insist on their abandoning beef consumption and, in fact, announced that he had shared his vegetarian meal with tribal participants at the conference.[43] Appealing to local religious customs among tribals, the RSS encourages local mores and indigenous religious beliefs, partly to reduce the chances of conversion to Christianity. There is even an organization (International Centre for Cultural Studies) started by senior RSS members and headquartered in Nagpur that has the preservation and revival of indigenous culture, both within and outside India, as its goal.[44] Reviving the memory of Gaidinliu, a twentieth-century female activist who sought to insulate the indigenous Haraka religious community from Christian missionary activity in the Christian-majority state of Nagaland, is one example of what the RSS wants to project culturally in India's Northeast. However, that indigenous cultural inheritance sometimes includes beef consumption. The RSS response to this cultural issue increasingly is to change behaviour voluntarily through example and education rather than coercive legal action.

Besides states in the Northeast, cow slaughter is also permitted in Kerala and, under certain conditions, in West Bengal, two states with large religious-minority populations. Despite its traditionally minuscule presence in both states, the BJP has since 2009 morphed into a party commanding about a tenth of the votes in national and local elections and has hopes of becoming much stronger. The RSS, however, has a relatively strong presence in both states, especially Kerala. O.M. Roopesh has argued that the surge in the number of temples in Kerala since the early 1990s and their involvement in a wide range of social activities have led to 'a certain process of homogenisation, wherein these communities begin to see temples as "Hindu" worship places [rather than discreet community efforts]'.[45] He further argues that the RSS is using this development to advance its cultural message as well as that of the larger sangh parivar.[46] Kerala, with about 5000 shakhas, has one of the highest densities of these daily-meeting centres among Indian states—even more than the four RSS administrative areas of BJP-ruled Maharashtra, which cumulatively boast some 4000 shakhas.[47] Journalist Varghese K. George, in a perceptive analysis of why the various elements of the sangh parivar are gaining ground in Kerala at the expense of the long-powerful political left, argues that its growth is linked to a rising concern across the Hindu caste spectrum that they are losing out economically and demographically to the growing and increasingly prosperous Muslim and Christian populations, who together now form slightly more than 40 per cent of the population.[48] An RSS pracharak from Kerala told us that the bulk of the organization's participants in Kerala are from the OBC category; relatively few are from the state's influential high-caste Namboodiri Brahmin and Nair communities. He also said that the RSS in the state emphasizes economic conditions rather than cultural issues such as cow protection.[49] The BJP in Kerala is beginning to register its presence politically, winning a seat for the first time in the 2016 Assembly elections with a cumulative total of slightly more than 10 per cent of the popular vote, about the same percentage it won in the 2014 parliamentary polls and up from 6 per cent in the 2009 parliamentary elections. Reflecting generally favourable popular views on eating beef, the party and the RSS in the state have taken a rather subdued stand on the cow protection issue. To clarify the party's neutrality on dietary restrictions, the state leadership of the BJP in early 2015 informed the press that the party does not object to what people eat.[50] This effort came in the wake of protests in Kerala over a raid on the Kerala House canteen in New Delhi to check on claims (false, as it turned out) that beef was being served there in a jurisdiction that bans the sale of beef.[51]

In West Bengal, the presence of the left and the Congress party has shrunk significantly since 2009, creating an opening for the BJP and other affiliated organizations to advance. Political scientist Biswanath Chakraborty argues that increasing polarization between Hindus and the large Muslim minority (about 30 per cent of the population) is benefiting the BJP, with Muslims shifting from the political left to the regional Trinamool Congress and Hindus gradually shifting to the BJP—demonstrated by the growing appeal of Hindu festivals like Ram Navami and Hanuman Jayanti that had not been popular earlier in West Bengal.[52] The RSS has doubled in size from some 900 shakhas in 2013 to about 1800 in 2016, according to one RSS state official.[53] The RSS in 2014 loaned Dilip Ghosh, a pracharak, to the BJP, and in 2015 he became state president to build the BJP organizational structure.[54] The state BJP increased its parliamentary representation in the 2009 elections from no seats, with about 6 per cent of the popular vote, to two of forty-two seats in 2014 with 17.02 per cent of the popular vote, a vote percentage slightly behind the formerly dominant Communist Party of India (Marxist) (22.9 per cent), and considerably ahead of the Congress party (9.6 per cent).[55] The BJP also won three of 294 seats in the Assembly elections two years later, going from no seats (4.6 per cent of the popular vote) in 2011 to over 10.7 per cent of the popular vote in 2016. It then came in second after the dominant regional Trinamool Congress in a prestigious Assembly by-election contest in 2017, edging out the formerly dominant Communist Party of India (Marxist) and the Congress,[56] prompting the national BJP to send senior figures to help prepare the party for further advances in the local elections of 2018 and national elections of 2019. The BJP now sees itself as a major political competitor to the regional Trinamool Congress, replacing both the communists and the Congress. The party president, Amit Shah, responding to questions on the BJP's views on cow vigilante violence during a visit to the state, said, 'No one should take law in their own hands. We have given them the message strongly and cases have also been registered and arrests have also been made.'[57] When asked the politically sensitive question of whether the BJP would ban cow slaughter if it came to power in West Bengal, Shah gave a very cautious answer that avoided taking a side, saying, 'This is for the elected government to decide.'[58]

The views of the RSS regarding cow slaughter are rooted in the nineteenth-century Hindu reform movement's use of cow veneration as a symbol to create a boundary marker that would help unify the fractured Hindu community.[59] Dayanand Saraswati, better known for establishing the Hindu reformist Arya Samaj in the late nineteenth century, also set up a cow protection society, the Gau Rakshini Sabha; it was aimed at mobilizing Hindus on a community basis, which was also a core objective of the Arya Samaj, but served as a source of recurrent tensions with Muslims.[60] Hundreds of gaushalas were built as part of its effort to drum up support for Hindu nationalism.[61] Cow protection, which was supported by Mahatma Gandhi, also had the backing of a significant part of the Congress party during the long period after Independence, when it dominated Indian politics.[62] After Article 48 of the Constitution made cow protection a state subject in India's federal system, several Congress-ruled states quickly passed laws banning cow slaughter, and some form of cow protection now exists in a large majority of India's thirty-six states and Union Territories.[63] India's Supreme Court in 1958 upheld state laws banning the slaughter of cows, and the calves of cows and of buffaloes, as consistent with Article 48 of the Constitution, but Article 48 cannot be used to mandate cow protection as it is only a guiding principle for legislative purposes.[64] Three-quarters of those states banning cow slaughter make it a cognizable offence, while in half it is a non-bailable offence. State laws currently vary widely, from a total ban on slaughter and on the consumption of beef to permission from state authorities to slaughter cows depending on issuance of differently defined 'fit-to-slaughter' certificates. Penalties also vary widely. Several states have no bans on cow slaughter and beef-eating. Since the BJP's landslide victory in the 2014 parliamentary elections and its subsequent state election victories, several states have toughened their laws on this issue. BJP-ruled Gujarat, for example, in March 2017 amended its Gujarat Animal Preservation Act of 1954—which criminalizes cow slaughter as well as transportation of cows for slaughter and possession of beef as non-bailable offences—by extending the maximum sentence for cow slaughter from seven years to life imprisonment, making it the state with the strictest cow protection laws. BJP-controlled legislatures in Maharashtra and Haryana also toughened cow protection legislation.[65]

Within the sangh parivar, the VHP and its affiliated groups, especially the Bajrang Dal and the Durga Vahini (youth organizations for young men and women, respectively), have taken the hardest line on cow slaughter. What sets the VHP apart tactically from the RSS (and the BJP) on cow protection is that it seems more willing than the RSS or its other affiliates to engage in agitation, and possibly violence, to enforce the bans against cow slaughter and the consumption of beef. Togadia said at a press conference on 14 April 2017 that the spike in cow vigilante activity was due to the failure of the states to frame laws to end illegal cow slaughter, and that the violence took place when cow vigilantes sought to protect cows.[66] About a year earlier, Rajesh Pandey, the national convener of the Bajrang Dal, had said in response to alleged government laxness on cow slaughter that his organization would 'have to create some kind of fear and pressure, as not even a single cow should fall into the hands of slaughterers', even citing the Dadri lynching as an example of the backlash that would occur if cow slaughter continued.[67] A VHP national secretary, Radha Krishna Manori, told the press on 16 April 2017 that the VHP affiliates Bajrang Dal and Durga Vahini in two years 'will stop beef eating in Goa', and moreover 'they do not need the help of the state's BJP government to do so'.[68] This threat suggests a conviction within the VHP that Goa's BJP government, which relies on some Christian support in a state that is one-quarter Christian, might oppose what the VHP demands, much in the way it did not go along with those who wanted to terminate state assistance to Christian schools that used English as the medium of instruction. The threat to use the Bajrang Dal and the Durga Vahini, groups that sometimes employ strong-arm tactics against opponents, could create a law-and-order crisis in Goa that pits two of the most prominent members of the sangh parivar against each other. If a crisis develops due to different approaches to important issues like cow protection, the RSS would probably seek, quietly and outside the public eye, to negotiate some kind of solution satisfactory to both sides, as it did on the ghar wapsi issue in Uttar Pradesh. Further complicating the situation in Goa is that one of the BJP government's major coalition allies, the Maharashtrawadi Gomantak Party (MGP), also wants a complete ban on cow slaughter in the state,[69] a demand reiterated by its erstwhile ally, RSS rebel Subhash Velingkar. Goa has laws punishing cow slaughter, but these laws also have provisions for a 'fit-for-slaughter' certificate, while beef imported into the state for consumption is permitted.

The cow protection issue, while publicized heavily because of vigilante activity, became less important in the sangh parivar since the late 1990s, as economic development rose to the top of the BJP's agenda, a priority supported by the labour affiliates of the RSS, especially the worker and farmer affiliates. The cultural affiliates, especially the VHP, however, continue to make cow protection a priority. The RSS has assumed its balancing role when there are different policy orientations among the affiliates. Possibly hoping to revive public interest in the issue, the VHP organized a conference, the Gau-Sanskriti-2006, in March 2006. In attendance were several hundred delegates, representing cow protection shelters from across the country, Hindu organizations like the Arya Samaj and the International Society for Krishna Consciousness (ISKCON), as well as over a hundred scientists and doctors whose aim was to pave the way for a research-and-development centre on the productive uses of the cow.[70] Perhaps reflecting national exhaustion over further politicization of the issue, the 'achievements' section of the report on this conference on the VHP website focuses not on lobbying for a national legislation or better adherence to existing laws on cow protection, but rather on its economic benefits.[71]

While the RSS has consistently called for legal action to end cow slaughter on a national basis, it has taken a low-key approach to the issue since the late 1990s. After the April 2017 spate of cow vigilante violence noted above, Bhagwat said that a ban on cow slaughter 'has to be carried out [by the states] while completely obeying the law and the Constitution'.[72] Focusing on a legalistic approach to the issue, he added that in states where politicians from the RSS have assumed power, the laws against cow slaughter have been tightened.[73] In short, he was repeating Golwalkar's earlier advice that persuasion and the ballot box—and not agitation—are the best routes to fundamental change. As the BJP has evolved politically, it has also become more sensitive to the negative impact of cow vigilantism on its efforts to portray Hindu nationalism as a moderate force. While continuing to support an end to cow slaughter, the issue is not near the top of its policy agenda and it has sought to avoid confrontation with groups in regions where beef consumption is a regular part of the diet, as in north-eastern India. The RSS, however, does not want the BJP's pursuit of votes and its focus on economic development—using the slogan 'Sabka Saath Sabka Vikas'—to sideline cow protection, as some calculate has happened with the Ram Janmabhoomi issue. With this in mind, the RSS has tacitly accepted the VHP's activism on behalf of the cow.[74] The VHP's activism also serves as a check on the political marginalization of these cultural Hindutva projects, while maintaining the RSS's moral standing to mediate differences within the sangh parivar. Compromise for the sake of unity has long been the guide for RSS decision-making regarding differences within the parivar and this applies to the subject of cow slaughter too. But like all issues of piety, the danger is that motivated outliers on the right in the name of devoutness will act in aggressive ways that will test both the BJP's and the RSS's ability—or will—to constrain them.

TWELVE

A Ram Temple in Ayodhya

The Dilemma

V.S. Naipaul in his book *India: A Wounded Civilization* wrote about the deep wounds on the Hindu psyche caused by centuries of Muslim and British rule, such as the colonial historians' portrayal of Hindu men as effete and lacking in martial virtues.[1] The Ram Temple movement, referred to as Ram Janmabhoomi (birthplace of Lord Ram), has been used since at least the late 1800s to create a metanarrative aimed at reviving Hindu consciousness and pride among all segments of Hindu society and to assert a collective Hindu identity, which is a goal that has animated many Hindutva intellectuals who otherwise have had little patience for confessional Hindu beliefs.[2] On being asked about the Babri Masjid demolition during his 2004 visit to the BJP office, Naipaul said, 'Ayodhya is a sort of passion to be encouraged. Passion leads to creativity among a section of the public.'[3] The dilemma for the sangh parivar is that, while the Ram Janmabhoomi movement may instil a Hindu consciousness among India's majority and may be effective in arousing passion among Hindus, it is on a site claimed by Muslims, and any move to build a temple at this site could trigger communal violence and thus have a negative impact on the BJP's own metanarrative of economic growth beneficial to all.[4] The problem is how to advance both metanarratives without one undermining the other.

191

Yogi Adityanath, a forty-four-year-old firebrand religious figure and the BJP's choice for chief minister after the 2017 Assembly elections in India's most populous state, Uttar Pradesh, at his first news conference on 20 March 2017 following his party's landslide electoral victory tried to advance both metanarratives.[5] He said very little about what had been one of his signature (and controversial) talking points, the immediate construction of a temple dedicated to Lord Ram on the site of a sixteenth-century Muslim religious structure, popularly referred to as the Babri Masjid, in the holy city of Ayodhya. The RSS has also taken a similarly muted approach to the Ram Janmabhoomi issue, which formerly had been one of the key points on its Hindutva agenda. Yet, who can doubt that a Hindu monk will put temple construction on his agenda—when the time is ripe. Senior RSS figures also regularly express their support for a grand temple at Ayodhya, but are similarly vague on when that is to happen.

The Babri Masjid was built in 1528 on the orders of a Mughal general, Mir Baqi, over what many Hindus believe was the site of a historic Hindu temple dedicated to Lord Ram. Controversy over this site dates back to the nineteenth century and it continued after Independence. The Babri Masjid was torn down by a Hindu mob on 6 December 1992. Since then, a drawn-out legal process eventually reaching India's Supreme Court has delayed any action on the conflicting claims by Muslim and Hindu groups over the rightful possessor of the site.[6]

Chief Minister Adityanath repeated his policy priorities of good governance and economic development in his first interview with the RSS-affiliated weekly *Organiser*, limiting his comments on Ram Janmabhoomi to a short statement saying the government is not party to the legal case and that the contesting parties should resolve the matter through dialogue.[7] However, the very fact that a senior Hindu monk in charge of a state government makes a statement that Hindu identity issues like building a temple at the site of Ram's nativity would not be ignored, is a message to the many Hindus who want construction to start immediately that building a temple remains on the agenda. In an interview with us, Chief Minister

Adityanath said that none of the original parties in the legal case before the Allahabad High Court sought to divide the disputed property. He further argued that the final Supreme Court decision should address whether a Ram Janmabhoomi structure existed at the disputed site and, in his view, the case had been made that there was a Ram Temple at the site.[8]

The Ram Janmabhoomi movement, spearheaded in 1984 by the VHP as an expression of pan-Hindu nationalism, demanded the building of a Ram Temple at the site of an existing Muslim structure, the Babri Masjid, and proposed relocating the masjid to a site in the nearby town of Faizabad. Explaining the religious importance of the disputed property, Champat Rai, a joint general secretary of the VHP, wrote, 'This place being the *Janmasthan* [birthplace] of Lord Ram is of special significance and the place itself is not a property but being sacred it is itself a deity and is also worthy of worship . . .'.[9] Justifying the demolition of the Babri Masjid, he writes that it was a 'signpost of slavery for over 450 years and the self-respecting Bharat wanted to undo that statement of national humiliation and shame'.[10] Further focusing on the nationalist reason for supporting a Ram Temple, a pamphlet published by a pro-RSS think tank asserted that the proposed temple is 'the manifestation of our national culture and its honour that is at the core of our country's identity, ethos, integrity, urge for freedom and vigour'.[11] The movement, at its emotional height in the late 1980s and early 1990s, was characterized by marches, protests and occasional violence.

Chief Minister Adityanath is also the *mahant* (chief priest) of the influential Gorakhnath *math* (monastery) in eastern Uttar Pradesh and his backing of a Ram Janmabhoomi is consistent with that of his two predecessors who had been among the most ardent advocates of the construction of a Ram Temple at Ayodhya.[12] Mahant Digvijay Nath (1894–1969) was a militant Hindu nationalist and a Hindu Mahasabha politician who in December 1949 organized a week-long recitation of the Ramayana to strengthen his support base in a city associated with Ram, an action that inadvertently created enhanced popular support for the construction of a temple at the site of Ram's birth.[13] This event drew attention to the fact that the site of the birthplace of Ram was occupied by a Muslim religious structure and, within days, a statue of the Ram *lalla* (Ram as a child) appeared in the Babri Masjid, a move that, on 24 December 1949, led the local government to lock the masjid as a security measure against Hindu–Muslim confrontations.[14] Two of the most capable RSS pracharaks, Chandikadas Amritrao (aka Nanaji) Deshmukh, the division pracharak of eastern Uttar Pradesh, and Muralidhar D. (aka Bhaurao) Deoras, Uttar Pradesh state pracharak, had since the 1940s forged close relations between the RSS and Mahant Digvijay Nath. Soon after the locks were installed, Deshmukh organized non-stop bhajans (devotional prayers) in December 1949 at the Ram Janmabhoomi site, which impressed religious leaders of Uttar Pradesh, including Digvijay Nath. When Golwalkar launched his massive signature campaign in 1953 to ban cow slaughter, Digvijay Nath was among his most enthusiastic backers. That campaign collected over 17 million signatures in a petition submitted to the President of India, and it helped to build Golwalkar's credibility among the Hindu ecclesiastical class. As a consequence of these events, the religious leaders were more prone to accept Golwalkar as a colleague, which helped him get their support when the VHP was launched in 1964.[15] A further indication of Digvijay Nath's close collaboration with the RSS was the establishment in Gorakhpur in 1951 of the first RSS-supported school (Saraswati Shishu Mandir), a school that was to serve as the model for what would become the largest system of private schools in India.[16] Former BJP Prime Minister Vajpayee first ran for Parliament in 1957 in the Balrampur constituency in eastern Uttar Pradesh, with the active support of Digvijay Nath who had already established himself as a political force in that area.[17] Digvijay Nath's successor, Avaidyanath (1921–2014), developed a close relationship with the VHP after its founding in 1964 as it began to organize Hindu clerics for a Hindutva agenda, including the Ram Janmabhoomi. He too was committed to using politics to advance the Hindutva cause—and represented his district in the Indian Parliament as a member of first the Hindu Mahasabha (1989) and then the BJP (1991 and 1996).[18] Adityanath assumed the mantle of mahant of Gorakhnath Math in

September 2014 after ten years as the chosen heir. Following in his predecessor's political footsteps, Adityanath contested (and won) a parliamentary seat on a BJP ticket as the youngest member of Parliament, the first of five victories in the same constituency won by his two predecessors.[19] Building the Ram Temple was at the core of the campaign rhetoric of Adityanath and his two predecessors. He also followed their efforts to build a close relationship with the country's Hindu ecclesiastical leadership, links that enhance his potential as a political figure with a national following, and he has cultivated these national contacts since becoming the chief minister of Uttar Pradesh.

The movement to construct the Ram Temple reached its height in the late 1980s and early 1990s. The government's sensitivity to popular support for a Ram Janmabhoomi shows up dramatically when neither the Uttar Pradesh state government nor the federal government, both controlled by the Congress party, moved to reverse the decision of a sessions judge on 1 February 1986, ordering the government of Uttar Pradesh to unlock the gates of the Babri Masjid for the first time since 1949, thus enabling Hindus to conduct prayers within the structure of the Babri Masjid.[20] The RSS itself used the Ram Janmabhoomi issue during the 1980s to galvanize the Hindu community and it looked to Moropant Pingle, a senior pracharak loaned to the VHP as a trustee in 1980, to provide strategic guidance to it, including using the Ram Temple issue to mobilize pan-Hindu support. Pingle worked with pro-Hindu Congress leaders to support the building of the Ram Temple and he conceived of the Ram yatras (marches in 1983–84) in Uttar Pradesh that portrayed Ram as a prisoner behind bars. He secured the support of pro-Hindu politicians in the ruling Congress party such as Karan Singh, the former maharaja of Kashmir who had been a cabinet member in a series of Congress governments at the Centre; Gulzari Lal Nanda, twice interim prime minister of India; and prominent Uttar Pradesh Congress leader Dau Dayal Khanna.[21] The first major effort to prepare the way for a Ram Temple was a botched move by Prime Minister Rajiv Gandhi to play a Hindu card in response to charges of a pro-Muslim bias by facilitating the opening of the locked Babri Masjid in 1986 to allow Hindu pilgrims to worship within the disputed structure.[22] With subsequent mounting criticism because of corruption charges, and with the 1989 national elections approaching, he moved again to play the Hindu card. He worked quietly with the head of the RSS to facilitate a VHP-organized function in 1989, featuring a foundation stone laying ceremony (*shilanyas*) for the proposed Ram Janmabhoomi as a signal to start construction, in return for RSS support for Congress candidates in the forthcoming parliamentary elections. This followed the apparent Congress collusion in unlocking the masjid, after which the RSS began to express the possibility of supporting the Congress in the polls.[23] Out of these talks between senior RSS officials and representatives of the Rajiv Gandhi government emerged a deal that the RSS would back Congress candidates in the 1989 parliamentary elections in exchange for it facilitating the start of the construction of a Ram Temple. Banwarilal Purohit, a senior Congress politician in Nagpur at the time of these strictly confidential negotiations, claims that Rajiv Gandhi had asked him to arrange a secret meeting between Bhanu Pratap Singh, a former cabinet member and the Maharaja of Narsinghgarh (in Madhya Pradesh), and RSS chief Deoras. Deoras, according to Purohit, agreed to consider the deal if construction were to take place.[24] This deal reportedly fell through in the wake of the shilanyas when the Congress, facing a Muslim backlash, pulled back from the second part (permitting construction to start) of the reported bargain. Whatever the impact of this poorly conceived plan, Rajiv Gandhi's Congress party lost to a coalition backed on the outside by the BJP. With the very good showing of the BJP in the 1989 parliamentary elections, RSS talk of backing the Congress ended. Soon after, and at the height of the Hindutva rallies for a temple, Prime Minister Chandra Shekhar in 1990 tried unsuccessfully to resolve the dispute.[25] Following a heated parliamentary debate on the fate of the disputed temple/masjid on 7 November 1990, the BJP withdrew its support and the government survived on the fragile backing of the Congress, ultimately stepping down on 13 March 1991.[26]

This growing pro-temple sentiment also prompted the BJP on the eve of the 1989 parliamentary elections to formally embrace the notion of a Ram Janmabhoomi at its annual national session at Palampur, Himachal Pradesh, and to make the Ram Temple the core issue of its campaign. Following through on its robust parliamentary performance (increasing its parliamentary representation from two to eighty-five seats), BJP President Advani in September 1989 launched a nationwide march to push the Ram Janmabhoomi cause. Pingle also managed the close VHP–RSS collaboration in 1989 to move bricks from thousands of villages across India to the construction site of the Ram Janmabhoomi at Ayodhya. This effort was opposed by the ruling Janata Party governments in Uttar Pradesh and Bihar, and these two state governments tried to prevent the marchers from reaching Ayodhya. In June 1991, the BJP took control of the state government in Uttar Pradesh and it provided the VHP a plot of land next to the Ram Janmabhoomi site so that it could start the construction process. The issue reached its emotional height on 6 December 1992, when the VHP organized a mass gathering at Ayodhya to pressure the Congress federal government of Prime Minister Rao to facilitate the construction of the Ram Temple. The plan for the day was for a *bhoomipujan* (a Hindu ritual marking the start of construction) in which the pilgrims were symbolically to cleanse the soil to enable construction to begin when it was legally permitted to do so. However, that morning, the crowd, much larger than expected, got out of hand, tore down the mosque, moved the idols for safekeeping and, the next day, built a temporary temple for the idols—and worship has continued till date in this 'temporary temple'.[27] With the security forces withdrawing from the scene, the RSS claims that its volunteers tried to prevent the destruction and that even the general secretary of the VHP and leader of the Ram Janmabhoomi effort, Ashok Singhal, was manhandled by an angry crowd.[28] The immediate consequences were a short-term ban on the RSS (and the VHP),[29] the removal of the BJP from power in the state and, following central rule, its loss of the state elections in Uttar Pradesh in 1993 and a rethink on tactics within the sangh parivar.

By the time the 2009 general elections were conducted, followed by the 2014 polls that brought the BJP to power at the national level, the Ram Janmabhoomi issue had lost much of its emotional fervour. The constituents of the sangh parivar—with the prominent exception of the VHP—had, after the destruction of the Babri Masjid, focused their efforts elsewhere as the case of legitimate ownership of the property languished in the legal system.[30] In 2015, on the first anniversary of Modi's BJP government, for example, Home Minister Rajnath Singh told reporters that the government had set development as its priority and that, as such, the matter of the Ram Temple, while important, is not the main concern.[31] At about the same time, RSS General Secretary Bhaiyyaji Joshi, in words similar to what the home minister had said, told the press that the RSS does not favour an agitational strategy for the Ram Temple.[32] The electoral results of 2014 and the subsequent state victories demonstrate that *vikas* (development) is now viewed as the principal means to retain power, even though support for the Ram Temple is used to mobilize voters on a pan-Hindu basis. Clearly, for many Hindus who constitute the support base of the BJP, development and ideology are not mutually exclusive categories. One can support development *and* Hindutva (in this case, the Ram Temple). But these two factors still present the RSS with a fundamental test of its leadership: balancing the governance imperatives of the BJP with the goal of unifying Hindu society. Its task is to make sure the latter does not undermine the former. If Chief Minister Adityanath successfully emulates Modi's example of combining economic development with a soft Hindutva message while he was chief minister of Gujarat, it would enhance his prospects as a future national leader. If Adityanath fails, the state could plunge into communal violence that will work against economic growth and ultimately undermine support for the party and the RSS. Adityanath's inaugural speech as chief minister suggests that he plans to follow Modi's model of economic development combined with soft Hindutva.

The task of Prime Minister Modi and Chief Minister Adityanath to combine development and soft Hindutva is made more complicated by powerful structural forces that have nudged

Indian politics to the right, a process revealed by BJP victories at the central and state levels since 2014. The BJP may not yet be the hegemonic party that the Congress was after Independence, but its evolution after the 2014 general elections has elements of what Rajni Kothari called the 'Congress System', a broad tent able to accommodate a wide range of groups.[33] Some commentators have already begun referring to 'Congress-ification of the BJP'.[34] The weakness of viable competitors at the national level and in an increasing number of states has led to an influx of many ambitious politicians into the BJP. As such, the BJP (and the RSS) has become an umbrella organization with many shades of opinion—centrist, centre-right and far right—contained within it. This growing variety in the RSS shows up in contradictory statements of senior figures of the sangh parivar on subjects such as ghar wapsi (conversion), homosexuality and caste reservations as well as in debates on how deeply it is to engage in the political process.

The political decline of the Congress and the left after 2014 means that the most likely challenge to the BJP could come from its right flank. The Ram Janmabhoomi is a potent issue for these right-wing forces to organize around and to challenge the generally pragmatic leadership of the BJP—and the RSS. Elements of the sangh parivar, especially within the ranks of the VHP, who may be disappointed with a lack of progress on their cultural agenda, could demonstrate their frustration by rallying to the Ram issue and demanding that the federal government and the state of Uttar Pradesh take concrete steps first to remove obstacles to the construction of a temple and then manage the construction of a temple befitting one of the most revered figures in Hinduism—who, for many Hindu nationalists, is also a potent symbol of the country. A growing number of advocates of the Ram Temple want construction to start immediately and, if negotiations fail, they will seek a legislative solution to authorize immediate construction. This demand fits into a pattern of challenges from the right and is demonstrated by the actions of the Hindu nationalist Shiv Sena, reportedly backed by the youth wing of the VHP, on 29 March 2017 to force the closure of restaurants, including such foreign chains as

Kentucky Fried Chicken (KFC), serving meat during the holy nine-day Hindu festival of Navratri in Gurugram, a bustling suburb of some 2 million people to the west of Delhi that represents India's economic growth and whose gleaming high-rises house the offices of many of the Fortune 500 companies that operate in India.[35] The Chaitra Navratri is a nine-day celebration (28 March–5 April in 2017) of the goddess Durga when many Hindus fast. The last day (Ram Navami) is celebrated as the birthday of Lord Ram. Similar far-right challenges to Modi elsewhere have focused on shutting slaughterhouses, pressuring publishing houses to pulp publications determined to be offensive, and stopping such 'foreign' events as Valentine's Day or the 'insulting' film (*Padmaavat*) that allegedly portrays a Hindu queen (though the story is fictional) in a demeaning fashion. On the agitation surrounding the film, the RSS's former press spokesman Manmohan Vaidya on behalf of the RSS publicly condemned violent protest as contrary to democratic norms.[36] He also distanced himself from the RSS's regional sanghchalak from the north-west, who described the film as an attempt to hurt public sensibilities and disturb social harmony.[37]

Constructing the Ram Temple in 2018 or beyond, while less emotional an issue than in the past, continues to be popular across the Hindu caste spectrum and has been used by the RSS to draw the diverse Hindu community closer together and to create a Hindu vote bank that is above caste, region, class and even religion, always a goal of the RSS. What is now similar to the period before the demolition of the Babri Masjid in late 1992 is that lack of a resolution on the temple issue itself serves an instrumentalist purpose of building up emotional pan-Hindu support against perceived Muslim intransigence. Jaffrelot, in his analysis of the Ram Janmabhoomi movement, argues that the destruction of the disputed structure in late 1992 deprived the sangh parivar of a powerful symbol around which to mobilize broad popular Hindu support.[38] As he points out, subsequent electoral results show that it was easier to mobilize Hindus 'against the Babri Masjid than for something else'.[39] This dilemma continues to exist regarding the debate over when to construct a Ram Temple at Ayodhya.

Dr Keshav Baliram Hedgewar, or Doctorji, the founding sarsanghchalak
of the Rashtriya Swayamsevak Sangh

Deen Dayal Upadhyaya, leader of the
Bharatiya Jana Sangh, forerunner of
the BJP

Lakshmi Bai Kelkar, founder of the
Rashtra Sevika Samiti

Atal Behari Vajpayee and Deen Dayal Upadhyaya

The first RSS shakha in Nagpur

International cricketer Shivnarine Chanderpaul with the Hindu Swayamsevak Sangh in Guyana

Relief work being carried out by the RSS

A school established by Vidya Bharati, the educational affiliate of the RSS

Dhwajavataran, or lowering of the flag, at the end of a shakha

Mohan Bhagwat at the Rashtrodaya Sammelan in Meerut in 2018

RSS members at the same meet in Meerut

A Vishva Hindu Parishad rally for the Ram Janmabhoomi temple at Ramlila Maidan in 1992

An RSS *gaushala*

When the sangh parivar judges the situation as sufficiently ripe to call for the construction of the Ram Temple, it will almost certainly seek a solution that minimizes social disruptions. That could include authorizing the construction of a temple through a court decision, by a parliamentary act, negotiations among the relevant parties or through statements of support from senior figures in the central government, as happened in the early 1950s when the historic Somnath Temple in Gujarat, a major Hindu pilgrimage site, was rebuilt with a generous outpouring of private contributions.[40] There is a mix of opinions within the RSS over when is a good time politically to push for a resolution of the temple issue. Among the factors to consider are BJP control of the upper house of Parliament (the Rajya Sabha), selection of a reliably pro-BJP President of India, and BJP control of most state governments. Some have also argued that, in addition, there should be substantial Muslim support for the Ram Temple and the pro-RSS MRM has included this as a key item on its agenda. Precipitous action in this case could not only endanger the development objective, but also almost certainly undermine popular support for the BJP and its affiliates, including the RSS, as happened after the violence that followed the destruction of the Babri Masjid. In the wake of the communal riots that broke out at that time, the RSS for a third time (and the VHP for the first time) was briefly banned.[41] On the other hand, delaying action until the situation is politically favourable preserves a mobilization strategy useful at time of elections. In the interim, the VHP can be relied on to remind Hindus that the parivar's long-term goal is the construction of a splendid Ram Temple at Ayodhya, not only to satisfy the religious demands of Hindus, but also to rectify a perceived wound on Hindu civilization.[42] The then working president, Togadia, told the press soon after the Uttar Pradesh 2017 elections that it would hold programmes at 5000 venues on 5 April 2017 to advocate the Ram Temple's construction, followed by a conference of religious figures in June 2017 with the goal of pressuring the Modi government to call for a parliamentary act to permit construction.[43] Neither the RSS nor the VHP supported Togadia's plan of action, suggesting his loss of standing in the sangh parivar that was to lead to the 2018 defeat of his hand-picked candidate for the highest office in the VHP. The choice of a well-known Hindu monk, an outspoken advocate of a Ram Temple, as chief minister of Uttar Pradesh is further evidence of this long-term commitment to a temple, but the era of mass protests, marches and violence no longer seems to be part of the strategy of the parivar, and not even of the VHP. The RSS and the VHP are now focused on handling the issue in the courts, perhaps because of greater confidence that the judgment will ultimately be favourable.

Adityanath's cursory remarks on the Ram Janmabhoomi issue at his first news conference is therefore not surprising. It fits the strategy of signalling support for a temple, but leaves the issue to the courts, to Parliament or outside negotiators to resolve at some unspecified future date while the government focuses on development. Even the most ardent believers, however, could not charge the yogi chief minister with being unconcerned about this important Hindu issue. But in the meantime he promises to focus on economic development, using the slogan 'Sabka Saath Sabka Vikas' (inclusive development for all) that Narendra Modi and his BJP had used so successfully in the 2014 parliamentary election that brought them to power at the Centre in New Delhi.[44] In dramatic contrast to his years of criticizing Islam and Muslims during his five terms as a member of Parliament from a district in eastern Uttar Pradesh, Adityanath as chief minister has adopted a much more conciliatory tone, arguing that he and his government would treat all groups fairly. While spelling out in some detail what he planned to do to improve the lives of the state's huge agricultural population, to create jobs for its massive young aspirant population, to improve the law-and-order situation, and to protect the safety of girls and women, Adityanath's only reference to the Ram Temple and other contentious Hindutva cultural issues in his inaugural 20 March 2017 press conference was to say they would be addressed at some unspecified future date as they are mentioned in the party's campaign manifesto. Left out was any indication of how the complicated legal issue would be resolved, a necessary first step before any construction could begin on the Ram Temple.

Fortuitously, the day after Adityanath's press conference, India's Supreme Court issued an opinion supporting an effort to resolve the long-festering legal case by out-of-court negotiations between the interested Hindu and Muslim parties, admitting that the issue is a 'sensitive and sentimental matter',[45] and suggesting that it would prefer to avoid ruling on a case based on an issue of faith, as that could have a high potential for generating violence. The ruling even suggested that the court might involve itself if the negotiations among the interested parties failed.[46] Adityanath himself issued a statement supporting the proposal for negotiations among all parties concerned on the very day the Supreme Court offered its suggestion.[47] The RSS sah karyavah, Hosabale, and other senior figures in the BJP also backed the idea of negotiations. Hosabale said the RSS would stand by any decision of Hindu religious leaders meeting at a dharma sansad (a convocation) organized by the VHP.[48]

Efforts at negotiations so far have been futile, as none of the major parties has been willing to compromise.[49] Almost two decades prior to the 2017 effort at negotiations, BJP Prime Minister Vajpayee had set up an Ayodhya cell in the Prime Minister's Office to manage talks with Hindu and Muslim leaders, but that too produced no consensus.[50] The Allahabad High Court of Uttar Pradesh, months before its September 2010 decision to split the contested land among three of the major parties, unsuccessfully tried to get their counsels to reach an amicable settlement.[51] After India's Supreme Court in May 2011 stayed the order of the Allahabad High Court and thus reinstated the status quo barring any religious activity imposed by the Supreme Court in 1994, the litigants tried—and failed—on three occasions to reach a settlement.[52] The Supreme Court argued that 'no religious activity by anyone be permitted or allowed to take place [at the disputed area]', though it directed that the 'pujas', religious ceremonies, usually by a priest, and darshan, prayers by devotees in the makeshift Ram Temple set up on the ruins of the Babri Masjid soon after its destruction could continue[53]—and worship has continued at that site since then.[54]

This 2017 effort at negotiations failed to bring the parties to an agreement. The Supreme Court again sought and failed to get the parties to negotiate a compromise deal. The Uttar Pradesh

convener of the Bajrang Dal, the youth front of the VHP, issued
a statement that a Muslim religious structure must not be built on
the site, considered the exact place where Lord Ram took human
form.[55] A further complication was the negative reaction by the
Babri Masjid Action Committee (BMAC), which has proposed that
a Muslim religious structure must be built on the disputed site and
rejected the Supreme Court's suggestion for outside negotiations.[56]
The BMAC convener, Zafaryab Jilani, proposed instead that the
matter be handled exclusively by the Supreme Court to determine
which party has rightful control of the contested site in the city of
Ayodhya.[57] Failure of the 2017 call for mediation left three options
to the Supreme Court: (1) ask the government to pass legislation;
(2) give a final decision on its own; (3) continue to let the matter
languish while the litigants argue their respective sides, a stance that
has characterized the Supreme Court's handling of the issue since
taking control of it from the Allahabad High Court in 2011. The
Supreme Court reopened the case on 5 December 2017, deciding
to hear all appeals, which includes an unresolved conspiracy case
against such prominent BJP politicians as Advani and Uma Bharti
as well as senior figures from the VHP.[58]

A resolution of the Ram Temple question, however, does not
end the larger temple issue. The early demands by the sangh parivar
for a Ram Temple were typically linked to restoring two other
historic Hindu temples in Uttar Pradesh, one in the city of Mathura
(Shrikrishna Janmasthan—or birthplace of Lord Krishna) and the
other in the holy city of Varanasi (Kashi Vishwanath—dedicated
to Lord Shiva, considered by many Hindus to be the Lord of the
Universe). At the second dharma sansad called by the VHP in
November 1985, the delegates demanded that the three sites, all
of which had allegedly been destroyed by Muslims and over which
Muslim holy places were built, be restored, but only called for an
active campaign on the Ram Temple.[59] This focus on Ram may be
attributed to his popularity as a religious figure among the Hindu
masses. Edged out by the Ram Janmabhoomi in Ayodhya, the
other two sites receded into the background for the sangh parivar.
However, restoring them to their former glory as Hindu temples

could become the rallying cry of the militant right in an effort to press for a broader Hindutva agenda.

How to handle the Ram Janmabhoomi question elicits a mixed response within the sangh parivar. As of early 2018, opinion is divided between the moderates (primarily within the BJP and some senior RSS figures) who regard the title to the land on which the temple is to be built as an issue primarily for the courts to decide and the hardliners who believe the courts should have no say in a matter of faith such as this. What makes the compromise complicated is the sharp communal polarization on the mandir–masjid issue. Opinion polls conducted in 2016 by the CSDS find that almost half of the Hindus in Uttar Pradesh want only a temple on the disputed site (vs only 31 per cent in 2012) and are unwilling to accept both a mosque and a temple at that site, a stance taken by the VHP as well.[60] Contrary to conventional wisdom, educated youth support the 'temple only' view even more strongly.[61] The moderate view might be willing to accept a compromise that was implied in the 2010 Allahabad High Court judgment that the land be divided between the Hindus and Muslims (with the area under the dome awarded to the Hindus for the construction of the Ram Janmabhoomi). But the hardliners believe that the site of Ram's birthplace is an important matter of faith and the courts have no legitimate jurisdiction and that the partition of the site is unacceptable.[62] They also tend to look at the issue as righting a historical wrong of the sort that Naipaul wrote about in his book when he focused on the wounded pride of Hindus. The VHP, for example, has repeatedly argued that no Muslim structure should be permitted at the holy site. These seem to be irreconcilable demands which make a negotiated settlement highly unlikely. These prospective demands from the ideological right will test the will of the RSS (and the BJP) to keep the focus on pragmatism and good governance. The widespread Hindu support for the Ram Janmabhoomi assures that the parivar will continue to push for construction. The key question is when.

THIRTEEN

A Rebellion in Goa

Test for the RSS Decision-Making System

In a relatively rare example of open rebellion within the RSS, the popular sanghchalak of the RSS in Goa, Subhash Velingkar,[1] was removed from his post by the national RSS leadership on 31 August 2016. Velingkar was charged with violating an RSS rule prohibiting its officers from taking part in politics while still actively serving in the RSS. This violation stems from Velingkar's leading role in forming a lobby group, the Bharatiya Bhasha Suraksha Manch (BBSM), to protest the policy of Goa's BJP-led government to provide government grants-in-aid to English-medium elementary schools, most of which are operated by the Roman Catholic Church.[2] Out of this movement emerged a political party, the Goa Suraksha Manch (GSM), that became the political face of the BBSM and fielded candidates to contest four of the state's forty constituencies separate from the BJP in the 4 February 2017 state Assembly elections. The GSM forged an electoral alliance with the MGP and the Shiv Sena, all of which took a similar stand on the language issue.[3] Even though all the GSM candidates lost (winning only 1.2 per cent of the total vote) and the BJP came back to power in a coalition that included the MGP,[4] Velingkar vowed to continue his opposition to the state providing financial support to English-medium schools.[5]

Velingkar had justified his pre-election rebellion by arguing that the BJP state government's language policy violated its 2012 campaign pledge to end funding for English-medium elementary schools, funding that had been implemented by Goa's previous Congress government. He irritated the BJP party leadership during the 2017 state Assembly elections by asserting that Defence Minister Manohar Parrikar—formerly a popular chief minister of Goa—betrayed his earlier pledge to terminate grants-in-aid to English-medium schools, and even accused Parrikar of lobbying the central leadership of the RSS to get him removed.[6] The question is why this policy difference turned into an unprecedented crisis involving such a senior RSS officer in Goa. Velingkar seems to have become publicly outspoken with Parrikar's move in March 2014 to join the cabinet of Prime Minister Modi—and his replacement by the rather lacklustre Laxmikant Parsekar. Parsekar lacked Parrikar's diplomatic skills that were required to keep the various party interests together, and lost decisively in the 2017 Assembly elections as did most of his cabinet ministers who were contesting.

Sumant Amshekar, Goa's *vibhag* pracharak, informed us that Velingkar's removal 'has nothing to do about opposing BJP or not'.[7] He said that the RSS even supported the BBSM, 'issuing statements [on the language issue], addressing press conferences and holding demonstrations'. The ABPS had in March 2015 passed a resolution on the language issue stating:

> RSS Akhil Bharatiya Pratinidhi Sabha is fully supportive of study of various languages including foreign languages, but it is its considered opinion that for natural learning and to enrich cultural moorings, the education, particularly elementary education should be in mother language or in state languages recognised in our Constitution.[8]

The education affiliate of the RSS, the Bharatiya Shikshan Mandal, has on several occasions advised the ministry of human resource development to nudge the states to adopt a mother-tongue policy in education.[9]

So it was not the robust advocacy of education in the mother tongue that led to the disciplinary action. It was not even the formation of a political party opposed to the BJP that was the source of the crisis. Rather, it was Velingkar's decision to work actively for a political party while retaining his RSS position.[10] While Goa's BJP government that came to power in 2012 had formally supported the BBSM's indigenous language demands, it in fact made only cosmetic adjustments to the policy of grants-in-aid to existing English-medium elementary schools, most importantly, denying grants to any new schools while continuing such grants to schools that were already receiving them. Despite pressure, it did not alter this policy.

The GSM's post-2017 poll announcement that it would sustain the protest movement was a warning to the new BJP government that a continuation of the funding policy for English-medium schools would be opposed. Given the BJP's reliance on Goa's Roman Catholic vote, it is unlikely that the BJP government there will change this policy, despite the RSS's strong support for mother tongue–medium education as an essential ingredient in strengthening the indigenous culture.[11] The new BJP government that came to office in March 2017—with Parrikar once more the chief minister[12]—may be even more dependent on the Roman Catholic vote than its predecessor and thus even less likely to cut off the grants to English-medium schools. In 2012, the BJP won a legislative majority on its own, with six of the BJP's twenty-one seats in those elections won by Roman Catholics; in comparison, six of the mere thirteen winning BJP candidates in 2017 were Roman Catholics. While the Congress won more seats than the BJP (seventeen to thirteen), it won a smaller part of the total popular vote than the BJP (28.4 per cent to 32.5 per cent). If the Hindu nationalist coalition comprising the GSM, the MGP and the Shiv Sena allied with the BJP (winning three seats with some 13 per cent of the popular vote), the chances were high that the BJP would have picked up between three and six additional seats. (See Appendix VIII for 2017 Assembly results.) The BJP, however, needed to cobble together a coalition by aligning with several smaller parties (like the MGP) and a few independents.[13] The MGP, having made language a rallying point in its campaign, could have a shaky run in the BJP-led coalition government if that issue again became contentious. While Velingkar had tapped into a genuine language grievance of many Goan Hindus, he lacked the political credibility to gain significant Hindu support for his party. In working out a coalition, Parrikar once again demonstrated his diplomatic and political skills.

Velingkar had forced the hand of the RSS against him, and the consequences of stepping across the line of permissible political action were severe. Manmohan Vaidya, the then national publicity chief of the RSS, affirmed on 31 August 2016, that '[Velingkar] has been relieved from his responsibilities. He wanted to get into some political activity. Being a Sangh leader, he can't do that.'[14] Velingkar's organizational superior, the Konkan prant chief (state sanghchalak), Satish S. Modh, had announced the day before that the RSS, while supporting the language objective of the BBSM, 'would have no role in the political endeavour of the BBSM' and that it was 'at a recent meeting of senior RSS office-bearers that the convener of the BBSM, Subhash Velingkar, had been relieved from his responsibilities as the Goa vibhag sanghchalak'.[15] Lakshman Behere on 1 September 2016 was selected as Velingkar's replacement, an appointment confirmed to the press by the RSS central public affairs spokesman.[16] A decision of this magnitude was almost certainly vetted by the leadership in Nagpur.

Velingkar, following his dismissal, almost immediately reinstated himself as head of a rebel Goan RSS, noting that it would function independently of the parent body at least until the 2017 state elections, and the press reported that a large part of Goa's mainstream RSS membership followed Velingkar's lead and supported his new breakaway group.[17] The Goa vibhag pracharak, Amshekar, however, informed us that the establishment RSS in Goa continued with its regular work in spite of the exodus. Moreover, he asserted that, 'There is no "so called Goa RSS" in Goa. Shri Velingkar has openly welcomed the new vibhag sanghchalak of Goa and has expressed desire to work under his leadership as RSS swayamsevak after the Goa election.'[18] Despite Amshekar's protestations, there were for a time two RSS units contesting for the support of the state's swayamsevaks. Some six months after declaring his rebellion against the RSS, however, Velingkar announced that he had consulted with his fellow dissenters, and dissolved his Goa RSS. This dissolution came on 7 March 2017, four days before the announcement of the Goa state election results; Velingkar reportedly promised 'never to leave the Sangh again'.[19] He also said that whatever the electoral results, he and his followers would continue to support the BBSM campaign to stop state grants to English-medium elementary schools. He did not mention any effort to resume his former RSS position.

What makes this event rather unique is that it is one of the very few instances in which a serving senior RSS officer openly declared his dissatisfaction with the central leadership of the RSS, going in this case to the unprecedented extreme of forming his own political party to oppose the BJP, an RSS affiliate. Of this radical act of independence, Amshekar asserted that, 'Nobody, no political body, can dictate policy to RSS,' and that, 'Policies can be changed [only] after consensus at the national level [of the RSS].'[20] Velingkar, taking the RSS central leadership to task on this point, told journalists during the 2017 Assembly campaign that, 'The overwhelming feeling among the cadre is that the RSS is taking BJP stands everywhere. The RSS doesn't have the courage to point out the BJP's flaws.'[21] In a separately reported discussion with journalists, Velingkar expressed his dissatisfaction with the central leadership of the RSS and suggested that his criticism of Nagpur extends beyond Goa, reportedly saying that, 'I will stay with the Sangh, but we do not want a weak and helpless leadership. I am getting phone [calls] from across India and [RSS] activists are restless. The Sangh these days has submitted to the BJP.'[22] One of the justifications for the creation of an independent RSS in Goa was that the RSS proper had opted to support the electoral compulsions of the BJP, even if winning involved compromising on its stand on education in the mother tongue.

RSS decision-making tends to be a slow and deliberate process of informal interaction among its central and state leaders to produce a consensus and so avoid an open fissure. When a consensus cannot be reached, the usual practice is to put the issue aside until a mutually acceptable compromise is possible. However, there are situations when delays in addressing grievances can trigger a revolt that forces the RSS leadership to take some dramatic steps—in this case, the removal of Velingkar from his position.

The rapid expansion of the RSS and its affiliates into almost every arena of activity over the past two decades has made it difficult for the organization to stay aloof from the political process and to maintain internal discipline. Three related and contradictory currents of RSS opinion are at stake here: the debate between pragmatists and ideological hardliners; the balancing of often-competing political imperatives from the BJP (for example, retaining office) with the demands of a large part of its base; and the debate over how much of the group's core values (for example, education in the mother tongue) should be compromised for the sake of inclusivity and, consequently, electoral success. Goa is an example of the dilemmas that are likely to arise from such conflicts. Velingkar pointed out the practical consequences of these dilemmas when he told a journalist that the national RSS leadership had condoned his language protests against Goa's BJP government right up until the eve of the state Assembly elections; once that happened, 'I got orders from above that I should not hold a press conferences [sic] or take [Defence Minister] Parrikar's name. Our fight was on principles. I told them when I was fighting against the Congress on the same issue you never said anything so why were they asking me to back down when I was speaking on the same issue against the BJP. They did not listen to me and removed me from my post.'[23]

Even if Velingkar was cautioned by the senior RSS leadership to stop his protests, he was not suspended for ignoring this advice.[24] Rather, Velingkar broke RSS discipline by forming and then leading what could only be characterized as a political party while still retaining his senior position as head of the RSS in Goa. The RSS decision on this case laid down a rather precise marker between permissible and impermissible dissension: actual involvement in an opposition political party while still serving as an RSS officer is impermissible.

From the time of India's independence in 1947, the issue of acceptable political involvement by RSS office-bearers has generated a debate. Golwalkar, the RSS head at the time of independence, had tried to keep the organization aloof from politics, fearing that political activities would interfere with its prime mission of training young men to advance the cause of Hindu consolidation. Events surrounding the partition of the country in 1947—the massive outbreaks of communal violence and then a year-long ban on the RSS imposed on 4 February 1948 (and lifted 11 July 1949)[25] for allegedly creating an environment for anti-Muslim violence— brought urgency to the debate on politics. Many full-time pracharaks used the RSS's major national media outlet, *Organiser*, to press Golwalkar for the RSS to become a political party, both to provide organized resistance against further moves to split the country as well as to protect the RSS from another ban. Golwalkar opted for a compromise by supporting a new nationalist political party— the BJS—organized by Syama Prasad Mookerjee, a prominent politician from the state of West Bengal and a Hindu nationalist in Nehru's first cabinet. Golwalkar dispatched some of his best young full-time RSS pracharaks to the new political party to manage its organizational groundwork while keeping the RSS removed from its day-to-day political operations. Following Mookerjee's death on 23 June 1953, the full-time pracharaks who had been loaned earlier, led by party general secretary Upadhyaya, established control over the party machinery and successfully introduced the sangathan mantri (organizational secretary) system, though Golwalkar sought to keep a distance from policymaking in the BJS, an approach that was later to be applied to other affiliates as well.[26]

Despite an elaborate decision-making process prescribed in the RSS constitution for matters of national importance, the removal of Velingkar demonstrates that decisions in the RSS and most of its affiliates are in fact characterized by informal and very private consultations among organizers to achieve a consensus and pass on a final recommendation to the central leadership. RSS practice also demands unquestioning obedience to a decision after it is made. As we noted in our earlier study of the RSS, these organizing secretaries (referred to as sangathan mantris) form a parallel body that manages the larger organization.[27] Bruce Graham, in his study of the early years of the BJS, argued that the party's electoral success was hindered by an RSS-trained leadership that was reluctant to accept compromises or provide a space in the management of the BJS to people from different backgrounds.[28] The RSS, however, since the 1950s has become progressively more political and inclusive, especially since the death of Golwalkar in 1973. Besides dispatching full-time workers, it now supplies campaign workers to the BJP, lends advice on policy and adjudicates personnel issues. But the RSS has generally remained firm that its pracharaks will not take an active role in party politics while serving as functionaries for the RSS. If they want to take part in politics, they must vacate any RSS position, as did Ram Madhav when he left his RSS position as press spokesman to become a general secretary in the BJP. This policy against dual RSS–BJP political responsibilities was, however, sometimes overlooked in the decade after Independence. Party-building sometimes meant that the new party and the RSS (weakened by the 1948–49 ban) were both understaffed; it was necessary to share the relatively small cadre of trained, full-time office-bearers to advance the dual causes of Hindutva and rebuilding the RSS.[29]

In the ninety-odd years of its history, there have been only a few cases of rebellion that resulted in the formal removal of an RSS officer, sometimes for assuming a political party position, as occurred in Goa. During the leadership of Hedgewar (1925–40), the RSS reduced the chances of dissidence by employing a highly selective process regarding who would be admitted. The RSS demanded two recommendations for every person seeking admission, a requirement dropped after the ban in 1948, as the organization sought to quickly rebuild its membership.[30] In addition, Hedgewar also chose for the position of sanghchalak influential men with a Hindutva reputation from a wide variety of backgrounds (for example, the Congress party, the Arya Samaj, the Hindu Mahasabha and so on) and often with no or little RSS training, both to enhance the respectability of the young RSS and to provide models for the young members.[31] There are examples where Hedgewar encouraged sanghchalaks to contest in district and Assembly elections in the Central Provinces and Berar without dropping their RSS positions, so that the RSS would have a voice to protect itself from restrictions on holding civil service and teaching positions.[32]

Despite efforts to reduce the chances of dissidence, there have been recurrent examples of discontent, some at high levels of the organization—like the Deoras brothers in the early 1950s, who withdrew from RSS activities on policy grounds to protest the group's alleged lack of activism.[33] But only in a few cases have these dissidents formed independent RSS-type units, as happened in Goa. Perhaps the first case of such dissidence occurred in 1929, when Ganesh (alias Anna) Sohni, a close colleague of Hedgewar at the time of the founding of the RSS, left the organization following Hedgewar's rejection of his proposal to establish an *akhara* (a traditional gym) in every shakha.[34] Sohni then went on to establish a Hindu nationalist gym in Nagpur that focused on martial arts.[35] Perhaps the most extensive example of rebellion occurred during the 1938–39 Hindu agitation against the government of the princely state of Hyderabad, whose Muslim ruler had banned the singing of a highly popular national song, 'Vande Mataram', in schools and colleges.[36] The Congress party had made the song, set to music by India's renowned poet Rabindranath Tagore, a national anthem. It had become virtually an anthem of nationalist protest against colonialism. Hindu nationalist organizations like the RSS were especially incensed at the ban as the words in the song were interpreted as referring to Mother India (and the title of the song literally means 'Praise to thee, O Mother') and hence considered insulting both to Hindus and to the demand for an independent India. What triggered the rebellion within the RSS, mainly among swayamsevaks who were college students, was Hedgewar's rejection of the request that the RSS commit itself to participate in this protest movement to which such Hindu nationalist organizations as the Hindu Mahasabha and the Arya Samaj were actively committed.[37] While members could in their individual capacity participate in the satyagraha, many RSS members close to the Hindu Mahasabha, mainly in western Maharashtra, went on to form parallel RSS groups, similar to other independent RSS-like groups that already existed. However, these local breakaway groups typically lacked a leadership cadre capable of sustaining themselves and they all eventually collapsed. In 1943, Nathuram Godse, Narayan Apte and J.D. Jogalekar—young RSS members who left the organization in 1938 after it refused to involve itself in the Hyderabad movement—formed the militant Hindu Rashtra Dal, with branches in western Maharashtra. They were upset that Golwalkar, who took charge of the RSS following Hedgewar's death in 1940, rejected militancy for the sake of organization-building, placing greater emphasis on spirituality than on militant patriotism.[38] Still another case of dissidence occurred a year later in 1944, when RSS members from the Kannada-speaking Lingayat community in a Marathi-speaking area of Bombay Presidency formed their own separate shakhas, charging that the regular RSS was dominated by Maharashtrian Brahmins.[39] Even in Nagpur, the RSS headquarters, a short-lived rebel RSS organization emerged in 1950–51 led by young adult members who felt that the mainstream group, so focused during the post-ban period on institution-rebuilding, provided insufficient opportunities for the membership to do social work.[40]

In several cases, the RSS leadership removed officials who openly took positions embarrassing to the organization. Two of the better-known cases were the removal in 1964 of the Pune district sanghchalak, N.G. Abhyankar, for participating in a welcoming ceremony celebrating the release of those jailed in connection with the 1948 assassination of Gandhi,[41] and the removal of the Pune pracharak V.V. Pendse in 1954 for his repeated and open criticism of the RSS leadership for an alleged lack of activism, a charge also levelled against the RSS by the often-competitive Hindu Mahasabha.[42]

The removal in 1955 of Vasant Rao Oke,[43] the RSS prant pracharak of the crucial Delhi unit (which at that time also included western Uttar Pradesh, Rajasthan and Hindi-speaking Punjab), reflects the often-porous boundaries in the 1950s between the RSS and its political affiliate, the newly formed BJS. During the colonial period and the first parliamentary elections in a free India, the RSS permitted sanghchalaks to contest, though with a few exceptions: in 1952 it did not extend this right to the full-time workers or pracharaks who represented the steel frame of the organization.[44] The question of RSS full-time workers in the new party came to a head with the 1953 death of Mookerjee, the BJS founder. Mauli Chandra Sharma, the new president of the BJS, needed to select a working committee in 1954; his nominees were essentially divided between Hindu nationalist politicians associated with Mookerjee and RSS pracharaks dispatched to the party. Sharma lacked the prestige to shape developments within the party and therefore had to pay closer attention to the wishes of pracharaks in the BJP.[45] Oke, despite his RSS background, tended to back Sharma and the other politicians, proposing that the party had to reach out well beyond its RSS workers to staff positions if it were to become politically competitive. He was the only prant pracharak in the party and, moreover, was not one of those assigned to it by Golwalkar. Oke's pro-politician stance was probably the major reason for RSS opposition to his inclusion on Sharma's proposed working committee. Sharma nonetheless decided to go forward with Oke, who was not forced to relinquish his RSS position.[46] Oke was subsequently dropped from his RSS position in 1955 for engaging in what was a much more direct rebellion against the national RSS leadership: he refused a new position as the *sharirik* shikshan pramukh (head of the RSS physical programme). The programme was headquartered in the south-eastern city of Chennai, far from the political centre in Delhi where Oke had a base of support and could play a role in the country's national politics.[47] Subsequently, he was involved in the June 1956 conclave discussing the formation of a new party, the short-lived National Democratic Front (NDF), composed mainly of those politicians who left the BJS to protest the new direction of the party. At the formation of the NDF later that year, he reportedly accused the RSS of interfering in the affairs of the BJS.[48] While he temporarily went back to the BJS when the NDF collapsed, he never again held a position in the RSS.

This post-Independence aversion to formal political participation by RSS office-bearers has its roots in the 1948–49 ban period, when the Government of India demanded that the RSS adopt a constitution; a draft was sent to the government on 11 April 1949. Among other stipulations, it pledged that the RSS would keep its office-bearers removed from politics.[49] The original RSS constitution[50] states in

Article 4 that, 'The Sangh is aloof from politics and is devoted to social and cultural fields only.' Later in Article 11, it states that 'He [a swayamsevak] who is an office-bearer of a political party, shall not be eligible as a candidate for election or as an appointee to any [RSS] post so long as he is such an office-bearer.' Article 17 stipulates that the state pracharak is appointed from the Centre in consultation with the state sanghchalak. (See Appendix IX for the current RSS constitution.) The formal adherence of the RSS to these constitutional provisions against political activity forms part of the RSS narrative about itself, a narrative echoed by every senior RSS figure we have met. It was considered one tool in the fight against another ban. However, the Goa example points out how narrow the definition of unacceptable political action has become. The Amshekar email to us claimed that the 'RSS is free to oppose or condemn or differ from a decision of any political party (even BJP) if deemed necessary in interest of nation.'[51] Velingkar and the Goa RSS, by this interpretation, therefore did not cross a prohibited line of action by backing (and even organizing) BBSM protests against a BJP government's language policy; nor, even, by protesting the visit of national BJP leaders. The labour affiliate, the BMS for example, has a history of organizing protests/strikes against what it considers anti-labour policies of any government, even a BJP government. No one has been disciplined for adopting such organized confrontational stances. What is prohibited is an RSS officer working within a political party without giving up his RSS position. To allow him to retain the RSS office would have undermined the legitimacy of the organization as a disinterested advocate of Hindutva and threatened its moral pre-eminence within the sangh parivar. Velingkar eventually 'returned' to the mother organization, almost certainly recognizing that his breakaway RSS lacked legitimacy among fellow swayamsevaks. The cautious RSS leadership at the centre and at the state level were careful not to expel him formally from the RSS, though he will almost certainly never again assume a senior position. On 7 November 2017, Velingkar announced the formation of an organization named 'Bharat Mata ki Jay' (Victory to Mother India) to push the issue of language and other Hindu nationalist concerns, but was careful to state that this new organization is 'apolitical', a formulation necessary if he or this new group is to have any future role in the RSS.[52]

The Velingkar rebellion again demonstrates that the sangh parivar resembles Rajni Kothari's post-Independence 'Congress system', characterized by a wide spread of opinion from right, left and centre.[53] We have argued that much of this difference is that the constituents of the 'family' represent different interests. Like the Congress, there is a robust contestation at each level of the 'family' and the RSS's role is to mediate internal differences. Its goal, as attempted in the Velingkar rebellion, is to mediate disputes to reduce the chances of publicizing differences and work out a compromise. But this case is interesting in that the RSS failed to work out a compromise acceptable to the pragmatists (the BJP) and the purists (Velingkar), and between the hardliners (Velingkar) and the moderates (the BJP). The pragmatic moderates ultimately won due to Velingkar's political inexperience and Parrikar's shrewd political instincts, but the worrying factor for the RSS is that the Velingkar rebellion might represent the proverbial canary in the coal mine. It portends the rise of the right flank in the sangh parivar, which might in other places and on other issues seek to harness the base to force the hand of a BJP government—and even force the RSS to take a stand that deviates from its normally cautious style. With more astute leadership, a hard-line ideological message could pose a threat if it appealed effectively to BJP activists on the right and the sangh parivar faithful. This could explain the RSS (and BJP) caution in handling the periodic roars from the right. This problem is analysed in the two previous case studies on conversion and the cow.

FOURTEEN

Bihar Elections, 2015

Stepping into the Breach

In a 25 September 2015 interview with the editors of *Organiser* and *Panchjanya*, two publications sympathetic to the RSS, Bhagwat made a passing remark on the issue of caste reservations. His comment ignited a political firestorm on the eve of the keenly contested October–November 2015 Assembly elections in the populous north Indian state of Bihar. The BJP was keen on winning the Bihar polls as this election was considered by many to be a referendum on the party's popularity sixteen months after coming to power at the Centre.[1] It had done very well in Bihar's 2014 parliamentary elections—winning, with its NDA allies, thirty-two of the forty seats in the lower house. It also wanted to come back to power in the state after the 2013 split of a coalition government in which it was a key constituent. Another victory by Chief Minister Nitish Kumar, formerly an alliance partner who had parted ways with the BJP after it announced that Modi would be its choice for prime minister, would give rise to the possibility of his organizing an opposition alliance against the BJP and Modi in the 2019 parliamentary elections. The state Assembly elections in Bihar are analytically germane, not only because the RSS chief's remark became a part of the election campaign, but also because of the sangh parivar's extensive involvement in the BJP's poll efforts.

The RSS's involvement in politics has gone up incrementally since India's independence. From considering electoral politics as unsavoury and morally corrupting to viewing it as one of the tools to catalyse social change, the RSS's perception of politics has indeed evolved. To be sure, it still believes that significant social change happens from the bottom-up. The RSS's involvement in the activities of its political affiliate predated Modi's ascension to the national stage. Its role typically entails mediation when there is a lack of consensus on internal personnel and policy questions. Our proposition here is that the sangh parivar gets more deeply involved in the BJP's electoral campaigns when the party's organizational infrastructure is weak, like it was in the Bihar BJP as it prepared for the 2015 Assembly elections.

The Indian political class viewed the Bihar elections as an important midterm test of the BJP government's popularity. A few months earlier, the BJP had won just three of the seventy seats in the Delhi Assembly—an outcome that was particularly humiliating as it had won all seven Lok Sabha seats in the city just nine months earlier, in May 2014. Bihar was a much larger and more politically important state. Important because of its complicated caste dynamics, Bihar was considered a bellwether state for the populous Hindi-speaking heartland of the country. These elections were also an important test of the Opposition's political strategy to create an alliance to take on an ascendant BJP. The Opposition parties in Bihar—the Congress, the Rashtriya Janata Dal (RJD) and the Janata Dal (United) (JD[U])—had formed an electoral coalition with this goal in mind. Because the BJP was facing a united Opposition, Amit Shah, the party president, compared the Bihar elections to the British victory in the Battle of Buxar.[2] In that historically significant battle, fought in October 1764, the armies of the Mughal emperor and the nawabs of Bengal and Awadh had joined forces to fight the British East India Company. Despite their numerical superiority—the strength of the combined indigenous forces was four times that of the Company's army—lack of coordination and flawed planning created disorder among the allied armies, leading to the victory of the British. Amit Shah believed that the antagonism between the social bases of the JD(U) and the RJD[3] would make their alliance incompatible. This view was widely shared by political observers, who noted that the *mahagathbandhan* (grand alliance of the Congress, the JD[U] and the RJD) had good arithmetic, but no social chemistry.[4]

Not wanting to take any risks after the Delhi setback, the RSS had resolved to play a role in the BJP's Bihar electoral campaign. Immediately after the Delhi Assembly results were declared, Hosabale, the organization's joint general secretary, caucused with BJP leaders, including the party's Bihar incharge, Bhupendra Yadav, on the election strategy for the state.[5] The RSS's decision may have been prompted by its perception, articulated in *Organiser*, that the Delhi electoral drubbing was caused by 'a lack of unity in the organization and [poor] planning'.[6]

It was in the context of this decision to be closely involved in the BJP's electoral strategy that Bhagwat's comment on reservation acquired political salience. He spoke to *Organiser* on the occasion of the birth centenary of BJP ideologue and RSS pracharak Upadhyaya, arguing for the creation of 'a committee of people genuinely concerned for the interest of the whole nation and committed for social equality, including some representatives from the society, they should decide which categories require reservation and for how long'.[7] The statement was ambiguous—unexceptionable, perhaps. But in the run-up to the keenly contested Bihar state elections, the RSS chief's remark quickly assumed political overtones. Lalu Prasad Yadav, the charismatic RJD head, used Bhagwat's comment to argue that the BJP was trying to 'end reservations'.[8] Nitish Kumar, the chief ministerial candidate and the putative leader of the Opposition alliance, contended that Bhagwat's scepticism of the reservation policy represented the BJP's stand on the issue.[9]

In Bihar, a society that is riven by caste conflict, reservations are a highly emotive issue as they represent government jobs and admittance to public educational institutions to those at the lower end of the Hindu caste hierarchy, who might otherwise not be able to get these benefits. To win the Bihar elections, the BJP, which is perceived in the state as a political party dominated by the upper castes ('*Brahmin-Bania*'), would need the support of a broad social coalition, including from the lower castes that benefited from reservations. The BJP's rise to political prominence in the 1990s was partly owed to its success in mobilizing the upper castes after Prime Minister V.P. Singh announced in 1989 that his government would implement the Mandal Commission Report, thereby extending to the OBCs reservations in educational institutions and public-sector jobs.[10] The party, to stay relevant politically, soon moved to support the expansion of quota benefits. Similarly, in Bihar, fearing the wrath of the numerous and politically powerful SCs and OBCs in the state, the BJP quickly distanced itself from Bhagwat's remark. Ravi Shankar Prasad, then Union telecom minister and a senior BJP leader from Bihar, declared in a hastily arranged press conference that, 'The BJP is not in favour of any reconsideration of reservations being extended to these groups: Scheduled Caste, Scheduled Tribes, and Other Backward Classes.'[11] Even the RSS walked back Bhagwat's remark. Bhaiyyaji Joshi, the RSS general secretary, said that 'whatever was said [by Mohan Bhagwat] was not presented in proper words. Nowhere was it said that there should be a review of the reservation policy. It is compulsory for society.'[12]

Indian political parties tend to have weak organizational structures. Pradeep Chhibber and Sandeep Shastri observe that the Indian National Congress's party organization weakened after Indira Gandhi's ascension to power in the late 1960s. Since then, members of the Nehru–Gandhi family centralized control of the party.[13] While the BJP has never been dominated by an individual or a family, its party organization has also been relatively weak. Only recently, under the leadership of Modi's long-time confidant Amit Shah, has the BJP begun to build an extensive grass-roots party setup. Even so, the strength of the BJP's party organization across India remains variable, and is contingent on the social context of the state.[14] In his seminal study on the subject, focusing on Uttar Pradesh, Paul Brass noted that maintaining a strong party setup in the context of ethnic fractionalization requires large resources as ethnic divisions increase the likelihood of factionalism and splintering.[15] In a competitive political environment, local influencers who act as conduits between the politicians and the public have an incentive to hedge between different party networks in order to negotiate the best rents for themselves.[16] As such, Indian socio-economic conditions lead to weakly organized political parties.

The social milieus of Bihar and Uttar Pradesh are similar—Bihar, in fact, is even more ethnically fragmented than Uttar Pradesh. The BJP has had a limited presence in Bihar. From 2005 to 2014, it remained a junior member in a coalition government with the JD(U). The BJP's support base was drawn primarily from urban upper castes and its presence in the state's vast rural hinterland was skeletal. The urbanization rate and per-capita income—two factors that correlate strongly with support for the BJP—are relatively low in Bihar. It is a rural state—according to the 2011 census, the urbanization rate of Bihar is 11.3 per cent against the national figure of 32 per cent.[17] It is also far poorer compared to the rest of the country. Its per-capita income in 2016–17 was Rs 35,590, a third of India's per-capita income of Rs 1,03,219.[18] Its relative underdevelopment, ethnic fragmentation and the lack of a socially diverse support base resulted in a weak BJP party organization in the state.

The 2015 election in Bihar is a case study of the sangh parivar, especially the RSS, playing a significant role that is traditionally performed by a party organization. The weakness in the BJP's organization in Bihar made the RSS's involvement in its election campaign critical. The RSS was involved in every aspect of the party's campaign, and RSS pracharaks and swayamsevaks were recruited to take part in a wide range of campaign functions: providing advice on candidates and issues, campaigning and mobilizing voters. The sangh parivar's extensive network was used to solicit feedback from the grass roots on issues of importance to local voters. For better mobilization of voters, Amit Shah divided Bihar into four sectors. In the absence of a strong party organization with a deep bench of leaders, two of the four sector heads were RSS pracharaks and one was a swayamsevak with a long history of ties to the parivar.[19] The sector heads were tasked with coordinating voter mobilization efforts and managing the party's campaign in their respective regions. The three sangh activists were chosen primarily for their organizational skills honed during their long tenure in the parivar. Groups of pracharaks and sanghchalaks were each assigned a cluster of Assembly seats to supervise.[20] Their responsibility included assessing the effectiveness of each party candidate's campaign and determining the salience of issues to aid voter outreach.[21] Saudan Singh, a senior RSS pracharak who served as the BJP's general secretary (organization), was entrusted with the responsibility of coordinating the activities of the RSS cadre.[22] Because of Saudan Singh's prominence in the RSS and his extensive organizational experience, he was a key strategist for the BJP's Bihar campaign. His RSS background was an asset because he did not have to rely on the BJP's weak and factionalized party organization in the state to get grass-roots feedback while formulating a poll strategy. In any case, the BJP's skeletal presence in Bihar's rural hinterland and the lack of a socially diverse cadre base had limited the party's ability to gauge the salience of issues in each constituency. Saudan Singh used the RSS network to identify key issues in every seat and relay feedback to candidates on how they could resonate with the voters.

Candidate selection was another vexing issue for the BJP. As Milan Vaishnav notes, a small group of elites—often a single individual—was empowered to make decisions on ticket distribution in Bihar.[23] 'Winnability' was the most important criterion for selection, but BJP party elites had limited means to gauge a candidate's ability to attract public support. The Bihar unit of the party was faction-ridden, which was one of the reasons the BJP did not declare a chief ministerial candidate before the elections.[24] Each faction would have jockeyed to nominate its own supporters as candidates.[25] Under these circumstances, the RSS played a role in BJP's candidate selection. The BJP decided candidates based on three surveys—two conducted by an external agency and one by the RSS.[26] The RSS's massive network and the swayamsevaks' superior local knowledge made their assessment of a candidate's viability more accurate than the often-faulty opinion polls. Moreover, the sangh parivar cadres are relatively insulated from groupthink that is a characteristic of political elites. As such, the parivar is an ideal channel for the BJP elites to receive grass-roots feedback to gauge a candidate's winnability, especially in Bihar where the party is factionalized.

Given the BJP's lack of social diversity among its cadre, the party had to rely on the sangh cadre to campaign among Muslims and Dalits, especially to counter the effects of Bhagwat's remark. The BJP had few Muslim members who could spearhead the party's outreach to the state's largest minority (an estimated 17 per cent of the state's population). The BJP's campaign among the Muslim community in Bihar was outsourced to the RSS's MRM.[27] The BJP relied on RSS swayamsevaks to counteract the effects on Dalits (some 15 per cent of the population) of Bhagwat's statement regarding reservations. Groups of RSS swayamsevaks campaigning for the BJP, carrying photos of Ambedkar, shared food with members of a Dalit household, and told them that the RSS rejected caste discrimination.[28] Consuming food in a Dalit household is symbolically important for it violates the perceived taboo about food purity and thus signifies a flattening of caste hierarchies. Ajay Kumar, an RSS pracharak campaigning in Bihar, noted the Opposition's dependence on OBCs and argued that Dalits would be safer and law and order better implemented with the BJP in power.[29] The swayamsevaks also raised issues of Hindutva and nationalism whose appeal transcends caste and community cleavages. Highlighting the corruption scandals among leading figures in the non-BJP coalition which, opinion polls suggest, has worked in favour of the BJP, put a premium on their perceived probity in public life. Lalu Prasad, the former chief minister of Bihar, for example, was convicted of corruption and sentenced to five years in prison by a court in September 2013.[30] The BJP also made an issue of political dynasties in the Congress and in regional parties.[31] With a few state party exceptions, neither the BJP nor the RSS has politically powerful families running the show. An RSS pracharak has no family ties or personal property, and thus is the ideal foil to the entrenched leadership in many other political parties.[32]

Much like in the 2014 Lok Sabha elections, the RSS cadre played a practical role in the 2015 Bihar state campaign. After their morning shakha, RSS swayamsevaks would go around their locality, usually in small groups, to campaign for BJP candidates.[33] Following Bhagwat's exhortation to the cadre about the apolitical nature of the RSS,[34] the swayamsevaks were careful to focus on issues such as nationalism and Hindutva, rather than on specific candidates. Anil Thakur, an RSS pracharak and the kshetra *sampark* pramukh (regional communications chief) noted that, 'During our baithaks [discussions] and jan sampark [public outreach], we explain Hindutva and our understanding of nationalism. The RSS is the mother organisation, so any support for us translates into support for the BJP.'[35] The RSS's strategy for the BJP was to keep the organization below the radar. As a swayamsevak noted, 'sangh activists may not carry the BJP flag but they have made sure each branch is aware of the importance of this election'.[36] Nonetheless, the swayamsevaks spread the message of Hindutva and nationalism to the voters in Bihar with the expectation that this would translate into votes for the BJP.[37]

The RSS's support is a major asset for the BJP as Indian electoral rules make political campaigns manpower intensive. The Election Commission regulations allow only two weeks of official campaigning, which ends forty-eight hours before the scheduled close of polling.[38] The compressed campaign schedule, compounded by a large population spread over a vast swathe of territory, makes voter outreach dependent on a large contingent of campaign workers with thorough knowledge of their own areas. As we have noted above, the rootedness of swayamsevaks in the local community makes the campaigning more effective; they are invaluable for voter mobilization on voting day. Amrendra Sinha, the Begusarai vibhag sanghchalak—Begusarai is a district in Bihar on the northern banks of the River Ganga—remarked that, 'We meet people to ensure they vote. We want them to turn out in large numbers. We will mobilize people to come out of their homes and vote.'[39]

The entire sangh parivar machinery participated in the election campaign. As we have noted elsewhere, the past decade witnessed a rapid expansion in the membership of the RSS's affiliate organizations, especially the labour union, students' union and service groups. At the time of its formation, the goal of the RSS, in the words of Hedgewar, was to 'organize the Hindu society spread from the Himalayas to the ocean'.[40] As we have discussed earlier, the RSS set up affiliates so it could spread its message into diverse segments of India's associational life. The affiliates enable the RSS to reach out to non-traditional constituencies and do so in a way that buffers it against charges of assuming a political role. At the time of elections, the affiliate organizations utilize their network to reach out to diverse social constituencies, especially to gauge voters' issue preferences.[41]

The RSS has always been concerned that its political involvement will impede what it believes to be the more important mission of bottom-up social transformation. Seeking to counter the perception that the RSS's involvement in the 2014 elections was unprecedented, Bhagwat had said, 'We are not in politics. Our work is not to chant "NaMo, NaMo" [i.e., campaign for Narendra Modi]. We must work towards our own goal.'[42] The RSS in Bihar nonetheless was focused on voter mobilization to ensure that BJP supporters went to cast their votes on election day. As a pracharak noted, its voter-contact programme was an 'invisible way' to garner support for the BJP.[43] Among the ordinary sangh workers, even those who might be wary of electoral politics or think of electoral politics as morally corrupting, the ability to 'unite the Hindu society' is a motivator for participating in voter mobilization for the BJP.

Media reports[44] make it clear that the swayamsevaks' involvement in the BJP election campaign was centrally coordinated. To give greater coherence to the RSS's involvement, senior pracharaks, including several from outside the state, and central leaders like Hosabale and Krishna Gopal, both joint general secretaries, were tasked with strategizing the voter outreach and mobilization efforts. They realized the importance of this election for the larger political success of the BJP at the national level. The 2015 Bihar election campaign demonstrates the nature of BJP–RSS coordination. Amidst reports of the BJP performing below expectations in the first two phases of Bihar's multi-phase election, the party, with inputs from the RSS, made a course correction to focus greater attention on pan-Hindu identity issues. The firestorm that followed Bhagwat's statement on reservations underscored the significance of his remark in the context of the political campaign. Prime Minister Modi himself felt it necessary to counter the charge that the BJP sought to eliminate reservation, declaring that the mahagathbandhan (grand alliance) was conspiring to take away 5 per cent of the quota from existing beneficiaries of reservations and give them to another unspecified community (most likely he meant Muslims).[45] In an election speech, Modi called the Opposition's alleged plan a '*paap ki yojna*' (conspiracy of sin).[46] The issue is politically salient as the Supreme Court has capped the quota at 50 per cent of the total seats in educational institutions or civil service jobs. Giving reservations to a new group would necessarily reduce the quota benefits among existing beneficiaries.

The seeming reorientation in the BJP's electoral strategy—a focus on pan-Hindu identity issues that transcend caste cleavages—was made with inputs from RSS leaders. A day before Modi's speech on 26 October 2015, senior RSS leaders, including Hosabale and Krishna Gopal, the RSS's joint general secretary and its point person for the BJP, met about seventy sangh leaders.[47] It was decided at this meeting to frame the Bihar elections as a '*Hindu swabhimaan ka chunav*' (an election for Hindu pride).[48] The strategy change was implemented to create a unified spectrum of Hindu voters, overcoming caste divisions, and to counter attempts by the Opposition to mobilize voters who did not approve of Bhagwat's comment on reservations. A few days after this meeting, on 29 October 2015, Amit Shah declared in a campaign speech that 'fire crackers will be burst in Pakistan if the BJP is defeated in Bihar'.[49] RSS workers went door to door, communicating to voters that a defeat for the BJP-led NDA in Bihar would be a 'blow to Hindu self-esteem' and compromise their safety.[50] RSS swayamsevaks employed the symbolism of the cow—widely revered as sacred among Hindus in India's Hindi-speaking heartland—as a pan-Hindu motif to transcend caste barriers.[51] RSS affiliates too were involved in transmitting this message to voters. The head of the DJS, a VHP affiliate focused on organizing highly controversial and polarizing religious reconversion campaigns, declared, 'We are telling people that for the first time a *kanya* pujan [a Hindu celebration of the creative power of the goddess] was held during Navratri [Hindu celebration of the goddess Durga] in government buildings this year and that Gita is being read and celebrated everywhere. This is the first time our country is holding its head high in the world. A defeat in Bihar will destroy this self-respect.'[52] The message, as a pracharak remarked, was to underscore to the Hindu voter that only a vote for the BJP 'will keep them safe in the country'.[53]

If the BJP wanted to communicate this message to the Hindu voters of rural Bihar, it could only be done effectively through door-to-door campaigning by people who knew the issues of importance to the residents. With a weak party organization, the BJP had to rely on RSS cadres for communicating this message verbally. Direct person-to-person campaigning is important in a state like Bihar which has a low literacy rate (66 per cent) and limited media penetration. The Boston Consulting Group, for example, estimates that only 9 per cent of Bihar's population is connected to the Internet.[54] On the other hand, there are over 1200 RSS shakhas scattered across the state. Five swayamsevaks from each shakha were given election-campaign duties.[55] Through door-to-door campaigning, RSS swayamsevaks exhorted voters to consider 'Hindu unity' when voting.

The BJP, despite the substantial support from the RSS 'family', suffered the ignominy of an unexpectedly large defeat in the Bihar elections. The Opposition won two-thirds of the seats in the Assembly. The prospect of the BJP's dominance and a concern for political survival had brought the JD(U), RJD and the Congress together to fight the BJP. Political observers predicted that a united Opposition was a blueprint that could be used to combat the BJP both at the state and national levels. Most notably, the Bihar elections underscored the BJP's inability to overcome the caste divisions in Indian society—a problem that was exacerbated by Bhagwat's words. The BJP, and the RSS, were anxious that the results could be a harbinger of future elections, a concern that has prompted the party, with RSS support, to strengthen its organizational base.

Political analysts disagree on the extent to which Bhagwat's remark hurt the BJP. Indian elections are a complex phenomenon. In a competitive polity, it is inaccurate to attribute election outcomes to monocausal factors. The CSDS survey indicated that 37 per cent of voters had not heard of Bhagwat's statement, and 7 per cent were ambivalent about the issue. The remaining 56 per cent were equally divided, and their voting intention for the NDA and the Opposition alliance was about the same.[56] But it is instructive to look at how the Opposition reacted to the RSS chief's statement: it used the remark to mobilize backward caste voters. After the election outcome, Lalu Prasad declared it as a loss specifically for the RSS and appealed to the Opposition parties to unite to 'defeat the nefarious ideology of RSS and BJP'.[57]

Bihar is not the only recent instance of the sangh parivar using its network to complement a weak BJP party organization. The RSS was also instrumental in the BJP's successes in the 2018 state Assembly elections in the north-eastern states of Tripura, Meghalaya and Nagaland. Nowhere was the RSS's support to the BJP's electoral campaign more apparent than in the Tripura Assembly elections. The party previously had a skeletal presence in the state—it had received a mere 1.5 per cent of the votes in the 2013 Assembly elections there. In 2018, the BJP won a majority of the Assembly seats on its own. With these three states, the BJP now controls seven of the eight north-eastern states either on its own or in coalition with local allies.[58] The RSS's expansion in Tripura preceded the political success of the BJP, as occurred elsewhere in the Northeast. Sunil Deodhar, an RSS pracharak from Maharashtra who headed the BJP's Tripura campaign, said that the number of RSS shakhas in the state increased from about fifty or sixty to 250 in just a few years—a significant jump given the recent entry of the RSS into the state.[59] Deodhar, who was assigned to the Northeast as a Meghalaya RSS pracharak, was sent to neighbouring Tripura a year before the election to help organize the campaign there. The prachar pramukh of the RSS in Assam, Shankar Das, dispatched a group of 250 workers to help with the establishment of additional shakhas in Tripura.[60] The expansion of the RSS enabled it to provide the BJP with local campaign workers that the party otherwise would have lacked during the elections. The RSS workers, aided by its affiliates which provide educational and health services to tribals, reached out to the substantial tribal population in the state. Sangh workers reportedly held meetings with 1 lakh households in just two days.[61] The RSS organized a Hindu Sammelan in the capital city, Agartala, on 17 September 2017, which reportedly was attended by 26,000 people from across the state.[62] The expansion of the

RSS shakha network and the sangh parivar's efforts to reach out to different segments of society are factors driving the BJP's political success in a region where it had been weak. To specifically rebut the argument that the RSS and, by extension, the BJP, would seek to alter local customs such as beef consumption, the RSS did not pressure the BJP to adopt a policy on beef. In fact, Himanta Biswa Sarma, a prominent BJP leader in the Northeast, told a reporter, 'India is a country which has diverse cultures. In some regions beef eating is considered taboo but in some parts of the country, mainly in the north-eastern region, this is not considered a taboo. You don't have to impose the culture of UP, Bihar or Maharashtra on the north-eastern region and vice versa. Rather you have to celebrate that diversity.'[63] Deodhar echoed this sentiment and reiterated that the BJP did not seek to impose a ban on cow slaughter in parts of the country where beef consumption is not a cultural taboo, as in the Northeast.[64]

In the overwhelmingly Christian-majority state of Meghalaya, the task of strengthening the BJP party organization was assigned to Ram Lal, Ram Madhav and Ajay Jamwal—RSS pracharaks who have been seconded to the national BJP.[65] Because of a lack of BJP presence in the state, the campaign heavily relied on RSS swayamsevaks and the goodwill earned by the extensive service network that the sangh parivar operates in the state. While the BJP could win only two seats, its alliance partner, the National People's Party, won nineteen of sixty seats and, with support from a few others, could cobble together a majority. A senior RSS official in the state openly stated that Meghalaya's swayamsevaks were working to build support for the larger 'family', which of course includes the BJP, and the BJP has benefited from this assistance. The BJP won a parliamentary by-election in 2015 and seats in three district councils in 2016. The RSS state organizing secretary admitted that the RSS needed to overcome biases of Christians against it to clarify that the sangh parivar did not seek to lure Christians from their faith, did not lobby for changing the traditional culture and accepted people of all faiths. He, moreover, added that 'local traditions have to be respected and preserved. If these disappear no diversity will remain.'[66]

In the case of the May 2018 elections in the south Indian state of Karnataka, the RSS also aided the BJP, especially in the state's coastal areas where it has a high concentration of shakhas. Coastal Karnataka is a region that also has a large Muslim and Christian population. Prabhakar Bhat, the kshetra karyakarni (zonal executive) member of the Karnataka RSS, claimed that 'while we [RSS] have worked for the Lok Sabha elections earlier, we have never involved ourselves in the state elections. But this time around, we are campaigning for the BJP to ensure it wins in Karnataka. BJP win in Karnataka will be a stepping stone for 2019 [parliamentary elections].'[67] Bhat acknowledged that the 2018 elections marked the first time he would campaign for the BJP instead of for individual candidates.[68] The decision by the Congress government to grant minority status to the Lingayat community, which the RSS perceived as an action intended to divide the Hindus, prompted a more active involvement by the RSS in the BJP's election campaign. Twenty-eight senior pracharaks from across India congregated to coordinate the activities of the RSS cadre.[69] Around 50,000 swayamsevaks reportedly campaigned for the BJP.[70] Media reports also suggest that around 3000 VHP and Bajrang Dal workers canvassed votes for BJP candidates in that area, a sure sign of the use of pan-Hindu identity issues in the campaign.[71]

The RSS campaign, according to a senior sangh functionary, helped the BJP's electoral prospects. Ram Madhav, now a senior BJP leader, conceded that 'in certain regions like coastal Karnataka, Parivar has helped us a lot'.[72] In coastal Karnataka, the BJP won seventeen Assembly seats out of twenty-one—an increase from four seats in 2013 and eleven in 2008.[73] The BJP won 51 per cent of the popular vote—more than in other regions of the state.[74] The Congress's apparent strategy to gain Lingayat votes by designating them as a separate religion seems to have failed—the BJP won 61 per cent of the Lingayat vote.[75] Coastal Karnataka is an instance where sangh parivar cadres played the role of party activists and were able to act as force multipliers.

Such close involvement of the RSS in the BJP's electoral activities is a recent phenomenon. While the organization has always been involved in the affairs of its political affiliate, its earlier interventions were largely limited to arbitrating personnel disputes in the BJP, especially in times of a leadership vacuum, and providing volunteers during political campaigns. The RSS leadership also provided inputs to the BJP governments of Vajpayee and Modi on cabinet selection. Kanchan Gupta, a Vajpayee aide who later joined the Prime Minister's Office, recounts an incident which demonstrates the substantial influence of the RSS in the BJP's cabinet choices. The day before the Vajpayee government's swearing-in ceremony in 1998, Sudarshan, the then joint general secretary of the RSS and the organization's liaison to the BJP, strongly opposed the inclusion of Jaswant Singh, who had lost his election, in the cabinet.[76] Jaswant Singh was something of an outsider as he had never been a swayamsevak, but he was later included in the cabinet with the influential portfolios of foreign affairs and finance at the insistence of Vajpayee. The RSS and some of its affiliates have also taken a critical populist stand on some of the BJP's policies, such as opposition to globalization. The RSS intervened to force the resignation of Advani—after he made remarks in Pakistan that controversially extolled Jinnah as secular— from the post of BJP president in 2005. Jinnah was a reviled figure among the sangh parivar faithful as an individual responsible for dismembering Bharat Mata. As we have noted elsewhere in the book, Advani had criticized the RSS's involvement in politics, exclaiming that 'the impression that [had] gained ground [was that] no political or organizational decision can be taken [by the BJP] without the consent of the RSS functionaries'.[77]

However, the RSS has always been ambivalent about its involvement in political activity. The fear of being embroiled in legal charges related to 'saffron terrorism' intensified the RSS's political activities. An authoritative RSS insider noted in an interview[78] that P. Chidambaram, the then Union home minister, directed the chiefs of security and intelligence agencies to remain vigilant against 'the recently uncovered phenomenon of saffron terrorism that has been implicated in many bomb blasts'.[79] He noted that the sangh did not fear a ban like in 1948 or 1975, but was worried about the demoralizing effect of being ensnarled in 'saffron terror' cases.[80] The RSS recognized that damage to its public image would impede efforts to mobilize non-traditional constituencies and the lower castes.

The RSS viewed the charge of 'Hindu terrorism' as a political challenge by the Congress to damage its social standing and erode its support base. The leadership recognized that this had to be countered by a more active involvement in electoral politics, which catalysed another strategic reorientation by the RSS. Only if the BJP captured state power could the RSS insulate itself from what it feared would be restrictions justified by 'saffron terrorism' charges. The shift became obvious at the RSS's annual meeting in the Maharashtrian city of Amravati in June 2013, when it decided to use the cadre network to help the BJP in the forthcoming parliamentary elections. The meeting was acrimonious, with dissenters arguing that electoral politics was morally corrupting and would impede the more important mission of character-building.[81] Notwithstanding the discordant voices, the RSS decided that its mission would be better accomplished under a BJP government. The RSS provided its imprimatur to the then Gujarat chief minister, Modi—who had both a charismatic appeal among the sangh cadre and a record as an efficient administrator—as the BJP's prime ministerial candidate, overruling objections from other BJP leaders and even some senior RSS figures.

The RSS's desire to remain relatively aloof from the day-to-day functioning of its affiliates, including the BJP, has prompted it to advise them to build up their own organizational infrastructure. Heeding the RSS's advice, Amit Shah has focused on attracting new members to the party and training them in the BJP's ideology as well as campaign strategy. While the accuracy of the contention is difficult to ascertain, the BJP now claims to be the largest political party in the world, with a membership of 100 million.[82] Energizing the party cadre enables the BJP to execute its much acclaimed booth-level strategy wherein it deputes *panna* pramukhs[83] to campaign and to ensure that BJP voters turn out on election day. As Prashant Jha notes in his perceptive book on the BJP's creation of an impressive organizational machine, the party has made recruiting activists at the booth level a major administrative objective.[84] If this strategy succeeds, it would reduce the party's dependence on the RSS, but it would also increase the possibility of power struggles that, ironically, would provide the RSS avenues to interfere in the affairs of its political affiliate. Even so, it is likely to be a while before the BJP establishes a booth-level organizational mechanism in every corner of the country. The RSS, therefore, will continue to assist the BJP in many areas, as it did in Bihar in 2015. In addition, the pracharaks, with a moral legitimacy bestowed by their training as well as their organizational experience, will almost certainly continue to play a pre-eminent role in the top echelons of the affiliates.

The RSS's view of politics has changed significantly since the formation of its political affiliate in the early 1950s. At that time, the RSS's attitude was that politics is morally corrupting and inimical to its goal of unifying Hindu society. The RSS's fear of restrictions being imposed on its activities is one of the major reasons for it to provide support to its political affiliate. Even so, the RSS has remained relatively aloof from electoral politics, and its leaders vehemently argue that it is not a political organization. The RSS forbids its senior officials from holding positions in a political party or elected office while they continue to serve as its functionaries. Nonetheless, it has agreed to help the BJP, especially where the party's organizational infrastructure is deficient, as seen during the 2015 Bihar elections, and uses its many affiliates to amplify the BJP's political message. There is no better indication of the RSS's increased influence across the Indian spectrum than the fact that Nitish Kumar, who in 2015 had issued a call for a 'sangh-*mukt* Bharat' (RSS-free India), dumped his anti-BJP poll partner and rekindled his alliance with the BJP in 2017. At the same time, he dropped his public criticism of the RSS. The growth of the RSS as well as the depth and breadth of the policy activism of the affiliates will, in our view, only increase the politicization of the sangh. But, more importantly, the RSS has internalized the perception that the BJP capturing political power is a necessary, but not sufficient, condition to achieve the desired bottom-up strategy for social change.

CONCLUSION

The RSS

Reshaping a Role for Itself in a Rapidly Changing India

The essence of Hindutva is loyalty to the nation. But the nation is a construct that incorporates a mix of several elements (for example, land, language, religion, cultural traditions, historical memories) and a sense of nation—and loyalty to it—grows out of the interaction of these variables over time.[1] The rationale for the formation of the RSS in 1925 was to train a cadre of men who would, motivated by that training (i.e., character-building), use these diverse cultural elements to forge a loyalty to a unified Indian state and thus advance the cause of independence. This identity could not be based primarily on religion, as Hinduism contains innumerable varieties and it possesses no structural mechanism to bring those elements together. The RSS for its part has never claimed to speak for Hinduism as a religion. Historical circumstances such as the freedom struggle, the violent partition of the country and the adoption of democracy were developments that helped shape the notion of a national Indian identity, though there were many, even after the secession of a large swathe of British India's Muslim population, who had a weak or non-existent sense of being Indian. Recognizing the cultural diversity of India, the RSS relied initially on Savarkar's notions of territorial nationalism in his treatise on the subject in his book *Hindutva*[2] and combined that with his views on the 'great' cultural tradition of Brahmanical Hinduism to define who a Hindu was. He excluded those whose

237

religions had a foreign origin (Parsis, Christians, Jews and Muslims) but included many groups outside the Brahmanical tradition that are rooted in India (Jains, Sikhs and Buddhists). The Indian government has also subscribed to a similar view, as witnessed by the definition of who is (and who is not) a Hindu in the Hindu Code Bills adopted in 1955–56. These bills, as pointed out by Kumkum Sangari, contributed significantly to the homogenizing of Hinduism.[3] Similarly, the national government followed this definition when it limited quota benefits to disadvantaged groups who fit into the characterization of who a Hindu is.

Critics of the RSS world view ask whether India in the twenty-first century requires a vision of Hindu unity based on culture to ensure a robust society that guarantees the territorial integrity of one of the world's most socially diverse populations. Why not, its critics ask, rather focus on an Indian unity grounded in civic values such as democracy, social equality and freedom of religious expression as a better way of guaranteeing territorial integrity.[4] The RSS's view of the critical importance of culture is more nuanced than it was when our first book on the RSS was published. As we note in the chapter on Hindutva (Chapter Five) here, its senior leadership has broadened the definition of Hindu to include most Christians and Muslims (and others as well) as long as they subscribe to what Upadhyaya in *Integral Humanism* described as the 'national soul', that unique element that gives life to a people's culture and institutions and provides the boundaries of what it is to be a member of the Hindu nation.[5] The term is a bit ambiguous and needs to be redefined depending on changing social circumstances—and the RSS considers itself well-situated to speak on this issue. The message that will likely win out at the popular level will depend, as we note in Chapter Five, on which message is better suited to meeting the demands of the Indian population. For the RSS, that may depend on whether the sangh parivar can respond better than its competition to cues (cultural, economic and political) that may have little to do with its larger ideological formulation, though the notion of a uniquely Hindu 'national soul' is the guiding cultural principle of the elites of the sangh parivar.

What has led to the greater RSS sensitivity to the diversity of India over the past three decades? The proliferation of RSS affiliates penetrating all parts of society and the political successes of the BJP all over the country have forced the RSS leadership to come to terms with the frequently conflicting policy and cultural interests in the country and the need to address these differences, often in the role of mediator between conflicting interests of its affiliates. Along with this has come an unprecedented interest in the political process while trying to stay above it. The shift of senior RSS leaders in the 1990s from Nagpur to Delhi for much of the year reflects the greater importance of politics and the tentative acceptance of the validity of the political vocation within the RSS.[6] The construction of state-of-the-art multistoreyed RSS facilities in the capital suggests that this shift is permanent. The RSS clearly wants the BJP to remain in power and is therefore certain to provide advice and warnings on how to satisfy the hopes and expectations of the larger public whose views on key national issues it is constantly monitoring. The RSS and the BJP have an implicit understanding that the party makes public policy and the RSS mediates disputes within the 'RSS family'. Part of its mediatory role is to balance the interests of the various affiliates to stabilize the functioning of the larger 'family'. Its goal of social harmony, the RSS's most important societal objective, is becoming increasingly difficult to achieve as a consequence of the success of Indian democracy which has politicized all parts of this diverse country as well as the increased wealth and population mobility which is changing traditional cultural perspectives.

The RSS's mediatory role has grown as a consequence of the BJP's political success. The RSS itself played an important role in bringing about Modi's ascent to power. Following a 2009 RSS decision to involve itself fully in the 2014 parliamentary elections,[7] its cadre were canvassed in 2013[8] on their views regarding Modi. The results were overwhelmingly in Modi's favour, both to lead the BJP campaign and to become prime minister if the BJP got a parliamentary majority in the 2014 elections. Modi, who was facing harsh criticism worldwide after the 2002 Gujarat riots, even by elements within his own party, was viewed by the cadre as the

victim of an unfair assault on Hindutva.[9] The BJP performed better
than what it—or the RSS—had expected, winning 282 of 543 seats
(with an additional fifty-four seats won by its National Democratic
Alliance partners), the first time any party had a parliamentary
majority on its own since 1984. A large part of that success can
be attributed to the help extended to the BJP by tens of thousands
of swayamsevaks involved in tasks ranging from distributing
campaign material to helping organize party meetings, and its IT
specialists (both from India and abroad) preparing sophisticated
electoral studies. Never before had the RSS membership worked so
hard—and so enthusiastically—on behalf of its political affiliate.[10]
And the results were deeply satisfying to it. Modi, the prime
minister, was an RSS pracharak; the Indian vice-president is an
RSS member, while the President is an RSS sympathizer. The BJP
is the largest party in the indirectly elected upper house and, due
to the party's strong showing in post-parliamentary state Assembly
elections, it will likely become a majority in 2018 in the Rajya
Sabha, the upper house of Parliament. Some two-thirds of the
population in mid-2017 lived in states where the BJP ruled either
alone or with alliance partners. The party has made major gains in
areas of the country where it had been weak (the Northeast and the
south). There are signs, however, that while the prime minister's
popularity exceeds that of any of his rivals, support for the BJP
might be flagging somewhat. In 2017, for instance, the BJP won
Gujarat, the prime minister's home state, by a narrower margin
than had been expected. In the same year, the BJP also lost two
Lok Sabha by-elections in Rajasthan, where it had won all twenty-
five constituencies in 2014. The BJP, in addition, in 2018, lost
three Lok Sabha by-elections in Uttar Pradesh, where it had won
an unprecedented seventy-two out of the eighty constituencies in
2014. Confirming the trend is a survey by CSDS which shows a
loss of voter support for the BJP in large parts of northern and
western India.[11] The CSDS polls suggest that the BJP's all-India
vote share had declined from 39 per cent in May 2017 to 32 per
cent in May 2018. Minorities, such as Christians and Muslims,
are reportedly opposed to the BJP government, and CSDS surveys

show that Dalit support for the BJP has declined from 33 per cent in May 2017 to 22 per cent in May 2018.

The signs in mid-2018 nonetheless point to the BJP emerging as the single largest party in the 2019 parliamentary elections—with the RSS continuing to support the BJP's efforts to remain in power, despite some grumbling around the edges.[12] According to the prestigious CSDS poll, Modi, four years into his tenure, remains the most favoured choice to be the next prime minister.[13] To be sure, while a BJP victory remains a likely outcome, recent electoral losses should make one circumspect about the BJP's prospects in 2019. As one astute observer of contemporary politics put it, after the Gujarat and Rajasthan poll results, 'Indian politics has opened up.'[14]

The Opposition in 2018, meanwhile, shows signs of coalescing against the BJP.[15] There are several unresolved problems that present long-term political problems for Prime Minister Modi and the BJP, perhaps the most serious being a set of economic challenges, such as the inability to create the necessary number of jobs to employ the hundreds of thousands entering the job market each month, agrarian distress, flagging exports and a lower than expected investment level. These issues (as of this writing) seem to be weighing on the favourability rating of the BJP. While the prime minister personally remains popular and the RSS's support of him continues to be enthusiastic, the party's election performance in 2017 and 2018 nonetheless threw a scare into party ranks.[16] The RSS sarsanghchalak, Bhagwat, in his annual Vijayadashami speech on 30 September 2017, viewed as an occasion to voice major concerns of the RSS, issued an implicit warning to the Modi government that its policies are not creating the promised jobs and suggested a more proactive RSS advisory role on government policies. Bhagwat's message was even more explicit in his 16 April 2018 speech to the business community in Mumbai. This more assertive stance seems partly intended to carry out the RSS's mediatory role as several of the affiliates, like the BMS and SJM, claim that the government's two signature policy moves (demonetization aimed at curbing corruption and the GST designed to integrate the economy) are hampering economic growth and thus harming vulnerable sections of the population whose interests they claim to represent. In his Vijayadashami speech, Bhagwat reminded the government that, 'Employment, that is, work for every hand and enough remuneration for sustainable livelihood is a major consideration for us.'[17] And in the same speech he leaves no room for doubt that he is concerned with particular groups that he identifies as the source of growth and social stability: 'the small, medium and handicrafts industry, retail or small self-employed businesses, cooperative sector and agro and agro-allied sector'.[18] These groups represent a large part of the RSS's support base. The speech also reflects a fundamental dilemma within the RSS: wanting to engage with politicians and bureaucrats to influence policy, while maintaining its traditional stand to keep a distance from politics in order to evaluate the actions of politicians more objectively in the public interest.[19] This distance is also justified in order to keep the RSS morally above the infighting, ambitions and ego that are said to characterize those involved in the political arena.

The BJP's growth over the last few years is altering the social composition of its support base as the party expands from its former upper-caste core to lower ranks in the traditional Hindu caste hierarchy, and draws increasing support from rural India. At the same time, the RSS is also changing as it too has been on a rapid growth trajectory since the 1990s, with a similar impact on its social base of support. If this process continues, as we think it will, the sangh parivar faces a situation that raises several key questions, the first being how it will handle the tensions between pervasive Hindu caste identities and the non-caste orientation of Hindutva. A related issue is how it will adjust itself to identities outside the traditional Hindu caste hierarchy. Its leaders have long recognized that the traditional caste hierarchy is a challenge to the desired goal of Hindutva, but they are less certain about how to handle regional and class identities among Hindus which pose questions not only of culture, but also of state-Centre relations. Even more problematic is how it will handle Indian minority groups such as Christians (2.3 per cent) and Muslims

(14.20 per cent) who were the only major groups to provide more votes to the Congress than to the BJP in the 2014 parliamentary elections, and who remain deeply suspicious of both the BJP and the RSS—and a reciprocal questioning if these minority religious populations will be loyal citizens. Yet another social issue that the RSS is beginning to address is how to reconcile the interests of the rapidly growing urban middle class (for whom development that carries with it jobs and a better lifestyle is a high priority) with those of the poor farmers in the villages (who demand infrastructure like healthcare, water, connectivity to markets and skill-based education). These conversations will shape the ongoing debate on how to make its educational system more relevant to the needs of students. RSS writers are against analysing these divisions on a class basis, but their increasing use of the terms 'India' (urban Western-educated India) vs 'Bharat' (rural India that is more traditional) suggests a growing recognition of class differences.

These issues also raise the question of what kind of nationalism the RSS will propagate as it continues to expand. Especially since the leadership of Madhukar Deoras, the RSS has increasingly favoured a cultural nationalist view that now includes Muslims and Christians. That view was clearly expressed by Bhagwat in his consequential 2017 Vijayadashami speech when he stated that, 'Our existence is based on Sanskriti [culture] and people which is unique and entirely different from the union-state concept rooted in power.' Further, he argues in the address that, 'Our Sanskriti . . . is our collective bonding spirit.'[20] Bhagwat has often reiterated that all Indians are culturally Hindu, which is likely to remain the RSS's stand on nationalism.[21]

The third question is about how the RSS will modify its 'character-building' agenda that has been at the core of its training efforts from the time of its founding in order to make itself more relevant in the twenty-first century. The question also involves how it will respond to the growing intra-parivar differences on public policy issues that reflect the increasing social complexity of the parivar. These differences over the ban of cow slaughter, the Ram Temple, participating in a coalition government in Kashmir, and religious conversion (ghar wapsi) and globalization are a reflection of disagreements over the terminology of Hindu nationalism. Will the organization's traditional mediation techniques work or will it require fresh approaches and institutional changes to handle the new and growing social nuances within the RSS itself? The government's role in regulating the economy and Indian foreign policy are among the issues on which the constituent groups of the parivar will disagree. Perhaps the most important point to consider is whether the RSS will be able to keep the dozens of affiliates, representing varied interests and often with very different policy perspectives, operating within the 'family'. Will the glue provided by a corps of similarly trained pracharaks who still dominate the top organizational ranks of the RSS and its affiliates continue to work even as many of the affiliates rely increasingly on experts knowledgeable in the technical details of their respective organizations? Will the change in the role of the pracharaks in the affiliates affect the RSS leadership's ability to mediate inter- and intra-parivar differences?

The most significant players in shaping the responses to these questions, at least over the next several years, will be Prime Minister Modi and RSS chief Bhagwat. They are both relatively young (both born in 1950) and healthy, with enormous energy. Neither has a viable competitor within their respective organizations. They have a long record of getting along with each other, in part because each understands the key role of the other in the sangh parivar. The prime minister, on behalf of the BJP, sets public policy and the RSS sarsanghchalak supervises the mediation of differences among the affiliates, a role that focuses on the political process since public policy has a direct impact on the functioning of many of the affiliates. The RSS is also entrusted with training the corps of men (the pracharaks) who will occupy the most senior administrative positions in the sangh parivar.

So the fourth question is how the RSS balances its goal of 'uniting Hindu society' through its tested agenda of 'character-building' with a growing involvement in politics that requires ideological compromises and a tolerance of behaviour it might otherwise consider unethical (for example, promises of contracts in return for campaign donations or acceptance of tainted or corrupt mass-based winnable leaders). How will it balance the demands of those who want to implement an ideological agenda with those who would prefer to make compromises, such as by keeping controversial issues on the back-burner, in order to maintain political power? In short, how will it meet the challenges of democracy?

On the issue of traditional Hindu caste hierarchy versus Hindutva, the RSS has faced the dilemma right from its inception of attracting backing for its nationalist programme from its original support base of high-caste Hindus while advocating a doctrine of social unity that undermines caste hierarchy and those located on its top rung. Up to Independence, it could live with this dilemma by focusing on a 'character-building' training programme that used many culturally Sanskritic elements of traditional high-caste Hinduism that appealed to its then largely upper-caste base, but with the goal of benefiting all Indians. With the introduction of democracy at the time of Independence, this papering over of the conceptual dichotomy would no longer work as the presumption of religious and social pre-eminence of the upper castes is bad politics for the large majority of voters who are from the lower castes and poor, and who would be increasingly politicized in India's robust democratic system. Passivity in mobilizing the lower castes would also stand in the way of the Hindutva goal of Hindu social unity. In fact, as many close observers of the RSS have noted, Hindutva is only marginally interested in the forms of worship and almost not at all in such metaphysical concerns as the religious justification of the caste hierarchy; it is interested in the strength and unity of Hindus. Hindutva, as Arun Swamy has noted, may have traitors, but not apostates.[22]

Therefore, the RSS began to work towards a programme that would both empower the lower castes and bring them closer to the parivar. As sarsanghchalak, Deoras, in the 1970s and 1980s, sought to integrate low-caste Hindus by advocating the removal of 'untouchability' and caste restrictions in temples and other holy places as well as promoting a set of service projects that benefited primarily those at the lower end of the Hindu caste hierarchy. He supported the formation of the Samajik Samrasta Manch (a group aiming to arrange the interaction of low-caste Hindus, Dalits and Vanvasis [tribals] with high-caste Hindus), backed the expansion of the ABVKA (an affiliate that works to enhance the social and economic status of tribals) and encouraged the setting up of the Seva Bharati (confederation of social service groups focused on working among poor and low-caste Hindus), which got the RSS directly involved in social services. The building of a Ram Temple at Ayodhya and providing security for the Amarnath yatra comprise a pan-Hindu cause to mobilize support across the caste spectrum and the RSS. In his twelve years at the helm of the Gujarat government, Modi, as chief minister, used investment and economic development as key tools to make the state a laboratory to replace the traditional hierarchical Hindu caste order with a reformist Hindutva that included economic investment. He relegated two large affiliates, the BKS and the VHP, to the sidelines in Gujarat, partly due to their criticism of his support for foreign investment as part of a larger economic development agenda,[23] a policy he believed was important politically because it played well electorally. In response, some state-level VHP leaders even campaigned against Modi in the Gujarat state elections. The VHP was especially incensed by the government of Gujarat's removal of temples to make way for infrastructure projects. Modi's inclusion of economic development as virtually a part of Hindutva, as he understands it, was a policy that appealed to the aspirations of young Indians from across the caste spectrum. It is a policy that seeks, with some success, to remove the lower-caste suspicions of the BJP as a party that backed the hierarchical social structure. Modi, himself a low-caste Hindu, showed that there was space in the BJP for Hindus from the lower rungs. The strategy seems to be working; according to one study, the BJP in 2014 won 24 per cent of the popular Dalit vote (vs 18.5 per cent for the Congress) and 37.5 per cent of the tribal vote (vs 28.3 per cent for the Congress).[24] It is instructive that the BJP calculated that it would be politically prudent in 2017 to choose a presidential candidate who is a Dalit—and an RSS sympathizer. The journalist Varghese K. George reports that as the prime ministerial candidate in the 2014 campaign, Modi appealed to a pan-Hindu audience by stating that, 'The next decade will belong to the Dalits and the backwards' while highlighting his own lower-caste origins.[25] Modi's frequent visiting of Hindu, Sikh and Buddhist places of worship both in India and abroad resembles the civic religion practised by the Lutheran leadership in the Scandinavian states rather than an expression of faith in the divine. In his analysis of the interaction of Hinduism and Hindutva, Ashis Nandy in the early 1990s wrote perceptively that, 'Hinduism and Hindutva now stand face to face, not yet ready to confront each other, but aware that the confrontation will have to come some day.'[26]

Advocacy of a comprehensive Hindu identity provides the RSS ideological justification for claiming that the myriad social groups loosely categorized as Hindu share more in common with each other culturally than with non-Hindus and non-Indians. The dilemma, however, is that the pan-Hindu tradition initially took on a highly Sanskritic cultural shape that was the preserve of the Brahmins at the top of the Hindu caste hierarchy and it was thus prone to be looked at suspiciously by both regional political leaders and low-caste Hindus. The leadership of the RSS for most of its existence drew largely from the Brahmin elites but, since the late 1980s, a growing number has been recruited from the lower Hindu castes, an indication of the expanding social support pool of the RSS.

The logic of the RSS's call for sangathan or unity demanded that it recruit members from the lower castes, including Dalits, and treat them as equals within the organization, practices that placed the RSS outside Hindu orthodoxy.[27] The decision soon after Independence to support a political party and other affiliates representing the interests of labour, students and farmers reinforced its policy of recruiting from across the Hindu spectrum (and indeed across the entire religious spectrum since there are no rules limiting membership to Hindus, in sharp distinction to the Hindu Mahasabha whose doors were open only to Hindus). Golwalkar, the RSS sarsanghchalak at the time of Independence, also advised the founder of the BJS to avoid a name that would give the party a sectarian orientation, and favoured the more inclusive Bharatiya in its name.[28] Thus, as Donald Smith has pointed out in his discussion of the RSS, the BJS adopted an inclusive view of nationhood covering all groups loyal to India that was incompatible with a Hindu *rashtra* (nation).[29] To back up his point, Smith quotes the 1960 party presidential speech of Pitamber Das in which he stated, 'A change of religion surely does not mean a change of our ancestors or a change of nationality.'[30] Since the time of Deoras, the third head of the organization, RSS leaders have used the term Hindu to cover all Indians, including Christians, Muslims and other religious minorities.[31] The one affiliate that has an exclusively Hindu religious base is the VHP, a group that works with the Hindu religious establishment on behalf of exclusively Hindu interests. This sectarian perspective has frequently put it at odds with the BJP that seeks the votes of all Indians, and tensions emerge on such issues as when to build the Ram Temple at Ayodhya, whether to provide financial support to Roman Catholic schools in Goa that use English as the language of instruction, whether to delay any action to abolish Article 370 of the Constitution (providing autonomy to Muslim-majority Kashmir), and how to handle the cow protection issue.

India is a federal system and the practice of democracy since Independence has strengthened regional identities as well as loyalty to the idea of India. In the face of secessionist movements in a few places, the central government has worked to secure territorial integrity and the RSS has always supported the objective of one state. In the language debates of the 1950s and 1960s, the ABPS called for all indigenous languages to be accorded equal status and the RSS has consistently called for public education in the regional mother tongue. Against the wishes of the Hindi-speaking population in Punjab, the RSS (and eventually the BJS) abandoned the idea that Punjab was a bilingual state of Hindus (Hindi-speaking) and Sikhs (Punjabi-speaking) and accepted the partition of the state into two: one (Punjab) with a substantial Sikh majority and the other (Haryana) with a Hindu majority.[32] This willingness to compromise sometimes went against the wishes of its natural ethnic support base, as in Punjab with urban Hindus who speak Hindi, but its goal of national unity has usually triumphed, as in this case, over narrow regional interests. On the issue of regional identities, leaders of the sangh parivar are virtually unanimous in stating that there is no inherent conflict between regional and national identities as long as secession is not part of any local political agenda. The BJS supported the formation of linguistic states in the 1950s and later the partition of Punjab on a linguistic basis.[33] The BJP has had no problems forming electoral alliances at both the Centre and in the states with regional parties, though there was some grumbling within the sangh parivar over the BJP's alliance with a party in Kashmir, the PDP, that draws its support almost exclusively from the state's Muslim majority. The RSS, despite some misgivings, has tended to follow a pattern of acquiescing to the party's electoral interests.

The RSS has established a pattern of accommodating regional religious and cultural traditions by claiming them as elements of the larger Bharatiya culture. In line with this effort, Modi, when chief minister of Gujarat, promoted distinctly regional festivals (Uttarayan and Navratri) as an integral part of the larger Hindu culture,[34] similar to what the RSS and its affiliates have done with regard to indigenous cultural practices in the Northeast. One research project reports that many RSS schools link the heroes of low-caste groups to the broader story of Hindu society. One example is that folk plays about the god-king Ram in Uttar Pradesh place low-caste actors at the forefront to build support across the caste spectrum for an integrated Hindu nation.[35] On state–Centre relations, Modi as chief minister had pushed Gujarat's economic interests, sometimes in opposition to the Centre. On the controversial Narmada River project aimed at providing additional irrigation and power to several states including Gujarat, for example, he portrayed himself as the protector of Gujarati interests. He also saw no contradiction between loyalty to regional identity and to the idea of India. During his long tenure as chief minister, he advocated a pride in Gujarati culture and identity—as well as loyalty to India. To demonstrate the importance of the state in the federal relationship, he employed the term 'cooperative federalism' during the campaign and created the National Institution for Transforming India (NITI) Aayog to give this notion an institutional framework once he assumed office.[36]

For the sangh parivar, more problematic than regional identity has been the accommodation of Muslims and Christians. The RSS's nation-building effort has been almost exclusively focused on promoting a sense of unity among Hindus. Regarding Muslims and Christians, there are two contradictory views within the RSS. One is that these non-Hindu groups are in fact ethnically Indian as the vast majority of them are converts and therefore to be won over. The opposing view is that they are the 'other' whose fundamentalist outlook has undermined the Indian state. On the issue of the 'other', the concern is that these groups will push for creating separate states. Muslim support for the creation of Pakistan in 1947 and subsequent calls for the secession of Muslim-majority Kashmir as well as efforts towards secessionist activities in Christian-majority states in the Northeast are seen as indications of the danger. There is a range of views even within the RSS. Golwalkar, in the major compilation of what he has said and written about Hindu nationalism, has chapters identifying Muslims and Christians as internal threats to national unity.[37] The pan-Hindu effort in addition puts Muslims and Christians outside the national narrative and, in fact, can take on an anti-Muslim character as demonstrated in the Ram Janmabhoomi marches in the 1980s and early 1990s that culminated in the destruction of the disputed Babri Masjid in 1992. Hindu nationalist organizations have portrayed the slaughter of cows, a venerated symbol within Hindu nationalism, as a marker that divides Hindus from non-Hindus, and this has informed attacks on Muslims suspected of either beef consumption or transporting cows to the market.

On the other hand, there is a growing effort within the sangh parivar to bring Muslims into a larger Indian cultural milieu, motivated partly by the fact that Muslims and Christians are considered ethnically similar to other Indians and partly by the political need of the BJP to win their support. The RSS's affiliate organizations, especially the labour and farmers' unions, have long worked with Indian minorities.[38] Hence the alliance with the PDP in Kashmir whose support base is Muslim and the decision in Goa to continue support for Roman Catholic schools to avoid antagonizing the large Roman Catholic population. To a large extent, this more moderate approach to non-Hindus is driven, as Ashutosh Varshney has pointed out, by electoral considerations.[39] In a democratic political system of many parties competing in first-past-the-post constituencies, Muslims with some 14 per cent of the national population constitute 20 per cent or more of the electorate in seventy to eighty of India's 543 elected parliamentary constituencies. Yet the BJP still has some distance to go in accommodating Muslims.

While there were coded Hindutva messages in the 2014 parliamentary campaign, the focus in those elections was on economic development and creating jobs. The party's campaign manifesto for those elections was largely lacking in Hindu nationalist themes while being explicit on enhancing the quality of life for Muslims. Nonetheless, this more moderate face at the top is sometimes ignored in the lower ranks of both the RSS and the BJP. The RSS leadership has repeatedly censured those engaged in violence against people suspected of consuming beef, the illegal transportation of cows, 'love jihad' and conversion as anti-socials who should be subject to legal action. But such admonition, often late in coming, has not substantially reduced the level of violence so far. Varshney in another place argues that Hindu–Muslim violence is relatively weak where there exists 'bridging ties' between the two communities in business, politics, education and so on.[40] Some of our interlocutors, basically agreeing with this formulation regarding the notion of 'bridging ties', used this theory to justify efforts to establish links with Muslims through the occupation-based affiliates like the BMS or direct-contact groups such as the MRM. The RSS, since the time of Deoras, has accepted non-Hindus at its daily shakhas and a few Muslims have risen through the three-tier training system to become pracharaks. Yet, the results so far are thin. This relative lack of success brings to mind the question of the RSS's commitment to secularism or at least as it is practised in India. Secularism is not, as in the US or France, considered as requiring a wall of separation between church and state, but the equal treatment of all religions. In spite of RSS opposition to public financial support to minority institutions, BJP state governments continue to provide monetary aid to Christian schools and Modi's national government extends financial support to Muslim educational institutions. The RSS looks at India's multiple indigenous religious traditions as part of the country's culture, but is wary of doing so for Christianity or Islam. This view has had an impact, for example, on the subject matter of history and social-science school texts recommended by the HRD ministry. Hindutva hardliners, in addition, demand that non-Hindus conform to cultural norms broadly defined as Hindu on such matters as their diet (for example, the consumption of beef). The recent controversy over the provenance of the Taj Mahal also raised questions on whether the BJP and the RSS believe in the indigenous roots of Indian Muslims. How the BJP government responds to outbursts of cultural intolerance will affect stability at home and the government's standing abroad. As long as economic growth remains a priority, the BJP government will probably try to marginalize the Hindutva hardliners in the sangh parivar, even if it does so cautiously and sometimes slowly. The BJP caution is prompted by the fine line it walks to satisfy four important groups: its economically aspirational supporters, its Hindu religious backers, the Hindu nationalists advocating a strong and unified India, and groups that prioritize their caste and regional identities. The RSS walks an equally fine line in reconciling the interests of its many constituents in the sangh parivar. It has sought to retain its moral standing among them by not interfering in their functioning and by staying aloof from specific policy discussions and balancing the differing interests of its constituents, such as the VHP and the BJP. As long as good governance and economic growth are key policy drivers of the BJP, the RSS is likely to use its moral standing within the sangh parivar to tone down the hard edges of the VHP without entirely abandoning key elements of the traditional Hindutva agenda, such as building the Ram Temple at Ayodhya.

On our third question of how the RSS is responding to a much expanded and changing membership, the leadership is conscious of the need to make the organization relevant in the twenty-first century, which includes addressing major social and economic challenges facing the country. This discussion must start with an explanation of the continuing importance of the traditional training system of the RSS, referred to as 'character-building', that takes place in the local shakhas (as well as in the training camps to prepare the top leadership ranks of the RSS and its affiliates, the pracharaks). Most shakha participants are in the grade-school or high-school age range. Many senior RSS leaders have told us that key to this system is a committed *mukhya shikshak* (shakha leader) whose actions are a model that determines whether the young boys and men will continue participating in the shakha. Mukhya shikshaks are required to complete at least the first-year camps. At the administrative apex of all the affiliates are the RSS-trained full-time workers, the pracharaks, who attain their position after training at all three levels, the most significant being the third year that takes place in Nagpur. This training system produces sufficient numbers of young men to fill the various leadership positions of the RSS, the most significant being those who finish the third year and agree to abandon family life to adopt an austere lifestyle and devote themselves to the RSS as full-time workers. The 2017 RSS general secretary's report notes that in the previous year some 17,500 participated in first-year camp; some 4130 in the second and 973 in the third. There were about 6000 pracharaks scattered through the sangh parivar in mid-2017.[41] (See Appendix I for statistics on training camp attendance from 1994 to 2015.) With the rapid expansion of the affiliates has also come a growing demand for staff, perhaps most acute in the BJP. While most of the groups have started their own training system, the top administrative positions in all of them are likely to remain full-time RSS pracharaks, which is a significant factor in keeping the various parts of the parivar together, as we demonstrated in our study of the language rebellion in Goa. The pracharak has a standing that those from the outside do not possess, a position somewhat analogous to the officers in the Indian and American foreign service who come through the traditional examination route. The pracharaks continue to interact with each other and collectively consider themselves members of a brotherhood with a common Hindutva mission, even though they may differ on policy perspectives.

One of the most significant innovations in the RSS has been a much greater willingness to have its leaders speak at public forums, to interact with the media and to use RSS-backed think tanks (perhaps the most consequential of these is the India Foundation, located in the national capital) to address issues of importance to the organization. Earlier, the RSS leadership had calculated that its activities were sufficient testimony to the good work it was doing. The real test of success was its ability to train young men who would, on the basis of their 'character-building' experience, take a leading role in nation-building. While there is still substantial support for this view now, the RSS core leadership has moved closer to the proposition that it is one of many interest groups in the country and thus needs to build public support. While quiet mediation out of the public glare is still perceived as the best way to produce a consensus, senior RSS figures have used the media to convey its standing on controversial issues as well as to balance the interests of affiliated groups, as it has done rather frequently where there are economic disagreements. A prominent example is Bhagwat's implicit criticism of the Modi government's economic policies in his 2017 Vijayadashami speech where he chastises the government for policies that do not address basic problems of the common man, the small-scale entrepreneur and the farmer.[42] He advises the NITI Aayog to 'come out of the same old economic "isms", and . . . integrate the most up-to-date economic experiences with the ground reality of our nation'.[43] These criticisms put Bhagwat and the RSS implicitly on the side of the BMS, the BKS and the SJM, against the government on controversial economic policies. Bhagwat's speech also calls on 'necessary Constitutional amendments' to completely assimilate Jammu and Kashmir, which puts him on the side of the VHP. Given the importance of this speech, it is likely that the concerns he raised had already been reviewed at the intra-sangh level. The GST Council, set up to formulate policy recommendations under the controversial GST bill, made several far-reaching decisions in late 2017 to ease tax compliance for taxpayers, provide faster refunds for exporters, ease the process of tax filing and slash the tax rate under GST for twenty-seven items including such significant areas as man-made yarn, stationery, diesel-engine parts, food items and printing.[44]

The RSS dilemma is that it bases its ideology on supreme loyalty to the state while it is at the same time wary of the state's ability to bring about the necessary changes to create a truly Indian community that sharply reduces social and economic inequality and is faithful to the country's cultural inheritance. Can it convince its partners to accept social and economic equality and put these notions into practice, something that has evaded every Indian government since Independence? Prime Minister Modi appears to have accepted the idea that rapid economic growth is necessary to bring about this transformation. But he faces the same problem that confronted the Chinese government after the adoption of market reforms in the late 1970s—reconciling goals of social and economic equality both to bring about desired growth rates and satisfy the interests of the new professional and managerial class. The compulsions of the BJP to accommodate India's diversity to remain in power and the RSS's commitment to a restraint on state power are likely to keep both committed to democracy. But these very factors, while good for democracy, could deepen tensions between the BJP and the RSS. The longer the BJP remains in power, the more likely it is to identify itself with the administrative state and its 'experts' that the RSS so deeply suspects. We already see that in the clash over globalism, growing economic inequality, the role of the state and issues of security and, perhaps most importantly for the two as organizations, career patterns for the swayamsevaks (i.e., party politics that provide access to the bureaucratic state or 'selfless' work within the sangh parivar).

The sangh parivar over the past three decades has been far more diverse in its membership, becoming an umbrella organization that resembles the post-Independence Congress party in that it has an ideological right, centre and left. It is less Brahmanical both ideologically and in membership. Definitions of Hindutva within it vary widely. On economic policy issues, the labour affiliates lean to the left, while cultural affiliates like the VHP veer to the right on social issues. The RSS itself has a similar ideological spread and definitions of Hinduism are similarly diverse. The RSS, contrary to much public discourse, is not the BJP, nor does the RSS desire to become like the BJP or assume control over the party. The RSS's views on politics, however, have evolved from one of disdain of what was perceived to be a morally corrupt system to the predominant current view that political power is a necessary, but not sufficient, means to achieve the desired bottom-up social change. It does want to influence the political arena to protect itself from restrictions as well as assist the affiliates to carry out their missions. The RSS differs from the BJP in several fundamental ways. It does not depend on periodic popular votes; it has a leadership cadre that stays in office longer and looks at its vocation as lifelong; it looks at the future over the long term; and it considers itself a significant moral voice in the country. It hopes to transmit this moral voice into practical measures by mediating intra-parivar disputes and balancing the parivar's policies through a slightly left-of-centre populist line on economic issues and a slightly right-of-centre one on socio-cultural matters. One significant aspect of its mediation is to keep its sometimes fractious 'parivar' together by working out a consensus on contentious issues and keeping differences within the 'family'. So far, this strategy has worked. India will continue to change; the question is whether the RSS is flexible enough to adapt to the needs of a rapidly modernizing society.

Appendix I

RSS Training Camps

Year	Shiksha Varg - 1st Yr	Shiksha Varg - 2nd Yr	Shiksha Varg - 3rd Yr
1994	9856	9856	932
1995	10387	3762	1136
1998	10729	3255	1036
1999	9815	4187	1993
2001	N/A	N/A	N/A
2006	12017	3300	945
2007	12140	3070	937
2008	N/A	N/A	N/A
2009	11082	2772	862
2010	N/A	N/A	N/A
2011	11556	2678	877
2012	11507	2781	732
2013	12549	3063	1003
2014	10435	2231	607
2015	15332	3531	709

Source: Organiser magazine, Rashtriya Swayamsevak Sangh. Data not available for 1996, 1997, 2000, 2001 to 2005, 2008 and 2010.

Appendix II

Organizations Where RSS Swayamsevaks Are Active and Their Area of Work

	Organization	Area
1.	Akhil Bharatiya Vidyarthi Parishad	Students
2.	Akhil Bharatiya Adhivakta Parishad	Advocates, judiciary
3.	Arogya Bharati	Public health
4.	Bharatiya Mazdoor Sangh	Labour
5.	Bharatiya Kisan Sangh	Farmers, agriculture
6.	Bharat Vikas Parishad	Social service
7.	Bharatiya Itihas Sankalan Yojana	History
8.	Balagokulam	Children's cultural organization
9.	Bharatiya Shikshan Mandal	Educationists
10.	Bharatiya Janata Party	Politics
11.	Deendayal Shodh Sansthan	All-round village development
12.	Gau Samvardhan	Cow protection
13.	Gram Vikas	Overall village development
14.	Grahak Panchayat	Customer interest

	Organization	Area
15.	Kutumb Prabodhan	Family values and communion
16.	Kushth Rog Nivaran Samiti	Leprosy patients
17.	Kreeda Bharati	Sports
18.	Laghu Udyog Bharati	Small industries
19.	National Medicos Organisation	Doctors
20.	Akhil Bharatiya Sainik Seva Parishad	Ex-servicemen
21.	Pragya Pravah	Academics and intelligentsia
22.	Rashtra Sevika Samiti	Women
23.	Rashtriya Shaikshik Mahasangh	Teachers
24.	Rashtriya Sikh Sangat	Religious solidarity
25.	Sahakar Bharati	Cooperatives
26.	Samajik Samrasta	Social unity
27.	Sahitya Parishad	Literature
28.	Seva Bharati	Service
29.	Seema Jankalyan Samiti	Border area development
30.	Sanskar Bharti	Arts and artists
31.	Sanskrit Bharti	Sanskrit language
32.	Swadeshi Jagran Manch	Development and economy
33.	Akhil Bharatiya Vanvasi Kalyan Ashram	Tribal welfare
34.	Vidya Bharati	Education
35.	Vishva Hindu Parishad	Religious
36.	Vigyan Bharati	Science, scientists

Source: Narender Thakur and Vijay Kranti (eds), *About RSS (Rashtriya Swayamsevak Sangh)*, Mahipalpur Extension (Delhi: Vichar Vinimay Prakashan, 2015).

Appendix III

Growth in the Number of Shakhas

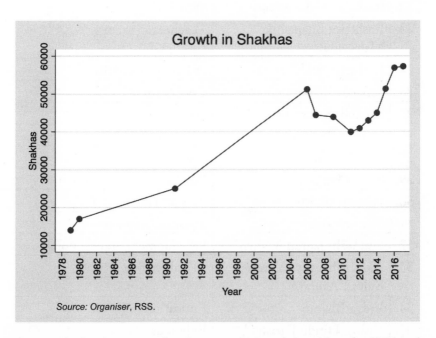

Source: Organiser, RSS.

Among the last ten years, the above graph doesn't have data for 2008 and 2010

Appendix IV

RSS Leadership

Dr Keshav Baliram Hedgewar (*Doctorji*)
Birthplace: Nagpur, Maharashtra
Years as head of RSS: 1925–40

Dr Hedgewar, a Telugu Brahmin, was a trained medical practitioner, and founded the RSS in 1925. As the founder, Dr Hedgewar's views and leadership have had a lasting impact on the ethos and organization of the RSS. Convinced that it was necessary to unify the deeply divided Hindu community to attain independence, he formulated a system to train a cadre of men to bring about Hindu unity. He worked to keep the RSS as an organization aloof from politics, though he permitted its members in their individual capacity to work towards a free India. Besides shaping the training system, he laid the groundwork for a network of full-time workers who would provide the administrative framework for the new organization. He became the model which his successors emulated. In addition, he formulated the guidelines which became a blueprint for the RSS's functioning from his time to the present.

M.S. Golwalkar (*Guruji*)
Birthplace: Ramtek near Nagpur, Maharashtra
Years as head of RSS: 1940–73

Golwalkar, trained as a biologist and professor of zoology, was Hedgewar's hand-picked successor. Dr Hedgewar set the precedent of the sitting sarsanghchalak choosing his successor. Golwalkar headed the RSS through the turbulent times of Independence and the partition of British India. Following the assassination of Mahatma Gandhi, the organization was banned from February 1948 to July 1949, during which time Golwalkar was arrested. The ban was lifted on 11 July 1949. However, the organization lost many of its members and Golwalkar saw it as his major mission to rebuild the RSS. At the same time, he made a compromise with those activist members who wanted to turn the RSS into a political party by backing a party formed by Syama Prasad Mookerjee, a member of India's first cabinet, and loaning full-time RSS workers to it. He oversaw the formation of several affiliates and similarly loaned pracharaks to them.

Madhukar Dattatreya Deoras (*Balasaheb*)
Birthplace: Nagpur, Maharashtra
Years as head of RSS: 1973–94

Deoras, a law-school graduate, was among the first full-time workers trained by the RSS founder, Dr Hedgewar. Deoras reoriented the RSS to include involvement in politics and social reforms. In fact, his disagreement with Golwalkar's view on activism was strong enough for Deoras and his brother, Muralidhar alias Bhaurao, to pull out of the daily functioning of the sangh for several years. Golwalkar's choice of Deoras as his successor marked the end of the organization's quietist rebuilding process and the start of a new and more assertive RSS. In his early speeches after becoming sarsanghchalak, he spoke of the need for the RSS to act assertively on behalf of the poor and disadvantaged. His open support of those opposing Prime Minister Indira Gandhi's Emergency (1975–77) underscored his interest in political activism. His denunciation of caste discrimination was a significant ideological shift within the RSS. Under him, the RSS also opened its doors to non-Hindus.

Prof. Rajendra Singh (*Rajju Bhaiyya*)
Birthplace: Shahjahanpur, Uttar Pradesh
Years as head of RSS: 1994–2000

Rajendra Singh, who held a doctorate in physics, was the first non-Brahmin head of the RSS. Deoras's choice of Singh, a native of Uttar Pradesh, underscored the growing importance of the Hindi-speaking heartland to the RSS. Singh continued the activism initiated by Deoras and stood out in shaping Hindu unity. As general secretary of the RSS in Uttar Pradesh as well as at the national level, he knew the leaders of the BJP as it gained popular support that led to its heading a national governing coalition in the closing years of the 1990s. By this point, the RSS had changed significantly and was much more entwined with the BJP, though there were several issues where it had substantial policy differences with the party. Therefore, Singh was a much more public persona than his predecessors in terms of interacting with the media and taking direct interest in the BJP's functioning. With the rapid growth of the RSS affiliates, he also put in place the organization's mediatory mechanisms to address policy differences among them.

K.S. Sudarshan
Birthplace: Raipur, Chhattisgarh
Years as head of RSS: 2000–09

K.S. Sudarshan, trained as an electronics
and telecommunications engineer, headed
the RSS during the BJP-led government of
Atal Behari Vajpayee and its defeat in 2004 by a Congress-led coalition.
During his tenure, the affiliates grew at an unprecedented rate, especially
the Bharatiya Mazdoor Sangh (its labour-oriented group) and the
Bharatiya Kisan Sangh (its farmer affiliate). He was sympathetic to
the economic affiliates' call for self-sufficiency and their opposition to
the BJP's increasing support for liberalization, including privatization
and economic globalization. He was instrumental in the creation of the
anti-globalist Swadeshi Jagran Manch. Under Sudarshan, there was a
shift in the RSS–BJP relationship, especially as he had been openly
critical of the party on several occasions. After the defeat of the BJP-led
coalition in the 2004 parliamentary elections, his blunt style was evident
when he suggested that the party's older leadership, represented by its
two most prominent stalwarts, Lal Krishna Advani and Vajpayee, step
down and let younger leaders take charge. Sudarshan, in an effort to
establish a dialogue with India's largest religious minority, midwifed
the formation of the Muslim Rashtriya Manch.

Mohan Bhagwat
Birthplace: Chandrapur, Maharashtra
Years as head of RSS: Incumbent since
21 March 2009

Mohan Bhagwat, trained in veterinary
science, was the first RSS head born after
Independence and the first from a family
of RSS activists. Unlike Sudarshan,
Bhagwat is a diplomat who intensified
the use of the mediation system to handle

policy differences, some of them significant, among the various RSS affiliates. Bhagwat is a pragmatist as reflected in his effort to make the RSS a big tent that can accommodate many different views. He recognized Modi's popularity among the RSS members and pushed him as the putative prime ministerial candidate of the BJP despite significant opposition from some RSS and BJP leaders. The RSS involved itself extensively on the BJP's behalf in the 2014 parliamentary elections. Bhagwat has sought to push the policy agenda of the BJP government in a more populist direction, thereby accommodating the views of the economic and cultural affiliates. Referring to Modi, Bhagwat has cautioned RSS members to be wary of a cult of personality, and reminded them that their first loyalty is to the RSS. This reflects his view, which is also the traditional view of the RSS, that durable change comes from the bottom-up and not from the government. He has used the RSS platform to try to work out a consensus among the various affiliates. Perhaps his two major challenges are to rein in the hard Hindutva right and to nudge the government on to a more populist policy path.

Appendix V

RSS Organization

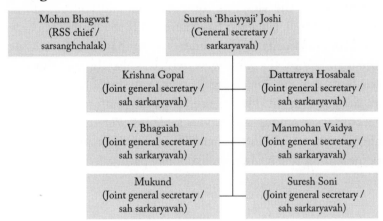

Mohan Bhagwat
(RSS chief /
sarsanghchalak)

Suresh 'Bhaiyyaji' Joshi
(General secretary /
sarkaryavah)

Krishna Gopal
(Joint general secretary /
sah sarkaryavah)

Dattatreya Hosabale
(Joint general secretary /
sah sarkaryavah)

V. Bhagaiah
(Joint general secretary /
sah sarkaryavah)

Manmohan Vaidya
(Joint general secretary /
sah sarkaryavah)

Mukund
(Joint general secretary /
sah sarkaryavah)

Suresh Soni
(Joint general secretary /
sah sarkaryavah)

Functional Departments

These seven departments are each headed by a senior pracharak

Sunil Kulkarni
Sharirik pramukh (physical education)

Swant Ranjan
Bouddhik pramukh (intellectual)

Mangesh Bhende
Vyavastha pramukh (general management)

Parag Abhyankar
Seva pramukh (services)

Anirudh Deshpande
Sampark pramukh (public relations)

Arun Kumar
Prachar pramukh (media)

Suresh Chandra
Pracharak pramukh (pracharak management)

Akhil Bharatiya Karyakari Mandal (Central Executive Committee)

The forty-eight-member executive committee consists of the RSS top leadership: the RSS chief, the general secretary, the six joint general secretaries, the seven functional heads and their deputies, senior pracharaks and sanghchalaks as well as select invitees. It meets twice a year and formulates policy recommendations which it submits to the Akhil Bharatiya Pratinidhi Sabha. A sub-group of the ABKM, referred to as the National Team (Rashtriya Toli) meets to discuss important issues as they arise.

Akhil Bharatiya Pratinidhi Sabha (RSS General Assembly)

The body, composed of some 1400 delegates, functions like a parliament of sorts. The ABPS debates issues in an effort to arrive at a consensus on the policy recommendations of the ABKM. It meets annually, and once every three years elects a general secretary. Each RSS prant (state, though not necessarily coinciding with states as designated in official maps) has a pratinidi sabha which elects delegates to the ABPS. Senior pracharaks who represent the affiliates also attend the national ABPS meetings.

Geographical divisions

Kshetra (region): 11
Prant (state, as defined by the RSS): 52
Vibhag (grouping of districts)
Zilla (district)
Nagar (city)
Mandal (10 or more shakhas)
Shakha (local unit)

Note: The March 2018 expansion in the number of sah sarkaryavahs (joint general secretaries) from four to six reflects the increased workload within the sangh parivar. The top leadership and the functional heads along with their deputies are senior pracharaks.

The functional heads have one or two (prachar and sampark) deputies. The assignment of two deputies to the prachar and sampark divisions reflects their increased workload as the RSS sheds its old trappings of insularity. The continuation of Suresh 'Bhaiyyaji' Joshi as the sarkaryavah (general secretary) suggests a preference for continuity.

Appendix VI

Parliamentary Performance of BJS/BJP

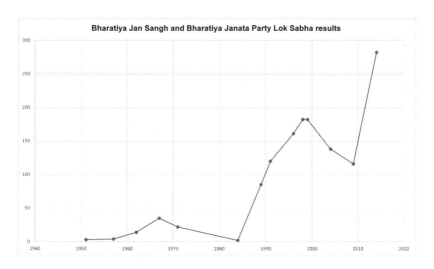

Bharatiya Jan Sangh and Bharatiya Janata Party Lok Sabha results

Source: Election Commission of India.

Appendix VII

Expansion of the Labour Affiliate, the Bharatiya Mazdoor Sangh

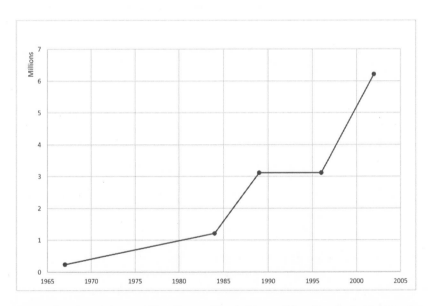

Source: BMS website and 'Big Rise in Trade Union Membership', *The Hindu*, 31 December 2006, http://www.thehindu.com/todays-paper/tp-national/ big-rise-in-trade-union-membership/article3041103.ece. BMS is one of the few RSS-affiliated organizations to maintain comprehensive membership records. Note that a major surge in membership occurs in the late 1990s and the early years of the new millennium.

Appendix VIII

Goa State Assembly Results 2012, 2017

Goa State Assembly Results of Major Parties, 2017			
Party	Seats Contested	Seats Won	Vote % in Seats Contested
BJP	36	13	36.06
INC	37	17	30.35
MAG	25	3	17.42
GFP	4	3	35.02
Others	116	4	27.17

Goa State Assembly Results of Major Parties, 2012			
Party	Seats Contested	Seats Won	Vote % in Seats Contested
BJP	28	21	50.17
INC	33	9	37.44
MAG	7	3	37.67
GVP	9	2	14.8
Others	84	5	47.22

Abbreviation	Party Name
BJP	Bharatiya Janata Party
INC	Indian National Congress
MAG	Maharashtrawadi Gomantak Party
GFP	Goa Forward Party
GVP	Goa Vikas Party
Others	Communist Party of India; Aam Aadmi Party; Nationalist Congress Party; Independents

Source: Election Commission of India

Appendix IX

संघाचे संविधान

ABBREVIATIONS

Sangh	:	Rashtriya Swayamsevak Sangh
A.B.P.S.	:	Akhil Bharatiya Pratinidhi Sabha
A.B.K.M.	:	Akhil Bharatiya Karyakari Mandal
P.K.M.	:	Prantiya Karyakari Mandal
K.M.	:	Karyakari Mandal

SHRI

THE CONSTITUTION OF THE RASHTRIYA SWAYAMSEVAK SANGH

(Translated from the original in Hindi)
(as adopted on 1st August 1949 and amended upto 1st July 1972)

PREAMBLE

WHEREAS in the disintegrated condition of the country it was considered necessary to have an Organisation,

(a) to eradicate the fissiparous tendencies arising from diversities of sect, faith, caste and creed and from political, economic, linguistic and provincial differences, amongst Hindus;

(b) to make them realise the greatness of their past;

(c) to inculcate in them a spirit of service, sacrifice and selfless devotion to the Society;

(d) to build up an organised and well-disciplined corporate life; and

(e) to bring about an all-round regeneration of the Hindu Samaj on the basis of its Dharma and its Sanskriti;

AND WHEREAS the Organisation known as 'RASHTRIYA SWAYAMSEVAK SANGH' was started on the Vijaya Dashami day in the year 1982 Vikram Samvat (1925 A.D.) by the late Dr. Keshav Baliram Hedgewar;

AND WHEREAS Shri Madhav Sadashiv Golwalkar was nominated by the said Dr. Hedgewar to succeed him in the year 1997 Vikram Samvat (1940 A.D.);

AND WHEREAS the Sangh had till now no written constitution;

AND WHEREAS in the present changed conditions, it is deemed desirable to reduce to writing the Constitution as also the Aims and Objects of the Sangh and its Methods of Work,

THE RASHTRIYA SWAYAMSEVAK SANGH hereby adopts the following Constitution:

ARTICLE 1

NAME

The name of the Organisation is 'RASHTRIYA SWAYAMSEVAK SANGH.'

ARTICLE 2

HEAD-QUARTERS

The Head-Quarters of the Akhil Bharatiya Karyakari Mandal is at NAGPUR.

ARTICLE 3

AIMS AND OBJECTS

The Aims and Objects of the Sangh are to weld together the various diverse groups within the Hindu Samaj and to revitalise and rejuvenate the same on the basis of its Dharma and Sanskriti, that it may achieve an all-sided development of Bharatvarsha.

ARTICLE 4

POLICY

(a) The Sangh believes in the orderly evolution of society and adheres to peaceful and legitimate means for the realisation of its ideals.

(b) In consonance with the cultural heritage of the Hindu Samaj, the Sangh has abiding faith in the fundamental principle of respect towards all faiths.

(c) The Sangh is aloof from politics and is devoted to social and cultural fields only. However, the Swayamsevaks are free, as individuals, to join any party, institution, or front, political or otherwise, except such parties, institutions, or fronts which subscribe to or believe in extra-national loyalties, or resort to violent and/or secret activities to achieve their ends, or which promote or attempt to promote, or have the object of promoting any feeling of enmity or hatred towards any other community or creed or religious denomination. Persons owing allegiance to the above-mentioned undesirable elements and methods of working shall have no place in the Sangh.

ARTICLE 5

DHWAJ

While recognising the duty of every citizen to be loyal to and to respect the State Flag, the Sangh has as its flag, the 'BHAGWA-DHWAJ'-the age-old symbol of Hindu Sanskriti which the Sangh regards as its 'GURU'.

ARTICLE 6

SWAYAMSEVAK

1 (a) Any male Hindu of 18 years or above, who subscribes to the Aims and Objects of the Sangh and conforms generally to

its discipline and associates himself with the activities of the Shakha will be considered as a Swayamsevak.

(b) A Swayamsevak shall be deemed to be an Active Swayamsevak if he pledges to devote himself for the furtherance of the Aims and Objects of the Sangh, and attends a Shakha regularly or performs any work duly assigned to him.

(c) A Swayamsevak shall cease to be a Swayamsevak if he resigns or is removed for any act prejudicial to the interests of the Shakha or the Sangh.

2. **Bal Swayamsevak** – Any male Hindu below the age of 18 may be admitted and allowed to participate in the Shakha programmes as a Bal Swayamsevak.

ARTICLE 7

SHAKHA

(a) Swayamsevaks desirous of propagating the Aims and Objects of the Sangh coming together in the form of a regular assemblage will form a Centre. Each Centre shall be a self-contained unit receiving its finances and making its own financial disbursements and is herein referred to as a 'SHAKHA'.

(b) Each such Shakha shall constitute the primary unit of the Sangh, which shall be an autonomous body in respect of its administration and finances.

(c) The Shakha shall function under the directions of its Karyakari Mandal.

ARTICLE 8

PROGRAMMES

For the fulfilment of the Aims and Objects as set out herein earlier, the Shakhas may undertake any or all of the following programmes:

'Arranging frequent discussions and lectures for imparting intellectual and moral education to Swayamsevaks and others and inculcating in them love for the Nation and the ideals of Hindu Dharma and Sanskriti.

'Establishing and running of Libraries and Reading Rooms for the benefit of the general public.

'Carrying on of activities or undertaking programmes for the welfare and benefit of the general public, such as extending medical care, propagation of literacy and improvement of living conditions of the poorer sections of the society; and flood and famine relief, study circles and free exhibition of educative films and advancement of other objects of general public utility, but not involving carrying on of activity for profit.

'Imparting physical education by means of exercises and games with a view to improving the physical and mental faculties of Swayamsevaks and others for the co-ordinated and disciplined development of the Society.

'Arranging periodical classes for Swayamsevaks to be trained as Instructors and Workers.

'Celebrating festivals of cultural importance with a view to providing opportunity for Swayamsevaks and others to imbibe the sublime cultural values of character, service and sacrifice to rededicate themselves to the cause of society.

'Adopting suitable means and establishing institutions to propagate the ideals and activities of the Sangh and to educate the people.

'Generally the Shakhas may do all such things as are considered necessary and are conducive directly or indirectly, to promoting and achieving any of the objects of the Sangh.'

ARTICLE 9

FINANCES

Any voluntary offering made with devotion before the BHAGWA-DHWAJ shall exclusively constitute the finances of the Shakha and shall belong to and be solely managed and disbursed by the Shakha for the promotion of the Aims and Objects of the Sangh and general advancement of Sangh work to be done by the Shakha according to the rules framed by it for that purpose.

ARTICLE 10

ELECTIONS

(a) Elections shall be held after every three years.

(b) The date, method and venue of election shall be determined by the concerned K.M. in consultation with the A.B.K.M.

ARTICLE 11

QUALIFICATION FOR VOTERS AND CANDIDATES FOR ELECTIONS AND APPOINTEES

(a) **VOTERS**

Every Active Swayamsevak of at least one-year standing immediately prior to the date of preparation of the Electoral lists for the election, shall be entitled to vote in the election.

(b) **CANDIDATES FOR ELECTIONS AND APPOINTEES**

(1) A Swayamsevak, who is an office-bearer of a political party, shall not be eligible as a candidate for election or as an appointee to any post so long as he is such an office-bearer.

(2) A candidate for election, or an appointee to any Akhil Bharatiya post, shall be an Active Swayamsevak of at least six years' continuous standing.

(3) A candidate or appointee for Sanghachalakship shall be an Active Swayamsevak of at least one-year standing.

ARTICLE 12

SARSANGHCHALAK

The late Dr. Keshav Baliram Hedgewar, the founder of the Sangh, was the Adya (First) Sarsanghchalak. He, in consultation with the then K.K.M., nominated Shri Madhav Sadashiv Golwalkar, who is the Sarsanghchalak since then. The Sarsanghchalak will nominate his successor as and when the necessity arises, with the consent of the then A.B.K.M.

The Sarsanghchalak is the Guide and Philosopher of the Rashtriya Swayamsevak Sangh. He may attend, summon or address any assembly of the Swayamsevaks, A.B.P.S. and Karyakari Mandals severally or jointly.

ARTICLE 13

SARKARYAVAHA

(a) The elected members of the Akhil Bharatiya Pratinidhi Sabha (vide Article 15a) shall elect the Sarkaryavaha.

(b) The Sarkaryavaha shall act in consultation with the Sarsanghchalak.

(c) In case of death, incapacity, or resignation of the Sarkaryavaha, the A.B.K.M. may appoint a person to discharge his duties until such time as his successor is elected.

ARTICLE 14

AKHIL BHARATIYA KARYAKARI MANDAL

(a) THE Sarkaryavaha shall form the Akhil Bharatiya Karyakari Mandal of which he shall be the Chairman with the following office-bearers duly appointed by him.

   i) One or more Sah-Sarkaryavahas.

   ii) Akhil Bharatiya Sharirik Shikshan Pramukh. (In-charge of guidance in physical education.)

   iii) Akhil Bharatiya Bouddhik Shikshan Pramukh. (In-charge of guidance in intellectual and moral instruction.)

   iv) Akhil Bharatiya Prachar Pramukh (In-charge of propagation of Sangh work and guidance to Pracharaks).

   v) Akhil Bharatiya Vyavastha Pramukh. (In-charge of general management).

and not less than five members chosen from among the Prantiya Karyakari Mandals.

(b) THE following will be the functions of the A.B.K.M. :

   i) The A.B.K.M is the co-ordinating body of all of the Shakhas in the country to carry out the policy and programmes laid down by the A.B.P.S.

   ii) The A.B.K.M. will frame rules and bye-laws in consonance with the Constitution for the purpose of regulating its own affairs and for the general functioning of the Sangh.

ARTICLE 15

AKHIL BHARATIYA PRATINIDHI SABHA

(a) THE delegates elected in accordance with Article 16 (a) and (i) and (ii) in a Prant shall elect from amongst themselves one tenth of their number as representatives of the Shakhas on the Akhil Bharatiya Pratinidhi Sabha.

(b) The A.B.P.S shall consist of –
   i)   Representatives of the Shakhas as elected in 15(a) above.
   ii) Sanghachalak and Pracharaks of Vibhags and Prants.
   iii) Members of the A.B.K.M.

(c) THE Sarkaryavaha shall be the chairman of the A.B.P.S.

(d) THE A.B.P.S shall meet at least once a year.

(e) THE A.B.P.S shall review the work and lay down policy and programmes of the Sangh.

ARTICLE 16

DELEGATES AND SANGHCHALAKS

(a) i)   Fifty or more Swayamsevaks entitled to vote in Shakha will elect from among themselves one for every fifty such Swayamsevaks as delegates of the Shakha.
   ii) Such of the Shakhas as are having less than fifty Swayamsevaks entitled to vote will come together to elect delegates.

(b) The delegates, as elected above, in a Jilla, in a Vibhag and in a Prant will elect the Jilla Sanghachalak, the Vibhag Sanghachalak and the Prant Sanghachalak, respectively.

(c) The Jilla Sanghachalak, in consultation with the Prant Sanghachalak and Prant Pracharak will nominate Sanghachalaks for the various Shakhas and groups of Shakhas within the Jilla.

(d) In case a suitable person is not available for the office of Sanghachalak, the Jilla Sanghachalak will appoint a Karyavaha.

(e) In case of death, incapacity or resignation of Prant, Vibhag or Jilla Sanghachalak the K.M. of the larger area may appoint a person to discharge the duties of the respective Sanghachalak until such time as his successor is elected.

ARTICLE 17

PRACHARAKS

(a) i) Pracharaks shall be full time workers selected from amongst those devoted workers of high integrity, whose mission is to serve the society through the Sangh and who, of their own free will, dedicate themselves to the Cause.

    ii) They will receive no remuneration. However their expenses will be met by the Shakhas.

(b) Appointment of Pracharaks –

    i) The Sarkaryavaha will appoint Prant Pracharaks on the advice of the Akhil Bharatiya Prachar Pramukh and in consultation with the Prant Sanghachalak concerned.

    ii) The Prant Sanghachalak on the advice of Prant Pracharak will appoint Pracharaks for different areas in the Prant for the assistance and co-ordination of the Shakhas in their respective areas.

ARTICLE 18

KARYAKARI MANDALS

(a) Sanghachalak of a Prant, Vibhag or Jilla elected in accordance with 16(b), or any group of Shakhas within the Jilla appointed in accordance with 16(c), will form a Karyakari Mandal of the respective area, of which he shall be the Chairman, consisting of the following office bearers duly appointed by him –

    i) Karyavaha

    ii) Pracharak (appointed under Article 17(b)(ii)

    iii) Sharirik Shikshan Pramukh.

    iv) Bouddhik Shikshan Pramukh.

    v) Vyavastha Pramukh.

(b) The Sanghachalak of a Shakha appointed in accordance with 16(c), will form a Karyakari Mandal, of which he shall be the Chairman, consisting of the following office-bearers duly appointed by him –

    i) Karyavaha

    ii) Sharirik Shikshan Pramukh.

iii) Bouddhik Shikshan Pramukh.
iv) Prachar Pramukh.
v) Vyavastha Pramukh.
vi) Nidhi Pramukh.

NOTE – In case suitable person/s is/are not available for appointment to any one or more of the above posts the same may remain vacant until suitable person/s is/are available.

(c) Each Karyakari Mandal shall also have in addition not less than three members chosen from amongst the other Karyakari Mandals within the area, if any.

(d) K.Ms. will be executive bodies in their respective areas, guided by the K.M. of the immediate larger area for implementing the policy and carrying out the programme laid down by the A.B.P.S.

(e) The K.M. of a Shakha will have the power to take disciplinary action against any individual Swayamsevak for breach of discipline or behaviour prejudicial to the interests of the Shakha or the Sangh. Such an action will be subject to confirmation by the Karyakari Mandal of the immediate larger area.

ARTICLE 19

QUORUM

ONE half of the total strength shall form the QUORUM for the meetings of the various Karyakari Mandals, and one fifth for the A.B.P.S.

ARTICLE 20

UNDEVELOPED PRANTS

IN case of prants in which the work has not yet developed to an appreciable level, the A.B.K.M may provide representation to them on the A.B.P.S in a manner it deems fit.

ARTICLE 21

INTERPRETATION AND AMENDMENTS TO CONSTITUTION

(a) The interpretation of the Constitution and its Articles by the A.B.K.M shall be final.

(b) An amendment to the Constitution not inconsistent with the Aims and Objects of the Sangh can be proposed at a convention specially convened for that purpose by the A.B.K.M on its own, or to the A.B.K.M by any P.K.M., or by any other Karyakari Mandal with the recommendation of the respective P.K.M., or by any twenty-five members of the A.B.P.S. The A.B.K.M after due consideration will put the proposal of such an amendment before the P.K.Ms. and the amendment will be deemed carried if two-thirds of the P.K.Ms. agree by simple majority.

(c) The decision of the P.K.Ms. regarding such amendments may be brought for reconsideration before the A.B.P.S. on a requisition by any twenty-five members of that Sabha. The decision of the A.B.P.S in this behalf, taken by a two-thirds majority shall be final.

Source: Sanjeev Kelkar, *Lost Years of the RSS* (New Delhi: Sage Publications, 2011), pp. 324–32.

Notes

Introduction

1. See report of this meeting at, Agencies, 'Top BJP Ministers Attend RSS Meet, Opposition Questions Govt's Accountability', *The Indian Express*, 3 September 2015, https://indianexpress.com/article/india/india-others/rss-bjp-meet-opposition-parties-slam-saffron-outfits-interference-in-governance/ (accessed 23 January 2017).
2. In an interview on 10 January 2018 in New Delhi, Virjesh Upadhyay, the general secretary of the BMS, noted that the sangh parivar had learnt from its experience during the Vajpayee government (1998–2004) and had worked to keep the channels of communication between the affiliates and the government open. The affiliates' access to the current government ministers and bureaucrats is also much better. This improved liaison was confirmed by the BKS's Badri Narayan Chaudhury in an interview in New Delhi on 16 January 2018.
3. For a comprehensive discussion of the organization and ideology of the RSS, see our study in, Walter Andersen and Shridhar Damle, *The Brotherhood in Saffron: The Rashtriya Swayamsevak Sangh and Hindu Revivalism* (Boulder: Westview Press, 1987).
4. Referred to in the RSS ecosystem as grihastha.
5. The idea of looking at an organization's decision-making process through several analytical lenses forms the basis of Graham Allison's study of the Cuban missile crisis, *Essence of Decision: Explaining the Cuban Missile Crisis* (New York: Little Brown, 1971, 1st edition).

6. Figures from the RSS general secretary's annual 2017 report. Figures available at, http://rss.org//Encyc/2017/3/23/rss-Annual-Report-2017-English.html (last accessed 12 July 2018).

7. Figures provided by Prafulla Ketkar—editor of *Organiser,* an English-language weekly publication associated with the sangh parivar—in a meeting in Delhi on 28 March 2016. Membership statistics are by necessity an estimate, as the RSS does not keep such statistics.

8. Shakha figures are reported and available in the annual report of the general secretary to the ABPS, the highest deliberative body of the RSS. For a summary of the rapid recent growth of the number of shakhas and service projects across the country, see, Indian Express News Service, 'Highest Growth Ever: RSS Adds 5000 New Shakhas in Last 12 Months', *The Indian Express,* 16 March 2016, https://indianexpress.com/article/india/india-news-india/rss-uniform-over-5000-new-shakhas-claims-rss/ (accessed 12 July 2018).

9. Venkatesh Raghavan, the Hindu Swayamsevak Sangh's pracharak for the eastern US, told us in a 6 November 2017 interview in Washington DC that about a quarter of the 6000 full-time pracharaks are in fact vistaraks, a designation used for full-time workers in their first year of RSS service. He estimated that some 75 per cent of the vistaraks continue their service after the first year, and that most serve for at least three years. The RSS also refers to people giving short-term service (for example, two to three months) as vistaraks. Still another vistarak category consists of college graduates who live in local RSS offices (*karyalaya*) and serve part-time. In all of these vistarak categories, the RSS evaluates performance and encourages those who do well and demonstrate initiative to continue serving, either in the RSS itself or in another parivar body.

10. For a more detailed discussion of the formation of the RSS, see, Andersen and Damle, *The Brotherhood in Saffron,* ch. 2.

11. Godse left the RSS in 1938 because he believed it was insufficiently involved in the Hindu Mahasabha–supported satyagraha against the allegedly anti-Hindu policies of the Muslim ruler of the princely state of Hyderabad. He formed the Hindu Rashtra Dal, modelled after the RSS organization, though with a much more politically activist orientation. This information taken from the court testimony of Nathuram Godse, published by his brother, Gopal Godse, in *May It Please Your Honour* (Pune: Vitasta, 1977), in which Nathuram Godse

analyses his political evolution and his drift away from the RSS for its perceived lack of political focus.

12. Prior to independence, politically active Marathi-speaking members of the RSS tended to participate in the Hindu Mahasabha; non–Marathi-speaking members instead tended to join the Congress party.

13. The RSS expected these three organizations to train their own cadre, a policy that was adopted by most of the affiliates formed later. However, pracharaks trained in the RSS still occupy senior administrative positions in almost all the affiliates. Information on this supplied during an interview with Professor Yeshwant Kelkar, an erstwhile pracharak and former national president of the ABVP, the student branch of the RSS, in Mumbai on 14 July 1983. A more recent interview on this issue was with Ramdas Pande, a founding member of the BMS, the labour affiliate of the RSS, in New Delhi on 21 January 2016. He said that the BMS primarily needed more workers with specialized experience/knowledge, but that pracharaks were still needed to expand the BMS because they had unique skills in organization-building and could devote all their time to it.

14. For a discussion of these efforts to organize college students, see ch. 2, 'Affiliates: The Public Face of the Parivar'.

15. Perhaps the most prominent of these affiliated organizations at that time, other than the BJS, were the ABMS and the ABVP, the labour and student affiliates respectively, and the VHP, which works with the Hindu ecclesiastical establishment.

16. C.P. Bhishikar, *Sri Guruji* (Pune: Bharatiya Vichar Sadhana, 1973, in Marathi).

17. Current statistics noted in *Sewa Kunj 2015: An Insight into Sewa Activities* (New Delhi: Aravali Printers and Publishers, 2015), p. 5.

18. Ibid.

19. Shreerang Godbole, 'Service and Social Harmony: An Enlightened Reformist', *Organiser*, 2017, http://www.hvk.org/2017/0417/13.html (accessed 28 January 2018).

20. The general secretary of the BJP, Ram Madhav, who was shifted to the party from the RSS only months before the September 2015 conclave, even wrote an analysis of this meeting involving the prime minister and several ministers in one of India's leading dailies. He wrote that this was just another of the meetings between leaders of the RSS and the

governing BJP and suggested that it would become a regular feature of the government as it reached out for information and advice. Looked at from another perspective, these meetings also gave the RSS a similar opportunity to reach out for information and a chance to influence policy. See, Ram Madhav, 'A Family Gets Together: RSS-BJP Relationship Is Unique. It Cannot Be Understood by Existing Models', *The Indian Express*, 15 September 2015, https://indianexpress.com/article/opinion/editorials/a-family-gets-together/ (last accessed 12 July 2018).

21. In answer to a question on how the RSS had changed, almost all the senior leaders interviewed at the Nagpur RSS headquarters in mid-2015 said that the reason for greater transparency was greater public acceptance of the RSS and, consequently, a reduced fear of another partisan ban. Interviews were conducted on 7–8 July 2015. Christophe Jaffrelot has given a timeline for the incremental political mainstreaming of the BJP that could also, to a certain extent, apply to the greater public. He argues that this development owes much to the acceptance of the RSS and its student affiliates in a national anti-corruption movement in the mid-1970s. Moreover, there were opportunities for the leaders of the RSS and the sangh parivar to develop personal links with a wide range of opposition political figures when activists from both sides were imprisoned during the 1975–77 Emergency declared by Prime Minister Indira Gandhi. See, Jaffrelot, 'Who Mainstreamed BJP?', *The Indian Express*, 21 July 2015, https://indianexpress.com/article/opinion/columns/who-mainstreamed-bjp/ (accessed 12 July 2018).

22. Andersen and Damle, *The Brotherhood in Saffron*, p. 7. The book presents the findings of a set of questions administered to RSS cadres in three regions to test, among other things, what shaped their ideological orientation.

23. An RSS pracharak from Rajasthan, for example, told us that equal inheritance of farmland was antithetical to Indian values because it created fissures between siblings.

24. We refer here to the period of 1997–98 to 2014–15.

25. See, World Bank reference for 1960 and 2015 in http://data.worldbank.org/indicator/SP.URB.TOTL.IN.ZS (accessed 29 July 2016). See the 1990 urbanization rate in http://wdi.worldbank.org/table/3.12 (accessed 29 July 2016).

26. McKinsey figures of middle class in, Diana Farrell and Eric Beinhocker, 'Next Big Spenders: India's Middle Class', McKinsey Global Institute,

https://www.mckinsey.com/mgi/overview/in-the-news/next-big-spenders-indian-middle-class (accessed 28 January 2016).

27. http://www.trai.gov.in/sites/default/files/PRNo35TSDReportJan23032018.pdf (accessed 1 February 2016).

28. Internet and Mobile Association of India, 'Internet Users in India Is Likely to Reach 478 Million by June', http://www.iamai.in/media/details/5008 (accessed 11 April 2018).

29. Ronald Inglehart, *Modernization and Postmodernization: Cultural, Economic and Political Change in 43 Societies* (Princeton: Princeton University Press, 1997).

30. Andersen and Damle, *The Brotherhood in Saffron*, p. 1. On this point, RSS chief Mohan Bhagwat in his 2016 Vijayadashami speech focused his comments on the critical importance of the family for social stability and what he called 'proper behaviour'. Bhagwat, 'Full text of #RSSVijayaDashmi2016 speech by RSS Sarasanghachalak', *Samvada*, 11 October 2016, http://samvada.org/2016/news/mohan-bhagwat-speech-rss-vijayadashami-nagpur/ (accessed 13 April 2018). For theoretical discussions of the social impact of rootlessness, see, Robert A. Nisbet, *The Quest for Community* (New York: Oxford University Press, 1971); Ted Robert Gurr, *Why Men Rebel* (Princeton: Princeton University Press, 1970), pp. 46–50; and Hannah Arendt, *The Origins of Totalitarianism* (Cleveland: Meridian Books, 1952), pp. 227–43.

31. Erikson's work in this area is perhaps best expressed in his book on Martin Luther, *Young Man Luther* (New York: Norton, 1958).

32. David D. Laitin, *Identity in Formation: The Russian-Speaking Populations in the Near Abroad*, (Ithaca: Cornell University Press, 1998), pp. 17–28.

33. This analysis of 'tips' and 'cascades' is developed in Thomas Schelling's *Micromotives and Macrobehavior* (New York: Norton, 1978). See an application of Schelling's analyses in Laitin's discussion of Russian minorities in the former Eastern Bloc states (the so-called 'near abroad'), in Laitin, *Identity in Formation*, pp. 21–24.

34. Ranju Dodam, 'Manmohan Vaidya: Beef Consumers Can Become RSS Members', *Northeast Today*, 9 December 2015, https://www.northeasttoday.in/manmohan-vaidya-beef-consumers-can-become-rss-members/ (accessed 13 April 2018).

35. Asian News International, 'No Beef Ban in North-east, As Majority of People Consume It: Sunil Deodhar', *Business Standard*, 14 March 2018,

http://www.business-standard.com/article/news-ani/no-beef-ban-
in-north-east-as-majority-of-people-consume-it-sunil-
deodhar-118031400057_1.html (accessed 13 April 2018).

36. Rupam Jain Nair et al., 'Special Report: Battling for India's Soul,
    State by State', Reuters, 13 October 2015, https://www.reuters.
    com/article/us-india-rss-specialreport/special-report-battling-for-
    indias-soul-state-by-state-idUSKCN0S700A20151013 (accessed 28
    January 2018).

37. Three of the more important works are: M.S. Golwalkar, *Bunch
    of Thoughts* (Bangalore: Vikram Prakashan, 1966); Deendayal
    Upadhyaya, *Integral Humanism* (Delhi: Navchetan Press, 1968);
    D.B. Thengadi, *Ekatma Manav Darshan* (Delhi: Suruchi, 1985).

38. We frequently heard RSS officials argue that the various social sciences
    had to be viewed from a uniquely Indian perspective, an approach
    similar to the Chinese assertion that the various social sciences need
    to be used in ways that reflect unique Chinese characteristics.

39. Ruhini Kumar Pegu, 'Hinduisation and Identity Conflict: The
    Mising Case', *IJCAES Special Issue on Basic, Applied & Social
    Sciences*, vol. 2, October 2012, https://pdfs.semanticscholar.
    org/0500/2e98456e1938780a6cf1eddab67514dae585.pdf (accessed
    13 April 2018).

40. Smita Gupta, 'How the RSS Grew Roots in the North-East', *The Hindu
    BusinessLine*, 9 March 2018, https://www.thehindubusinessline.
    com/blink/know/how-the-rss-grew-roots-in-the-north-east/
    article22991950.ece (accessed 13 April 2018).

41. For a theoretical discussion of identity formation, and especially these
    contrasting aspects of identity, see, Richard Jenkins, *Social Identity*
    (London: Routledge, 1966), p. 4.

42. For a discussion of 'social engineering' by the sangh parivar, see,
    Christophe Jaffrelot, 'The Sangh Parivar between Sanskritization
    and Social Engineering', in Thomas Blom Hansen and Christophe
    Jaffrelot (eds), *The BJP and the Compulsions of Politics in India* (New
    Delhi: Oxford University Press, 1998), pp. 22–71.

43. Interview with Narendra Modi in New Delhi on 15 November 2013.

44. Aadhaar (meaning 'foundation') is a twelve-digit unique identity
    number assigned to every resident of India after recording biometric
    and demographic data. Because every resident has a unique Aadhaar
    number, it has been used to eliminate ghost beneficiaries in many
    government welfare schemes.

45. Surya Rao, 'This Theory Explains Why BJP Won in Muslim Dominated Areas', *RightLog*, 12 March 2017, https://rightlog. in/2017/03/muslim-bjp-area-win/ (accessed 29 January 2018).

46. An interesting analysis of the tensions between employing strategies of identity and economic nationalism in the US, another socially complex country, in Jonathan Rauch, 'Speaking as a . . .', *New York Review*, 9 November 2017, vol. LXIV, no. 17, pp. 10–13.

Chapter One: *A Growing Involvement in the Policy Process*

1. At the beginning of our research, we interviewed the senior leadership of the RSS at its Nagpur headquarters on 7–8 July 2015. We began all the interviews by asking how the RSS had changed since our previous book three decades ago. Among those interviewed were Mohan Bhagwat (sarsanghchalak), Suresh 'Bhaiyyaji' Joshi (sarkaryavah), Dattatreya Hosabale (sah sarkaryavah) and Manmohan Vaidya (the then prachar pramukh, now sah sarkaryavah).

2. The full text is available at, *The Times of India*, 'Text of RSS Chief Mohan Bhagwat's Vijayadashami Speech', 3 October 2014, https://timesofindia.indiatimes.com/india/Text-of-RSS-chief-Mohan-Bhagwats-Vijayadashami-speech/articleshow/44199148.cms (accessed 9 October 2017).

3. See an analysis of the keen interest of the Indian press in Bhagwat's politically oriented Vijayadashami speech in, Ratan Sharda, 'RSS Chief Advocates Inclusive Approach to Economic Issues', Newsbharati.com, 2 October 2017, http://www.newsbharati.com/Encyc/2017/10/2/RSS-chief-advocates-inclusive-approach-to-economic-issues.html (accessed 10 November 2017).

4. A description of the impact of the revision in GST rates made by the GST Council in, Soumya Gupta, 'What the Revision in GST Rates Means for Consumers', LiveMint, 12 November 2017, http://www. livemint.com/Companies/6yNnNILs0kTeseNGKmhINO/What-the-revision-in-GST-rates-means-for-consumers.html (accessed 13 November 2017).

5. Information from an interview with Ram Madhav, BJP general secretary and former RSS spokesperson, on 23 October 2017, in Washington DC.

6. See a more elaborate description of RSS activities during the Emergency in, Walter Andersen and Shridhar Damle, *The Brotherhood*

in *Saffron: The Rashtriya Swayamsevak Sangh and Hindu Revivalism* (Boulder: Westview Press, 1987), pp. 210–13.

7. The ban was lifted on 21 March 1977, after the Congress's loss in the parliamentary elections.

8. Sharad Hebalkar, *Shri Balasaheb Deoras* (Pune: Bharatiya Vichar Sadhana, 2000), pp. 158–59 in Marathi. Also Seshadri Chari (ed.), *Fruitful Life* (Delhi: Bharat Prakashan, 1996), p. 20.

9. Inder Malhotra, a prominent Indian journalist and biographer, described the satyagraha and its participants. See his book, *Indira Gandhi: A Personal Political Biography* (London: Hodder and Stoughton, 1989), p. 178. See an account of the RSS's role in *Hebalkar, Shri Balasaheb Deoras*, pp. 165–66. We also talk about this in Andersen and Damle, *The Brotherhood in Saffron*, pp. 210–13.

10. Statistics from, http://eci.nic.in/eci_main/StatisticalReports/LS_1977/Vol_I_LS_77.pdf#page=89&zoom=auto,-85,834.

11. Press Trust of India, 'Narendra Modi Gets Clean Chit in SIT Report', *The Times of India*, 10 April 2012, https://timesofindia.indiatimes.com/india/Narendra-Modi-gets-clean-chit-in-SIT-report-on-gujarat-riots/articleshow/12612345.cms (accessed 13 November 2017). This legal exoneration enhanced Modi's standing among swayamsevaks as a person who had emerged unscathed from public criticism (the word they use for this is *agnipariksha*, to express the notion of an 'acid test'). Modi, meanwhile, projected himself as a long-suffering (and falsely persecuted) martyr.

12. Ibid. The RSS spokesperson in Delhi explained that the parallel network set up by the RSS was aimed at getting people to the polls. Its first step was to enrol voters, second was person-to-person canvassing to convince people to vote and third was to take them to the polling booth.

13. Shantanu Guha Ray, 'Narendra Modi May Not Wait till 2019 for General Elections: Will India Hold "Dual" Polls with States in 2018?', Firstpost, 23 May 2017, www.firstpost.com/politics/narendra-modi-may-not-wait-till-2019-for-general-elections-will -India-hold-dual-polls-with-states-in-2018-3473100.html (accessed 14 November 2017). This report states that the national BJP has sent almost 2500 volunteers (whom it calls vistaraks) to spend a year training local workers for booth-level management for the 2019 parliamentary elections.

14. Andersen and Damle, *The Brotherhood in Saffron*, pp. 43–45. The RSS conducted protracted negotiations with Home Minister Vallabhbhai Patel to lift the ban in 1949. Among other things, it pledged to prepare a written constitution which would explicitly state that the RSS would not involve itself in political activities—indeed, the present RSS constitution states that the organization's activities will be devoted entirely to cultural work.

15. For reference to these RSS dissident groups, see, Andersen and Damle, *The Brotherhood in Saffron*, pp. 108–10, 145. Additional information from an interview with Professor Madhav G. Vaidya, the first spokesperson for the RSS, in Nagpur on 6 March 2016.

16. See an insightful discussion of the more activist transition of the RSS under Balasaheb's leadership in Pralay Kanungo, *RSS's Tryst with Politics: From Hedgewar to Sudarshan* (Delhi: Manohar Publishers, 2002), ch. VI. For a study supporting Deoras's greater activist orientation (and strong opposition to Golwalkar's apolitical orientation) see, Sanjeev Kelkar, *Lost Years of the RSS* (New Delhi: Sage Publications, 2011).

17. Vidya Bharati on its website claims that it has 12,364 schools, 1,46,643 teachers, and 34,52,615 students, http://vidyabharti.net/ (accessed 19 February 2016). Schools affiliated to the RSS were started in the early 1950s, and the rapid expansion of this network of schools led to the formation of the Vidya Bharati in 1977. The explanation of its philosophy says it has its 'roots in Hindutva'. For information about its formation and goals, see the website for its national publication at, http://www.vidyabharti.net/organization.php (accessed 1 February 2016). This RSS focus on education, especially in tribal areas, is further demonstrated by the sangh's support of two other affiliates that specialize in education as a means of tribal outreach—the ABVKA and the Ekal Vidyalaya Foundation of India.

18. As an example of this, Golwalkar was reportedly very angry at Deoras's interview 'Next Move of RSS', published in the annual 1949 issue of *Yughdharma*, which called for greater RSS activism in society and politics and expressed surprise that Golwalkar did not recognize the need to be more active in these fields. It is widely believed that Golwalkar had the editor fired as a message to Deoras to be more cautious. Report of this in the Marathi book, Gangadhar Indurkar, *Rashtriya Swayamsevak Sangh, Kal, Aaj, aani Udya* (Pune: Shri Vidya Prakashan, 1983), pp. 36–46.

19. This speech by RSS chief Deoras was delivered in Pune on 8 May 1974, and published in pamphlet form as 'Hindu Organization and Social Equality' (New Delhi: Suruchi Prakashan, 1991). It was first published in Marathi, the language in which the speech was delivered. This reference is to the English translation of the speech.

20. The speech was delivered at Vasant Vyakhyanmala (Spring Lecture Series), held in Pune each year. The series was started by Justice M.G. Ranade, a famous Indian social reformer. The choice of this venue underscored the importance Deoras assigned to this speech; he linked it to the tradition of social reform.

21. Interview with Mohan Bhagwat in *Organiser*, reported in *Samvada*, 31 March 2017, http://samvada.org/2017/news/drbhagwat-interview-organiser/ (accessed 26 April 2018).

22. Interview with Suresh 'Bhaiyyaji' Joshi, RSS general secretary, at the RSS headquarters in Nagpur on 8 July 2015.

23. In the wake of the June 1975 decision of the Allahabad High Court that Prime Minister Indira Gandhi's election should be set aside because of electoral law violations, the prime minister declared a national state of Emergency. A renowned Gandhian, Jayaprakash Narayan, founded the Lok Sangharsh Samiti (LSS) to coordinate the activities of the Opposition, and Deoras, himself under arrest, decided to allow senior RSS workers to cooperate closely with the LSS; following Narayan's arrest, a series of senior figures in the sangh parivar took over the management of the LSS.

24. See, Andersen and Damle, *The Brotherhood in Saffron*, pp. 216–20.

25. Ibid., p. 228.

26. The RSS considered Deendayal Upadhyaya's *Integral Humanism* (Delhi: Navchetan Press, 1968) the most authoritative presentation of Hindutva. Upadhyaya argued that Western concepts such as Marxism and capitalism both put an unhealthy focus on materialism that generated greed, individualism and social conflict. He, like Golwalkar, believed that a lasting improvement in the human condition was not possible without the transformation of man, a task which the RSS saw as its unique responsibility. Golwalkar's major theoretical work, *Bunch of Thoughts* (Bangalore: Vikram Prakashan, 1966), makes a similar argument.

27. http://eci.nic.in/eci_main/StatisticalReports/LS_1989/Vol_I_LS_89.pdf#page=97&zoom=auto,-80,795.

28. See, Andersen and Damle, *The Brotherhood in Saffron*, pp. 135–36 for a discussion of these VHP efforts to mobilize support for the restoration of Hindu temples. The conversion in early 1981 of several hundred Hindu Dalits to Islam in the southern state of Tamil Nadu triggered an organized effort at reconversion. This reconversion effort was later to be referred to as *ghar wapsi* (or literally to return home). A prominent figure in the VHP-led campaign for reconversion, Lala Harmon (VHP general secretary and a wealthy businessman), told us in an interview on 24 January 1988 in Delhi that the RSS took up the issue nationally because the conversions had aroused significant Hindu concern and thus provided the RSS an opportunity to reach out to non-RSS groups. He even stated that Prime Minister Indira Gandhi, after the issue broke in 1981, sent an emissary to the VHP saying that she sympathized with their efforts.

29. Newly deputed RSS pracharak Narendra Modi organized the Gujarat link of L.K. Advani's Ram Yatra so successfully that he caught the attention of senior RSS and BJP leadership.

30. The BJP, emulating Rajiv Gandhi's 1989 election campaign, gave a speech from Ayodhya referring to Ram Rajya (the rule of Ram). Aviral Virk, 'Ayodhya Part III: Ram Mandir First Politicized by Congress', The Quint, 3 December 2015, https://www.thequint.com/videos/short-dogs/ayodhya-deqoded-part-3-ram-mandir-first-politicised-by-congress (accessed 14 November 2017).

31. S.P. Udayakumar, *Presenting the Past: Anxious History and Ancient Future in Hindutva India* (Westport: Praeger Publishers, 2005), p. 128.

32. See discussion of this claim in, Madhav Godbole, *Unfinished Innings* (Delhi: Blackswan, 1996), ch. 9. Also see a comprehensive 11 February 2017, NDTV panel discussing former Prime Minister Narasimha Rao's alleged sympathy to Hindutva, with panel members being former Congress cabinet member Jairam Ramesh, former Home Department Secretary Madhav Godbole and Rao biographer Vinay Sitapati. The claim was made during this discussion that Rao in 1992 did not take sufficient preventive actions to save the Babri Masjid in Ayodhya, https://youtube.be/h/kikpyoim (accessed 15 November 2017).

33. Vinay Sitapati, *Half Lion: How P.V. Narasimha Rao Transformed India* (Gurgaon: Penguin Random House India, 2016).

34. Vinay Sitapati, 'Personal Doctor Says Narasimha Rao's Reaction to Babri Demolition Was Honest Agitation', *The Indian Express*, 26 June 2016, https://indianexpress.com/article/india/india-news-india/babri-masjid-p-v-narasimha-rao-vishwa-hindu-parishad-vhp-along-with-babri-it-was-me-they-were-trying-to-demolish-2875958/ (accessed 12 July 2018).

35. Ibid.

36. Hansen and Jaffrelot report that such hard-line public speakers as Uma Bharti and Sadhvi Rithambara stopped addressing BJP national meetings. See, Thomas Blom Hansen and Christophe Jaffrelot (eds), *The BJP and the Compulsions of Politics in India*, (New Delhi: Oxford University Press, 1998), p. 6.

37. See, Golwalkar's discussion of this issue in Madhav Sadashiv Golwalkar, 'Integral Man: Bharatiya Concept', in Devendra Swarup (ed.), *Integral Humanism* (Delhi: Deendayal Research Institute, 1929), pp. 63–69. We also interviewed Golwalkar and other national leaders from 16–19 April 1969, at the RSS headquarters in Nagpur. In many hours of conversation, Golwalkar's concern about the adverse impact of Western consumerism on Indian society was a prominent theme. By contrast, he supported small-scale economic units controlled by their own labour, a theme that also comes through in an interview we had with Dattopant Thengadi, long-time head of the BMS (the labour affiliate of the RSS), on 10 April 1983 in Pune.

38. An excellent analysis of the differing economic views within the parivar in, Thomas Blom Hansen, 'The Ethics of Hindutva and the Spirit of Capitalism', in Hansen and Jaffrelot, *The BJP and the Compulsions of Politics in India*.

39. See discussion of the formation and goals of the SJM in Isabelle Boutron, 'The Swadeshi Jagran Manch: An Economic Arm of the Hindu Nationalist movement', in Christophe Jaffrelot (ed.), *The Sangh Parivar: A Reader* (Delhi: Oxford University Press, 2005), ch. 18. In an interview with us on 13 February 2016 in Delhi, Ashwani Mahajan (the national coordinator of the SJM and an economics professor at Delhi University) said one of the major reasons for starting the SJM was to provide a public platform for a wide variety of groups—including Gandhians, communists and academics—opposed to the market reforms adopted by the Rao government.

40. The first two chiefs of the RSS died in office. Starting with Deoras, the next three have stepped down because of illness.

41. Rajendra Singh was a high-caste Thakur (Rajput) from an educated family. His father was a senior engineer who was a civil servant. Singh himself had been head of the prestigious physics department at Allahabad University, and his doctoral dissertation guide was C.V. Raman, Nobel laureate, which gave him a rather high status in RSS circles, where educational pedigree is highly regarded.

42. Election Commission of India, General Elections, 'Performance of National Parties via-a-vis Others', 1999, http://eci.nic. in/eci_main/StatisticalReports/LS_1999/Vol_I_LS_99. pdf#page=92&zoom=auto,-80,783.

43. National Democratic Alliance, *For a Proud, Prosperous India: An Agenda*, Election Manifesto, Lok Sabha Elections, 1999, p. 1.

44. For a statistical analysis of the BJP's ability to expand its support base, see, Yogendra Yadav, Sanjay Kumar and Oliver Heath, 'The BJP's New Social Bloc', *Frontline*, 19 November 1999, pp. 31–40.

45. Kanungo reports that shortly before leaving office, Rajendra Singh rescued the Vajpayee government from a controversial circular which permitted government employees to participate in RSS activities by suggesting that the RSS would not oppose a withdrawal of the circular; the circular was duly withdrawn. See, Kanungo, *RSS's Tryst with Politics*, p. 269.

46. Sudarshan was a Kannadiga Brahmin born and brought up in Raipur, Madhya Pradesh (now Chhattisgarh). He was an engineer by training and became a pracharak in 1954. At the time of his appointment, he was the sah sarkaryavah (joint general secretary), and was designated the RSS liaison with the BJP.

47. See report of the RSS reaction to Advani's visit in, Radhika Ramaseshan, 'Advani Salutes "Secular" Jinnah', *The Telegraph*, 5 June 2005, http://www.telegraphindia.com/1050605/asp/nation/ story_4828954.asp (accessed 19 February 2016). The RSS press spokesman's statements can be found in, Neena Vyas, 'RSS Questions Advani's Remarks', *The Hindu*, 5 June 2005, http://www.thehindu. com/2005/06/05/stories/2005060506111000.htm (accessed 10 February 2016). Pravin Togadia, a prominent national figure in the VHP, went even further, virtually denouncing Advani as a 'traitor' for making a remark that undermined the RSS's vision of a united South Asia or Akhand Bharat. See his remarks in, Soutik Biswas, 'How Indians See Jinnah', BBC, 7 June 2005, http://news.bbc.co.uk/2/hi/ south_asia/4617667.stm (accessed 10 February 2016).

48. News item on this in, Neena Vyas, 'Advani to Step Down, Criticises RSS', *The Hindu*, 19 September 2005, http://www.thehindu. com/2005/09/19/stories/2005091907280100.htm (accessed 29 July 2016).

49. See, Kingshuk Nag, *The NaMo Story: A Political Life* (New Delhi: Roli Books, revised edition 2014). This is one of the best analytical biographies of Modi.

50. Ibid., p. 39. For Modi's early activities in the RSS, see ch. 2.

51. A senior BJP operative told us that Modi is a tough taskmaster who can be dismissive of incompetence. He also noted that Modi can be vindictive towards those who stand in his way or disagree on policy issues.

52. Nag, *The NaMo Story*, p. 71.

53. Ibid., p. 73.

54. Ibid., pp. 81–89.

55. Nag gives a balanced account of the conflicting evidence. Ibid., pp. 90–91. There is similarly conflicting evidence regarding Modi's efforts to restore order. However, no court has held him responsible for the violence.

56. The home ministry report in the Rajya Sabha records can be accessed at   http://164.100.47.5/EDAILYQUESTIONS/sessionno/204/ uq11052005.pdf (accessed 29 July 2016).

57. Ibid., pp. 100–02.

58. The BJP won 127 of 182 seats, ten more than it had won in the 1998 elections.

59. Nag has a comprehensive discussion of the 'Vibrant Gujarat' effort, *The NaMo Story*, pp. 106–23.

60. There is a debate over how much credit Modi should get for Gujarat's very robust economic growth rates. An argument for his importance can be found in, Arvind Panagariya, 'Here's Proof That Gujarat Had Flourished under Modi', *Tehelka*, 29 March 2014, http://www.tehelka. com/2014/03/heres-proof-that-gujarat-has-flourished-under-modi/ (accessed 10 November 2017). On the other side, M. Ghatak and S. Roy, 'Modinomics: Do Narendra Modi's Economic Claims Add Up?', *The Guardian*, 13 March 2014, https://www.theguardian.com/ commentisfree/2014/mar/13/modinomics-narendra-modi-india-bjp (accessed 10 November 2017).

61. Sheela Bhatt, 'Why Modi Had to Get Rid of Harin Pathak', *India Abroad*, 4 April 2014, pp. 22–23.

62. See Walter Andersen's discussion of Modi's consolidation of power within the BJP in, 'The Bharatiya Janata Party: A Victory for Narendra Modi', in Paul Wallace (ed.), *India's 2014 Elections: A Modi-Led Sweep* (New Delhi: Sage Publications, 2015), pp. 50–55.

63. Advani and Vajpayee had formed the leadership team of the BJP since its founding in 1980, but by this time Advani was discredited and Vajpayee was ill and effectively retired from active politics.

64. For a report of the close relationship of Gadkari and Bhagwat, see, Aditya Menon, 'The Rise and Rise of Nitin Gadkari', *India Today*, http://indiatoday.intoday.in/story/the-rise-of-president-nitin-gadkari/1/226559.html (accessed 11 February 2016). Reportedly, the BJP followed RSS advice that the party amend its constitution to permit a second term for Gadkari in 2012. See, Press Trust of India, 'BJP Amends Constitution Allowing Nitin Gadkari to Get a Second Term', Sify News, 28 September 2012, http://www.sify.com/news/bjp-amends-constitution-allowing-nitin-gadkari-to-get-a-second-term-news-national-mj2uBzccbdhsi.html (accessed 9 February 2016).

65. Bhavna Vij-Aurora, 'Burden of Gadkari', *India Today*, 25 January 2013, https://www.indiatoday.in/india/corruption-charges-against-nitin-gadkari/story/the-burden-of-gadkari-152504-2013-01-25 (accessed 17 April 2018).

66. Bhagwat at a press conference on 8 December 2009 in Chandigarh warned the BJP leadership to overcome the factionalism that characterized the party at that time, https://www.youtube.com/watch?v=8xb2JGND88Yd-list=PL755691AE8F586ECB (accessed 14 November 2017).

67. These high-level and periodic intra-parivar meetings were established by Balasaheb Deoras during his tenure as sarsanghchalak as an organizational response to the rapid growth of the parivar. Formerly, the chief deliberative body of the RSS, the ABPS, was the venue for such discussions, but this met only once a year and could not handle both BJP and RSS issues. The ABKM, the RSS executive body, meets twice a year. There are a range of other intra-parivar bodies.

68. The press report of the establishment of this BJP–RSS coordination committee is in Press Trust of India, 'Top BJP Leaders, RSS Functionaries Discuss Better Coordination', *The Indian Express*, 24 July 2014, https://indianexpress.com/article/india/politics/top-bjp-leaders-rss-functionaries-discuss-better-coordination/ (accessed 12 July 2018).

69. See discussion of the national RSS leadership and Modi in, Andersen, 'The Bharatiya Janata Party', in Wallace (ed.), *India's 2014 Elections*, pp. 52–53.

70. *Caravan* magazine has a comprehensive analysis of the RSS perception of the importance of the 2014 elections. See, Dinesh Narayanan, 'RSS 3.0', *Caravan*, 1 May 2014, http://www.caravanmagazine.in/reportage/rss-30 (accessed 29 July 2016).

71. Discussion with Manmohan Vaidya, the prachar pramukh (chief spokesperson) since 2000, at the RSS office in Delhi on 11 July 2015. It was our view that Vaidya, who sat in on most of our interviews with the senior leadership, is highly esteemed by his colleagues. In March 2018, Vaidya was named one of two new joint general secretaries.

72. Ibid. Bhagwat made these comments in an address to the RSS's chief deliberative body in Bangalore on 9 March 2013. He was perhaps reacting to a comparison of Modi to Lord Ram by some BJP and RSS figures. For many, this praise was a dangerous display of the type of personality cult that the RSS has always opposed. It prefers to emphasize such iconography as the RSS flag and Bharat Mata, a symbol of the united Indian nation.

Chapter Two: Affiliates

1. For a discussion of this strategy, see, Tariq Thachil, *Elite Parties, Poor Voters: How Social Services Win Votes in India* (New York: Cambridge University Press, 2014).

2. Express News Service, 'Modi Appeals for Moratorium on Communalism But Is His MP Listening?', *The Indian Express*, 16 August 2014, https://indianexpress.com/article/india/india-others/modi-appeals-for-moratorium-on-communalism-but-is-his-mp-listening/ (accessed 12 July 2018).

3. Pracharaks bring to their position a legitimacy (in RSS circles) that derives from their willingness to sacrifice potentially lucrative personal careers to work for the nation instead. In addition, as bachelors with no family responsibilities, they can devote themselves fully to their work. It is our experience that pracharaks, working closely with and dependent on the membership of the group to which they are assigned, tend to identify with the interests of the particular stratum of society they represent.

4. Narender Thakur and Vijay Kranti (eds), *About RSS* (New Delhi: Vichar Vinimay Prakashan, 2015), pp. 71–72.

5.   See Appendix II for the list of affiliated organizations. Not all groups working with the RSS are considered members of the parivar. Among those not counted is the MRM, which has received considerable RSS attention since its founding in 2002.

6.   Other prominent groups not included as affiliates are: the Hindu Swayamsevak Sanghs (the overseas groups linked to the RSS); the International Centre for Cultural Studies (which works to revive the culture of indigenous Indian communities); Sewa International (which deals with overseas volunteer work); and the Hindu Councils of Kenya, Malaysia and Mauritius (which organize and advocate for Hindus in those countries), as well as many others. Generally, the RSS does not count as an affiliate any group that works overseas.

7.   There have been several RSS initiatives to work with various Christian denominations since the early 1980s, but they have all failed. Information on these efforts from Madhav G. Vaidya, first RSS spokesperson, on 6 March 2016 in Nagpur. Vaidya himself was one of three RSS figures that took the lead in these initiatives. The other two were K.S. Sudarshan (later head of the RSS) and Sripati Shastri (head of the history department, University of Pune).

8.   See our analysis of the organization in Walter Andersen and Shridhar Damle, *The Brotherhood in Saffron: The Rashtriya Swayamsevak Sangh and Hindu Revivalism* (Boulder: Westview Press, 1987), pp. 38–39. Also Paola Bacchetta, 'Hindu Nationalist Women as Ideologues: The "Sangh", the "Samiti" and Their Differential Concepts of the Hindu Nation', in Christophe Jaffrelot (ed.), *The Sangh Parivar: A Reader* (Delhi: Oxford University Press, 2005), ch. 4.

9.   A detailed discussion of the talks between Kelkar and RSS chief Hedgewar on establishing the samiti in, Suneela Sovani, *Hindutvacha Prakashat Stree Chintan* (Pune: Bharatiya Vichar Sadhana, 2007, in Marathi), pp. 201–06.

10. The most authoritative biographies of Kelkar report that she also met with Mahatma Gandhi to seek his advice, but was discouraged by his pacifism as well as his distaste for the martial arts, one of the cornerstones of the RSS and the samiti. The first is by her son, Dinkar Kelkar, *Stree Shakticha Sakshatkar* (in Marathi), and the second by senior samiti leader Sushila Mahajan, *Deepjyoti Namostute* (in Marathi).

11. A discussion of the RSS's support for the samiti and its encouragement of female empowerment group Stree Shakti from an interview with senior RSS Maharashtra official Damodar 'Damuanna' Date on

15 February 1991, in Pune. He later went on to establish the Samajik Samrasta Manch (Social Oneness Platform), which encourages cross-caste interaction with low-caste Hindus, Dalits and tribals.

12. In a section of *Bunch of Thoughts* entitled 'Call to Motherhood', Golwalkar talks of motherhood as the highest goal of women, and advises women to avoid the fashionable trends of 'modernism'. M.S. Golwalkar, *Bunch of Thoughts* (Bangalore: Vikram Prakashan, 1966).

13. RSS General Secretary Bhaiyyaji Joshi's report to the ABPS in March 2016 is noted in, 'RSS National Meet ABPS Endorses Entry of Women to Temples without Any Discrimination', *Samvada*, 11 March 2016, http://samvada.org/2016/news-digest/rss-on-women-entry-to-temple/ (accessed 8 June 2016).

14. Figures from the samiti website at rashtrasevikasamiti.org (accessed 22 July 2016).

15. Prominent Congress figures who supported Apte as he established this news service were Rajendra Prasad (later President of India), Jagjivan Ram (Nehru cabinet minister), Sampurnanand (chief minister of Uttar Pradesh) and Purushottam Das Tandon (Congress party president).

16. Information on these new RSS media activities from an interview with the RSS's former spokesperson Manmohan Vaidya on 9 July 2015 in Delhi.

17. See discussion of the debate within the RSS in our book, Andersen and Damle, *The Brotherhood in Saffron*, ch. 4. We referred to those sangh members who supported expanding the group's programmes beyond character-building as 'activists'; 'traditionalists' were those wary of this reorientation of the RSS.

18. The RSS stayed aloof from the Quit India movement, a decision compatible with Golwalkar's aversion to political activism. However, many RSS members—including its many new, young entrants during the war—sympathized with that movement and some even participated in it.

19. Syama Prasad Mookerjee (1901–53), a lawyer trained in London and the youngest vice chancellor of Calcutta University, came from one of united Bengal's most prominent families. He joined the Hindu Mahasabha in 1939 and became an advocate of the Bengali Hindu community's interests during Partition. Prime Minister Nehru asked him to join India's first cabinet as minister of industry and supply. He resigned in 1950 over disagreements with Nehru

regarding relations with Pakistan, and soon moved to establish a nationalist alternative to the Congress. He also disagreed with the government's decision to grant autonomous status to the state of Jammu and Kashmir, including that state's right to determine who could enter from India. Mookerjee in 1953 entered the state without permission and was promptly arrested; he died while in detention.

20. Nana Deshmukh, *R.S.S., Victim of Slander: A Multi-dimensional Study of RSS, Jana Sangh, Janata Party, and the Present Political Crisis* (New Delhi: Vision Books, 1979), ch. 6.

21. M.G. Vaidya, the first spokesperson of the RSS and a confidant of Golwalkar and subsequent RSS heads, mentioned to us that Golwalkar supported a party open to everyone, and thus the RSS avoided adopting a sectarian title. M.G. Vaidya is among the most respected figures within the RSS and is acknowledged as one of its most influential ideological proponents since Upadhyaya. He also said Golwalkar suggested that Mookerjee's proposed name for his organization, the Indian People's Party, should be rendered in the indigenous language equivalent, BJS, to underscore the genuine cultural identity of the new India. Information from an interview with Vaidya on 7 July 2015 in Nagpur.

22. At a time when most pracharaks were from Maharashtra and Punjab, Golwalkar was likely attracted to the fact that Deendayal Upadhyaya was from India's Hindi-speaking heartland which plays a pre-eminent role in Indian politics. Still another difference that may have attracted Golwalkar to Upadhyaya was his rural background.

23. For an analysis of the sometimes fractious interaction between pracharaks and traditional politicians in Mookerjee's BJP, see, Christophe Jaffrelot, *The Hindu Nationalist Movement in India* (Delhi: Thomson Press, 1996), pp. 116–23. An excellent discussion of their contrasting organizational and programmatic goals in, Bruce Graham, 'The Leadership and Organization of the Jana Sangh, 1951 to 1967', in Jaffrelot (ed.), *The Sangh Parivar*, ch. 11.

24. The Congress won a large majority in those elections, with 364 of 489 seats. The BJP won only 3.06 per cent of the popular vote, in contrast to the 44.9 per cent won by the Congress.

25. For a brief review of the circumstances leading the post-Partition RSS leadership to branch out into activities beyond shakha character-building, see, M.G. Vaidya, *Understanding RSS* (New Delhi: Vichar Vinimay Prakashan, 2015), pp. 37–45.

26. For an analysis of the founding of the ABVP, see, Andersen and Damle, *The Brotherhood in Saffron*, pp. 117–28.

27. The ABVP differs from communist students' unions in that it advocates collaboration between the various parts of the university, including teachers, staff and students. This non-confrontationist philosophy has its roots in the RSS message of pan-Hindu unity.

28. See discussion of the formation of the VHP in, Andersen and Damle, *The Brotherhood in Saffron*, pp. 133–37.

29. The four Shankaracharyas are the leaders of the four non-dualist Advaita Vedanta monastic orders, which date back to the sixth century AD. RSS ideologues have tended to support Advaita Vedanta as it fits the widely accepted notion within the RSS that all living beings contain a spark of the divine, a notion that is compatible with the RSS's views on nationalism.

30. For a discussion of Shivram Shankar Apte's efforts to gain the support of modern Hindu religious figures, such as Swami Chinmayananda (who sought to make Hinduism more appealing to India's educated middle class), see, Jaffrelot, *The Hindu Nationalist Movement in India*, pp.194–204. Also see, the VHP website's discussion of this effort to make Hinduism more relevant to India's growing urban population at http://vhp.org/organization/org-inception-of-vhp (accessed 15 November 2017).

31. Sudarshan Rambadran, 'Swami Chinmayananda: The Spiritual Giant', *Organiser*, http://organiser.org//Encyc/2016/5/9/Swami-Chinmayananda---The-Spiritual-Giant.aspx (accessed 17 May 2016).

32. For a discussion of the two VHP-sponsored international conferences, see, Christophe Jaffrelot, 'The Vishwa Hindu Parishad', in Jaffrelot (ed.), *The Sangh Parivar*, ch. 13.

33. This resolution also advocated that two other Hindu holy sites (the birthplace of Krishna in Mathura and the Shaivite temple in Benares) be restored to Hindu control. This proposal was extremely controversial, as at the time all three sites were administered by Muslim religious bodies.

34. The RSS's support for these marches is described in detail by Champat Rai (general secretary of the VHP) in 'Moment of Resurgence', *Organiser* (special issue, 11 December 2016), pp. 52–53.

35. In launching this protest movement, the RSS had to decide which of the three proposed temples would be its object. We were told by Moropant Pingle (then a trustee of the VHP) that the RSS chose

the Ram site in Ayodhya because Ram is the most revered religious figure in northern India. Interview with Pingle on 11 September 1993 in Pune.

36. The full reason for the resolution can be found at the BJP website's 'Articles' section at, www.bjp.org/index.php?option=com_conte nt&view=article&id=298:resolution-on-the-issue-of-shri-ram-janmabhoomi-at-national-executive-meeting-raipur-july-18-20-2003&catid=87&Itemid=503 (accessed 15 November 2017).

37. Information regarding the anger this incident inspired in the karsevaks from an interview with Anirudha Pande (one of the karsevaks arrested in Uttar Pradesh) on 7 February 1991 in Nagpur.

38. *The Times of India*, 'Text of Allahabad High Court Order on Ayodhya Dispute', 30 September 2010, https://timesofindia.indiatimes.com/india/Text-of-allahabad-high-court-order-on-Ayodhya-dispute/articleshow/6659163.cms (accessed 18 November 2017). Mohan Bhagwat reportedly told diplomats at a 13 September 2017 meeting that the RSS would be bound by the Supreme Court's verdict, whatever it might be. Statement reported at, Liz Mathew, 'RSS Bound by Supreme Court Order on Ayodhya: Bhagwat', *The Indian Express*, 13 September 2017, https://indianexpress.com/article/india/rss-bound-by-supreme-court-order-on-ayodhya-mohan-bhagwat-4840926/ (accessed 12 July 2018).

39. Taken from the VHP website's section 'Nation Re-Building through SEWA', http://www.vhpsewa.org/inner.php?pid=11 (accessed 10 May 2016).

40. Taken from the VHP website, http://www.vhpsewa.org/inner.php?pid=1 (accessed 6 May 2016).

41. Togadia is no longer a VHP office-bearer.

42. The more moderate orientation of the new VHP leadership is reflected in an interview with the *Hindustan Times* correspondent Smriti Kak Ramachandran, published on 20 April 2018. In that interview, Alok Kumar, the new international working president of the VHP, makes no reference to the contentious cow issues and briefly alludes to Ram Janmabhoomi, https://www.hindustantimes.com/india-news/no-compromise-on-ram-temple-says-vhp-working-president-alok-kumar/story-5jJD4uqYnlzJH1XTQf4vvM.html (accessed 26 April 2018).

43. For a study of the impact of the Bajrang Dal on the VHP, see, Manjari Katju, 'The Bajrang Dal and Durga Vahini', in Jaffrelot (ed.),

The Sangh Parivar, ch. 14. Also see, Katju's book on the VHP, *Vishwa Hindu Parishad and Indian Politics* (Hyderabad: Orient Longman, 2003).

44. Information from the VHP website's section 'Youth–Bajrang Dal', http://vhp.org/vhp-glance/youth/dim1-bajrang-dal/ (accessed 16 November 2017).

45. For the listing, see the VHP website's section 'Youth', http://vhp.org/vhp-glance/youth/ (accessed 21 May 2016).

46. Ibid. This same website has a section devoted to the Durga Vahini, http://vhp.org/vhp-glance/youth/durga-vahini/.

47. See our discussion of the importance of college students in the spread of the early RSS in Andersen and Damle, *The Brotherhood in Saffron*, pp. 117–28.

48. In an interview with ABVP Organizing Secretary Sunil Ambekar on 28 July 2015 in Delhi, he informed us that the ABVP organized a voter registration campaign on college campuses prior to the 2014 parliamentary elections. By the same token, BJP politicians supported ABVP candidates in students' union elections.

49. See discussion of the ABVP's association with Jayaprakash Narayan's anti-corruption movement in Jaffrelot, *The Hindu Nationalist Movement in India*, ch. 7. See also our discussion in Andersen and Damle, *The Brotherhood in Saffron*, pp. 120–22.

50. Ranade dispensed this advice in his keynote speech at the Silver Jubilee session of the ABVP in 1974.

51. This is taken from the 'History' section of the ABVP website, http://abvp.org/history (accessed 3 June 2016).

52. Smriti Kak Ramachandran, 'The Rise of ABVP and Why It Attracts the Youth', *Hindustan Times*, 9 March 2017, http://www.hindustantimes.com/india-news/the-rise-of-abvp-and-why-it-attracts-the-youth/story-EINVYG4o21aDovqD3f6IcK.html (accessed 17 November 2017).

53. A good background on this educational affiliate, the Vidya Bharati Akhil Bharatiya Shiksha Sansthan, can be found at http://svmmunger.org/about-vidya-bharti/ (accessed 12 May 2016).

54. For a discussion of the educational experience within an RSS-affiliated school, see, Christophe Jaffrelot, 'Educating the Children of Hindu Rashtra', in Jaffrelot (ed.), *The Sangh Parivar*, ch. 8.

55. Over the past two decades, we have visited several such schools in different states—and the education is remarkably similar at each institution.

56. These are noted in the section on 'Philosophy, Aims and Objectives' on the Vidya Bharati website, http://vidyabharti.net/EN/AimAndObjective and http://vidyabharti.net/EN/Philosophy (accessed 12 July 2018).

57. Ibid.

58. Reported in the section on 'Statistics: Formal Education' on the Vidya Bharati website.

59. See Hindi report in http://www.amarujala.com/tags/muslim-children-studying-in-rss-schools (accessed 4 June 2016).

60. Laxmanrao Joshi, *Vanayogi* (Nagpur: Nachiketa Prakashan, 2013, in Marathi).

61. Figures taken from Akhil Bharatiya Vanvasi Kalyan Ashram: Annual Report 2015–16. Besides its educational endeavours, the report notes that the ABVKA also runs medical centres that service over 1 million patients, as well as 2398 sports centres, 5018 devotional centres, and over 200 hostels with some 7500 residents.

62. Report of the minister's comments in, Mohua Chatterjee, 'Bharatiya Mazdoor Sangh Turns Down RSS's Persuasion; Plans Holding Strikes against Modi Government's Policies', *The Economic Times*, 20 May 2015, http://economictimes.indiatimes.com/news/politics-and-nation/Bharatiya-Mazdoor-Sangh-turns-down-RSS-persuasion-plans-holding-strikes-against-Modi-governments-policies/articleshow/47352920.cms (accessed 13 May 2016).

63. For a report on the opposition to the Modi government's proposed land acquisition bill by certain RSS affiliates, including the ABVKA, see, Press Trust of India, 'RSS Affiliates Oppose Changes in Land Bill', *Deccan Herald*, 22 June 2015, https://www.deccanherald.com/content/485049/rss-affiliates-oppose-land-bill.html (accessed 26 April 2018). We were told that the lack of internal consensus in the parivar was one of the major reasons the Modi government decided to outsource this proposal to the states; some states have passed legislation lowering these requisite percentages. Interview with Ram Madhav, general secretary of the BJP on 6 December 2016 in Washington DC.

64. See our discussion of the founding of the BMS in Andersen and Damle, *The Brotherhood in Saffron*, pp. 129–33. Also see, Christophe Jaffrelot's study of the BMS in his 'Ideology and Strategies of the BMS', *The Sangh Parivar*, ch. 16.

65. Taken from the section 'At a Glance', on the BMS website, http://bms.org.in/pages/BMSATGlance.aspx (accessed 20 May 2016).

66. Neena Vyas, 'Swadeshi Gives Way to the Reforms Juggernaut', *The Hindu*, 27 May 2001, http://www.thehindu.com/2001/05/27/ stories/05271344.htm (accessed 3 June 2016).

67. United News of India, 'RSS Ideologue Blasts Vajpayee; PM Is Petty Says Dattopant Thengadi', Rediff, 16 February 1999, http://www. rediff.com/news/1999/feb/16bjp.htm (accessed 3 June 2016). Media reports suggest that the RSS had used the BMS to pressure the Vajpayee government on multiple occasions.

68. The objective of this 'New Industrial Policy' can be found on the BMS website, http://bms.org.in/pages/BMSATGlance.aspx (accessed 11 September 2017).

69. Letter from BMS President C.K. Saji Narayanan to Prime Minister Manmohan Singh, available on the BMS website, http://bms.org.in// Encyc/2013/9/23/BMS-Letter-to-PM.aspx (accessed 11 September 2017).

70. Information on the meetings regarding the land acquisition bill comes from four sets of interviews. The first was with two BMS officials, Krishna Chandra Mishra (organizing secretary) and Devender Kumar Pandey (general secretary) on 16 July 2015 in New Delhi; the second with Prabhakar Kelkar (vice president of the BKS) and Ganesh Kulkarni (assistant organizing secretary of the BKS) on 17 July 2015 in New Delhi; the third with Ashwani Mahajan (professor of economics and general secretary of the SJM) in New Delhi on 13 January 2018; and the fourth with Bajrang Gupta (former zonal sanghchalak for the RSS and adviser to the BMS, BKS and SJM) on 28 July 2015 in Mumbai. They all reported that they had met with government officials during both BJP and non-BJP governments. Under previous administrations, they would only meet with cabinet ministers, and there was very little follow-through and, therefore, confrontations would often erupt. Under the Modi government, however, they meet with both ministers and departmental secretaries, and have found this a better format for discussion. On the land bill specifically, they had six meetings and, as a result, had narrowed down their problems with the bill from eleven issues to just two: one related to rehabilitation and compensation for those displaced by the government, and the other to the percentage of farmers and farm workers required to agree to the sale.

71. An example of one such palliative effort was the reported discussion between three cabinet ministers and various representatives of the

BMS following major changes in 2016 in FDI rules (allowing 100 per cent foreign investment in defence production and e-commerce). Taken from, Rahul Shrivastava, 'Top Ministers at RSS Mediation Session for New Foreign Investment (FDI) Rules', NDTV, 26 July 2016, www.ndtv.com/india-news/top-ministers-at-rss-mediation-session-for-new-foreign-invesment-fdi-rules-1436505 (accessed 26 July 2016).

72. Figures taken from section on 'Organizational Growth' on the BMS website.

73. See analysis of this class dilemma within the sangh parivar in Thomas Blom Hansen, 'The Ethics of Hindutva', in Jaffrelot (ed.), *The Sangh Parivar*, ch. 17.

74. Among those intellectuals were S. Gurumurthy, a chartered accountant and a financial journalist who writes extensively on trade and the dangers of foreign penetration in the Indian economy; M.G. Bokare, an economist who was formerly a member of the now-defunct national Planning Commission; Bajrang Gupta, an economics professor at Delhi University; and Bhagwati Sharma, an economics professor who writes extensively on globalization and intellectual property rights.

75. For an account of the philosophy and goals of the BKS, see the 'About Us' section of its website: http://en.bharatiyakisansangh.org/static/about.aspx (accessed 1 June 2016).

76. Ibid.

77. Smita Mishra, '8 Reasons Why Modi Needs to Worry about RSS Post Delhi', Bhupendrachaubey.com, http://www.bhupendrachaubey.com/news/8-reasons-why-Modi-needs-to-worry-about-RSS-post-Delhi (accessed 23 May 2016).

78. See the 'Achievements' section of the Laghu Udyog Bharati website: http://lubindia.com/laghu-udyog-bharati/achievements (accessed 3 June 2016).

79. See the 'Home' section of the Laghu Udyog Bharati website.

80. See report of the Laghu Udyog Bharati's three-year-old protest against BJP-led state government in Madhya Pradesh in, BS Reporter, 'Laghu Udyog Bharti to Intensify Stir against Harsh MSME Policies', *Business Standard*, 3 April 2016, http://www.business-standard.com/article/current-affairs/ladhu-udyog=bharti-to-intensify-stir-against-harsh-msme-policies-116040300531_1.html (accessed 23 May 2016).

81. The Hindi terms for these core management positions are sangathan mantri (organizing secretary), karyavah (general secretary), and sah karyavah (joint general secretary).

82. As the RSS does not collect caste data, our statement on the increasingly diverse social representation among pracharaks is based on the opinion of the dozens of RSS swayamsevaks we consulted during our research.

Chapter Three: The RSS Overseas

1. See a good summary of Modi's 28 September 2014 visit to New York City in, Nikhil Kumar, 'India's Modi Comes Full Circle at Madison Square Garden', *Time*, 28 September 2014, http://time.com/3442490/india-narendra-modi-madison-square-garden/ (accessed 15 November 2017). Overall coordination was arranged by the Indian American Community Foundation (a group expressly created for this event), working closely with the Indian embassy and more informally with the HSS and VHP. Thousands more spectators, unable to get tickets, stood on the streets and watched the events on massive screens either outside the Garden or farther down the island in Times Square. Vikas Deshpande, assistant spokesperson of the HSS in the US, told us that more than 300 volunteers had worked for over three months to organize the event, which included selecting invitees from over 70,000 applications. Telephone interview with Deshpande on 21 November 2017.

2. Modi had a rich record of foreign travel even before assuming his position as prime minister—indeed, even before assuming the chief ministership of Gujarat in 2001. He visited the US in 1993, for example, to attend the Global Vision Conference in Washington DC and Chicago, Illinois. (The conference celebrated the centenary of Swami Vivekananda's speech at the World Parliament of Religions on 11 September 1893.) Modi, during his visit to the US, established contact with non-resident Indian RSS members in the US, a linkage that was to serve him well when he began his visits as prime minister. Modi was also dispatched by the BJP to the US in 1998 to review the activities of the Overseas Friends of BJP (OFBJP), which was experiencing a serious internal struggle at that time. Modi was then a general secretary of the party. We were told by Vikas Deshpande, who accompanied Modi on both visits to the US, that Modi asked

'a volley of questions' regarding American politics, business, social issues and journalism, as well as the views of non-resident Indians regarding India, raising children in the US and adjusting to life in America. Telephone interview with Deshpande in Chicago on 10 June 2014.

3. On 9 January 2015, the Indian government merged the Person of Indian Origin visas with the Overseas Citizen of India visas.

4. See reference in, Kalyani Shankar, 'Modi's Engagement with Diaspora Needs a Rethink', ABP Live, 17 November 2015, http:// www.abplive.in/blog/modis-engagement-with-diaspora-needs-a-rethink (accessed 26 June 2016).

5. Ullekh N.P. writes of this effort to mobilize the talents of overseas Indians in *War Room: The People, Tactics and Technology behind Narendra Modi's Win* (New Delhi: The Lotus Collection/Roli Books, 2015), pp. 133–34.

6. The summary of Modi's speech on Pravasi Bharatiya Divas, 2015, available at, Indo-Asian News Service, 'PM Narendra Modi at Pravasi Bharatiya Divas 2015 Says, "Diaspora's Strength Can Be Driving Force for India"', India.com, 9 January 2015, http://www.india.com/news/india/pm-narendra-modi-at-pravasi-bharatiya-divas-2015-says-diasporas-strength-can-be-driving-force-for-india-242732/ (accessed 15 June 2016).

7. Reference to this effort in, Ronak D. Desai, 'Modi's NRI, NRI's Modi', *The Indian Express*, 2 December 2014, https://indianexpress.com/article/opinion/columns/modis-nri-nris-modi/ (accessed 12 July 2018).

8. The term used for overseas branches, the Hindu Swayamsevak Sangh, differs from the parent Rashtriya Swayamsevak Sangh in that 'Rashtriya' refers to the organization in what is territorially India.

9. Vijay Chauthaiwale, appointed as coordinator of the OFBJP shortly after the 2014 parliamentary elections, described to us his role in these overseas rallies in a conversation at the BJP headquarters in New Delhi on 27 March 2014. Chauthaiwale is an RSS member and participated with his family in the American HSS before he moved back to India.

10. An account of these early RSS efforts in Africa reported in A.E. Purushothama Rao, *Inception and Expansion of Sangh in Kenya* (Nairobi: ND). Also see, Jagdish Chandra Sharda Shastri, *Memoirs of a Global Hindu* (New Delhi: Vishwa Niketan, 2008), pp. 23–37. Shastri started the RSS's work in Africa.

11. This lecture was part of a collection of Golwalkar's writings and lectures. It is in the first chapter of Golwalkar's book, *Bunch of Thoughts*, entitled 'World Mission'. See the 1966 edition of this book published by Vikram Prakashan, Bangalore, pp. 5–10.

12. Benedict Anderson, 'The New World Disorder', *New Left Review*, May/June 1992, no. 193, pp. 4–11.

13. This cyclone relief effort was the first case in which RSS members in the USA involved themselves directly in relief efforts in India, including the rehabilitation of a whole village. This effort was organized as the India Relief Fund, set up under the aegis of the VHP in the USA. The Indian Relief Fund later changed its name to the India Relief and Development Fund, and still exists under that name, though it is much less active than in the past. Many of its service activities were assumed by Sewa International to provide a greater scope for relief activities.

14. See, Ullekh, *War Room*, ch. 7, 'Diaspora Power'. In addition, we heard from Mahesh Mehta at a September 2013 ceremony memorializing Swami Vivekananda's 125th birth anniversary that some 1200 people from the HSS and other pro-Hindutva groups in the US volunteered to work on the 2014 parliamentary campaign. Those who could not go to India, he said, were tasked to contact people in non-BJP ruled states—some 20 million people were apparently contacted thus.

15. Ibid., pp. 127–31.

16. News analysis of the growth of overseas RSS in, Zeeshan Shaikh, 'RSS Expands Overseas: Opens *Shakhas* in 39 Countries including Middle East', India.com, 21 December 2015, http://www.india.com/news/india/rss-expands-overseas-opens-shakhas-in-39-countries-including-middle-east-802587/ (accessed 10 June 2016). There is no consensus on the number of countries in which the RSS operates. It is estimated to be somewhere between thirty-five and forty. Manmohan Vaidya, the former publicity chief of the RSS, claims the number is thirty-five. He notes this in his discussion of the growth of the RSS in *Understanding RSS (Rashtriya Swayamsevak Sangh)* (New Delhi: Vichar Vinimay Prakashan, 2015), pp. 37–42.

17. Documentation on the overseas RSS in, http://samvada.org/2011/news/widening-horizons-a-book-on-genesis-philosophy-methodology-progress-the-thrust-of-the-rss/ (accessed 26 June 2016). Also see the US HSS website, http://www.hssus.org (accessed 18 November 2017).

18. The results of this 2014 Pew study on population can be accessed at http://www/pewforum.org/religious-landscape-study/immigrant-status/ (accessed 18 October 2017).

19. http://www.pewforum.org/religious-landscape-study/educational-distribution/ (accessed 13 June 2017). The next highest group is Jewish Americans at 60 per cent.

20. http://www.pewforum.org/religious-landscape-study/income-distribution/ (accessed 3 July 2017).

21. http://www.pewforum.org/religious-landscape-study/religious-tradition/hindu/ (accessed 4 July 2017).

22. Interview with Venkat Raghavan, a pracharak assigned to eastern US, on 6 November 2017, in Fairfax, Virginia.

23. As of 2016, the global coordinator is New Jersey-based Soumitra Gokhale, and the joint coordinators are Ravi Kumar (Australia), Ram Vaidya (UK) and Sadanand Sapre (Bhopal, India). In 2018, Kumar and Sapre were replaced by Rajendran and Anil Vartak.

24. A total of thirty-two vistaraks and vistarikas have served in the American HSS since the mid-1990s. This information was revealed at an HSS long-term planning session in Chicago in 2014. The objective of this session, which we attended, was to formulate goals for the next quarter century.

25. Interview with Venkat Raghavan in Fairfax, Virginia, on 6 November 2017.

26. Our host was Rohit Deshpande, and he organized for us a meeting at his home with several of the active members of the parivar in the Washington DC area. He then took us to his shakha at a nearby high school.

27. Information regarding the HSS organization in the US from a conversation with Bhanu Gouda, assistant general secretary of the DC area shakhas, in Great Falls, Virginia, on 23 July 2016.

28. The salute in the US is different from that in Indian shakhas. In the US, participants fold their hands in front of them, while in India, participants salute with right hand, palm down.

29. This organization, the Samskrita Bharati, is international in scope; the speaker at this shakha was Padma Kumar, a pracharak assigned to the American branch, which he claimed had thirty-five chapters (one in the Washington DC area), as well as online Sanskrit courses. The RSS considers the group a member of the sangh parivar. The shakha secretary, Rohit Deshpande, told us that this shakha (named the Ram

Krishna Shakha) is part of a region that covers Virginia, DC, and Maryland. He said there are eight shakhas functioning in this area, with two more in the early stages of development. He estimated that some 500 people regularly attended these shakhas in 2015, and some 2000 people participated in the six festivals that are part of the RSS festival year all over the world. This particular shakha celebrated three additional festivals, in fact: a Ganesh festival, International Yoga Day and Diwali.

30. We were told that about half the audience could follow the talk, though most had a sense of what he was saying. The speaker said the purpose of speaking in Sanskrit is to get people to realize that Sanskrit, far from being a dead language, can be spoken in everyday circumstances.

31. Information on the establishment of the American VHP in an interview with Mahesh Mehta in Chicago on 10 September 1984. He was the then president of the VHP in the US.

32. See 'Coalition of Hindu Youth' section of the VHP of America website at, http://www.vhp-america.org/activities/coalition-hindu-youth-chy (accessed 26 June 2016).

33. This conference was reported as the largest overseas Hindu gathering. Attending it was RSS General Secretary H.V. Seshadri, underscoring the importance the RSS placed on the American VHP's activities.

34. Information provided by Mahesh Mehta in an interview in Chicago on 10 September 1984.

35. Figures from the annual report of the Ekal in the US, https://www.ekal.org/annual-reports/usa/ekal-usa-annual-report-2016.pdf (accessed 22 November 2017).

36. Information from the website of the US branch of the VHP at, https://www.vhp-america.org/milestones (accessed 20 November 2017).

37. Ibid.

38. See 'Who is a Hindu?' section of the VHP of America website at, http://www.vhp-america.org/aboutus/who-is-a-hindu (accessed 26 June 2016).

39. Ibid.

40. For a discussion of the Pravasi Bharatiya Divas and its mission, see, Priya Prakashan, 'Pravasi Bharatiya Divas 2015: All You Need to Know about 13th Pravasi Bharatiya Divas (PBD)', India.com, 7 January 2015, http://www.india.com/news/india/pravasi-bharatiya-

divas-2015-all-you-need-to-know-about-13th-pravasi-bharatiya-divas-pbd-241048/ (accessed 15 June 2015).

41. Ibid.
42. For a review of the OCI system, see, http://www.theindianpanorama. news/india/pravasi-bharatiya-divas-format-change-47594/ (accessed 15 June 2016).
43. Account of VHP involvement in, Katju, p. 156.
44. Information from Rao, *Inception and Expansion of Sangh in Kenya*, p. 18.
45. For a rather objective account of that controversy, see, Jennifer Medina, 'Debate Erupts in California over Curriculum on India's History', *The New York Times*, 5 May 2016, https://www.nytimes. com/2016/05/06/us/debate-erupts-over-californias-india-history-curriculum.html (accessed 13 June 2016). A comprehensive account of the HAF's involvement in the textbook controversy can be found in its pamphlet, 'The Coalition against Genocide: A Nexus of Hinduphobia Unveiled' (Washington DC: Hindu American Foundation, 2014), pp. 22–27. Digital copy at, https://www.scribd. com/document/191868816/The-Coalition-Against-Genocide-CAG-A-Nexus-of-HinduphobiaUnveiled.
46. Reference to Gabbard's letter to California's Instructional Quality Commission in, https://gabbard.house.gov/news/in-the-news/broad-coalition-supports-equity-hindus-ca-textbooks (accessed 22 January 2018).
47. The HAF pamphlet 'The Coalition against Genocide', besides narrating the HAF's active role in the California textbook controversy, purports to be an exposé of the Coalition Against Genocide (CAG), an anti-Hindutva coalition organized in the wake of the 2002 Gujarat riots. According to the HAF's review of the CAG's activities, most of these groups exist only on paper, represent a narrow and radical leftist ideology, and come alive periodically to support such measures as H.Res.417, a bill sponsored by Joseph Pitts (R-PA) and Keith Ellison (D-MN) that attacked India's human rights record. The HAF was one of several groups to lobby against this measure, which was eventually abandoned.
48. The four Vedas are the most ancient Hindu scriptures.
49. Report of the controversy from the HAF perspective in the 'Updates' section of its website, http://www.hindueducation.org/india-restored-in-california-textbooks/ (accessed 12 June 2016).

50. Sunita Sohrabji, 'California Board of Education Votes on New Framework for Textbooks, Opposing Sides Claim Victory', *IndiaWest*, 20 July 2016, http://www.indiawest.com/news/global_ indian/california-board-of-education-votes-on-new-framework- for-textbooks/article_85be1b92-4ea0-11e6-87ae-4399fe84d0e3. html?utm_source=Newsletter++2016+-+July+20&utm_ campaign=DNL+July+20%2C++2016&utm_medium=email (accessed 15 November 2017). Another account of the controversy in, Theresa Harrington, 'After Hours of Testimony, California State Board Rejects Two History Textbooks,' EdSource, 9 November 2017, https://edsource.org/2017/after-hours-of-testimony-state- board-rejects-two-history-textbooks-approves-10-others/590118 (accessed 21 November 2017). Yet another report of this controversy in, Press Trust of India, 'Hindu Groups Claim Win in California Textbooks Case over Portrayal of Hinduism,' *Hindustan Times*, 12 November 2017, www.hindustantimes.com/world-news/hindu- groups-claim-win-in-california-legal-case-on-textbooks/story- 4jsKcUardvG5nKHPIM2KLL.html (accessed 27 November 2017).

51. Report of the 14 July 2016 decision in *India Abroad*, 29 July 2016, p. A10.

52. Ibid.

53. Telephone conversation with Samir Kalra, senior director and human rights fellow for HAF and a leader on the textbook issue in California, on 29 July 2016.

54. https://www.hssus.org/about-us (accessed 22 June 2016).

55. For a review of HSS activities in the US, see, https://www.hssus.org/ about-us (accessed 22 June 2016).

56. Ibid.

57. Ibid.

58. The full letter, as well as a list of its signatories, was printed in the blog of *Academe* magazine, a publication of the American Association of University Professors. It can be accessed at, https://academeblog. org/2015/08/27/faculty-statement-on-modi-visit-to-silicon-valley/ (accessed 27 June 2016). Opinions in *Academe*, the publication is predictably careful to note, represent the views of the contributors and not necessarily those of the magazine.

59. Ibid.

60. For accounts of the counter-petition, see, 'Indian-American Academics Spar over PM Narendra Modi's Visit to Silicon Valley',

Silicon India, 4 September 2015, http://www.siliconindia.com/news/
usindians/IndianAmerican-Academics-Spar-Over-PM-Narendra-
Modis-Visit-To-Silicon-Valley-nid-186827-cid-49.html (accessed
28 June 2016).

61. Quoted in ibid.

62. This response was also published in *Academe* and is available at, https://
academeblog.org/2015/09/15/faculty-response-to-harassment-by-
hindu-nationalist-organizations/ (accessed 28 June 2016).

63. See its website at http://www.hindunet.org/hvk/ (accessed 28 June
2016).

64. See description of its activities on the HAF website, http://www.
hafsite.org/ (accessed 28 June 2016).

65. See http://www.hafsite.org/about-us/who-we-are (accessed 30 June
2016).

66. See https://www.scribd.com/document/191868816/The-Coalition-
Against-Genocide-CAG-A-Nexus-of-HinduphobiaUnveiled
(accessed 22 January 2018).

67. See http://www.hafsite.org/about-us/who-we-are (accessed 30 June
2016).

68. The HAF's activities are listed and explained on its website, http://
www.hafsite.org/our-work (accessed 1 July 2016).

69. Interview with Jay Kansara, the HAF's director of government
relations, at the group's DC office, on 26 July 2016.

70. In the American HSS, one administrative position, referred to
as the samiti pramukh, was established to handle the women's
training camps; this position is currently held by Anjali Patel. She is
considered the Rashtra Sevika Samiti's representative in the US. In
other countries with a samiti branch, the organization is known as the
Hindu Sevika Samiti.

71. The samiti, while not functioning in the US, does operate in other
countries like the UK.

72. Manoj Anand, 'RSS Strength Not to Domineer but to Make India
Vishwa Guru: Mohan Bhagwat', *Deccan Chronicle*, 21 January 2018,
https://www.deccanchronicle.com/nation/current-affairs/210118/
rss-strength-not-to-domineer-but-to-make-india-vishwa-guru-
mohan-bhagwat.html (accessed 19 April 2018).

73. This visit by Mohan Bhagwat and Dattatreya Hosabale was not,
however, the first time senior RSS leaders visited the UK—or
other Western countries. In 1977, Moropant Pingle (the pracharak

pramukh) visited the US; Dattopant Thengadi (founder of the BMS) visited the US in 1978; Bhaurao Deoras (sah sarkaryavah and brother of the sarsanghchalak Deoras) visited the US in 1980; Rajendra Singh (the sarkaryavah) visited the US in 1982 and Seshadri (sarkaryavah) visited the US in 1984 to attend the first mass rally of the American VHP. All of these leaders also visited the UK on these visits. While there has been a steady stream of visits to the US and UK, which contain the two largest diasporic populations, the visit of Bhagwat and Hosabale to the UK was the first time the two most senior officials of the RSS travelled together; it was also the first time that RSS figures met the leading political, academic, religious and business leaders of the UK as equals.

74. Golwalkar would have been the first RSS head to go overseas in 1963, but he was denied a passport by the Indian government for a scheduled visit to Myanmar. Professor Rajendra Singh in 1998 was the first RSS head to go abroad, at the invitation of the HSS in the UK. Regarding Singh's groundbreaking overseas visit, see, Ratan Sharda, *Professor Rajendra Singh ki Jeevan Yatra* (in Hindi). The text was sent to us via email by the author.

75. Interview with Yogi Adityanath at his office in Lucknow, Uttar Pradesh, on 18 January 2018.

76. The ICCS was established by Yashwant Pathak, a former pracharak who worked among tribals in north-eastern India and South Africa, thereafter establishing an Afro-Hindu Study group in Nagpur. Information on the group provided by Radheshyam Dwivedi, president of ICCS USA.

Chapter Four: 'Indianizing Education'

1. Information based on a telephone interview with Sharad Kunte on 22 August 2017. Kunte is the Vidya Bharati president of India's western zone.

2. The choice of this school that announced the RSS's entry into the field of education was influenced by the fact that Kurukshetra is considered the site of the great battle as narrated in the Mahabharata. The school was named after the Bhagavad Gita, the most widely accepted holy book of Hinduism.

3. The Vidya Bharati website recognizes the Hindu-oriented educational contributions of several Hindu groups in the pre-independence period, such as the Brahmo Samaj, the Ramakrishna Mission and the

Bharat Sevashram Sangha, as well as Hindu nationalist leaders who established schools, such as Lala Lajpat Rai (in Punjab), Lokmanya Tilak (in Maharashtra), Subramania Bharati (in Tamil Nadu) and Narayan Guru, a Dalit educationist in Kerala. See, 'Philosophy: Aims and Objectives' section of the website http://www.vidyabharti.net (accessed 24 August 2017).

4. For a study of schools in pre-Independence India, see, Susanne H. Rudolph and Lloyd I. Rudolph (eds), *Education and Politics in India: Studies in Organization, Society, and Policy* (Cambridge: Harvard University Press, 1972), pp.13–24. A good discussion of the Arya Samaj education system in, Kenneth W. Jones, *Arya Dharm: Hindu Consciousness in 19th-Century Punjab* (Berkeley: University of California Press, 1976).

5. These schools were called Saraswati Shishu Mandirs; the use of the word 'mandir' (temple) directed attention to the focus that would be given to Hindu culture. The choice of the feminine goddess Saraswati—rather than the male equivalent Ganesha—in the name reflects the emphasis in the RSS on the nurturing power of the feminine aspects of the divinity. Similarly, there is a focus within the RSS on the feminine to refer to the country (Bharat Mata), the cow (Gau Mata) and the holy Ganga River (Ganga Mata). This use of the feminine is in marked contrast to Savarkar's use of the masculine to refer to the country.

6. See the discussion of this debate within the RSS in Walter Andersen and Shridhar Damle, *The Brotherhood in Saffron: The Rashtriya Swayamsevak Sangh and Hindu Revivalism* (Boulder: Westview Press, 1987), pp. 43–56. Fuelling support for the activist cause within the RSS was the Congress party's decision to exclude RSS members from its many affiliated groups. While the decision was soon withdrawn, our RSS contacts tell us that the action led to the formation of several RSS affiliates.

7. A good discussion of the motivation behind the formation of these RSS-affiliated schools in, Tanika Sarkar, 'Educating the Children of the Hindu Rashtra: Notes on RSS Schools', in Christophe Jaffrelot (ed.), *The Sangh Parivar: A Reader* (New Delhi: Oxford University Press, 2005), pp. 197–201.

8. Figure from Christophe Jaffrelot, *The Hindu Nationalist Movement in India* (Delhi: Thomson Press, 1996), p. 531.

9. Statistics from the website of Vidya Bharati, the major RSS affiliate engaged in education, and available at http://www.vidyabharti.net/statistics.php (accessed on 18 August 2017).

10. Figures from the Ekal Vidyalaya website, https://www.ekal.org/our-schools (accessed on 24 August 2017). Education is only one part of the Ekal endeavours which include such development activities as teaching modern agricultural methods. The Ekal mission also includes a cultural component that appears to combine local indigenous customs with elements of the great tradition of Hinduism in the songs and stories that are part of the Ekal's instruction. This fits the objective of yet another RSS affiliate to preserve indigenous cultures. A study of RSS-affiliated schools among tribals in, Thomas Blom Hansen, 'Hindu Missionaries at the Frontier', in Jaffrelot (ed.), *The Sangh Parivar,* pp. 207–10.

11. These books are used as extracurricular assignments as well as for general reading. There are other affiliated educational groups that run schools besides the Vidya Bharati and Ekal Vidyalaya; they are the ABVKA which also works among tribals as well as private educational trusts operated by RSS members and coaching classes run as a service project by RSS volunteers.

12. For a report on these activities, see, Basant Kumar Mohanty, 'Irani Backs NCERT', *The Telegraph,* 31 July 2014, https://www.telegraphindia.com/1140731/jsp/nation/story_18671675.jsp (accessed 23 August 2017).

13. From a reference to the committee report in a discussion of this issue in Partha S. Ghosh, *BJP and the Evolution of Hindu Nationalism: From Periphery to Centre* (New Delhi: Manohar Publishers, 1999), p. 240.

14. The quotes from the 1964 Education Commission in ibid., p. 241.

15. Danish Raza, 'Saffronising Textbooks: Where Myth and Dogma Replace History', *Hindustan Times,* 8 December 2014, http://www.hindustantimes.com/india/saffronising-textbooks-where-myth-and-dogma-replace-history/story-CauM4dmmsPGrjZ3APAvNxO.html (accessed 18 August 2017).

16. Ibid.

17. 'ABISY: Visions and Objectives', http://itihasabharati.org/index.php?option=com_content&view=article&id=114&Itemid=134 (accessed 23 August 2017).

18. See a report of coaching classes run in Delhi by the RSS for Indian Administrative Service aspirants, where the group provides mock interviews as part of the class and offers meals and housing during the training period. The group, called Samkalp Bhawan in the Paharganj neighbourhood of Delhi, reported that some 800 of the 1800

examinees for the 2007 tests enrolled at Samkalp and that some 300 of them were successful. Pallavi Singh, 'In a Paharganj Lane, Sangh Coaches IAS Aspirants, a Third of This Year's Batch Trained There', *The Indian Express*, 19 May 2008, http://archive.indianexpress.com/news/in-a-paharganj-lane-sangh-coaches-ias-aspirants-a-third-of-this-year-s-batch-trained-there/311504/ (accessed 12 July 2018).

19. Reports of these meetings respectively in (1) Express News Service, 'PM Modi Urges Vidya Bharati Schools to Aim for Excellence', *The Indian Express*, 13 February 2016, https://indianexpress.com/article/india/india-news-india/vidya-bharati-akhil-bharatiya-shiksha-sansthan-pm-modi-urges-vidya-bharati-schools-to-aim-for-excellence/ (accessed 12 July 2018); (2) 'Vidya Bharti Can Be a Catalyst for Change', OneIndia, 12 February 2016, *https://www.oneindia.com/india/vidya-bharti-can-be-a-catalyst-for-change-modi-2011205.html* (accessed 12 January 2018); (3) Prakash Waghmare, 'Ekal Vidyalaya Adopting New Methodology', India Post, 4 October 2016, http://www.indiapost.com/ekal-vidyalaya-adopting-new-methodology/ (accessed 23 January 2018).

20. ABPS 2008, 'Evolve a System of Education in Tune with National Ethos'.

21. See an analysis of the difficulty the sangh parivar faces in mobilizing support from India's intellectuals written by the working president (external) of the VHP, Ashok Chowgule, for the Hindu Vivek Kendra website, 'The Hindu Right Does Not Know How to Manage Intellectuals', http://hvk.org/2015/1115/17.html (accessed 23 August 2017).

22. In an article generally critical of the professional credentials of the Modi government's appointments to academic and cultural bodies, the historian Ramachandra Guha also wrote that 'contrary to the impression Congressmen may now convey, academic appointments during the UPA regime [dominated by the Congress party] were often influenced by political considerations'. He further argues that previous federal governments have 'sought to undermine the autonomy of institutions that promote culture and scholarship'. While asserting that the BJP-led NDA and the Congress-led UPA governments both engaged in partisan appointments, he wrote, 'What is new about the appointments made by this NDA regime is that they have chosen individuals in contempt by their fellow professionals.' Ramachandra Guha, 'Some Thoughts on the Closing of the Indian

Mind', *Hindustan Times*, 21 May 2017, http://www.hindustantimes.
com/columns/some-thoughts-on-the-closing-of-the-indian-mind/
story-SuSWIqYttjOV7qCk6uLtBM.html (accessed 20 August
2017).

23. Leading advocates for the publication of these seminal works of
the RSS's Hindutva ideology were K.S. Sudarshan, the bouddhik
karyavah (intellectual secretary) and later sarsanghchalak, H.V.
Seshadri, the sarkaryavah (general secretary) and two senior
pracharaks Ranga Hari (Kerala) and Suryanarayan Rao (Tamil
Nadu). All four were non-Maharashtrian activists. At that time, the
conservative elements in the RSS, advocating a virtually exclusive
focus on its 'character-building' training programme in the shakha,
tended to come from its ethnic Maharashtrian core. The Upadhyaya
collection is a set of seven volumes, each written by a prominent
RSS intellectual. It was first published in Marathi, then in Hindi
and finally in English. We have used the English-language version.
Pandit Deendayal Upadhyaya, *Ideology and Perception* (New Delhi:
Suruchi Prakashan, 1988). Golwalkar's twelve-volume collection
is available only in Hindi and other Indian languages. We have
used the Hindi-language version. *Sree Guruji Samagra* (New Delhi:
Suruchi Prakashan, 2015).

24. For an example of a review of the controversy from a view sympathetic
to Murli Manohar Joshi, see, Rakesh Sinha, 'Red Green Clubs',
The Telegraph, 30 June 1998, available on the Hindu Vivek Kendra
website which states that it is 'a resource centre for the promotion of
Hindutva'. The website contains several articles addressing the debate
over Joshi's choices to the ICSSR, the ICHR and the NCERT,
from a Hindutva perspective. Available at http://www.hvk.org/
specialarticles/ichr/0005.html (accessed 18 August 2017).

25. Dina Nath Mishra, 'HRD Minister Does a Pokhran in ICHR', *The
Observer*, 18 June 1998, available on the Hindu Vivek Kendra website,
http://hvk.org/1998/0698/0093.html (accessed 18 August 2017).

26. An excellent review of the Hindu nationalist effort to influence the
content of Indian history texts in the context of the debate over
rival versions of Indian history in William Dalrymple, 'India: The
War over History', *New York Review of Books*, 7 April 2005, http://
www.nybooks.com/articles/2005/04/07/india-the-war-over-history/
(accessed 18 August 2017).

27. 'RSS Leaders Meet Smriti Irani, Seek Revamp of India's Education System', *India Today*, 30 October 2014, http://indiatoday.intoday. in/story/rss-leaders-meet-smriti-irani-revamp-of-india-education-system/1/398247.html (accessed 18 August 2017).

28. Press Trust of India, 'BJP-ruled States Discuss Education and Cultural Policy, RSS Present', *India Today*, 6 September 2015, http://indiatoday.intoday.in/story/bjp-ruled-states-discuss-edu-andamp-cultural-policy-rss-present/1/466853.html (accessed 18 August 2017).

29. Irani was involved in several of the controversial cultural struggles that embarrassed the new Modi government, such as the JNU students' agitation over the issue of nationalism, the protests surrounding the death of a graduate student at Hyderabad University, a controversial appointment of the chairman of the Film and Television Institute of India. She was shifted to the position of minister of textiles. Shortly afterwards, she was elevated to the important cultural position of minister of information and broadcasting.

30. RSS Joint Secretary Krishna Gopal (in charge of RSS liaison with the BJP) and BJP President Amit Shah were reportedly at the 27 July 2016 meeting.

31. Ritika Chopra, 'Prakash Javadekar Meets RSS, Its Affiliates to Discuss New Education Policy', *The Indian Express*, 28 July 2016, https://indianexpress.com/article/education/prakash-javadekar-meets-rss-its-affiliates-to-discuss-new-education-policy-2939600/ (accessed 12 July 2018).

32. Abid Shah, '2.5 Lakh RSS Course to "Train" Future Leaders', *National Herald*, 3 June 2017, https://www.nationalheraldindia.com/ campus/indian-rupee25-lakh-rss-course-to-train-future-leaders-sangh-parivar-rss-rambhau-mhalgi-probodhini (accessed 18 August 2017).

33. Praful Bidwai, 'India: How the Hindu Right Is Taking over Institutions in Education and Culture', South Asia Citizens Web, 31 December 2014, http://www.sacw.net/article10301.html (accessed 18 August 2017).

34. Sidharth Bhatia, 'FTII Controversy: A Case of Very Bad Casting', *Hindustan Times*, 22 June 2015, http://www.hindustantimes. com/ht-view/ftii-controversy-a-case-of-very-bad-casting/story-0fwS2CoyHsl1Sb7PTCSjpL.html (accessed 19 August 2017).

35. Those cooperating included director Madhur Bhandarkar, actors Jackie Shroff, Paresh Rawal and Anupam Kher.

36. For a discussion of the pressure from the far right on issues related to education, see, Ram Puniyani, 'India: What Is RSS Agenda in Education?', South Asia Citizens Web, 16 August 2017, http://sacw. net/article13429.html (accessed 19 August 2017).

37. Other RSS-affiliated think tanks in the Delhi area include the Forum for Integrated National Security, Dr. Syama Prasad Mookerjee Research Foundation, India Policy Foundation, Forum for Strategic and Security Studies, Policy Research Centre and Centre for Policy Studies.

38. Interview in New Delhi dated 16 January 2018.

39. BMS's Badri Narayan told us in an interview in New Delhi on 16 January 2018 that the organization's research head, an agronomist, was among those who had attended a meeting with the bureaucrats to discuss the draft fertilizer policy. SJM's Ashwani Mahajan in an interview in New Delhi on 13 January 2018 confirmed that the in-house expertise developed in the SJM over the years is used while lobbying government officials.

40. OBC benefits have, in addition to 'backwardness', included an economic criterion, unlike Dalits who are listed in the Constitution. The right to do this is confirmed by the case of *Indra Sawhney v. Union of India* where the Indian Supreme Court argued that 'backwardness' is not the sole criterion for OBCs. However, the court did not define precisely what it meant and left it to the states to decide, a policy that has given rise to periodic attempts by various groups to be included. See decision in *Sawhney v. Union of India*, AIR 1993 SC 477.

41. A prominent RSS activist and former editor of the *Panchjanya*, Tarun Vijay, was attacked by a mob for escorting a low-caste Hindu into a temple. See, Press Trust of India, 'Mob Attacks BJP MP Tarun Vijay outside Uttarakhand Temple', NDTV, 21 May 2016, https://www. ndtv.com/india-news/bjp-mp-tarun-vijay-injured-in-fight-outside-uttarakhand-temple-report-1408268 (accessed 21 November 2016).

42. M.S. Golwalkar elaborates on the notion of equality in a chapter entitled 'Children of the Motherland' in his major work on the RSS belief system, *Bunch of Thoughts* (Bangalore: Vikram Prakashan, 1966), pp. 97–120.

43. A compendium of RSS resolutions from 1950–2007, including the two 1981 resolutions on reservations, in 'R.S.S. Resolves:

1950-2007: Resolutions Passed by A.B.P.S. and A.B.K.M. of R.S.S. from 1950-2007' (New Delhi: Suruchi Prakashan, 2007). There were also resolutions in 1989, 1990 and 2005 against extension of reservations to those Dalits or tribals converting to Islam or Christianity.

44. Ibid.
45. Ibid.
46. Prafulla Ketkar, 'Strengthening the Weakest Link Will Lead the Nation to Development', *Organiser*, 21 September 2015, http:// organiser.org//Encyc/2015/9/21/'Strengthening-the-weakest-link-will-lead-the-nation-to-Development-.aspx (accessed 23 August 2017).
47. Shyamlal Yadav, 'Why RSS Changed Its Stand on Reservation', *The Indian Express*, 3 November 2015, https://indianexpress.com/article/ explained/why-rss-changed-its-stand-on-reservation/ (accessed 12 July 2018).
48. Mahim Pratap Singh, 'RSS Quotes BR Ambedkar to Say Reservation Should Go, Clarified Not against Quota', *The Indian Express*, 21 January 2017, https://indianexpress.com/article/india/rss-quotes-br-ambedkar-to-say-quotas-should-go-clarifies-not-against-quota-4484573/ (accessed 12 July 2018).
49. Newsagency, 'Hosabale Clarifies on RSS View on Reservations', India Live Today, 21 January 2017, http://www.indialivetoday. com/hosabale-clarifies-on-rss-view-on-reservation/104091.html (accessed 24 August 2017).
50. Special correspondent, 'No Move to Review Quota Policy, Jaitley Assures MPs', *The Hindu*, 15 March 2016, http://www.thehindu. com/news/national/no-intention-to-change-reservation-policy-jaitley-clarifies-in-rajya-sabha/article8351849.ece# (accessed 24 August 2017).
51. Gadkari made this comment in a speech at a BJP Maharashtra state conference on 22 June 2016. See the YouTube video from the Marathi language channel, IBN Lokmat, https://www.youtube.com/ watch?v=WRncdzyLT9Y (accessed 15 August 2017).
52. Special correspondent, 'RSS Stint Behind PM's Success: Bhagwat', *The Hindu*, 12 July 2017, http://www.thehindu.com/news/national/ rss-stint-behind-pms-success-bhagwat/article19265379.ece (accessed 23 August 2017).
53. The BJP in the 2014 parliamentary elections won sixty-six of 131 seats reserved for the two groups; forty-seven seats are reserved for

tribals and eighty-four seats for Dalits. These figures provide only an approximate picture of Dalit and tribal support as all voters are eligible to vote in reserved constituencies.

54. See analysis of the issue of politicization in India's institutions of higher learning in Susanne H. Rudolph and Lloyd I. Rudolph (eds), *Education and Politics in India: Studies in Organization, Society, and Policy* (Cambridge: Harvard University Press, 1972), pp. 25–34. A 2008 ABPS resolution addressed the issue of government influence on education, arguing that, 'In view of the crucial importance of education for national development, it is necessary to keep it free from the influence of changing political situations as well as bureaucratic control.' Contained in 'R.S.S. Resolves: 1950-2007: Resolutions Passed by A.B.P.S. and A.B.K.M. of R.S.S. from 1950-2007' (New Delhi: Suruchi Prakashan, 2007). Responding to this potential development, RSS interlocutors typically mention that the financial independence of its affiliated schools provides protection from such interference.

Chapter Five: What Does Hindutva Mean?

1. See website, http://rss.org/Encyc/2015/4/7/1254694.aspx (accessed 23 February 2016).

2. Pratap Bhanu Mehta, 'Hinduism and Self-Rule', *Journal of Democracy*, vol. 15, no. 3, July 2004, pp. 109–10.

3. For a discussion of the important role of the legislative branch of government regarding Hindu personal law, see, Donald Eugene Smith, *India as a Secular State* (Princeton: Princeton University Press, 1963), pp. 277–91.

4. Manmohan Vaidya mentioned this to us in an email dated 2 March 2018, which was a response to a set of questions posed to him.

5. Some quasi-religious symbolism continues to be commonly used in the RSS, such as pictures of Bharat Mata (the feminine personification of India) and symbols of the sacred sound 'om', though these tend to be interpreted as symbols of patriotism and not religion. At public RSS events, pictures of Bharat Mata and the first two heads of the RSS, Hedgewar and Golwalkar, are prominently displayed side by side. The main reception area of the RSS headquarters in Nagpur, however, has just two large painted portraits of the first two heads of the RSS; the walls are otherwise bare. To reinforce the notion

of Bharat Mata as a patriotic and cultural symbol, the iconography represents an undivided India, as it was before Partition in 1947. After India's independence, the RSS would often express the desire to unite India and Pakistan once more, but that proposal has long since been dropped, and the term 'Akhand Bharat' (united India) now has a cultural rather than political connotation, one of uniting Hindus wherever they live. The RSS itself has long since given up the call for a united India as impractical. Some prominent writers, like Upadhyaya and Advani, have raised the idea of a voluntary confederation of India, Pakistan and Bangladesh—but even that more limited notion is not part of the agenda of either the RSS or the BJP. The RSS mission statement does not even mention Akhand Bharat as a goal.

6. Vaidya email interview, 2 March 2018.
7. M.S. Golwalkar, *Bunch of Thoughts* (Bangalore: Vikram Prakashan, 1966), p. 24. Also see our discussion of what the RSS means by 'Hindu' in our previous book, Walter Andersen and Shridhar Damle, *The Brotherhood in Saffron: The Rashtriya Swayamsevak Sangh and Hindu Revivalism* (Boulder: Westview Press, 1987), ch. 3.
8. Ibid., pp. 24–25.
9. Interview with Mohan Bhagwat at the RSS headquarters in Nagpur in July 2015. The term Hindu is highly ambiguous and has been used in very different ways over the past two centuries. As we noted in our previous book, Hindu symbolism differed in the various cultural regions of India as late as the closing decades of the nineteenth century and it was not until the early twentieth century that revivalist organizations succeeded in giving the term a national reference. See our discussion in Andersen and Damle, *The Brotherhood in Saffron*, pp. 16–20.
10. Ajay Singh, 'Mohan Bhagwat's "Hinduism vs Hindu-ness" Statement Is Old Rhetoric; Does Not Signal Change in RSS' Stand', Firstpost, 16 September 2017, https://www.firstpost.com/politics/no-shift-in-rss-position-mohan-bhagwats-hinduism-vs-hindu-ness-postulation-is-old-hat-4046753.html (accessed 9 May 2018).
11. Vinayak Damodar Savarkar, *Hindutva—Who Is a Hindu?* We relied on the version published by Veer Savarkar Prakashan in Mumbai, 1969.
12. C.C. Basu, *Old Hindu's Hope: Proposal for Establishment of Hindu National Congress* (Calcutta: C.C. Basu, 1888). The original

manuscript was part of a larger discussion in the late nineteenth century about who a Hindu is, and involved differing interpretations of that question. For an analysis of Basu's contribution to this debate, see, Makarand R. Paranjape, 'Hindutva before Savarkar: Chandranath Basu's Contribution', *DNA*, 22 April 2017, http://www.dnaindia. com/analysis/column-hindutva-before-savarkar-chandranath-basu-s-contribution-2411145 (accessed 10 December 2017).

13. An excellent discussion of the importance Savarkar gave to subjective feelings of identity with the Hindu nation in Thomas Blom Hansen, *The Saffron Wave: Democracy and Hindu Nationalism in Modern India* (Princeton: Princeton University Press, 1999), pp. 77–80.

14. Sumit Sarkar, for example, has written that what mattered to Savarkar 'was not content or status, but authentic indigenous origin of *Bharatvarsha* (classical India)'. Quote taken from Sumit Sarkar, 'Indian Nationalism and the Politics of Hindutva', in David Ludden (ed.), *Making India Hindu: Religion, Community, and the Politics of Democracy in India* (New Delhi: Oxford University Press, 2005), p. 289.

15. Dhananjay Keer, *Savarkar and His Times* (Bombay: India Printing Works, 1950), p. 164. His chapter on 'Social Revolution', ch. IX, analyses Savarkar's progressive social agenda, which upset conservative Hindu orthodoxy.

16. Ibid.

17. Savarkar's manuscript, entitled *Hindutva* and written under the pen name Mahratta, was sent to V.V. Kelkar, a Hindu Mahasabha leader in Nagpur, for publication. Hedgewar was a prominent Hindu activist in the city and read the manuscript. His biographer, H.N. Palekar, writes that Hedgewar was highly impressed by the manuscript and reportedly found in it an ideological justification for creating the RSS. Palekar's biography is *Dr. Hedgewar* (Poona: Hindustan Sahitya, 1960, in Marathi).
Deen Dayal Upadhyaya translated this book into Hindi, reflecting its importance in RSS circles. Manmohan Vaidya in a discussion with us said that if we wanted to have a reliable perspective on the RSS, we should read the book.

18. This is a quote from a booklet of statements by Hedgewar assembled by the RSS under the title *Pathey*. *Pathey* (New Delhi: Shri Vishwa Niketan, 2015, translated into English from Marathi), p. 4, in a section entitled 'Our Hindu Nation'. Originally Marathi publication,

P.G. Sahasrabuddhe (ed.), *Pathey* (Nagpur: Bharat-Bharti Bal Pustakmala Prakashan, 1989).

19. Golwalkar, *Bunch of Thoughts*, pp. 142–43. This book was edited by a team of RSS intellectuals and the content was based mainly on Golwalkar's speeches, as noted on p. vi of the first edition, published in 1966. One of those team members, senior Kerala RSS leader Ranga Hari, explained in an email that the reference in the 'Contents' (p. vii) of the book to Muslims and Christians as 'internal threats' would be changed to 'Islamic fundamentalism' and 'missionary evangelism' in the next edition of the book, as these new terms are more accurate renditions of what Golwalkar had in mind. Hari explained that this change was necessary, as 'critics dub the RSS as anti-Muslim and anti-Christian . . . [which does] injustice to Guruji the spiritual personality'. Hari also told us that, as the editor of the compilation of Golwalkar's complete works in Hindi, he could not find any derogatory reference by Golwalkar against either religion in all of those documents. He did say, however, that Golwalkar criticized 'anti-national and unpatriotic behavior' of people regardless of their claimed religious faith, but he never criticized the faith itself.
20. Ibid., p. 178.
21. Ibid., p. 180.
22. *Pathey*, p. 17.
23. See his discussion of the RSS as a Hindu sect in 'The RSS: A Hindu Nationalist Sect', in Christophe Jaffrelot (ed.), *The Sangh Parivar: A Reader* (New Delhi: Oxford University Press, 2005), pp. 56–102.
24. Andersen and Damle, *The Brotherhood in Saffron*, pp. 94–98.
25. This speech is referenced in Jaffrelot, 'The RSS: A Hindu Nationalist Sect', in Jaffrelot (ed.), *The Sangh Parivar*, p. 64.
26. Interview with Prafulla Ketkar, editor of *Organiser*, in Delhi on 28 March 2015. One prospective means of addressing this issue is to introduce an economic quota alongside the caste-based one, though this has not been formally proposed by the RSS, given the political sensitivity of the issue.
27. Smita Gupta, 'How the RSS Grew Roots in the North-East', *The Hindu Business Line*, 9 March 2018, https://www.thehindubusinessline.com/blink/know/how-the-rss-grew-roots-in-the-north-east/article22991950.ece (accessed 9 May 2018).
28. We were told that in the southern state of Kerala, which has a large Christian population, there are Christian RSS members and there are

even Christian regional leaders. We were also told that most of these Christian members belonged to the Syriac Orthodox Church, one of the several large Christian denominations in the state.

29. Indresh Kumar told us this in an interview at the MRM office in Delhi on 28 March 2016. Kumar is from Kashmir and is an RSS pracharak who had for many years been the state pracharak for Kashmir. In his office were the usual icons of the RSS: a poster of Bharat Mata and pictures of Hedgewar and Golwalkar, as well as a picture of Swami Vivekananda. In a separate 1 July 2015 interview with Kumar, he told us that an RSS-affiliated organization for Christians had been considered, but RSS leaders felt the time was not ripe, as large parts of the Indian Christian community are opposed to the RSS, though the RSS has been in dialogue with Christian leaders since the 1980s.

30. Golwalkar, *Bunch of Thoughts*, p. 87.

31. Ibid., p. 120.

32. Ibid., p. 165.

33. Interview in Lucknow, Uttar Pradesh, on 18 January 2018.

34. Bhagwat gave this broadened definition of nationalism in a June 2016 speech in Delhi. He is the first RSS head to talk specifically about the environment and social service as a patriotic duty. See YouTube clip of his 12 September 2016 speech, https://www.youtube.com/watch?v=9jQCRgx88O0 (accessed 3 January 2018).

35. Mohammed Afzal Guru was sentenced to death on 18 December 2002 as an accomplice in the 13 December 2001 attack on the Indian Parliament. This decision was upheld by India's Supreme Court in August 2005. Human rights groups in India and elsewhere appealed for clemency, arguing that the trial was flawed and unfair, but the ministry of home affairs in June 2010 and again in August 2011 advised the President of India to reject any petition for mercy. After further delays, Indian President Pranab Mukherjee asked the ministry of home affairs of the Congress-led coalition government to review the decision, and it again recommended execution. The President consequently rejected another mercy petition on 3 February 2013, and Afzal Guru was executed six days later. Protest demonstrations broke out on the campus of JNU, led by students from the state of Jammu and Kashmir and backed by students from the Communist Party of India (M-L) and the People's Union for Democratic Rights. Meanwhile, student groups associated with the sangh parivar

(ABVP and the Bajrang Dal) engaged in counter-demonstrations at the JNU campus. The third anniversary of the execution, in early February 2016, witnessed similar counter-demonstrations involving the same groups on the JNU campus.

36. The ABVP had charged that the marchers shouted, 'Our war will continue until India is destroyed' and 'Death to the Indian Army.' Kanhaiya Kumar denied making any such any such anti-national statements, though the issue is complicated by the apparent doctoring of at least some of the videos of the event. See summaries of the event in, Press Trust of India, 'Court's Order Vindicates Our Stand: ABVP', OneIndia.com, 3 March 2016, http://www.oneindia.com/india/court-s-order-vindication-our-stand-abvp-2030837.html (accessed 3 March 2016), and 'Protests Paralyze India's JNU as Government Cracks Down on Dissent', DW.com, 15 February 2016, http://www.dw.com/en/protests-paralyze-indias-jnu-as-government-cracks-down-on-dissent/a-19049950 (accessed 3 March 2016).

37. See a report on the judgment of the Delhi High Court in, Scroll staff, 'Delhi HC Gives Kanhaiya Kumar Bail Quoting Bollywood Song and Calling Slogans an "Infection"', Scroll, 2 March 2016, http://scroll.in/article/804489/delhi-hc-gives-kanhaiya-kumar-bail-quoting-bollywood-song-and-calling-slogans-an-infection (accessed 9 March 2016). His two compatriots arrested at the time, Anirban Bhattacharya and Umar Khalid, were later released on the same conditional terms as Kumar.

38. For a discussion of the tensions between the protest leaders and the JNU administration, see, Shreya Roy Chowdhury, 'JNU Protest: Administration Threatens Student Union President of Disciplinary Action', The Times of India, 2 January 2017, http://timesofindia.indiatimes.com/city/delhi/jnu-protest-students-union-president-receives-letter-and-police-presence-sought-for-ec-meeting-on-tuesday/articleshow/56297058.cms (accessed 10 January 2017).

39. Discussion of the Delhi High Court's decision in, Press Trust of India, 'JNU Row: Delhi High Court Dismisses Plea for Action against Kanhaiya Kumar', India.com, 15 March 2016, http://www.india.com/news/india/jnu-row-delhi-high-court-dismisses-plea-for-action-against-kanhaiya-kumar-1033415/ (accessed 6 January 2017).

40. For the speech by Kanhaiya Kumar, see, http://www.ndtv.com/india-news/full-speech-kanhaiya-kumar-out-on-bail-speaks-of-azadi-on-jnu-campus-1283740 (accessed 9 March 2016).

41. Chawla's article in *Organiser*, vol. 67, no. 36, http://epaper. organiser.org/epaper.aspx?lang=4&spage=Mpage&NB=2016-02-29#Mpage_22 (accessed 9 March 2016).

42. Editorial can be found at http://organiser.org//Encyc/2016/2/29/Editorial----Different-Layers-of-Anti-Nationals.aspx (accessed 9 March 2016).

43. The rationale for an alliance between the BJP and the PDP was given to us by Ram Madhav, a BJP general secretary who had previously been press spokesman for the RSS, in an interview in New Delhi on 27 June 2015. Prime Minister Modi had tasked Madhav with working out the modalities of such an alliance. This was not the first alliance between the BJP and a largely Muslim party in the state; it had also formed an alliance with the Jammu and Kashmir National Conference party in 1998. Madhav had been in talks with both the National Conference and the PDP prior to the formation of the most recent alliance.

44. The RSS, however, considers Sikhs to be a part of the larger Hindu community.

45. For the full text of the Political Resolution Number 2 Passed by BJP National Executive Meeting, 20 March 2016, on the issue of nationalism, see, http://www.bjp.org/media-resources/press-releases/political-resolution-passed-in-bjp-national-executive-meeting-at-ndmc-convention-centre-new-delhi-20-03-2016 (accessed 12 January 2018).

46. Ibid.

47. The ABPS is the RSS's annual national assembly (refer to Appendix V for details); it announces RSS policy and every three years elects the RSS general secretary, who in turn appoints the various heads of the departments. It hosts some 1500 representatives from the RSS and each of the affiliate organizations, as well as some special invitees. The ABKM is a much smaller group of fifty-two heads of the zonal and state branches of the RSS, including a national 'core group' consisting of the sarsanghchalak (RSS head), the sarkaryavah (the general secretary), five sah karyavahs (assistant general secretaries) and the heads of the RSS departments. The ABKM formulates resolutions for the ABPS. The sequence of meetings of these groups begins on 7 March, with the inaugural meeting between the core group and senior state and zonal RSS leaders. On 8 March, the core group meets with state RSS leaders. On 9 March is a meeting of only

the core group to review issues to present to ABKM. On 10 March, the ABKM meets to prepare the resolutions it will present to the RSS general assembly from 11–13 March. The presentations start with the general secretary's report on the state of the RSS; this is followed by a select number of senior full-time RSS workers presenting the formal resolutions for deliberation, followed by an often-robust discussion and then a vote (usually unanimous). In addition, representatives from the various affiliate groups present reports on their own organizations.

48. The material here is drawn from the RSS official website for that meeting of the ABPS, http://samvada.org/2016/news/rss-abps-begins/ (accessed 22 March 2016).

49. A summary of the report can be found in, Mahim Pratap Singh, 'RSS Calls for Strict Action against "Anti-National" Forces in Universities', *The Indian Express*, 12 March 2016, https://indianexpress.com/article/india/india-news-india/govt-should-check-anti-nationals-in-universities-rss/ (accessed 12 July 2018).

50. The Allahabad High Court addressed the Ram Temple dispute and in a 30 September 2010 decision ruled that evidence suggested there had once been a temple on the disputed site. Because of this, the RSS was confident that the ultimate decision on this issue would be in favour of Hindus and therefore continued agitation while the issue was still before India's Supreme Court would not be necessary. Nonetheless, the VHP continued to talk about the issue, with some of its leaders even lobbying the government to pass legislation to return the land to the Ram Janmabhoomi Trust. See the VHP website, which gives details on the VHP's policies regarding the temple dispute, www.vhp.org/wp-content/uploads/2010/10/rjb-hc-verdict.pdf (accessed 28 July 2016).

51. During the BJP national executive meeting of 19–20 March 2016, Prime Minister Modi reportedly told party workers not to get involved in any controversy thrown up by critics and rather focus on development. Yet the party at this same meeting moved a political resolution advising the BJP to focus on nationalism and Dalit entrepreneurship as it gears up to expand its support in the forthcoming Assembly elections in five states. See reports in *The Economic Times* (New Delhi), 21 March 2016, p. 2.

52. Prime Minister Modi in a 2013 meeting with us suggested that economic development was at the core of his views regarding Hindu nationalism.

53. Press Trust of India, 'Business Should Be Considered a Dharma, Says RSS Chief Mohan Bhagwat at BSE', News18, 25 January 2018, http://www.news18.com/news/business/business-should-be-considered-a-dharma-says-rss-chief-mohan-bhagwat-at-bse-1641929.html (accessed 25 January 2018).

54. See the discussion of his criticism of hardline Hindutva statements during the campaign in chapter 1. We have heard several justifications for the prime minister's reluctance to speak out more promptly and forcefully; the most convincing to us is that he calculates that he could lose support among his core Hindu followers if he adopts a harsh response. Perhaps another reason, mentioned to us by a senior RSS figure, is that the RSS's method of handling internal disagreements is private consultation with the aim of changing behaviour, rather than public reprobation.

55. We talked to several delegates at the end of that 23 March 2016 meeting in New Delhi. Several senior RSS officials, such as Joint General Secretary Hosabale, were at that meeting.

56. For a report of his comments against forcing people to chant 'Bharat Mat ki Jai', see, Rajiv Srivastava, 'Chanting of "Bharat Mata Ki Jai" Can't Be Forced on Others: RSS Chief', *The Times of India*, 28 March 2016, https://timesofindia.indiatimes.com/india/Chanting-of-Bharat-Mata-Ki-Jai-cant-be-forced-on-others-RSS-chief/articleshow/51585274.cms (accessed 9 May 2018).

57. Ibid.

58. Ibid.

59. For studies of sangh parivar activities among Dalits, tribals and other disadvantaged groups, see, Tariq Thachil, 'Elite Parties, Poor Voters', (London: Cambridge University Press, 2014).

60. See reports of efforts by the sangh parivar to include Ambedkar among the revered figures of Hindutva nationalism in *The Economic Times* (New Delhi), 24 March 2016, p. 2.

61. Ibid.

62. Ibid.

63. In an interview with the editors of RSS-affiliated *Panchjanya* (a Hindi weekly) and *Organiser* on 27 September 2015, Bhagwat said he had proposed that a committee of experts should re-evaluate the basis of reservations because of the proliferation of demands for being included as beneficiaries. He also drew attention to the fact that

present beneficiaries are disproportionately from the 'creamy layer' (that is, the socially and economically advantaged segment of the Dalit population).

64. Smriti Kak Ramachandran, 'We Never Thought of RSS as a Custodian of Religion: RSS' Manmohan Vaidya', *Hindustan Times,* 20 March 2016, https://www.hindustantimes.com/india/we-never-thought-of-rss-as-a-custodian-of-religion-rss-manmohan-vaidya/story-VLN01dCxL09MDJbnvBS1WM.html (accessed 9 May 2018).

65. DNA web team, 'Even Beef-Eaters Can Be RSS Members, Says Senior Leader Manmohan Vaidya', *DNA,* 10 December 2015, http://www.dnaindia.com/india/report-even-beef-eaters-can-be-rss-members-says-senior-leader-manmohan-vaidya-2154163 (accessed 28 July 2016).

66. DNA web team, 'Dadri Lynching: Govt Can't Decide What People Should Eat, Says BJP Leader Nitin Gadkari',
DNA, 4 October 2015, https://indianexpress.com/article/india/india-news-india/dadri-lynching-govt-cant-decide-what-people-should-eat-says-bjp-leader-nitin-gadkari/ (accessed 12 July 2018).

67. Speed News Desk, 'Homosexuality Is Not a Crime. It Is Socially Immoral, Psychological Problem', Catch News, 14 February 2017, http://www.catchnews.com/national-news/homosexuality-not-a-crime-requires-psychological-treatment-rss-1458291055.html (accessed 28 July 2016). In a 28 December 2015 interview at Indore, Madhya Pradesh, Hosabale told us that the RSS neither condemned nor condoned homosexuality.

68. Express News Service, 'Mohan Bhagwat: Don't Force Anyone to Say "Bharat Mata ki Jai"', *The Indian Express,* 29 March 2016, https://indianexpress.com/article/india/india-news-india/no-need-to-force-anyone-to-chant-bharat-mata-ki-jai-focus-on-building-great-india-mohan-bhagwat/ (accessed 12 July 2018). This was reportedly stated at a private meeting of parivar participants and released publicly by the BKS.

69. Interview with Prafulla Ketkar at the *Organiser* office in Delhi on 29 March 2016.

70. For a study of the popular impact of non-ideological cues within ideological organizations in the context of US politics in the late 1960s, see, Louis Menand, 'Been There: The Presidential Election of 1968', *The New Yorker,* 8 January 2018, pp. 69–75.

Chapter Six: The Muslim Rashtriya Manch

1. http://muslimrashtriyamanch.org/Encyc/2016/1/13/About-us.aspx (accessed 15 February 2017).
2. Charu Kartikeya, 'RSS Is Lying: Muslim Rashtriya Manch Is As Much an RSS Outfit as BJP', Catch News, 15 July 2016, http://www.catchnews.com/politics-news/rss-is-lying-muslim-rashtriya-manch-is-as-much-an-rss-outfit-as-bjp-1467992819.html (accessed 12 July 2018).
3. Reported in *The Hindu* (Chennai), 1 July 2015. M.G. Vaidya in an interview with us in Nagpur on 10 July 2015 explained that the MRM (originally named the Rashtravadi Muslim Andolan) was officially launched on 24 December 2002 at the request of several Muslim leaders who approached the RSS. Among the prominent Muslims at its launch were the president of the All India Imams Council and the shahi imam of the Fatehpuri Masjid. The then head of the RSS, K.S. Sudarshan, demonstrated his support by attending the inaugural event, as did M.G. Vaidya, the first spokesperson of the RSS. See MRM website for information on who attended, http://muslimrashtriyamanch.org/Encyc/2016/1/13/About-us.aspx (accessed 27 February 2017).
4. For an account of the 2002 formation of the Muslim Rashtriya Manch, see its website, http://muslimrashtriyamanch.org/Encyc/2016/1/13/About-us.aspx (accessed 28 January 2017). The organization changed its name to the present one in 2005.
5. We were informed by both Manmohan Vaidya and Hosabale that the MRM is one of several organizations started by members of the RSS, but is independent of the sangh. The official MRM narrative is somewhat different, stating that several influential Muslim figures approached the RSS for help starting the organization. Most of the other unaffiliated organizations are located outside India, and we address them in another chapter. Interview in Delhi with Vaidya on 10 July 2015, and Hosabale on 21 July 2015.
6. While RSS head Sudarshan attended each MRM annual conference from the time of its formation in 2002 until his death in 2012, his successor, Bhagwat, has not attended any of the annual conferences. Hosabale attended the sessions from 2009 to 2016. Bhagwat did, however, attend an MRM meeting in Lucknow on 2 December 2016 with a large number of Muslim intellectuals to discuss how Muslims and Hindus can bridge the cultural gap that now separates them. Information

on this meeting provided to us by Virag Pachpore in an email message on 11 January 2017. He also told us that two other senior RSS leaders attended that December 2016 session: Suresh 'Bhaiyyaji' Joshi (general secretary of the RSS) and Krishan Gopal (RSS assistant general secretary and BJP liaison), signalling that the RSS leadership strongly backed the MRM's efforts to advance a nationalist message among Muslims.

7. Information on Golwalkar's thoughts about why his outreach failed is discussed in volume seven of his collected works, *Sree Guruji Samagra* (New Delhi: Suruchi Prakashan, Hindu year 5016), p. 157 (in Hindi). Golwalkar expressed his views on why his outreach to Muslims had failed in an interview to an Iranian journalist in 1971.

8. The BJS group aimed at Muslims was the Muslim Morcha and was established in the mid-1960s. The BMS group is the Sarva Panth Samdar Manch set up in 1994.

9. Report of the MRM working for the BJP in Gujarat in Tanvir Siddiqui, 'Gujarat Assembly Elections 2017: RSS-backed Muslim Outfit to Seek Votes for BJP', *The Indian Express*, 22 November 2017, https://indianexpress.com/elections/gujarat-assembly-elections-2017/rss-backed-muslim-outfit-to-seek-votes-for-bjp-4948804/ (accessed 12 July 2018).

10. Of the seven BJP Muslim nominees, three were from the Valley of Kashmir, two were from West Bengal, and one from the Lakshadweep Islands.

11. Tanvir Siddiqui, 'In Muslim-dominated Jamalpur, BJP Candidate Says: "You Are My Family, Not My Voters"', *The Indian Express*, 20 November 2017, https://indianexpress.com/elections/gujarat-assembly-elections-2017/in-muslim-dominated-jamalpur-bjp-candidate-says-you-are-my-family-not-my-voters/ (accessed 12 July 2018).

12. Heptulla comes from a very prominent Indian Muslim family. She is the grand-niece of Maulana Abul Kalam Azad, formerly a cabinet member and president of the Congress party and a colleague of Mahatma Gandhi in India's struggle against colonialism. His was a family of renowned Islamic scholars.

13. The discussion of the ministry's goals can be accessed at http://minorityaffairs.gov.in/sites/default/files/pm15points_eguide.pdf (accessed 25 November 2017).

14. Madhav S. Golwalkar, *Bunch of Thoughts* (Bangalore: Vikram Prakashan, 1966), pp. 167–77.

15. Madhav S. Golwalkar, *We or Our Nationhood Defined* (Nagpur: Bharat Prakashan, 1947, 4th edition), pp. 55–56. Any reference to Golwalkar's authorship of this book must come with a caveat, as it is widely believed that he did not write it all. For example, former *Panchjanya* editor Professor Swaroop Agarwal wrote that Golwalkar penned only the first and last chapters of the book; the remainder, he maintains, was the English translation of a Ganesh (Babarao) Damodar Savarkar's book, *Rashtra Mimansa*, written in Marathi in 1934. Agarwal's book is in Hindi *Sangh Beej se Vriksh* (Delhi: Prabhat Prakashan, 2017).

16. See, Walter Andersen and Shridhar Damle, *The Brotherhood in Saffron: The Rashtriya Swayamsevak Sangh and Hindu Revivalism* (Boulder: Westview Press, 1987), pp. 26–40.

17. A.G. Noorani, *The Muslims of India: A Documentary Record* (New Delhi: Oxford University Press, 2003), p. 1.

18. Golwalkar discusses this issue at some length in *Sree Guruji Samagra*, vol. 9, pp. 105–10, 182–84, 186–95.

19. We were told by barrister Narendrajit Singh, sanghchalak of Uttar Pradesh, that Golwalkar, in choosing a successor, was required by the RSS constitution to consult members of the RSS executive council (ABKM). The final two candidates, according to Singh, were Madhukar Deoras and Eknath Ranade, former general secretary of the RSS. Ranade was the quintessential organization man. Singh told us that he advised Golwalkar that Deoras would be a better pick 'from a practical and organizational point of view'. Interesting in this advice is that Singh left out the issue of ideology as a criterion for the new sarsanghchalak. Interview with him in Kanpur on 23 March 1991.

20. One of the major moves Golwalkar made was to add a spiritual element to Hindutva to bring it more in line with Swami Vivekananda's message that good deeds done selflessly on behalf of humanity constitute the essence of philosophic Hinduism. Golwalkar made a reference to Vivekananda's views during a 1953 speech to RSS state-level pracharaks. Information in Golwalkar's collected works in *Sree Guruji Samagra*, vol. 2, pp. 111–21.

21. Among those committed to continuing the reconstruction phase were Ranade, Yadavrao Joshi (one of the first pracharaks and instrumental to the growth of the RSS in south India) and Madhavrao Mulye (an early RSS pracharak in charge of building the RSS in Punjab, Delhi

and Kashmir). All three were initially groomed by the RSS founder, Hedgewar.

22. The two Deoras brothers as well as other activist pracharaks withdrew from RSS organizational work between 1953 and 1957 to protest what they considered Golwalkar's overemphasis on inward-oriented reconstruction, wanting instead for the RSS to assume a more activist stand to address various problems in society. Information on the tensions regarding Golwalkar's reconstruction activities from a conversation with Malhar Kale, a publisher of Golwalkar's *We or Our Nationhood Defined*, in Nagpur on 12 July 1983. Kale told us that he delivered Golwalkar's plea to the Deoras brothers to resume their organizational work. On Golwalkar's fear of another ban, there was discussion of a possible second ban starting after the 1969 Congress party split into two factions, one led by Indira Gandhi.

23. The Jamaat-i-Islami was especially opposed to the Indira Gandhi government's policy of non-consensual sterilization, as well as its slum removal programme, both of which affected Muslims disproportionately.

24. The three major figures advocating a more open RSS were Jayaprakash Narayan (the Janata Party's major ideologue), M.C. Chagla (a former cabinet member and judge) and J.B. Kripalani (a former president of the Congress).

25. For a discussion of this pressure, see, L.K. Advani, *My Country, My Life* (New Delhi: Rupa Publications, 2008).

26. Quotation from Narayan H. Palkar, *Dr. Hedgewar* (Pune: Bharatiya Vichar Sadhana, 1960), p. 219. This book was translated by Deendayal Upadhyaya from Marathi into Hindi.

27. Golwalkar, *Sree Guruji Samagra*, vol. 9, pp. 105–20.

28. K.R. Malkani, *The RSS Story* (New Delhi: Impex India, 1980), p. 139.

29. This information was provided in an email message from Virag Pachpore, national co-convener of the MRM and a former RSS pracharak on 19 January 2017. The information is also in Sanjeev Kelkar, *The Lost Years of the RSS* (Delhi: Sage Publications, 2011), p. 147.

30. http://mrm.testbharati.com//Encyc/2016/7/12/National-Conventions.aspx (accessed 15 February 2017).

31. Ibid.

32. Heena Kausar, 'Muslim Rashtriya Manch to Help BJP in Wooing Muslims in Poll Bound Jharkhand and J and K', *India Today*, 19 November 2014, https://www.indiatoday.in/india/story/mrm-

to-woo-muslims-to-see-lotus-bloom-227727-2014-11-19 (accessed 19 February 2017).

33. Mohan Bhagwat mentioned Golwalkar's advice to Mookerjee to us in an interview in Nagpur on 7 July 2015.

34. The Urdu writer Imdad Sabri rose to be the BJP mayor of the Delhi Metropolitan Council. In addition, a Muslim candidate contested (and lost) a state Assembly seat from Ajmer, Rajasthan, in 1952. There were also Muslims in the early 1960s who were vice presidents of BJS state units in Delhi, and another Muslim was president of the party's Jammu and Kashmir unit. Information about this can be accessed at the *Organiser* website, http://organiser.org//Encyc/2017/1/9/A-Page-From-History-Jana-Sangha-Muslims.asbx (accessed 26 February 2017).

35. Information taken from the BJP 2014 Election Manifesto, *Ek Bharat Shreshtha Bharat: Sabka Saath Sabka Vikas* (New Delhi: Bharatiya Janata Party, March 2014), p. 42, available at, https://www.bjp.org/images/pdf_2014/full_manifesto_english_07.04.2014.pdf (accessed 10 January 2015).

36. The figures are from an article written by Sanjay Kumar, director of the Centre for the Study of Developing Societies, perhaps the most reliable source on voting statistics in India. Sanjay Kumar, 'Who Did Muslims Vote for in General Election?', BBC, 30 May 2014, http://www.bbc.com/news/world-asia-india-27615592 (accessed 25 November 2017). Kumar cautions that the BJP and its allies received a comparable percentage in 1998, 1999 and 2004. He adds that there was, however, a decisive shift towards the BJP in Uttar Pradesh and Bihar—two states that represent about 20 per cent of the MPs in the Lok Sabha—among low-caste Hindus and Dalits.

37. Syed Kahlique Ahmed, 'Gujarat Local Body Polls: Over 200 Muslim BJP Candidates Victorious', *The Indian Express*, 5 December 2015, https://indianexpress.com/article/cities/ahmedabad/gujarat-local-body-polls-over-200-muslim-bjp-candidates-victorious/ (accessed 12 July 2018).

38. M.G. Vaidya told us in an interview in Nagpur on 9 March 2016 that senior RSS leadership was concerned about stabilizing relations between Hindus and non-Hindus, especially Muslims.

39. Tarun Vijay, 'KS Sudarshan—A Leader Who Broke Barriers', *Samvada*, 17 September 2012, http://samvada.org/?p=12241 (accessed 25 February 2017).

40. Email to us from Dr Shreerang Godbole on 21 November 2016.

41. The RSS tends to translate ghar wapsi (literally 'homecoming') as 'reconversion', arguing that most Muslims in India are descendants of Hindu converts.

42. Godbole email message on 21 November 2016.

43. Ibid.

44. Virag Pachpore, 'Muslim Rashtriya Manch: Rekindling Hindu Muslim Synergy', *Organiser*, 27 June 2016, http://organiser.org// Encyc/2016/6/27/Muslim-Rashtriya-Manch---Rekindling-Hindu-Muslim-Synergy.aspx (accessed 19 February 2017).

45. Ibid.

46. http://muslimrashtriyamanch.org/ (accessed 12 July 2018).

47. Ibid.

48. The MRM website contains an extensive review of its activities, http://muslimrashtriyamanch.org/Activity.aspx (accessed 19 August 2017).

49. Kedar Nagarajan, 'Scholarships, Nationalism and Peace: Scenes from the RSS's Event for Outreach to Kashmiri Students', *Caravan*, 8 January 2017, http://www.caravanmagazine.in/vantage/rss-kashmir-muslim-wing-students (accessed 22 February 2017).

50. Danish Raza, 'The Saffron Muslim', *Hindustan Times*, 19 January 2014, http://www.hindustantimes.com/india/the-saffron-muslim/story-sxdXyHOdasvoBCnV858EWL.html (accessed 15 November 2017).

51. The pamphlet is *Gaay aur Islam* (Cow and Islam) (New Delhi: Goraksha Prakosth, 2016).

52. Mohammad Ali, 'RSS Muslim Affiliate to Hold Clerics' Meet', *The Hindu*, 31 October 2016, http://www.thehindu.com/news/national/other-states/RSS-Muslim-affiliate-to-hold-clerics%E2%80%99-meet/article16085423.ece (accessed 22 February 2017).

53. Mushirul Hasan, *Legacy of a Divided Nation: India's Muslims since Independence* (Delhi: Oxford University Press, 1997), p. 167.

54. Nilanjan Mukhopadhyay, 'Muslim as Chief Guest at RSS Function: Political Compulsion or a Paradigm Shift?', *The Economic Times*, 25 September 2017, https://economictimes.indiatimes.com/news/politics-and-nation/muslim-as-chief-guest-at-rss-function-political-compulsion-or-a-paradigm-shift/articleshow/60820620.cms (accessed 1 October 2017).

55. Ibid.

56. Kamal Saiyed, 'Dawoodi Bohra Head Praises PM Modi in Muharaam Speech', *The Indian Express*, 30 October 2014, https://indianexpress. com/article/india/gujarat/dawoodi-bohra-head-praises-pm-modi-in-muharaam-speech/ (accessed 12 July 2018). Even though Bohras also suffered casualties in the 2002 Gujarat riots, Bohra leadership had clearly calculated that it was prudent to get along with Modi, and probably recognized that he too was reaching out to them.

57. We attended those events and were struck by the genuinely friendly interaction between Modi and the Bohra delegation.

58. These figures are compiled by a Shia charitable trust (Alimaan) and can be found at, http://www.alimaan.org/whyindia.html (accessed 27 November 2017).

59. Shreyas Sardesai, 'Lok Sabha 2014—A Further Marginalisation of Muslims?' *The Hindu*, 9 June 2014, http://www.thehindu.com/ opinion/op-ed/lok-sabha-2014-a-further-marginalisation-of-muslims/article6100764.ece# (accessed 29 November 2017).

60. Our correspondent, 'Shias Inch Closer to BJP', *The Sunday Guardian*, 10 September 2017, https://www.sundayguardianlive.com/news/ 10800-shias-inch-closer-bjp (accessed 10 November 2017).

61. Suchandana Gupta, 'No One Has a Right to Measure Other's Patriotism: Mohan Bhagwat', *The Times of India*, 12 February 2017, http://timesofindia.indiatimes.com/city/bhopal/no-one-has-a-right-to-measure-others-patriotism-mohan-bhagwat/ articleshow/57103204.cms (accessed 22 February 2017).

62. Press Trust of India, 'Muslims Are Hindus by Nationality, Says RSS Chief Mohan Bhagwat', India TV, 9 February 2017, https:// www.indiatvnews.com/politics/national-muslims-are-hindus-by-nationality-says-rss-chief-mohan-bhagwat-368215?HPT=1 (accessed 23 February 2017).

Chapter Seven: Jammu and Kashmir Quandary

1.   For the BJP press conference addressed by Ram Madhav announcing the break-up of the coalition, see https://www.youtube.com/ watch?v=kQMIr8jIuwY (accessed 20 June 2018).

2.   Press Trust of India, 'Afternoon Call from Governor Vohra That Ended Mehbooba Mufti's CM Tenure', ABP News, 19 June 2018, http:// www.abplive.in/india-news/afternoon-call-from-governor-vohra-ended-mehbooba-mutis-cm-tenure-713002 (accessed 20 June 2018).

3. Vasudha Venugopal, 'Past 2 BJP-RSS Meets Focussed on Worsening Kashmir Situation', *The Economic Times,* 20 June 2018, https://economictimes.indiatimes.com/news/politics-and-nation/ past-2-bjp-rss-meets-focussed-on-worsening-kashmir-situation/ articleshow/64656955.cms (accessed 21 June 2018).

4. Prashant Jha and Kumar Uttam, 'Why BJP Pulled the Plug on PDP: Rainbow Alliances Are Short Lived, Says Ram Madhav', *Hindustan Times,* 21 June 2018, https://www.hindustantimes. com/india-news/why-bjp-pulled-the-plug-on-pdp-it-was-a-rainbow-alliance-rainbows-don-t-last-says-ram-madhav/story-JtuXifiLC8n934q6CkQC3N.html (accessed 21 June 2018).

5. Vajpayee at that time proposed substituting Bharatiya as a term for the ideological formulation rather than Hindutva, as the sense Bharatiya conveyed was more inclusive. For more about Vajpayee's efforts to make the BJP more inclusive, see, Sudheendra Kulkarni, 'What Made Bharat Ratna Vajpayee an Extraordinary Leader', NDTV, 27 March 2015, https://www.ndtv.com/opinion/what-made-bharat-ratna-vajpayee-an-extraordinary-leader-750011 (accessed 20 June 2018).

6. Respect for Mufti Mohammad Sayeed in the sangh parivar is demonstrated by the invitation to him to speak at the 2015 India Ideas Conclave, Goa, organized by the RSS-sympathetic India Foundation, where Ram Madhav plays a prominent role. We attended that speech and witnessed the rousing reception Mufti received. His speech, entitled 'Kashmiriyat, Jamhuriyat, Insaniyat' was met with resounding applause. In his speech, he praised the composite culture of Jammu and Kashmir and compared it to that of India. For his speech, see, https://www.youtube.com/watch?v=dRFA6uP1zIQ (accessed 20 June 2018).

7. The RSS leadership has moved rather far in the past few years to accept compromises to back up the BJP's efforts to form governments that could stay in power. The BJP governments under Atal Behari Vajpayee (1996 and 1998–2004) also compromised on a range of Hindu nationalist issues—such as Article 370—but at that time there was considerable open grumbling about what many considered a betrayal of the core elements of Hindu nationalism. Today there is less.

8. The RSS has in the past rejected the notion of territorial nationalism in defining what it is to be a 'Hindu'. With the BJP's ascent to power, the RSS has begun to look at Hindu ethnicity within the confines of the territory controlled by India. The RSS defines Hindu culture

and philosophy in a broader international context, arguing that it has universal applicability.

9. The Hindu nationalist notion of kinship and cultural ties creating a distinct Indian ethnic group is discussed in Pratap Bhanu Mehta, 'Hinduism and Self-Rule', *Journal of Democracy* (vol. 15, no. 3, July 2004), pp. 108–21.

10. Savarkar's argument is spelt out in his book *Hindutva*, and we rely on the version that is published in volume six of his works in *Samagra Savarkar Wangmaya: Hindu Rashtra Darshan* (Pune: Maharashtra Prantik Hindusabha, 1964), pp. 1–91. Also see, our discussion of the issue in Walter Andersen and Shridhar Damle, *The Brotherhood in Saffron: The Rashtriya Swayamsevak Sangh and Hindu Revivalism* (Boulder: Westview Press, 1987), pp. 33–34.

11. The MRM has published a booklet arguing that yoga exists as a part of the Muslim tradition, using the example of namaz. See, Dr Imran Chaudhry and Abhijit Singh (eds), *Yoga and Islam* (Delhi: Muslim Rashtriya Manch, 2015).

12. RSS writers often point to the continued use of Hindu cultural elements in Muslim-majority Indonesia, such as the adaptation of the classic epics, to explain the cultural assimilation they hope to achieve among India's large Muslim community.

13. Prime Minister Modi mentioned the relationship between infrastructure development and closer emotional integration of Kashmiris into the Indian Union in his Independence Day speech on 15 August 2017.

14. See report of the extensive CMP in '15 Highlights of PDP-BJP Government Agenda in Jammu and Kashmir', *India Today*, 1 March 2015, http://indiatoday.intoday.in/story/pdp-bjp-government-jammu-and-kashmir-common-minimum-programme-afspa-article-370/1/421696.html (accessed 4 August 2017).

15. Jha and Uttam, 'Why BJP Pulled the Plug on PDP: Rainbow Alliances Are Short Lived, Says Ram Madhav', *Hindustan Times*.

16. Assisting Madhav were BJP President Amit Shah and Finance Minister Arun Jaitley. It is likely that Indresh Kumar, the national convener of the MRM, and the Kashmir prant pracharak, Arun Kumar (who was simultaneously the head of an RSS think tank on Kashmir), were also involved.

17. Ram's unique role in the RSS is reflected by the fact that he was selected in 2003 as the second media spokesman in the executive

of the RSS. The first media spokesperson was Prof. M.G. Vaidya, the father of two sons who have played a prominent role in the contemporary RSS: Manmohan Vaidya, earlier the RSS national prachar pramukh and now the sah sarkaryavah, and Ram Vaidya, assistant world coordinator of the HSS.

18. Hanging over the talks was a possible alliance of the three so-called secular parties: the PDP with twenty-eight seats; the Jammu and Kashmir National Conference with fifteen seats; and the Congress with twelve. Intense rivalry between the leaders of the first two prevented such an alliance from forming.

19. Bharat Mata arose as a nationalist icon in the late nineteenth century, and served to arouse opposition to the British colonial presence. It is not a traditional representation of the goddess, but Mahatma Gandhi in 1936 dedicated a Bharat Mata temple in Benares, containing only a marble-embossed map of India. The RSS itself has defended its use as a symbol of the unity among Hindus in India—and increasingly as a symbol of unity of all Indians. A controversy arose in 2016 when a Muslim member of Parliament refused to use it as the patriotic chant ('Bharat Mata ki Jai', or 'victory to Mother India').

20. Taken from 'RSS Annual Report Akhil Bharatiya Pratinidhi Sabha 2015', http://rss.org//Encyc/2015/3/13/rss-annual-report-2015.html (accessed 6 August 2017).

21. Press Trust of India, 'RSS Says No Change in Stand on Article 370; Wants Jammu and Kashmir Experiment to Succeed', India. com, 13 March 2015, http://www.india.com/news/india/rss-says-no-change-in-stand-on-article-370-wants-jammu-and-kashmir-experiment-to-succeed-315108/ (accessed 8 August 2016).

22. Ibid.

23. Ibid.

24. The 2011 Census of India reports that 68.31 per cent of the population is listed as Muslim and 28.44 per cent as Hindu (slightly more than 30 per cent if Sikhs and Jains are included in that reckoning). For statistics by district in the state, see http://www.censusindia.gov. in/2011-prov-results/prov_data_products_J&K.html (accessed 15 May 2017). Jammu and the Valley also differ in language, with a Punjabi dialect dominant in Jammu, and Kashmiri in the Valley. Bhoti, a Tibetic language is dominant in sparsely populated Ladakh.

25. Press Trust of India, 'RSS Says No Change in Stand on Article 370; Wants Jammu and Kashmir Experiment to Succeed', India.com.

26. 'No Separatist Will Be Released without Consultation: Sayeed to Rajnath', Zee News, 10 March 2015, http://zeenews.india.com/ news/jammu-and-kashmir/no-separatist-will-be-released-without-consultation-sayeed-to-rajnath_1559023.html (accessed 4 August 2017).

27. For details of the tension, see, Muzamil Jaleel, 'PDP-BJP Alliance Govt Turns Three in J-K: A Look at What Keeps Them Together', *The Indian Express*, 25 March 2018, https:// indianexpress.com/article/india/jk-delhi-tightrope-narendra-modi-mehbooba-mufti-india-pakistan-bjp-pdp-alliance-5076885/ (accessed 12 July 2018).

28. A particularly good review of this violence reported in Pakistan's major English-language daily, *Dawn*, can be found at, AFP, 'Clashes as Kashmir Marks Burhan Wani's Death Anniversary', *Dawn*, 8 July 2017, https://www.dawn.com/news/1344017 (accessed 5 August 2017).

29. In the 1990s, the RSS played a major role in popularizing religious tourism to the Amarnath cave as an act that combines devotion and patriotism.

30. Reported in the *Indian Express* App and can be found at, http:// trueviralnews.com/36-attacks-on-amarnath-yatra-in-27-years-53-pilgrims-killed (accessed 6 August 2017).

31. The VHP circular was entitled 'Time for Strongest Action against Jihadist Terrorism in Kashmir', and released in New Delhi on 11 July 2017.

32. See the Jammu and Kashmir Constitution, Part III (Permanent Residents), http://www.jklegislativeassembly.nic.in/Costitution_ of_J&K.pdf (accessed 9 August 2017).

33. The Jammu and Kashmir Centre's website is http://www. jkstudycentre.org.

34. References to the legal action against Article 35A can be found in, Ishfaq-ul-Hassan, 'Mufti Mohammad Sayeed Government Vows to Protect Article 370', *DNA*, 7 October 2015, http://www.dnaindia. com/india/report-mufti-mohammad-sayeed-government-vows-to-protect-article-370-2132281 (accessed 9 August 2017).

35. Ibid.

36. Vinod Sharma, 'Mehbooba's Message Deserves Reciprocation Not Belligerence', *Hindustan Times*, 2 August 2017, http://www.hindustantimes.com/opinion/mehbooba-s-

message-deserves-reciprocation-not-belligerence/story-EMoUpzOjFpCbFrJt2yZDNL.html (accessed 10 August 2017).

37. HT Correspondent, '"Larger Debate" Needed on Constitution's Article 35A: Govt Tells Supreme Court', *Hindustan Times*, 17 July 2017, http://www.hindustantimes.com/india-news/larger-debate-needed-on-constitution-s-article-35a-govt-tells-supreme-court/story-wL93eMNNAC6w8vSyYmbmkL.html (accessed 10 August 2017).

38. Report on these infrastructure projects in Kashmir in, FE Online, 'After Chenani-Nashri Tunnel, Here Are Narendra Modi's Top Infrastructure Projects for Jammu and Kashmir', *The Financial Express*, 3 April 2017, http://www.financialexpress.com/india-news/after-chenani-nashri-tunnel-here-are-narendra-modis-top-infrastructure-projects-for-jammu-and-kashmir/612847// (accessed 11 August 2017).

39. Ibid.

40. Following the model of establishing service activities to build support for the sangh parivar in the Northeast, the RSS could use the same tactic in the Valley to build support among Muslims.

41. Figures from 'Economic Survey Report 2016', Government of Jammu and Kashmir.

42. The third-year Officer Training Camp (OTC) is called the Sangh Shiksha Varg and is a critical element in the training of RSS pracharaks. It is held at the RSS headquarters in Nagpur and is the longest and most substantive of the three sets of training camps. Officers selected to attend it are those who have successfully completed the first- and second-year training camps and have demonstrated leadership capabilities. RSS national leaders attend and pay close attention to these prospective future leaders.

43. The order of senior annual national deliberations is: the Akhil Bharatiya Karyakari Mandal (the executive arm of the RSS, a conclave of about fifty delegates who formalize resolutions presented to the ABPS), held once a year close to the Hindu festival of Diwali; the Akhil Bharatiya Pratinidhi Sabha (a kind of parliament of some 1400 delegates that discusses national issues) which is held once a year, usually in March.

44. An excellent analysis of the politicization of religious tourism can be found in, Raksha Kumar, 'India Is Weaponizing Its Spiritual Tourists', *Foreign Policy*, 9 August 2017, http://foreignpolicy.com/2017/08/09/

india-is-weaponizing-its-spiritual-tourists/ (accessed 10 August 2017).

45. Ibid.

46. Quoted in Kumar, ibid.

47. Pravin Togadia, the former international working president of the VHP, said, 'The Yatra is very much a spirituo-patriotic pilgrimage and mountain adventure. It strengthens national unity and territorial integrity. The two-month long Yatra mobilises people from all nooks and corners of the country thereby strengthening national unity.' For details, see, 'Amarnath Yatra: A Militarized Pilgrimage', *Equitable Tourism*, 10 June 2017, https://www.equitabletourism.org/files/fileDocuments5925_uid32.pdf (accessed 10 February 2018).

48. See the Amarnath Shrine website for details on the substantial support for the annual pilgrimage at, http://shriamarnathjishrine.com/DarshanFiguresYatra2016.html (accessed 10 August 2017). Figures for the 2017 pilgrimage season are taken from the website. There were over 3,52,000 pilgrims in 2015; this number declined to 2,20,000 in 2016, probably owing to the fear of militant attacks, but increased some 20 per cent in 2017.

49. For the press account of the three-day conclave, see, Arvind Sharma, 'RSS Meet Discusses Plans to Set Up Base in Kashmir', *Greater Kashmir*, 19 July 2017, http://www.greaterkashmir.com/news/jammu/rss-meet-discusses-plans-to-set-up-base-in-kashmir/255128.html (accessed 11 August 2017).

50. Kedar Nagarajan, 'Scholarships, Nationalism and Peace: Scenes from the RSS's Event for Outreach to Kashmiri Students', *Caravan*, 8 January 2017, http://www.caravanmagazine.in/vantage/rss-kashmir-muslim-wing-students (accessed 11 August 2017).

51. The RSS designated Kashmir as part of the Punjab region until 1947, when it was made a separate administrative unit.

52. An excellent analysis of the early political activities of the RSS in Jammu and Kashmir can be found in, Navnita Chadha Behera, *State, Identity and Violence: Jammu, Kashmir and Ladakh* (Delhi: Manohar Publishers, 2000), pp. 84–87. Balraj Madhok's activities in Kashmir are analysed in Craig Baxter, *The Jana Sangh: A Biography of an Indian Political Party* (Philadelphia: University of Pennsylvania Press, 1969), p. 59. Madhok was expelled from the state in 1948 by the National Conference government for his role in organizing protests against Kashmir's autonomy. His forced move to Delhi led this dynamic organizer to find a role coordinating the new BJS.

53. Balraj Madhok, the first general secretary of the Praja Parishad, provides an authoritative account of its formation in his book *Kashmir: Centre of New Alignments* (New Delhi: Deepak Prakashan, 1963), pp. 37–39.

54. For a discussion of the legal, political and strategic moves by India that brought Jammu and Kashmir into the Indian Union as an autonomous state, see, Behera, *State, Identity and Violence*, ch. 4, 'Dreams Gone Sour'.

55. The Hindu Maharaja Hari Singh, unlike most of the Indian ruling princes, had not joined the Indian Union at Independence. But the attacks on his forces from Muslims fighters from Pakistan soon after Independence prodded him to ask India for assistance and to agree to the accession of Jammu and Kashmir to the Indian Union.

56. Behera reports that a large majority of the critical bureaucratic cadre at the time of Independence comprised Hindu Kashmiri Pandits, a small high-caste community residing mainly in the Valley that was disproportionately influential due to its education and support from the royal order. She also notes the major turnaround in ethnic power that occurred when the National Conference took over the state from the Dogra Maharaja, virtually excluding the Jammu region from government by manipulating the system to win seventy-three of seventy-five contested seats and selecting only one cabinet member from the region. See, Behera, *State, Identity and Violence*, pp. 82–84.

57. Ibid., p. 84.

58. An analysis of the 1952–53 Kashmir protest in Craig Baxter, *Jana Sangh*, pp. 116–28.

59. Behera, *State, Identity and Violence*, p. 100.

60. The state's autonomy has been gradually whittled down since the 1950s so that now Kashmir resembles an ordinary Indian state.

61. Security presence in Kashmir is likely to remain as long as there is a militant threat from across the border in Pakistan.

62. For a review of the steps leading to the appointment of a Kashmir interlocutor, see, 'Can Dineshwar Sharma End the Violence?', Rediff.com, 6 November 2017, http://www.rediff.com/news/special/can-dineshwar-sharma-end-the-violence-in-kashmir/20171106.htm (accessed 28 December 2017).

63. Bharti Jain, 'Govt Restarts Kashmir Dialogue with Former IB Chief at the Helm', *The Times of India*, 24 October 2017, https://timesofindia.indiatimes.com/india/govt-appoints-former-ib-director-dineshwar-sharma-as-special-interlocutor-on-kashmir/articleshow/61187478.

cms (accessed 30 December, 2017). In 2001, Prime Minister Vajpayee had appointed the deputy chairman of the Planning Commission, K.C. Pant, to manage talks. Pant was the first of several people subsequently chosen to conduct such talks, though Sharma was the first with direct experience of Kashmir as well as the first intelligence officer.

64. Ibid.

65. Jha and Uttam, 'Why BJP Pulled the Plug on PDP: Rainbow Alliances Are Short Lived, Says Ram Madhav', *Hindustan Times*.

66. There is a vast literature on the Kashmir dispute. Some of the better books are Robert G. Wirsing, *Kashmir in the Shadow of War: Regional Rivalries in a Nuclear Age* (Armonk: M.E. Sharp, 2003) and Ashutosh Varshney, 'Three Compounded Nationalisms: Why Kashmir has been a Problem', in Raju Thomas (ed.), *Perspectives on Kashmir: The Roots of Conflict in South Asia* (Boulder: Westview, 1992), pp. 192–234.

67. For a discussion of these efforts from the Pakistani perspective, see Web Desk, 'Pakistan, India Almost Sign Win-Win Kashmir Deal in 2007', *Express Tribune*, 16 June 2018, https://tribune.com.pk/story/973934/pakistan-india-almost-signed-win-win-kashmir-deal-in-2007-ex-envoy/ (accessed 4 January 2018). For a comprehensive analysis of the secret talks, see, Steve Coll, 'The Back Channel: India and Pakistan's Secret Kashmir Talks', *New Yorker*, 2 March 2009, https://www.newyorker.com/magazine/2009/03/02/the-back-channel (accessed 3 January 2018).

68. For a review of the terms of the proposal which were never formally discussed between the two sides, see, 'Musharraf Pushes Shared Kashmir Sovereignty Proposal', *Voice of America*, 31 October 2009, https://www.voanews.com/a/a-13-2006-12-05-voa22/324253.html (accessed 31 December 2017).

Chapter Eight: A Debate on Economic Self-Sufficiency

1. Express Web Desk, 'Full Text: PM Narendra Modi's Keynote Speech at Plenary Session of WEF in Davos', *The Indian Express*, 24 January 2018, https://indianexpress.com/article/india/full-text-pm-modis-keynote-speech-at-plenary-session-of-davos-wef-5036533/ (accessed 12 July 2018).

2. Report taken from Raj Kumar Ray, 'India's FDI Inflows at a Record \$60.1 Billion in 2016-17', *Hindustan Times*, 19 May 2017,

http://www.hindustantimes.com/business-news/india-s-fdi-inflows-at-a-record-60-1-billion-in-2016-17/story-7a8pt2u7e8IJttptDQcwhO.html (accessed 29 August 2017).

3. Express News Service, 'RSS-Affiliated BJS, SJM Term FDI Reforms "Betrayal" of Trust', *The Indian Express*, 21 June 2016, https://indianexpress.com/article/business/economy/rss-affiliated-bjs-sjm-term-fdi-reforms-betrayal-of-trust-2865487/ (12 July 2018).

4. SJM Press Release, 'Put on Hold the Decision to Ease FDI Norms, Demands SJM', http://www.swadeshionline.in/press-release-eng/put-hold-decision-ease-fdi-norms-demands-sjm (accessed 30 August 2017).

5. The speech delivered in Hindi (with English translation) is available on YouTube at, https://www.youtube.com/watch?v=dGJd9Jl1mOE (accessed 24 January 2018).

6. Kirtika Suneja, 'Customs Hike to Hit $65 Billion Imports, May Lead to WTO Dispute', *The Economic Times*, 5 February 2018, https://economictimes.indiatimes.com/news/economy/indicators/customs-hike-to-hit-65-billion-imports-may-lead-to-wto-dispute/articleshow/62784304.cms (accessed 25 April 2018).

7. Arun Jaitley, Budget 2018-2019 Speech, ministry of finance, Government of India, 1 February 2018, https://www.indiabudget.gov.in/ub2018-19/bs/bs.pdf (accessed 25 April 2018).

8. Arvind Panagariya, 'Return of Protectionism: Panagariya Sounds Alarm over Modi's New Trade Template for India', *The Economic Times*, 12 February 2018, https://economictimes.indiatimes.com/news/economy/policy/budget-2018-has-ensured-the-return-of-protectionism/articleshow/62876012.cms (accessed 25 April 2018).

9. Anurag Joshi, 'India Cuts Levy on Fuel to Ease Inflation after Oil Prices Surge', Bloomberg, 3 October 2017, https://www.bloomberg.com/news/articles/2017-10-03/india-cuts-levy-on-fuel-to-ease-inflation-after-oil-prices-surge (accessed 25 April 2018).

10. Press Trust of India, 'Just 4 States Cut VAT on Petrol, Diesel: Dharmendra Pradhan', *The Economic Times*, 5 February 2018, https://economictimes.indiatimes.com/industry/energy/oil-gas/just-4-states-cut-vat-on-petrol-diesel-dharmendra-pradhan/articleshow/62791588.cms (accessed 25 April 2018).

11. Himanshu Upadhyaya, 'Anger over Agrarian Distress Is behind BJP's Poor Performance in Saurashtra', The Wire, 20 December 2017,

https://thewire.in/206694/saurashtra-gujarat-bjp-agrarian-distress (accessed 25 April 2018).

12. Jaitley, Budget speech, https://www.indiabudget.gov.in/ub2018-19/bs/bs.pdf (accessed 25 April).

13. Mohan Bhagwat's speech is available at, https://www.youtube.com/watch?v=Tr3NfnaPQT8.

14. Vajpayee forced Govindacharya to step down as the party's general secretary when the latter reportedly stated that the prime minister was but a mask fronting for more intellectually substantive people. Though he claimed that he had been misquoted, Vajpayee was in no mood to be lenient towards this hard-line Hindutva critic within the party.

15. Pralay Kanungo, *RSS's Tryst with Politics: From Hedgewar to Sudarshan* (Delhi: Manohar Publishers, 2002), pp. 260–61.

16. 'Swadeshi', A.B.K.M.: 1998, in *R.S.S. Resolves 1950–2007: Resolutions Passed by A.B.P.S. and A.B.K.M. of R.S.S. from 1950 to 2007* (New Delhi: Suruchi Prakashan, 2007).

17. 'Resolution on WTO (World Trade Organization)', in *R.S.S. Resolves.*

18. Ibid.

19. 'Review of the Provisions of W.T.O.', A.B.P.S.: 1999, in *R.S.S. Resolves.*

20. A review of the FDI debate within the BJP, see, Partha S. Ghosh, *BJP and the Evolution of Hindu Nationalism: From Periphery to Centre* (New Delhi: Manohar Publishers, 1999), pp. 279–312.

21. See our detailed analysis of the formation of the BMS and its ideology in Walter Andersen and Shridhar Damle, *The Brotherhood in Saffron: The Rashtriya Swayamsevak Sangh and Hindu Revivalism* (Boulder: Westview Press, 1987), pp. 129–33.

22. The best sources for Thengadi's philosophy on labour that are still considered authoritative within the sangh parivar are the books he wrote, especially *Labour Policy* (Nagpur: Bharatiya Mazdoor Sangh, 1968), *Focus on Socio–Economic Problems* (New Delhi: Suruchi Prakashan, 1972). *Labour Policy* was originally a submission to India's First Commission on Labour in 1969 and reissued as a book.

23. For a review of BMS activities against the 'dangers' of foreign involvement in the India economy, see, 'Multi-faceted Achievements of BMS', BMS.org.in, http://bms.org.in/pages/Achievements.aspx (accessed 2 September 2017).

24. Ibid.
25. Ibid.
26. Ibid.
27. The samanvay samiti is a forum of representatives of the sangh parivar and meets at different levels. At the city level it meets once a month, at the state level quarterly and at the national level at least three times. Separate from this are consultations between federal ministers and their staff with parivar organizations involved in the issues covered by the minister. There is a counterpart of this at the state level.
28. The importance of social and economic equality to Upadhyaya discussed in Walter Andersen, 'Political Philosophy of Deendayal Upadhyaya', in Raje Sadhakar (ed.), *Destination* (Delhi: Deendayal Institute, 1978), pp. 43–48.
29. See the 'Philosophy' section of the Swadeshi Jagran Manch website, http://www.swadeshionline.in/content/philosophy (accessed 30 August 2017).
30. Ibid.
31. Many in the RSS were uncomfortable with the term 'Gandhian socialism' because they saw it as the incorporation of a foreign concept (socialism) in the sangh parivar's thinking on the Indian economy. Socialism was widely interpreted in RSS circles to mean government control of industry and collective farming. At the time, the RSS accepted the ideology of a 'mixed economy' giving the government control of large-scale industry and infrastructure.
32. For a discussion of the debate within the BJP on economic reforms, see, S. Ghosh, *BJP and the Evolution of Hindu Nationalism*, pp. 306–12.
33. Bharatiya Janata Party, *Economic Policy Statement, 1992: Our Commitment to Antyodaya—Human Approach to Economic Development (A Swadeshi Alternative)* (New Delhi, 1992), pp. 10–11.
34. Ibid.
35. National Democratic Alliance, *For a Proud, Prosperous India: An Agenda*, Election Manifesto, Lok Sabha Elections, 1999.
36. Ibid.
37. Bharat Jhunjhunwala, 'Dealing with Harmful Consumption?', Swadeshi Jagran Manch, http://www.swadeshionline.in/article-author/dealing-harmful-consumption (accessed 1 September 2017).
38. Rahul Kanwal, 'RSS Views Now More Aligned with Modi's? Mohan Bhagwat Says Sangh Not Opposed to FDI, Liberalisation', *India*

Today, 2 November 2013, https://www.indiatoday.in/india/story/rss-mohan-bhagwat-narendra-modi-fdi-bjp-216245-2013-11-02 (accessed 28 April 2018).

39. Ibid.

40. Ibid.

41. These groups taking part in the formation of the SJM were the BMS (labour), the BKS (farmers), the ABVP (students), the Akhil Bharatiya Grahak Panchayat (consumer protection) and the Sahakar Bharati (federation of cooperatives). More were to join and the SJM website claims that there are fifteen supporting bodies, almost all affiliated to the RSS. See 'Introduction', https://www.swadeshionline.in/content/introduction (accessed 29 August 2017).

42. While these accusations (which require a First Information Report) were never presented in formal legal proceedings against it, the RSS and its affiliates feared an unfriendly government might try to implicate its leaders in the bombings. Chief Minister Modi of Gujarat was similarly accused of triggering violence in the 2002 communal riots in Gujarat and, despite legal scrutiny, was exonerated of the charge of neglect of duty. This gave him all-India recognition and significant support among Hindu nationalists who saw him as a victim able to overcome what they interpreted as politically motivated slander.

43. India Today Online, 'BJP and RSS Are Promoting Hindu Terrorism: Home Minister Shinde', *India Today,* 20 January 2013, http://indiatoday.intoday.in/story/bjp-and-rss-are-promoting-hindu-terrorism-home-minister-shinde/1/243040.html (accessed 5 September 2017).

44. Ibid.

45. Of those polled by CSDS, 34 per cent prefer Narendra Modi for prime minister while 24 per cent opt for Rahul Gandhi. This represents a slight decline for Modi and an increase for Rahul Gandhi.
     India Today, 'Narendra Modi's Popularity as PM Dips to 34%, Rahul's Rises to 24%', 25 May 2018, https://www.indiatoday.in/india/story/narendra-modi-rahul-gandhi-prime-ministerial-popularity-1241741-2018-05-25 (accessed 26 May 2018).

46. Press Trust of India, 'RSS Proud of "Strong Leader" Modi's *Swayamsevak* Background', *The Hindu,* 7 March 2014, http://www.thehindu.com/news/national/rss-proud-of-strong-leader-modis-swayamsevak-background/article5760884.ece# (accessed 4 September

2017). Several RSS leaders have told us that the organization had ordered a canvas of the membership on Modi and the results showed strong support for him as leader of the party and next prime minister, a factor in the decision of the leadership to swing behind him.

47. *The Indian Express*, 'Bhagwat Cautions RSS Cadres against Crossing Limits for BJP, Says Can't Chant "Namo Namo"', 11 March 2014, https://indianexpress.com/article/india/politics/bhagwat-cautions-rss-cadres-against-crossing-limits-for-bjp-says-cant-chant-namo-namo/ (accessed 12 July 2018).

48. News18, 'Read Full Text of RSS Chief Mohan Bhagwat's Vijaya Dashami Speech', 4 October 2017, http://www.news18.com/news/india/read-full-text-of-rss-chief-mohan-bhagwats-vijaya-dashami-speech-1532625.html (accessed 4 October 2017).

49. For an analysis of BJP pro-growth strategy in the campaign, see, Walter Andersen, 'The Bharatiya Janata Party: A Victory for Narendra Modi', in Paul Wallace (ed.), *India's 2014 Elections* (New Delhi: Sage Publications, 2015), pp. 46–63.

50. The phrase that the BMS and other affiliates use to describe the effort to work out a consensus with the government on policy issues is 'responsive cooperation'.

51. Mohua Chatterjee, 'Saffron Trade Union Snubs RSS, to Join Protest against Govt', *The Times of India*, 20 May 2015, http://timesofindia.indiatimes.com/india/Saffron-trade-union-snubs-RSS-to-join-protest-against-govt/articleshow/47350063.cms (accessed 2 September 2017).

52. Archis Mohan and Somesh Jha, 'Sept 2 Strife: BMS Breaks Ranks with Other Unions', *Business Standard*, 29 August 2015, http://www.business-standard.com/article/current-affairs/in-a-first-bms-breaks-trade-union-ranks-115082900615_1.html (accessed 2 September 2017).

53. Comptroller and Auditor General of India, '"Conclusions and Recommendations", Performance Audit of Allocation of Coal Blocks and Augmentation of Coal Production', ministry of coal, 11 May 2012, pp. 43–44, http://www.cag.gov.in/sites/default/files/audit_report_files/Union_Performance_Commercial_Allocation_Coal_Blocks_and_Production_Ministry_Coal_7_2012_chapter_6.pdf (accessed 28 August 2017).

54. Krishnadas Rajgopal, 'Supreme Court Quashes Allocation of 214 Coal Blocs', *The Hindu*, 24 September 2014, http://www.thehindu.com/

news/national/supreme-court-quashes-allocation-of-all-but-four-of-218-coal-blocks/article6441855.ece (accessed 10 September 2017).

55. Express News Service, 'BMS Joins Other Trade Unions to Oppose Coal Bill', *The New Indian Express*, 15 December 2014, http://www.newindianexpress.com/states/odisha/2014/dec/15/BMS-Joins-Other-Trade-Unions-to-Oppose-Coal-Bill-694402.html (accessed 26 September 2017).

56. Gangadhar Patil, 'Battle for Coal: It's RSS vs Modi Sarkar', Newslaundry, 5 January 2015, https://www.newslaundry.com/2015/01/05/battle-for-coal-its-rss-vs-modi-sarkar (accessed 27 September 2017).

57. Ibid.

58. Indo-Asian News Service, 'Coal India Unions on Four Day Strike from Tuesday', *The Hindu*, 5 January 2015, http://www.thehindu.com/business/Economy/coal-india-unions-on-five-day-strike-from-tuesday/article6757194.ece (accessed 29 September 2017).

59. Manish Basu, Ruchira Singh and Utpal Bhaskar, 'Coal India Workers Call Off Strike', *Mint*, 8 January 2015, http://www.livemint.com/Companies/LMCxATYqfRLqcy5DOxHOyI/Coal-India-strike-said-to-shut-off-half-of-output-shipments.html (accessed 26 September 2017).

60. Shreya Jai, 'Cabinet Ends Coal India Monopoly, Allows Commercial Mining by Private Firms', *Business Standard*, 20 February 2018, http://www.business-standard.com/article/economy-policy/cabinet-ends-coal-india-monopoly-allows-commercial-mining-by-private-firms-118022000501_1.html (accessed 25 April 2018).

61. Mandira Kala and Prachee Mishra, 'Legislative Brief: The Right to Fair Compensation and Transparency in Land Acquisition, Rehabilitation and Resettlement (Second Amendment) Bill, 2015', PRS Legislative Research, Institute for Policy Research Studies, 17 July 2015, http://www.prsindia.org/administrator/uploads/media/Land%20and%20R%20and%20R/Brief%20-%20LARR%20Bill_2015.pdf (accessed 29 September 2017).

62. Ibid.

63. Vivek Deshpande, 'Amid Protests over Land Bill, Amit Shah Meets RSS Chief Mohan Bhagwat', *The Indian Express*, 17 May 2015, https://indianexpress.com/article/india/india-others/amid-protests-over-land-bill-amit-shah-meets-rss-chief-mohan-bhagwat/ (accessed 12 July 2018).

64. Ibid.

65. *The Telegraph*, 'Land Bill Reprieve from Farmer Wing', 12 June 2015, https://www.telegraphindia.com/1150612/jsp/frontpage/story_25285.jsp (accessed 30 September 2017).

66. Smita Mishra, '8 Reasons Why Modi Needs to Worry about RSS Post Delhi', BhupendraChaubey.com, http://www.bhupendrachaubey.com/news/8-reasons-why-Modi-needs-to-worry-about-RSS-post-Delhi (accessed 30 September 2017).

67. Ravish Tiwary, 'Land Bill Gets a Bharatiya Kisan Boost: Dilutes Opposition to Social Impact Assessment and Consent Clause', *The Economic Times*, 11 June 2015, http://economictimes.indiatimes.com/news/politics-and-nation/land-bill-gets-a-bharatiya-kisan-sangh-boost-dilutes-opposition-to-social-impact-assessment-and-consent-clause/articleshow/47622127.cms (accessed 30 September 2017).

68. Somesh Jha, 'Modi's "Make in India" bats for GM food crops', *Business Standard*, 29 November 2014, http://www.business-standard.com/article/economy-policy/modis-make-in-india-bats-for-gm-food-crops-114112800933_1.html (accessed 29 September 2017).

69. Ashwani Mahajan, 'Don't Follow MNC-Promoted GM Crop Science Blindly', Swadeshi Jagran Manch, https://www.swadeshionline.in/content/%E2%80%98don%E2%80%99t-follow-mnc-promoted-gm-crop-science-blindly%E2%80%99 (accessed 20 September 2017).

70. Mayank Bhardwaj, Rupam Jain and Tom Lasseter, 'Seed Giant Monsanto Meets Its Match as Hindu Nationalists Assert Power in Modi's India', Reuters, 28 March 2017, http://www.reuters.com/investigates/special-report/monsanto-india/ (accessed 21 September 2017).

71. Ibid.

72. Sayantan Bera and Shreeja Sen, 'Govt Cuts Cotton Royalty by 74%', LiveMint, 10 March 2016, http://www.livemint.com/Politics/NdDYRxsayfh2655qOqy7mI/Centre-notifies-Bt-cotton-seed-prices-slashes-royalty-fees.html (accessed 21 September 2017).

73. As of the writing of this draft in October 2017, the issue is currently pending a judicial review.

74. Aditya Karla, 'Ban on Foreign Funds for Non-Profit May Hurt India Health Programs', Reuters, 30 May 2017, https://www.reuters.com/article/us-india-health-ban/ban-on-foreign-funds-for-non-profit-may-hurt-india-health-programs-idUSKBN18Q1DK (accessed 2 November 2017).

75. Anubhuti Vishnoi, 'Centre Shuts Health Mission Gate on Bill and Melinda Gates Foundation', *The Economic Times,* 9 February 2017, https://economictimes.indiatimes.com/news/politics-and-nation/centre-shuts-gate-on-bill-melinda-gates-foundation/articleshow/57028697.cms (accessed 2 November 2017).

76. Marya Shakil, 'RSS-Affiliate Wants Government to Ban Gates Foundation in India', CNN-News18, 6 June 2016, https://www.news18.com/news/india/rss-affiliate-wants-government-to-ban-gates-foundation-in-india-1252971.html (accessed 3 May 2018).

77. Atul Chaurasia, 'We Shouldn't Look to Harvard and Columbia to Formulate Policy for India: Swadeshi Jagran Manch Snubs Panagariya', Newslaundry, 3 August 2017, https://www.newslaundry.com/2017/08/03/harvard-columbia-policy-india-swadeshi-jagran-manch-snubs-arvind-panagariya-resignation-niti (accessed 6 November 2017).

Chapter Nine: China

1. 'Bharat's Policy vis-a-vis Chinese Aggression', A.B.K.M.: 1959, in *R.S.S. Resolves 1950-2007: Resolutions Passed by A.B.P.S. and A.B.K.M. of R.S.S. from 1950 to 2007* (New Delhi: Suruchi Prakashan, 2007).

2. 'Statement Bharat's Policy vis-a-vis Chinese Aggression', A.B.K.M.: 1962, in *R.S.S. Resolves.*

3. 'Colombo Conference', A.B.P.S.: 1963, *RSS Resolves.*

4. See account of its participation in the 1963 Republic Day parade in, Pralay Kanungo, *RSS's Tryst with Politics: From Hedgewar to Sudarshan* (Delhi: Manohar Publishers, 2002), p. 58.

5. A good report of this conference in, 'VHP Organized World Hindu Congress Begins at New Delhi; RSS Chief Bhagwat, HH Dalai Inaugurates', Samvada, 21 November 2014, http://samvada.org/2014/news/vhp-world-hindu-congress-begins/ (accessed 2 September 2017).

6. For a detailed description of the RSS's role in the founding of the Bharat-Tibbat Sahyog Manch, see, '5 Years of Bharat Tibbat Sahyog Manch, a Mass Movement for Tibet', Phayul, 25 May 2005, http://www.phayul.com/news/article.aspx?id=9877 (accessed 20 July 2017). Indresh Kumar came in contact with Tibetans when he headed the RSS in Kashmir. Soon after launching the BTSM, he had in 2004 helped form the Indo-Tibetan Friendship Society to acquaint

Indians with what he called the colonial status of the Tibetans under Chinese rule.

7. HT Correspondent, 'India Won't Compromise on Defense, National Security Anymore: Mohan Bhagwat', *Hindustan Times*, 5 September 2017, http://www.hindustantimes.com/lucknow/india-won-t-compromise-on-defence-national-security-anymore-mohan-bhagwat/story-BMaPy2q1leM3ABr36bEe3O.html (accessed 9 September 2017).

8. These observations are based on the experiences of one of the authors, Walter Andersen, who has taught in China since 2012.

9. Dipanjan Roy Chaudhury and Vasudha Venugopal, 'Boycott Chinese Goods: RSS-Affiliated Organisations', *The Economic Times*, 11 July 2017, http://economictimes.indiatimes.com/news/politics-and-nation/boycott-china-goods-rss-affiliated-organisations/articleshow/59535684.cms (accessed 8 September 2017).

10. Kapil Dave, 'Drive to Boycott Chinese Products', *The Times of India*, 24 August 2017, http://timesofindia.indiatimes.com/city/ahmedabad/drive-to-boycott-chinese-products/articleshow/60199431.cms (accessed 9 September 2017).

11. Special Correspondent, 'VHP, Bajrang Dal Launch Campaign against Chinese Goods', *The Hindu*, 2 September 2017, http://www.thehindu.com/news/cities/Mangalore/vhp-bajrang-dal-launch-campaign-for-boycott-of-chinese-goods/article19605109.ece (accessed 8 September 2017).

12. Tribune News Service, 'VHP Calls for Boycott of Chinese Goods', *The Tribune*, 28 June 2017, http://tribuneindia.com/news/nation/vhp-calls-for-boycott-of-chinese-goods/428522.html (accessed 3 September 2017).

13. Sheela Bhatt, Interview with Shivshankar Menon, 'Do Not See Cross-LoC Strikes Minimising Pak Bid to Stir Up Trouble, Spread Alienation in J&K: Former NSA Shivshankar Menon', *The Indian Express*, 24 November 2016, https://indianexpress.com/article/india/india-news-india/shivshankar-menon-former-nsa-interview-do-not-see-cross-loc-strikes-minimising-pak-bid-to-stir-up-trouble-spread-alienation-in-jammu-kashmir-4387756/ (accessed 12 July 2018).

14. 'Belt and Road Attendees List', *The Diplomat*, 12 May 2017, https://thediplomat.com/2017/05/belt-and-road-attendees-list/ (accessed 27 September 2017).

15. Ministry of external affairs, Government of India, 'Official Spokesperson's Response to a Query on Participation of India in OBOR/BRI Forum', http://mea.gov.in/media-briefings.htm?dtl/ 28463/Official+Spokespersons+response+to+a+query+on+ participation+of+India+in+OBORBRI+Forum (accessed 12 July 2018).

16. Narayani Basu, 'China Buys Hambantota Port: Should India Be Concerned?', *The Diplomat*, 29 July 2017, https://thediplomat. com/2017/07/china-buys-hambantota-port-should-india-be-concerned (accessed 10 October 2017).

17. Rajiv Ranjan, 'Border Row: India Must Avoid the Trap Set by China's Bombastic English Language Media', Quartz, 19 July 2017, https:// qz.com/1033019/doklam-and-sikkim-row-india-must-avoid-the-trap-set-by-chinas-bombastic-english-language-media/ (accessed 5 November 2017).

18. Ibid.

19. Bhairavi Singh, 'Hindu Nationalism Risks Pushing India into War: China State-Run Media', NDTV, 20 July 2017, http:// www.ndtv.com/india-news/chinese-media-attacks-pm-narendra-modi-over-doklam-stand-off-1727159 (accessed 9 September 2017).

20. For more details of the commentary from Chinese state–run media during the Doklam standoff, see, Ranjan, 'Border Row', Quartz.

21. Sumit Pande, 'Business First: 3 Ministers of Modi Govt Travelled to China This Week', News18, 6 July 2017, http:// www.news18.com/news/india/business-trumps-rhetoric-3-ministers-of-modi-govt-travelled-to-china-this-week-1454049.html (accessed 22 September 2017).

22. Ibid.

23. US-India Joint Statement, 'United States and India: Prosperity through Partnership', The White House, 26 June 2017, https:// www.whitehouse.gov/briefings-statements/united-states-india-prosperity-partnership/ (accessed 12 July 2018, emphasis authors').

24. Rex Tillerson, 'Remarks on "Defining Our Relationship with India for the Next Century"', US Department of State, 18 October 2017, https://www.state.gov/secretary/remarks/2017/10/274913.htm (accessed 5 November 2017).

25. Ibid.

26. David Brunnstrom, 'U.S. Seeks Meeting Soon to Revive Asia-Pacific "Quad" Security Forum', Reuters, 28 October 2017, https://www.reuters.com/article/us-usa-asia-quad/u-s-seeks-meeting-soon-to-revive-asia-pacific-quad-security-forum-idUSKBN1CW2O1 (accessed 5 November 2017).

27. Asian Investment and Infrastructure Bank, 'Members and Prospective Members of the Bank', Asian Investment and Infrastructure Bank, 21 March 2018, https://www.aiib.org/en/about-aiib/governance/members-of-bank/index.html (accessed 23 September 2017).

28. Tencent and Alibaba have each invested over $1 billion in India. Other major investors have been Shanghai Electric which has provided several billion dollars for the construction of hydroelectric facilities in India.

29. See this story on increased interest by Tencent and Naspers (Tencent's largest investor) as well as Alibaba and Softbank (Alibaba's largest investment) in India's internet market, Mihir Dalal and Anirban Sen, 'Tencent Scouts for More Start-Up Deals, Tracking Alibaba in India', *Mint*, 6 October 2017, https://www.livemint.com/Companies/ZWjVhFAMeQ2fsuMRoS2EoM/Tencent-scouts-for-more-startup-deals-tracking-Alibaba-in.html (accessed 12 July 2018).

30. Ruchika Chitravanshi, 'Led by Chinese, Nearly 600 Companies Line Up $85 Billion Investments in India', *The Economic Times*, 16 October 2017, https://economictimes.indiatimes.com/news/economy/finance/led-by-chinese-nearly-600-companies-line-up-85-billion-investments-in-india/articleshow/61093929.cms (accessed 6 November 2017).

31. Subrata Majumder, 'India Emerges as Battleground for Chinese and Japanese Investment—Analysis', *Eurasia Review*, 28 March 2017, https://www.eurasiareview.com/28032017-india-emerges-as-battleground-for-chinese-and-japanese-investment-analysis/ (accessed 12 July 2018).

32. EshaDoot News, 'Brics 2017: Summit Declaration Names Lashkar, Jaish as Terror Concerns', 4 September 2017, http://eshadoot.com/2017/09/04/brics-2017-summit-declaration-names-lashkar-jaish-terror-concerns/ (accessed 8 September 2017). The final declaration does mention the Pakistan-based groups, though not Pakistan itself.

33. Satish Kumar, 'BRICS Summit: Rectifying Himalayan Blunder', *Organiser*, 17 September 2017, http://organiser.org//

Encyc/2017/9/11/BRICS-Summit---Rectifying-Himalayan-Blunder.aspx (accessed 11 September 2017).

34. Press Trust of India, 'Pakistan Should Resolve Kashmir Bilaterally with India: China', *The Times of India*, 22 September 2017, http://timesofindia.indiatimes.com/india/resolve-kashmir-issue-bilaterally-with-india-china-tells-pakistan/articleshow/60796366.cms (accessed 25 September 2017).

35. Sudesh Verma, *Narendra Modi: The Game Changer* (New Delhi: Vitasta Publishing, 2014), pp. 254–55.

36. Ibid., p. 255.

37. Ibid., p. 362.

38. Ram Madhav analyses the often-tense China–India relationship in his book *Uneasy Neighbours: India and China 50 Years of the War* (New Delhi: Har-Anand Publications, 2014).

39. Ibid., pp. 11–12.

40. Ibid., p. 14.

41. Ibid., p. 19.

42. Ibid. Madhav's rather extensive critical treatment of Nehru's handling of China on pp. 26–51.

43. M.S. Golwalkar, *Bunch of Thoughts* (Bangalore: Vikram Prakashan, 1966), p. 269. Golwalkar's argument for militarizing the country to counter what he was convinced would be the continuing threat from China is contained in a chapter of this book entitled 'Fight to Win'.

44. Ibid., p. 283.

45. About one-third of Madhav's book (six of twenty-one chapters) is an analysis of the likely continuation of Indo-Chinese tensions and the need therefore for India to develop its own strategic response to what he views as an increasingly assertive China that would challenge Indian interests.

46. Madhav, *Uneasy Neighbours*, p. 227.

47. Jaideep Mazumdar, 'Swarajya Exclusive: Ram Madhav on Kashmir, Northeast, Foreign Policy and Going Back to the Roots', *Swarajya*, 2 September 2017, https://swarajyamag.com/politics/swarajya-exclusive-ram-madhav-on-kashmir-north-east-foreign-policy-and-going-back-to-the-roots (accessed 10 September 2017).

48. Ibid.

49. Press Trust of India, 'India Assumes Responsibility in Indo-Pacific: Ram Madhav', NDTV, 22 November 2016, http://www.ndtv.com/

india-news/india-assumes-responsibility-in-indo-asia-pacific-ram-
madhav-1628455 (accessed 8 September 2017).

50. For a discussion of the support for Hindu radicalism and the
terrorism that often accompanied it, see, Barbara D. Metcalf and
Thomas R. Metcalf, *A Concise History of Modern India* (Cambridge:
Cambridge University Press, 2002), pp. 153–60. As they note, the
triggering mechanism for much of the radicalism in Bengal was
the British decision in 1905 to partition Bengal into a Muslim-
majority east and a Hindu-majority west, a move interpreted by
the rising middle class as a deliberate decision to undermine their
influence.

51. For a discussion of the nationalist urge for modernity to transform
Indian society in the late nineteenth century and early twentieth
century, see, Manu Goswami, 'From Swadeshi to Swaraj: Nation,
Economy, Territory in Colonial South Asia 1870–1907', *Comparative
Studies in Society and History*, vol. 40, no. 4, October 1998. Charles
H. Heimsath has a similar focus in his book *Indian Nationalism and
Hindu Social Reform* (Princeton: Princeton University Press, 1964).

52. Subhas Chandra Bose, *An Indian Pilgrim: An Unfinished Autobiography
and Collected Letters 1897–1921* (New York: Asia Publishing House,
1965), p. 2.

53. This quote is taken from Nirad C. Chaudhuri's memoirs, *Thy Hand,
Great Anarch!*, and cited in an article by Saswat Panigrahi, 'Hindutva
and Cultural Nationalism: The Missing Chapter in Netaji's Life',
Swarajya, 23 January 2017, https://swarajyamag.com/culture/
hindutva-and-cultural-nationalism-the-missing-chapter-in-netajis-
life (accessed 11 September 2017).

54. This quote is taken from a translation of Rash Behari Bose's
Japanese-language March and April 1939 biographical articles on
Savarkar in the Japanese magazine *Dai Ajia Shugi* as reported in,
Saswati Sarkar, Shanmukh Jeck Joy and Dikgaj, 'Rashbehari Bose:
India's Messenger in Japan', DailyO, 25 April 2016, http://www.
dailyo.in/politics/rashbehari-bose-indian-freedom-struggle-india-
japan-ties-british-raj-mahatma-gandhi-toshiko-soma-netaji-
subhas-chandra-bose-propaganda/story/1/10257.html   (accessed
11 September 2017).

55. National Archives of India, 23 January 2016, http://nationalarchives.
nic.in/content/release-declassified-files-relating-netaji-subhas-
chandra-bose-shri-narendra-modi-0 (accessed 18 February 2017).

56. HT Correspondent, 'Netaji's Grand Nephew Chandra Bose Joins BJP', *Hindustan Times*, 25 January 2016, https://www.hindustantimes. com/india/netaji-s-grand-nephew-chandra-bose-set-to-join-bjp-in-amit-shah-s-presence/story-tMInhEscITKFSjXyKtccbJ.html (accessed 18 February 2017).

Chapter Ten: Ghar Wapsi *(Homecoming)*

1. Singh told the press that his leaving was his own decision and that it was due to illness. His comments on this reported in, Piyush Srivastava, 'Conversion Row: Dharm Jagran Samiti Chief Rajeshwar Singh Goes on Leave,' *India Today*, 2 January 2015, http://indiatoday. intoday.in/story/rajeshwar-singh-dharm-jagran-samiti-djs-hindu-rashtra-love-jehad-reconversion-rss-vhp/1/410923.html (accessed 3 April 2017).

2. There are in fact two organizations within the sangh parivar involved in reconversion (ghar wapsi). One, a semi-autonomous group launched by the RSS, calls itself the Dharma Jagran; the other is referred to as Dharma Jagran Samiti and is a part of the VHP. The RSS's Dharma Jagran is a part of what is called *gati vidhi* (planned social movements); its goal is better family integration, which is considered the bedrock of social stability and, by extension, results in improved social integration of those who are reconverted. The semi-autonomous groups within the gati vidhi are involved in: family counselling (*kutumb prabodhan*), social harmony (*samajik samrasta*) imparted by working with leaders of different castes to reduce inter-caste differences and tensions, village development (*gram vikas*) and cow protection (*gauraksha*). For the RSS, the activities of these groups are important as they address what is essential to achieve social unity and a perception of oneness, the major goal of Hindutva.

3. Lalmani Verma, 'RSS Wing Launches Rakhi Crusade against "Love Jihad"', *The Indian Express*, 11 August 2014, https://indianexpress. com/article/cities/lucknow/rss-wing-launches-rakhi-crusade-against-love-jihad/ (accessed 12 July 2018).

4. Religious figures from the 2011 Census of India, available at http://censusindia.gov.in/Census_And_You/religion.aspx (accessed 10 April 2017). Though the Muslim increase at 24.67 per cent from the 2001 to the 2011 census was considerably higher than the 16.8 per cent growth rate of Hindus in that same period, the

increase over this decade for Muslims was less than in the previous ten years. The figure that was most disturbing to some Hindu nationalists was that Hindu percentage in 2011 had dropped below 80 per cent; in fact, it has dropped in every census since the 84.1 per cent figure in 1951.

5.   Ibid.

6.   Piyush Srivastava, '"We Will Free India of Muslims and Christians by 2021": DJS Leader Vows to Continue "Ghar Wapsi" Plans and Restore "Hindu Glory"', *Mail Today*, 19 December 2014, http://www.dailymail.co.uk/indiahome/indianews/article-2879597/We-free-India-Muslims-Christians-2021-DJS-leader-vows-continue-ghar-wapsi-plans-restore-Hindu-glory.html (accessed 3 April 2017).

7.   FP Politics, 'Bye, Bye Ghar Wapsi? RSS Dumps Rajeshwar Singh after Modi Meet', Firstpost, 2 January 2015, http://www.firstpost.com/politics/bye-bye-ghar-wapsi-rss-dumps-rajeshwar-singh-after-modi-meet-2026443.html (accessed 3 April 2017).

8.   Togadia quit the VHP following the loss of his candidate for the position of the president of the VHP. On 15 April 2018, Togadia announced his departure from the VHP. His sidelining within the VHP was likely driven by his hardline stance and his relentless opposition to Prime Minister Modi.

9.   See a report of his statistics on ghar wapsi in, Press Trust of India, '7.5 Lakh Muslims, Christians Re-converted to Hinduism in Last 10 Years: Praveen Togadia', Zee News, 8 January 2016, http://zeenews.india.com/news/india/7-5-lakh-muslims-christians-re-converted-to-hinduism-in-last-10-years-praveen-togadia_1843165.html (accessed 10 April 2017).

10. Report on the conversion of the Goan Gaudas in Marathi fortnightly *Sanskrutik Vartapatra*, December 2010, p. 112. A description of the devalsmriti rituals aimed at reconverting Sindhis who had converted to Islam after the eighth century is available in the journal *Ithihas*, https://ithihas.wordpress.com/2013/09/10/dharma-shastras-legal-literature-of-ancient-india/ (accessed 13 April 2017).

11. Interview with the late guide of the RSS Dharma Jagran, Mukundrao Panshikar, in Mumbai on 27 July 2015. He told us that reconversion is a very private act, one fraught with possible adverse social reaction if handled badly. He was therefore critical of efforts to publicize ghar wapsi.

12. The RSS has made clear that within the sangh parivar the VHP is tasked to address Hindu socio-religious issues.

13. Press Trust of India, '"Ghar wapsi" Is Natural Process, RSS Leader Vaidya Says', *The Times of India*, 3 January 2015, http://timesofindia. indiatimes.com/india/Ghar-wapsi-is-natural-process-RSS-leader-Vaidya-says/articleshow/45743075.cms (accessed 5 April 2017).

14. Ibid.

15. See an analysis of this belief in an age of bliss before the entry of Muslim and Christian powers into the subcontinent in, Alok Rai, 'Religious Conversions and the Crisis of Brahmanical Hinduism', in Gyanendra Pandey (ed.), *Hindus and Others: The Question of Identity in India Today* (New Delhi: Penguin Books India, 1993), pp. 225–37.

16. For a discussion of how the early-twentieth-century Hindu nationalists, Savarkar among them, related Hinduism to nationality, see, Pralay Kanungo, *RSS's Tryst with Politics: From Hedgewar to Sudarshan* (Delhi: Manohar Publishers, 2002), pp. 104–12.

17. Dhananjay Keer, *Savarkar and His Times* (Bombay: India Printing Works, 1950), p. 164.

18. Interview with Balasaheb Deoras, RSS sarsanghchalak, in Nagpur, Maharashtra, on 25 February 1988.

19. Interview with the Late Mukundrao Panshikar, a senior RSS pracharak who was at the time the guide of the Dharma Jagran Samiti, in Mumbai, Maharashtra, on 27 July 2015.

20. M.S. Golwalkar, *Bunch of Thoughts* (Bangalore: Vikram Prakashan, 1966), pp. 192–93. We were told in 2016 by Ranga Hari, a senior RSS intellectual who was one of the editors of *Bunch of Thoughts*, that the book is in fact a compilation of Golwalkar's lectures. The editors provided titles to the various chapters and were considering title changes in the next edition that would be less controversial.

21. Ibid., chs. 11 and 12.

22. Ibid., pp. 168–73.

23. Ibid., pp. 184–85.

24. Ibid., pp. 192–93.

25. More than a quarter of *Bunch of Thoughts* is focused on the 'character-building' activities of the RSS, far more attention than is given to any other subject.

26. Except the VHP, all the RSS affiliates (and the RSS itself) are open to all religious groups in India.

27. In the mid-1980s the RSS established the Rashtriya Sikh Sangat for Indian Sikhs, and the VHP established an equivalent group for Indian Buddhists.

28. See our discussion of this equalitarian undercurrent in RSS writings in Walter Andersen and Shridhar Damle, *The Brotherhood in Saffron: The Rashtriya Swayamsevak Sangh and Hindu Revivalism* (Boulder: Westview Press, 1987), pp. 79–83.

29. Golwalkar, *Bunch of Thoughts*, p. 107.

30. Ibid., p. 401.

31. See, Gene Thursby, *Hindu-Muslim Relations in British India: A Study of Controversy, Conflict and Communal Movements in North India: 1923-1928* (Leiden: E.J. Brill, 1975).

32. This suggestion was proposed by Girish Prabhune, an author and RSS activist who worked among low-caste nomadic groups, in 2014 Diwali issue of the *Vivek* (Mumbai), a Marathi weekly. This proposal triggered a robust debate within the RSS but, lacking a consensus, it has not formally acted on this proposal.

33. Bhagwat in 2010, after becoming head of the RSS, told the press that inter-caste marriage is very common among RSS members and he considers this a positive development. Printed in the 7 September 2012 issue of the Marathi daily *Loksatta* (Mumbai). One argument against this conversion to Buddhism is that it would in fact result in a neo-Buddhist Dalit group and thus bring no real change in social status.

34. A common narrative in the RSS is that most conversions in the past, especially during periods of Muslim rule, were the result of either force or the lure of social and financial gain.

35. A good study of the Arya Samaj and its founder, Dayanand Saraswati, can be found in Charles H. Heimsath, *Indian Nationalism and Hindu Social Reform* (Princeton: Princeton University Press, 1964), ch. V.

36. See, Pandey (ed.), 'Which of Us Are Hindus?', in *Hindus and Others*, for discussion of the 'discovered' text, the *Deval Smriti*, p. 254.

37. For a discussion of the limitations of conversion in India, see Laura Dudley Jenkins, 'Legal Limits on Religious Conversion in India', *Law and Contemporary Problems*, Spring 2008, vol. 71, pp. 109–27.

38. Quoted in Jenkins, ibid., p. 114.

39. Jenkins notes that the Supreme Court decision echoed a critical 1956 report on missionary activity, *The Report of the Christian Missionary Activities Enquiry Committee* (sometimes referred to as the Niyogi Report after its author, Bhawani Shankar Niyogi, a retired chief justice of the Nagpur High Court). The report talked harshly about

conversion as a threat to public order and national unity. Ibid., pp. 114–15.

40. Ibid., pp. 120–22.

41. An excellent analysis of this perceived Hindu vulnerability is available in Christophe Jaffrelot, *The Hindu Nationalist Movement in India* (Delhi: Thomson Press, 1996), ch. 10.

42. Quoted by Jaffrelot, ibid., p. 342.

43. Frank Fanselow, 'The Rise of Communalism in Tamilnadu', *Eastern Anthropologist*, vol. 43, October 2000, p. 9, http://www.academia. edu/1346645/The_Rise_of_Communalism_in_Tamilnadu, pp. 23 (accessed 15 April 2017).

44. Ibid.

45. Ibid.

46. http://vhp.org/conferences/dharmasansads/dharma-sansad-1/ (accessed 10 April 2017).

47. Ibid.

48. The unity conferences also had the support of several prominent Congress figures, like Gulzari Lal Nanda—twice interim prime minister of India (1964 and 1966)—and Karan Singh, the former maharaja of Jammu and Kashmir, who with RSS support established the Virat Hindu Sammelan to work against conversion to non-Hindu faiths.

49. See discussion of the organizational background of the first VHP-managed religious parliament in, Jaffrelot, *The Hindu Nationalist Movement in India*, pp. 346–55.

Chapter Eleven: Protecting the Cow

1. This was the first instance of the RSS conducting a mass movement for cow protection. However, the RSS encouraged a popular Hindu religious leader, Prabhudutta Brahmachari, to contest the 1952 Allahabad (Prayag) parliamentary seat against Prime Minister Jawaharlal Nehru. Prabhudutta, with the encouragement of the RSS leadership as well as many Hindu clerics, made cow protection the major issue in his campaign.

2. The RSS discovered in this campaign that cow protection was a popular political issue, especially in rural areas.

3. An excellent analysis of the pre-independence cow protection movement in Sandra Freitag, 'Sacred Symbol as Mobilizing Ideology: The North Indian Search for a Hindu Community', *Comparative Studies in Society and History*, October 1980, vol. 22, no. 4, pp. 597–625.

4. The BJS only won three of ninety-four contested seats (of 489 total) in the 1951–52 parliamentary contests. It also won thirty-five state Assembly seats of the 727 that it contested (3283 total).

5. For a discussion of the reasons that the young BJS had virtually no relations with the Hindu Mahasabha and the Ram Rajya Parishad, see, Bruce Graham, *Hindu Nationalism and Indian Politics: The Origins and Development of the Bharatiya Jana Sangh* (Cambridge: Cambridge University Press, 1990), pp. 26–27.

6. For a discussion of how the sangh parivar has tried to avoid the charge of radicalism on the cow protection issue, see, ibid., pp. 147–57.

7. This regulation was issued under authority of a parliamentary act, the Prevention of Cruelty to Animals (PCA) Act of 1960.

8. See press report of order in, Praveen Shekhar and Reema Parashar, 'Government Bans Sale of Cows for Slaughter at Cattle Markets, Restricts Trade', *India Today*, 26 May 2017, http://indiatoday. intoday.in/story/sale-of-cattle-for-slaughter-banned-at-markets-across-the-country-environment-ministry/1/963683.html (accessed 30 May 2017).

9. Togadia also advocated a law mandating life imprisonment for those engaged in cow slaughter. See, Press Trust of India, 'VHP Demands Nationwide Ban on Cow Slaughter', *Hindustan Times*, 19 July 2017, http://www.hindustantimes.com/india-news/vhp-demands-nationwide-ban-on-cow-slaughter/story-N4Il6neJ1CYeHhXV7fT19J.html (accessed 30 May 2017).

10. Mayank Bhardwaj and Suchitra Mohanty, 'India's Top Court Suspends Ban on Trade in Cattle for Slaughter', Reuters, 12 July 2017, https://in.reuters.com/article/cow-cattle-trade-slaughter-rules-india/supreme-court-suspends-ban-on-trade-in-cattle-for-slaughter-idINKBN19X0HA (accessed 12 July 2018).

11. Ibid.

12. The goals of the Go-Vigyan Anusandhan Kendra are described in the 'About Us' part of the website, http://govigyan.com/pages/about-us (accessed 29 May 2017).

13. Vishva Hindu Parishad website, 'Cow Protection', http://vhp.org/vhp-glance/dimensions/cow-protection/ (accessed 9 July 2018).

14. See a review of the politicization of the cow issue in Aravindan Neelakandan, 'Hindutva and the Politics of Beef', *Swarajya*, 30 October 2015.

15. ET Bureau, 'Mohan Bhagwat Condemns Violence by Cow Vigilantes', *The Economic Times*, 10 April 2017, http://economictimes.

indiatimes.com/news/politics-and-nation/mohan-bhagwat-pitches-for-all-india-law-against-cow-slaughter/articleshow/58092540.cms (accessed 20 April 2017). The press reports that on 1 April 2017, a crowd of some 200 cow vigilantes attacked six vehicles carrying cattle in Rajasthan, a state that bans the slaughter of cows, and beat up the drivers, and one of them, a dairy farmer, died a few days later as a result of the beating. The family of the deceased said that the cattle were to be sold, not slaughtered.

16. Ibid.

17. Ellen Barry, 'Narendra Modi, India's Leader, Condemns Vigilante Cow Protection Groups', *The New York Times*, 7 August 2016, https://www.nytimes.com/2016/08/08/world/asia/narendra-modi-indias-leader-condemns-vigilante-cow-protection-groups.html (accessed 12 July 2018).

18. Aloke Tikku, 'Endgame: New UP Police Chief Sulkhan Singh's Message for Criminals, Gau Rakshaks', NDTV, 22 April 2017, http://www.ndtv.com/india-news/endgame-new-up-police-chief-sulkhan-singhs-message-for-criminals-gau-rakshaks-1684607?pfrom=home-lateststories (accessed 22 April 2017). This was part of a statement addressing the larger question of restoring law and order in the state. This particular order included action against vigilantism on conversion.

19. Express News Service, 'Control Illegal Activities in Name of Cow Protection, Religious Conversion: UP DGP', *The Indian Express*, 5 May 2017, http://epaper.indianexpress.com/1196989/Indian-Express/May-06,-2017#clip/18841217/64725d77-9e2e-4d9c-a01d-a4d2804f6189/613.3333333333333:469.1488469601677/topclips (accessed 6 May 2017).

20. Syed Masroor Hasan and Md Hizbullah, 'Cow Vigilante Attacks Are Anything but Spontaneous, Reveals India Today Sting', *India Today*, 20 April 2017, http://indiatoday.intoday.in/story/cow-vigilante-gau-rakshak-attacks-india-today/1/934085.html (accessed 23 April 2017).

21. 'Supreme Court Asks States to Curb Violence in Name of Cow Protection', DD News, 6 September 2017, http://www.ddinews.gov.in/national/supreme-court-asks-states-curb-violence-name-cow-protection (accessed 15 December 2017).

22. Express News Service, 'Dadri Lynching: Govt Can't Decide What People Should Eat, Says BJP Leader Nitin Gadkari', *The Indian Express*, 4 October 2015, https://indianexpress.com/article/india/

india-news-india/dadri-lynching-govt-cant-decide-what-people-should-eat-says-bjp-leader-nitin-gadkari/ (accessed 12 July 2018).

23. Ranju Dodum, 'RSS Warms to Beefeaters', *The Telegraph*, 9 December 2015, https://www.telegraphindia.com/1151209/jsp/northeast/story_57428.jsp#.WPvTW4WcHSE (accessed 21 April 2017).

24. Ibid.

25. Ratnadip Choudhury, 'BJP Okays Beef on Meghalaya's Political Platter for Now', NDTV, 10 April 2017, http://www.ndtv.com/india-news/bjp-okays-beef-on-meghalayas-political-platter-for-now-1679270 (accessed 20 April 2017). Sarma is chairman of the BJP ally in Assam, the Northeast Democratic Alliance (NEDA).

26. M. Aamir Khan, 'In Valley, Kisan Sangh to Focus on Cow-Based Organic Farming', *The Tribune*, 19 October 2015, http://www.tribuneindia.com/news/jammu-kashmir/community/in-valley-kisan-sangh-to-focus-on-cow-based-organic-farming/147745.html (accessed 22 December 2017).

27. Bhardwaj and Mohanty, 'India's Top Court Suspends Ban on Trade on Cattle for Slaughter', Reuters.

28. Amy Kazmin, 'Modi's India: The High Cost of Protecting Holy Cows', *Financial Times*, 21 November 2017, https://www.ft.com/content/63522f50-caf3-11e7-ab18-7a9fb7d6163e (accessed 20 December 2017).

29. Rakesh Dixit, 'Battle of Bovines', India Legal, 14 November 2017, http://www.indialegallive.com/commercial-news/states-news/anti-cow-slaughter-law-in-madhya-pradesh-battle-of-bovines-39146 (accessed 20 December 2017).

30. The RSS fear of India losing a part of this north-eastern frontier region was underscored by the pre-Partition referendum in Sylhet, a slice of territory that bordered Bengal and had a Muslim-majority population.

31. For an analysis of the challenges to Hindu nationalism in the Northeast, see, Malini Bhattacharjee, 'Tracing the Emergence and Consolidation of Hindutva in Assam', *Economic and Political Weekly*, 16 April 2016, vol. LI, no. 16, pp. 80–87.

32. See discussion of this effort of the sangh parivar in the Northeast to appropriate local heroic figures to advance cause of Hindutva in V. Bijukumar, 'Politics of Counter-Narratives and Appropriation', *Economic and Political Weekly*, 6 May 2017, vol. LII, no. 18.

33. Ibid., p. 82: Bijukumar notes that the schools set up by the RSS's educational affiliate place pictures of traditional local religious figures alongside that of images drawn from Hindu nationalism, such as Bharat Mata.

34. The RSS administratively is divided into a prant (state units) for six of the seven states in the Northeast and two prants in Assam, the seventh.

35. Zeeshan Shaikh, 'Assam: Two Cattle Thieves Killed in Nagaon District by Cow Vigilantes', India.com, 30 April 2017, http://www.india.com/news/india/assam-two-cattle-thieves-killed-in-nagaon-district-by-cow-vigilantes-2085669/ (accessed 12 May 2017). It is unclear from the report what the thieves intended to do with the cows.

36. See a review of the RSS in the Northeast in, Simantik Dowerah, 'Rise of Hindutva in North East: RSS, BJP Score in Assam, Manipur but Still Untested in Arunachal', Firstpost, 21 April 2017, http://www.firstpost.com/politics/rise-of-hindutva-in-north-east-rss-bjp-make-a-mark-in-assam-manipur-but-poll-waters-still-untested-in-arunachal-3391504.html (accessed 3 May 2017).

37. Ibid.

38. Ibid.

39. Ibid.

40. Ibid.

41. Ibid. The Vivekananda Kendra, started by Eknath Ranade, the former general secretary of the RSS, has a strong presence in Arunachal Pradesh, where it runs English-medium schools. In addition, the Sewa Bharati, a federation of RSS-linked service projects, provides free coaching classes in mathematics and free orientation classes for aspiring civil servants.

42. Noted in Bhattacharjee, 'Tracing the Emergence and Consolidation of Hindutva in Assam', *Economic and Political Weekly*, p. 84. The food at the conference was, however, vegetarian in conformity with traditional Hindu food practices.

43. On the subject of toleration towards eating habits, Golwalkar told an RSS worker, 'Our value system is not a hard and fast set of rules and in our plural society there are different kinds of people with different food habits.' Taken from *Sree Guruji Samagra* (New Delhi: Suruchi Prakashan, Hindu year 5016), vol. 9, p. 120.

44. For a description of its activities focusing on preserving and strengthening indigenous cultures, see the International Centre for

Cultural Studies (ICCS) website, http://iccsglobal.org/?page_id=26 (accessed 6 May 2017). The website states that the ICCS supports 'projects that help empowering native and local communities, preserving world's cultures and traditions, as well as help reconnect people with their natural environment through ancient wisdom'. Its activities tend to focus on cultures prior to the appearance of Christianity and Islam.

45. O.M. Roopesh, 'Temple as the Political Arena in Kerala', *Economic and Political Weekly*, 22 April 2017, vol. 52, no. 16. The RSS has organized a movement called 'Temple for Devotees' whose message is to oppose government and private involvement in the functioning of temples, emphasizing that temple governance and the choice of activities be determined by people who actually worship at the temple. It also favours a priestly training system that is open to all social groups and provides an education that would make them influential community leaders.

46. Ibid. A key theme of the RSS is that the diverse Hindu communities are in fact a single community and temples in Kerala help advance that message.

47. Press Trust of India, 'RSS Strengthening Base in Kerala, Number of Shakhas Rising', *Financial Express*, 14 February 2017, http://www.financialexpress.com/india-news/rss-strengthening-base-in-kerala-number-of-shakhas-rising/550827/ (accessed 12 May 2017). Uttar Pradesh and Madhya Pradesh, with much larger populations, have more shakhas than Kerala. The article, however, incorrectly mentions that there are 45,000 shakhas all over India; the RSS General Secretary Report 2017 notes instead that there are 78,000 shakhas of all kinds (including some 58,000 daily shakhas). Figures available at RSS.org.

48. Varghese K. George, 'Red Fades to Saffron in Kerala', *The Hindu*, 29 August 2015, http://www.thehindu.com/opinion/op-ed/red-fades-to-saffron-in-kerala/article7591378.ece (accessed 12 May 2017).

49. Interview with Bhaskar Rao Kalambi in Mumbai on 15 June 1983. Kalambi was the Kerala prant pracharak of the RSS at the time we met him. He later became organizing secretary of the ABVKA and increased its influence in tribal areas all over India.

50. M.B. Rajesh, 'The BJP, Beef and the Battle of Kerala House', The Wire, 1 November 2015, https://thewire.in/politics/the-bjp-beef-and-the-battle-of-kerala-house (accessed 12 May 2017).

51. Ibid.

52. Suhrid Sankar Chattopadhyay, 'West Bengal—Disturbing Rise of Religion-based Nationalism', kractivist.com, 7 May 2017, http://www.kractivist.org/west-bengal-disturbing-rise-of-religion-based-nationalism/ (accessed 12 May 2017).

53. Milinda Ghosh Roy, 'Now, RSS Hopes to Storm Mamata's Stronghold West Bengal', The Quint, 12 April 2017, https://www.thequint.com/india/2017/04/12/rss-bjp-growth-west-bengal (accessed 12 May 2017). Information provided to the press by Jishnu Basu, a senior West Bengali RSS official. One can peg the number of young men participating in the daily shakha activities at about 90,000 (assuming about fifty participants per shakha).

54. In an interview with us in Chicago in September 2016, Ghosh told us that the BJP needed to conduct an aggressive campaign to establish itself as a formidable party ready to come to power, rather than perpetuating the accommodative policy (with regional parties) that had failed to produce a majority in the 2015 Bihar Assembly elections.

55. Figures taken from the Election Commission of India and available at http://eci.nic.in/eci_main1/ElectionStatistics.aspx (accessed 3 May 2017).

56. The Trinamool Congress won the Dakshin Kanthi by-election with 95,369 votes, while the BJP got 52,843 and the communists and the Congress were far behind, giving some credence to BJP's claim that it has already become the major Opposition party in the state. For figures see fn. 48.

57. Indo-Asian News Service, 'Action Being Taken against Cow Vigilantes: Amit Shah', Zee News, 26 April 2017, http://zeenews.india.com/india/action-being-taken-against-cow-vigilantes-amit-shah-1999604.html (accessed 10 May 2017).

58. Ibid.

59. For a comprehensive historical view of the cow protection issue from a friendly perspective, see, Neelakandan, 'Hindutva and the Politics of Beef', Swarajya. The RSS leadership from the time of Hedgewar looked on cow protection as a Hindu duty and therefore as a core element of Hindutva. Not all, however, looked at the cow as holy (for example, Vinayak D. Savarkar and B.R. Ambedkar).

60. For a discussion of the Arya Samaj cow protection movement in the nineteenth century, see, Peter van der Veer, Religious Nationalism: Hindus and Muslims in India (Berkley: University of California Press, 1994), pp. 83–94.

61. An account of the nineteenth-century efforts using the issue of cow protection noted in *Report of the National Commission on Cattle* (Government of India: Ministry of Agriculture, 2002), ch. 1. This chapter was written by Justice Guman Mal Lodha, acting chairman of the National Commission on Cattle.

62. The provision in the Indian Constitution regarding cow protection is noted as a Directive Principle of State Policy and not as a fundamental right as was demanded by its proponents. This reflects a debate on the issue with the liberal Prime Minister Jawaharlal Nehru who successfully lobbied to make the cow protection issue only an advisory one and provided states, rather than the Centre, the power to legislate on it. Gandhi, while against a legislative ban, reportedly stated, 'As for me, not even to win Swaraj, will I renounce my principle of cow protection.' See, *Report of the National Commission on Cattle*, ch. 1.

63. A discussion of the widespread popular support for cow protection within the ruling Congress and the many efforts to make it a federal subject discussed by Donald Eugene Smith, *India as a Secular State* (Princeton: Princeton University Press, 1963), pp. 483–89.

64. *M.H. Quareshi v. State of Bihar*, S.C.J., 1958. The ruling also justified a total ban on she-buffaloes, breeding bulls, and working bullocks, but did not apply the same ruling of usefulness to cow protection.

65. For a review of tougher state legislation since the election of Modi, see, Saptarishi Dutta, 'Where You Can and Can't Eat Beef in India', *The Wall Street Journal*, 6 August 2015, https://blogs.wsj.com/indiarealtime/2015/08/06/where-you-can-and-cant-eat-beef-in-india/ (accessed 1 May 2017).

66. Agencies, 'VHP Demands National Level Law to Ban Cow Slaughter', *The Echo of India*, http://echoofindia.com/jamshedpur-vhp-demands-national-level-law-ban-cow-slaughter-126144 (accessed 13 May 2017).

67. Press Trust of India, 'Those Involved in Cow Slaughter Will Not Be Spared, Dadri Incident Is an Example: Bajrang Dal', *DNA*, 5 August 2016, http://www.dnaindia.com/india/report-those-involved-in-cow-slaughter-will-not-be-spares-dadri-incident-is-an-example-bajrang-dal-2241614 (accessed 14 May 2017).

68. Press Trust of India, 'VHP Will Ban Cow Slaughter, Beef Consumption in Goa in 2 Yrs', *Hindustan Times*, 16 April 2017, http://www.hindustantimes.com/india-news/vhp-will-ban-cow-slaughter-beef-

consumption-in-goa-in-2-yrs/story-gXGsdBbf1tZ7NSIhBy3PXP. html (accessed 20 April 2017).

69.   Nidhi Sethi, 'Now BJP's Coalition Partner MGP Wants Ban on Cow Slaughter in Goa,' NDTV, 12 Aril 2017, https://www.ndtv. com/goa-news/now-bjps-coalition-partner-wants-ban-on-cow-slaughter-in-goa-1680411 (accessed 12 July 2018).

70.   Information taken from the VHP website available at, http://vhp.org/ vhp-glance/dimensions/cow-protection/ (accessed 24 April 2017).

71.   Ibid.

72.   Times News Network, 'RSS Chief: Violence Only Defames Effort of Cow Protectors', *The Times of India*, 10 April 2017, http://timesofindia. indiatimes.com/india/rss-chief-calls-for-all-india-ban-on-cow-slaughter/articleshow/58099954.cms (accessed 20 April 2017).

73.   Ibid. Bhagwat may be proved wrong if the BJP continues to grow in the north-eastern states, many of which have large Christian populations and lack legislation banning cow slaughter.

74.   The VHP was highly critical of the Vajpayee government for refusing to address such issues as Ram Janmabhoomi and cow protection, and for using the argument that coalition politics compelled it to take this approach.

Chapter Twelve: A Ram Temple in Ayodhya

1.   V.S. Naipaul, *India: A Wounded Civilization* (New York: Knopf, 1977).

2.   For a scholarly analysis of the Ram Janmabhoomi movement, see, Ashis Nandy, Shikha Trivedy, Shail Mayaram and Yagnik Achyut, *Creating a Nationality: The Ramjanmabhumi Movement and Fear of the Self* (Delhi, Oxford University Press, 1995).

3.   William Dalrymple, 'Trapped in the Ruins', *Guardian*, 20 March 2004, https://www.theguardian.com/books/2004/mar/20/india. fiction (accessed 12 January 2018).

4.   For a Muslim perspective of the mandir–masjid issue, see, Harsh Narain, *The Ayodhya Temple-Mosque Dispute: Focus on Muslim Sources* (Delhi: Penman Publishers, 1993).

5.   News conference available at, 'Exclusive: Yogi Adityanath's First Press Conference as the New CM of UP', Aaj Tak, 19 March 2017, https:// www.youtube.com/watch?v=9y2AEqhx53k (accessed 29 January 2017).

6.   Soon after the masjid was demolished, Hindu devotees constructed a temporary temple on the site containing idols of Ram as a baby. It has been open on an all-day basis ever since.

7. 'Interview: We Strive for Corruption-Free UP', *Organiser*, 3 April 2017, http://www.organiser.org//Encyc/2017/4/3/Interview-We-Strive-for-Crime-and-Corruption-free-UP-Yogi.html (accessed 10 April 2017). In answer to the question on what his focus as chief minister is, Adityanath responded it would be 'good governance', making society 'corruption free' and following the policy example of the Modi government at the Centre. No Hindutva issues are mentioned in his statement of priorities.

8. Yogi Adityanath's interview with us in Lucknow on 18 January 2018.

9. Champat Rai's extensive analysis of the Ram Janmabhoomi case in, 'Verdict of Lucknow Bench of Allahabad High Court on Sri Rama Janma Bhumi Based on Facts', http://vhp.org/wp-content/uploads/2010/10/RJB-HC-Verdict.pdf (accessed 22 March 2017). Champat Rai was a joint general secretary of the VHP at the time he wrote this analysis; he is now the vice president of the VHP.

10. Ibid.

11. Quote taken from the pamphlet *Ayodhya Verdict: Faith or Law* (New Delhi: India Foundation, 2010), p. 5.

12. For a review of the Ram Janmabhoomi efforts of the mahants of the Gorakhnath math over the past several decades, see analysis of Christophe Jaffrelot, 'The Other Saffron: Adityanath Belongs to a Distinct Ideological Tradition that Is Growing More Assertive', *The Indian Express*, 6 October 2014, http://indianexpress.com/article/opinion/column/the-other-saffron/ (accessed on 28 March 2017).

13. Information about the circumstances regarding the appearance of the idol in 1949 can be found in Krishna Pokharel and Paul Beckett, 'Ayodhya, the Battle for India's Soul: The Complete Story', *Wall Street Journal*, 31 March 2017. This article first appeared in a *Wall Street Journal* series that ran on 3–8 December 2012.

14. It remained locked until 1 February 1986 when a local district judge ordered it to be opened at the height of the Ram Janmabhoomi movement.

15. Information about the growing relationship between the RSS and Digviyay Nath based on an interview we had with Nanaji Deshmukh in Delhi on 25 June 1983. These bhajans continued up to 1986 when the lock was removed. This complex arrangement demonstrated the impressive social network among the general Hindu population that the RSS was able to put together in eastern Uttar Pradesh.

16. The Vidya Bharati, the educational affiliate of the RSS, notes that there are over 3 million students in schools from the primary to the post-secondary level, making it by far the largest private school system in India. Statistics available on its website, 'Statistics', http://www.vidyabharti.net/statistics.php (accessed 8 December 2017).

17. In those elections Vajpayee contested from three different seats, winning only Uttar Pradesh's Balarampur parliamentary seat where Digvijay Nath was an influential political figure.

18. Prior to serving in the Indian Parliament, Mahant Avaidyanath had won five elections to the state Assembly from Gorakhpur district in Uttar Pradesh.

19. The BJP, however, lost this seat in the 2018 parliamentary by-election to a Samajwadi Party candidate. RSS interlocutors tell us that the defeat in what had been a safe constituency reflected overconfidence and infighting within the local BJP.

20. See a discussion of the political collusion of the ruling Congress with the growing sentiment for a Ram Temple in Jaffrelot, *The Hindu Nationalist Movement in India* (Delhi: Thomson Press, 1996), ch. 11.

21. The Congress party at the time, both at the state and central levels, decided for political reasons to play a Hindu card in the face of a growing Hindu concern over the mass conversion of low-caste Hindus in Tamil Nadu to Islam, a Sikh secessionist movement in Punjab and the surge of anti-Indian violence in Kashmir. At the same time, many RSS leaders were disappointed with anti-RSS sentiment in the Janata government (1977–79) and were also concerned by some views of the new BJP, specifically the party's adoption of Gandhian socialism rather than the pro-Hindutva 'Integral Humanism' of Upadhyaya and the inclusion of a green strip in the party's flag. Uttar Pradesh Congress party figure, Dau Dayal Khanna, had raised the proposal for Ram Janmabhoomi in the 1982 Hindu Conference, a conference also attended by former Prime Minister Nanda. The attendance of these senior Congress figures could not have happened without the implicit support of Prime Minister Indira Gandhi.

22. A comprehensive review of Prime Minister Rajiv Gandhi's failed efforts to prepare the way for a Ram Temple can be found in, 'How Rajiv Gandhi Set the Ball Rolling for Ayodhya Temple—President Mukherjee Recalls in His Memoirs', *Nagpur Today*, 21 March 2017, http://www.nagpurtoday.in/how-rajiv-gandhi-set-the-ball-

rolling-for-ayodhya-temple-president-mukherjee-recalls-in-his-memoirs/03212006 (accessed 30 March 2017). The account of Gandhi's facilitating the opening up of the Babri Masjid for Hindu pilgrims in 1986 is attributed in part to the information from the second volume of memoirs by President Pranab Mukherjee, *The Turbulent Years: 1980–1996* (Delhi: Rupa, 2016). That opening breathed life into the VHP's Ram Janmabhoomi campaign and prompted the massive drive to send bricks and donations from all over India to the contested site.

23. For a discussion of the impact on the RSS of a Congress party more sympathetic to Hindu causes in the late 1980s, see, Jaffrelot, *The Hindu Nationalist Movement in India*, pp. 370–75.

24. Details of the negotiations from an interview with Banwarilal Purohit in Nagpur on 5 March 2016. Purohit told us that there was a second meeting in Delhi between Home Minister Buta Singh and a senior RSS functionary, Rajendra Singh (who was to follow Deoras as sarsanghchalak), when the deal between the RSS and the Gandhi government was finalized. Several years later, Purohit went public with the details of the botched deal and supplied us with the press documentation, including, most prominently, articles in two Nagpur dailies, *Lokmat Times*, 26 April 2007, and *The Hitavada*.

25. A review of several failed government attempts at mediation found in, Jagdeep Chokkar, 'Sentiment and Justice', *The Indian Express*, 27 March 2017, https://indianexpress.com/article/opinion/columns/ayodhya-dispute-supreme-court-babri-masjid-ram-janmabhoomi-4586845/ (accessed 12 July 2018).

26. For the complicated set of details leading to the fall of the Chandra Shekhar government, see, Barbara Crossette, 'India Disbands Parliament: Vote in May Seen', *The New York Times*, 14 March 1991, http://www.nytimes.com/1991/03/14/world/india-disbands-parliament-vote-in-may-seen.html (accessed 15 December 2017).

27. For the BJP's analysis of the destruction of the Babri Masjid, see the *BJP's White Paper on Ayodhya and the Rama Temple Movement* (New Delhi: Bharatiya Janata Party, 1993). A more neutral explanation is available in the government-appointed Liberhan Commission report issued by the Government of India, ministry of home affairs, on 24 November 2009, the full text of which can be accessed at http://www.thehindu.com/news/Report-of-the-Liberhan-Ayodhya-

Commission-of-Inquiry-Full-Text/article16894055.ece (accessed 10 December 2017).

28. See report of that day's violence in, 'December 26, 1992: That Day, That Year', *India Today*, http://indiatoday.intoday.in/gallery/babri-masjid-demolition-1992/4/5982.html (accessed 10 December 2017).

29. This ban was revoked on 4 June 1993, by a tribunal set up by law to investigate unlawful activities and had absolved the RSS of all charges. See an analysis of the lifting of the ban in, 'Since Inception, RSS Banned Thrice', *The Times of India*, 31 August 2009, http://www.epaper.timesofindia.com/Repository/getFiles.asp?Style=OliveXLib:LowLevelEntityToPrint_TOINEW&Type=text/html&Path=CAP/2009/08/31&ID=Ar01302 (accessed 10 December 2017).

30. Comprehensive reviews of the complex legal history of the Ram Temple issue can be found in, Koenraad Elst, *Ram Janmabhoomi vs. Babri Masjid. A Case Study in Hindu–Muslim Conflict* (Delhi: Voice of India, 1990) and Vijay Chandra Mishra and Parmanand Singh (eds), *Ram Janmabhoomi Babri Masjid, Historical Documents, Legal Opinions and Judgements* (Delhi: Bar Council of India Trust, 1991).

31. Bharti Jain, 'Ram Temple Not Priority Development', *The Times of India*, 30 May 2015, http://timesofindia.indiatimes.com/india/Ram-temple-not-priority-development-is-Rajnath-Singh-says/articleshow/47476835.cms (accessed 28 March 2017). At that press briefing, Home Minister Singh also noted that amending Article 370 of the Indian Constitution that provides autonomous powers to the Muslim-majority state of Jammu and Kashmir is not a priority, suggesting that this may not be a good time politically to address the issue as the BJP had just formed a coalition in the state with a party whose core base is the Muslim population in the Valley of Kashmir.

32. His comments made at the end of the annual 2015 conclave of the ABPS, the highest decision-making body of the RSS. Ramu Bhagwat, 'RSS Confirms Ram Temple Is on the Back Burner', *The Times of India*, 16 March 2015, http://timesofindia.indiatimes.com/india/RSS-confirms-Ram-temple-is-on-the-back-burner/articleshow/46577067.cms (accessed 28 March 2017).

33. See, Rajni Kothari, 'The Congress "System" in India', *Asian Survey*, December 1964, vol. 4, no. 12.

34. See a discussion in Rajdeep Sardesai, 'The Congress-ification of the BJP', http://www.rajdeepsardesai.net/columns/congress-ification-bjp (accessed 10 December 2017).

35. 'Shiv Sena Forces 300 Gurgaon Meat Sellers, Including KFC, to Close for Navratras', Wionews, 29 March 2017, http://www.wionews.com/south-asia/shiv-sena-forces-300-gurgaon-meat-sellers-including-kfc-to-close-for-navratras-13931 (accessed 2 April 2017). The protesters reportedly also demanded that the restaurants close every Tuesday, a day that many Hindus in north India fast.

36. Rumu Banerjee, 'Violence Can't Be Condoned: RSS Speaks out against Fringe', *The Times of India*, 26 January 2018, https://timesofindia.indiatimes.com/india/violence-cant-be-condoned-rss-speaks-out-against-fringe/articleshow/62658299.cms (accessed 30 January 2018).

37. Ibid.

38. Jaffrelot, *The Hindu Nationalist Movement in India*, ch. 13.

39. Ibid., p. 458.

40. Support for the construction on the ruins of the ancient Somnath Temple, destroyed several times, was part of a revived Hindu nationalism in post-Independence India. It is believed to be one of the twelve places where Lord Shiva took the physical form of a column of light and is hence of religious importance. Its reconstruction was also a reflection of a Hindu nationalist call to right a historic wrong on Hindu civilization. The reconstruction was proposed in 1947 by Home Minister Sardar Vallabhbhai Patel, himself from Gujarat, and approved by Mahatma Gandhi, also from Gujarat. The temple was built with private funds under the supervision of two cabinet members and was dedicated in May 1951 by Rajendra Prasad, the President of India. It is managed by a private trust, of which Prime Minister Modi has been a member since 2009. Other members as of 2017 include Amit Shah and Advani. The prime minister at the time of reconstruction, Nehru, however, was reportedly wary of any ministerial involvement in the reconstruction as he feared that it could encourage the political religious revivalism which he opposed. Advani was one of the first BJP politicians to advocate that the Somnath example be the model for the construction of a Ram Temple at Ayodhya. For an analysis of the comparative strategy for construction of the Ram Temple, see, Special Correspondent, 'Why Not Allow Temple Reconstruction As Was Done at Somnath', *The Hindu*, 26 September 2009, http://www.thehindu.com/news/national/

Why-not-allow-temple-reconstruction-as-was-done-at-Somnath/
article16883492.ece (accessed 27 March 2017). For scholarly studies
of the religious and nationalist significance of the temple, see, Richard
H. Davis, *Lives of Indian Images* (Princeton: Princeton University
Press, 1997) and Romila Thapar, *Somanatha: The Many Voices of
History* (New Delhi: Penguin Books India, 2004).

41.   The ban lasted only six months and the RSS did not shut down its
      activities and no RSS official was arrested.

42.   The VHP has already put in place plans for constructing a temple at
      short notice. In the late 1980s, the VHP organized *shila puja* (brick
      ceremony) in which villages from all over India were asked to send a
      brick and a donation for a Ram Temple. The VHP website says that
      at that time it had collected some 2,75,000 bricks domestically and
      abroad as well as funds so that there would be sufficient supplies and
      money to begin construction immediately.

43.   'VHP Bats for Law to Construct Ram Temple in Ayodhya, Lines
      Up Programmes to Push Demand', *Hindustan Times*, 10 April 2017,
      http://www.hindustantimes.com/india-news/vhp-bats-for-law-to-
      construct-ram-temple-in-ayodhya-lines-up-programmes-to-push-
      demand/story-HHwDDVa3pe9sZaOaUjshqL.html (accessed 27
      March 2017). Togadia reminded the VHP that the BJP in 1987 had
      recommended the construction of a Ram Temple by enacting a law on
      the subject, perhaps making an incorrect comparison to the decision
      to start construction of the Somnath Temple in the late 1940s. In that
      case, there was no parliamentary act authorizing construction.

44.   See fn. 5 for reference to Adityanath's inaugural speech.

45.   Anusha Soni, 'Supreme Court Suggests Out-of-Court Settlement of
      Ayodhya Dispute, Calls Ram Mandir Matter of Sentiment', *India
      Today*, 21 March 2017, https://www.indiatoday.in/india/story/
      ayodhya-supreme-court-ayodhya-issue-babri-masjid-demolition-
      case-bjp-ram-mandir-966721-2017-03-21 (accessed 12 July 2018).

46.   Ibid.

47.   See his comments supporting the Supreme Court's suggestion for an
      out-of-court mediation in, Express Web Desk, 'Ram Temple Issue:
      Agree with SC That Both Sides Must Sit Down and Find Solution,
      Says Yogi Adityanath', MSN, 23 March 2017, https://indianexpress.
      com/article/india/ram-temple-issue-both-sides-must-sit-down-
      and-find-solution-agree-with-sc-says-yogi-adityanath-4579277/
      (accessed 12 July 2018).

48. Hosabale issued his statement welcoming the Supreme Court's suggestion of a negotiated decision between the parties involved, while attending the RSS ABPS meeting on 19–20 March 2017 in the south Indian city of Coimbatore. His comments reported in the RSS-affiliated magazine *Samvada*, 21 March 2017, and can be read at, http://samvada.org/2017/news/datta-pc/ (accessed 23 March 2017).

49. While the temple issue has not been resolved, a succession of governments since 1986 permitted some form of Hindu worship at the site to continue.

50. Ibid. There have been no public reports on the outcome of this cell's efforts.

51. The Allahabad High Court had authorized an archaeological and scientific survey of the disputed property and accepted that a Hindu religious structure had existed at the site of the Babri Masjid and that, in a three-way division of the disputed area to litigants, Hindu worship would be permitted in that part where tradition says Lord Ram took human form, but none of the litigants accepted a division of any part of the disputed land. This decision was stayed and the issue of Lord Ram's nativity at this precise site is under review by India's Supreme Court. For details of the decision, see, Rupali Pruthi, 'Resolve Ram Temple Dispute outside the Court: SC', *Jagran Josh*, 21 March 2017, http://www.jagranjosh.com/current-affairs/resolve-ram-temple-dispute-outside-the-court-sc-1490091000-1 (accessed 28 March 2017).

52. Ibid. Those three occasions were 24 February 2015, 10 April 2015 and 31 May 2016.

53. J. Venkatesan, 'Supreme Court Stays Allahabad High Court Verdict on Ayodhya', *The Hindu*, 9 May 2011, http://www.thehindu.com/news/national/Supreme-Court-stays-Allahabad-High-Court-verdict-on-Ayodhya/article10751917.ece# (accessed 28 March 2017).

54. The Lucknow bench of the Allahabad High Court on 1 January 1993 gave permission to hold non-stop pujas at the site. See information on the history of the effort to build a temple at the site on the VHP website, http://vhp.org/wp-content/uploads/2010/10/AT-A-GLANCE-RJB.pdf (accessed 28 March 2017).

55. Ishita Bhatia, 'Will Not Let Babri Masjid Come Up Anywhere in India: VHP', *The Times of India*, 24 March 2017, http://timesofindia.indiatimes.com/india/will-not-let-babri-masjid-

come-up-anywhere-in-india-vhp/articleshow/57801796.cms (accessed 23 March 2017).

56. 'Ayodhya Dispute: Babri Action Panel Rejects SC Advice of Amicable Solution, BJP Hails Offer', *Hindustan Times*, 4 April 2017, http://www.hindustantimes.com/india-news/ayodhya-dispute-babri-action-panel-rejects-sc-advice-of-amicable-solution-bjp-hails-offer/story-fjuoaSoBIhSYcj4Cp9SqsL.html (accessed 24 March 2017).

57. Ibid.

58. A comprehensive report on the revived case in Inderjit Badhwar, 'Babri Masjid Demolition Case: India Legal Leads Again', *India Legal*, 19 April 2017, http://www.indialegallive.com/letter-from-the-editor-inderjit-badhwar/babri-masjid-demolition-case-india-legal-leads-23540 (accessed 15 December 2017).

59. Information from the VHP website in a section dealing with the second Dharma Sansad, http://vhp.org/conferences/dharmasansads/dharma-sansad-2/ (accessed 2 April 2017).

60. Rahul Varma and Pranav Gupta, 'In the Ruins of Babri', *The Indian Express*, 7 December 2016, https://indianexpress.com/article/opinion/columns/babri-masjid-demolition-uttar-pradesh-kar-sevaks-4414170/ (accessed 12 July 2018).

61. Ibid.

62. Recall, Uttar Pradesh Chief Minister Adityanath told us that the 2010 high court decision to partition the site is wrong. Interview with him in Lucknow on 18 January 2018.

Chapter Thirteen: A Rebellion in Goa Tests the RSS Decision-Making System

1. The sixty-eight-year-old Subhash Velingkar, a high school teacher and a member of the RSS since 1962, was selected as the Goa vibhag sanghchalak in 1996. However, he was not a pracharak.

2. Information on the formation and tactics of the BBSM can be found on its website, http://goabbsm.org/ (accessed 28 February 2017). Velingkar established the BBSM in 2011 when the then Congress government in the state decided to give grants to English-medium private schools. While the language issue was his pre-eminent cause, Velingkar also had a broader nationalist agenda; he opposed proposals for dual citizenship (Portuguese and Indian, of Goans born before 1961) as well as plans to provide funds for colonial-era festivals.

3. Circumstance of its formation in, Sanjay Jog, 'Rebel Goa RSS Leader Velingkar Launches Goa Suraksha Manch', *Business Standard*, 2 October 2016, http://www.business-standard.com/article/ politics/rebel-rss-leader-subhash-velingkar-floats-goa-suraksha- manch-116100200435_1.html (accessed 10 October 2017). The MGP campaign manifesto, however, did not include the language issue, though it was identical to the platforms of its two partners on other issues.

4. For a good review of the election outcome, see, Press Trust of India, 'Election Results 2017: BJPs Vote Share More Than That of Congress in Goa', *The Indian Express*, 12 March 2017, https:// indianexpress.com/elections/goa-assembly-elections-2017/election- results-bjp-vote-share-congress-4566386/ (accessed 12 July 2018).

5. For a discussion of GSM's post-election actions, see an interview with party president Anand Shirodkar, Express News Service, 'Goa Suraksha Manch Hits Out at Ally for Insult; Congress Legislators Fault Top Brass', *The New Indian Express*, 14 March 2017, http:// www.newindianexpress.com/nation/2017/mar/14/goa-suraksha- manch-hits-out-at-ally-for-insult-congress-legislators-fault-top- brass-1581079.html (accessed 14 March 2017).

6. *The Hindu*, 'Lakshman Behare Is New RSS Goa Chief', 11 September 2016, http://www.thehindu.com/news/national/other-states/ Lakshman-Behare-is-new-RSS-Goa-chief/article14633028.ece# (accessed 2 March 2017). The RSS leadership had consulted with Velingkar several times, according to RSS sources, when he used the BBMS to criticize Goa's BJP government, including demonstrating against BJP president Amit Shah, during a visit to the state. But it waited to act until he actually floated a political party to remove him from his position.

7. This message was part of an email correspondence we had with Amshekar, the Goa vibhag pracharak. The quote taken from a 17 November 2016 response to a set of questions from us.

8. ABVP resolution reported in, 'RSS ABPS Passes Resolution-2: "Elementary Education in Mother Language"', *Samvada*, 15 March 2015, http://samvada.org/2015/news/rss-abps-resolution-2- education-in-mother-language/ (accessed 30 November 2017).

9. See the Bharatiya Shikshan Mandal website for a discussion of this issue, http://bsmbharat.org/Articles.aspx (accessed 20 November 2017).

10. What Amshekar does not address in his correspondence with us is the BJP's efforts to get senior Roman Catholic clerics to help them retain

the substantial support of Goa's large Roman Catholic minority (a quarter of the state's population). He said this was an issue for the BJP to decide.

11. Despite the cordial relations between Parrikar and the Roman Catholic leadership, a case has been filed by a member of the RSS, Vinay Joshi, against Goa's Roman Catholic archbishop for allegedly appealing to voters to defeat the BJP candidate for a 2017 by-election, Chief Minister Parrikar, and thus violating the Representation of People's Act 1951 which prohibits religious figures from favouring or opposing the activities of a political party. Joshi has also filed a case against the Roman Catholic archbishop of Gujarat for similarly advising Catholics on how to vote in the 2017 Gujarat Assembly elections. Information from a telephone interview with Vinay Joshi on 6 December 2017. He told us that the RSS as an organization did not back him, though some members may have communicated their support to him.

12. Parrikar easily won his by-election Assembly contest, again underscoring his personal popularity among all segments of the population.

13. These allies were the MGP, the Goa Praja Party, and the Shiv Sena. The MGP won three seats (and 11.3 per cent of the vote), while the others won none. The MGP was part of the BJP-led 2012–17 government and had earlier been the state's ruling party. Its support base is now limited to one largely middle-class, Hindu, Marathi-speaking area in North Goa.

14. Press Trust of India, 'RSS Sacks Its Goa Chief Subhash Velingkar after He Openly Takes Anti-BJP Stance', India.com, 31 August 2016, http://www.india.com/news/india/rss-sacks-its-goa-chief-subhash-velingkar-after-he-openly-takes-anti-bjp-stance-1448457/ (accessed 28 February 2017).

15. The exact wording of the announcement dropping Velingkar from his position, signed by the Konkan Prant sanghchalak Satish S. Modh, can be found at, https://rsschennai.blogspot.com/2016/09/statement-of-rss-goa-on-bbsm-stand.html (accessed 3 March 2017).

16. *The Hindu*, 'Lakshman Behare Is New RSS Goa Chief'.

17. News on this new rebel RSS unit in the Goan press, and can be found in, GoaNews Desk, 'Rebel Goa RSS to Join Nagpur after Defeating "Pro-Minority" BJP', GoaNews, 11 September 2016, http://m.goanews.com/news_details.php?id=7452 (accessed 28 February 2017).

18. Taken from Sumant Amshekar's 17 November 2016 email response to us. In other words, Amshekar is saying that Velingkar continued to owe allegiance to Nagpur even while forming a separate RSS in Goa.

19. Murari Shetye, 'Goa RSS Rebel Faction Dissolved, Merged with Parent Organisation', *The Times of India*, 7 March 2017, http://timesofindia.indiatimes.com/city/goa/goa-rss-rebel-faction-dissolved-merged-with-parent/articleshow/57503590.cms (accessed 7 March 2017).

20. Ibid.

21. Vijay de Souza and Gauree Malkarnekar, 'Subhash Velingkar: RSS Acting Like BJP Slave, Scared of Manohar Parrikar', *The Times of India*, 25 January 2017, http://timesofindia.indiatimes.com/city/goa/velingkar-rss-acting-like-bjp-slave-scared-of-parrikar/articleshow/56768232.cms (accessed 3 March 2017). In that same meeting with journalists, Velingkar reportedly asserted that the problem of RSS submission to the BJP, as demonstrated in the language issue in Goa, began when Deoras stepped down from his position of sarsanghchalak in 1994.

22. Zeeshan Shaikh, '"Sangh Has Submitted to BJP . . . Whatever Paap BJP Does, Sangh Will Support": Subhash Velingkar', *The Indian Express*, 18 January 2017, https://indianexpress.com/article/india/sangh-has-submitted-to-bjp-whatever-paap-bjp-does-sangh-will-support-subhash-velingkar-4479359/ (accessed 12 July 2018).

23. Ibid.

24. Several RSS interlocutors deny that any such order was issued against the language protests by higher RSS authorities, though it is possible that (in the informal policy discussions that are common among senior RSS figures) some may have advised him that his protests could have the unwanted consequence of the BJP losing much of its Hindu vote base. The results indicate that the BJP did lose a considerable part of its Hindu vote base to various Opposition parties in the 2017 Assembly polls. An analysis of the loss of Hindu votes in Goa can be found in, S.K. Prabhu, 'Parrikar Government in Goa Again', *Vivek* (Marathi-language weekly), 20 March 2017, Prabhu also argues that the BJP government could continue to lose Hindu support if it does not change its current language policy.

25. The ban imposed in 1948 was lifted as there was no convincing legal evidence that the RSS had any involvement in the assassination of Mahatma Gandhi.

26. There are a number of very good accounts of the debate within the RSS over the level of its political involvement. Among the best are, Craig Baxter, *The Jana Sangh: A Biography of an Indian Political Party* (Philadelphia: University of Pennsylvania Press, 1969), ch. 3; Bruce Graham, *Hindu Nationalism and Indian Politics: The Origins and Development of the Bharatiya Jana Sangh* (Cambridge: Cambridge University Press, 1969), ch. 2; Christophe Jaffrelot, *The Hindu Nationalist Movement in India* (New York: Columbia University Press, 1996), ch. 3.

27. Walter Andersen and Shridhar Damle, *The Brotherhood in Saffron: The Rashtriya Swayamsevak Sangh and Hindu Revivalism* (Boulder: Westview Press, 1987), pp. 247–54.

28. Bruce Graham, *Hindu Nationalism and Indian Politics*, pp. 91–93.

29. For a discussion of this calculation of building apolitical party organization modelled after that of the RSS, even if it produced short-run challenges to winning elections, discussed in Jaffrelot, *The Hindu Nationalist Movement in India*, pp. 128–29.

30. Information on RSS practices written in Narayan H. Palkar, *Dr. Hedgewar* (Pune: Bharatiya Vichar Sadhana, 1960), p. 239.

31. Ibid., pp. 330–32.

32. Ibid., pp. 251–56. This tactic was continued in post-Independence India in the 1952 state elections in the Bombay Presidency. Three sanghchalaks contested as part of an effort to protect the post-ban RSS from further restrictions in a state where much of its leadership had been arrested during the ban. The three were S.A. Modak (Satara district), Dr Mule (Sholapur district) and Advocate Bhausaheb Deshmukh (Pune district). All three lost. Information on the nominations of sanghchalaks to elective offices was noted in a series of articles recommending changes in RSS policy by a dissident RSS pracharak, D.V. Gokhale, in the Marathi-language biweekly *Kesari*, May 1952. Gokhale along with at least two other pracharaks in western Maharashtra left the RSS shortly after the lifting of the ban in 1949. Gokhale later went on to be the news editor of the prestigious Marathi-language daily, *The Maharashtra Times*. The other two were B.K. Kelkar, who later became the chief of the Maharashtra Information Centre in Delhi, and Vidyadhar Gokhale, later editor of the Marathi-language daily *Loksatta* and a Shiv Sena Rajya Sabha member.

33. The Deoras brothers withdrew from active involvement in the RSS because of their sense that the RSS was not reaching out socially,

nor taking on new responsibilities in a changing India. Gangadhar Indurkar, *Sangh, Kal, Aaj, ani Udya* (Pune: Sree Vidya Prakashan, 1983, in Marathi), pp. 178–82. Indurkar was an RSS activist-member who wrote the first biography of Golwalkar, and for a period was editor of the RSS Hindi-language daily *Swadesh*.

34. Palkar, *Dr. Hedgewar*, p. 193.

35. There was a surge in the founding of akharas in the Nagpur area after the 1923 Moplah communal riots in Kerala. Also see the study of the rise of akharas in the 1920s in, D.E.U. Baker, *Changing Political Leadership in an Indian Province: The Central Provinces and Berar, 1919-1939* (Delhi: Oxford University Press, 1979), p. 71. Also see, Andersen and Damle, *The Brotherhood in Saffron*, pp. 34–35.

36. An account of this protest movement in, Guruprakash B. Hugar, 'Vande Mataram Movement in Hyderabad Karnataka 1938-1939', in *International Research Journal of Social Sciences*, September 2015, vol. 4/9, pp. 30–33. For an analysis of the nationalist significance of Vande Mataram, see, Haridas Mukherjee and Uma Mukherjee, *'Bande Mataram' and Indian Nationalism* (Calcutta: Firma K.L. Mukhopadhyaya, 1957). One of the students involved in this Vande Mataram agitation was P.V. Narasimha Rao, then a student in Hyderabad University from which he was expelled. He then shifted to Nagpur University where he came into contact with the Deoras brothers and Pingle, who later became a senior figure in the VHP.

37. Baker, *Changing Political Leadership in an Indian Province*, p. 333.

38. See our reference on this dissidence in Andersen and Damle, *The Brotherhood in Saffron*, pp. 108–10.

39. Taken from Anand Hardikar, *Rambhau Mhalgi* (Pune: Snehal Prakashan, 1993), p. 97.

40. Interview with M.G. Vaidya, a former all-India RSS spokesperson, in Nagpur on 6 March 2016. Similar examples of dissidence over RSS policy occurred in Bombay city.

41. For a review of this incident, see, https://indiankanoon.org/doc/383735/ (accessed 4 March 2017). This provides detailed information on those controversial celebrations.

42. Reference to this in, Swarnalata Bhishikar, *Appasaheb Pendse* (Pune: Snehal Prakashan, 1992), p. 93.

43. Oke was one of those early pracharaks from Nagpur trained by Hedgewar; he sent Oke to Delhi in 1937 to start an RSS group there. Oke, while there, expanded the RSS training format by starting shakhas tailored for senior government officials. As head of the RSS

unit in Delhi, Oke was in direct touch with the nation's political leaders as well as with senior figures in the Jana Sangh, access to which led some of his colleagues to refer to him as a 'kingmaker'. Details from a 25 March 2017 telephone conversation with Dr D.V. Nene, a journalist and doctor who wrote extensively on the RSS. His articles on the RSS appeared in the Marathi-language weekly *Sobat* in the late 1960s and 1970s, under the pseudonym 'Dadumiya'. These articles are highly critical of Golwalkar for his alleged lack of involvement in social and political issues.

44. Until the 1960s, sanghchalaks were often prominent local figures and not necessarily members (swayamsevaks) when they were appointed. Therefore their contesting elections was not perceived as an act that would undermine the work of the RSS. After the late 1960s, the sanghchalaks were almost all people who had gone through RSS training, and the RSS no longer gives permission for sitting sanghchalaks to hold any kind of political office or official position. If sanghchalaks do occupy a political office, they are required to relinquish their RSS position.

45. A very good summary of these divisions between RSS workers and the politicians in Graham, *Hindu Nationalism and Indian Politics*, pp. 56–68.

46. The issue of Oke's backing of Sharma in a crucial test of strength between the RSS and BJP politicians discussed in Baxter, *The Jana Sangh*, pp. 134–36. Also see the articles by Dr Nene. Oke's dual political/RSS responsibilities were probably not the major reason for the opposition of the RSS leadership to his inclusion in the working committee. The third president of the BJS, Prem Nath Dogra (1954–56), was in fact simultaneously the sanghchalak of Jammu and Kashmir, and he did not have to vacate that position. Further, Dogra was the long-time head of the Praja Parishad political party in Jammu and Kashmir, and was in fact asked to become sanghchalak of that state while continuing to hold his political office.

47. Oke was replaced as the prant pracharak of the Delhi unit in March 1956 by Madhav Mulye, also an early pracharak trained by Hedgewar. Many RSS members in Delhi, loyal to Oke, left the RSS to protest the removal. Information on Oke's refusal to go to Chennai in articles by Dr Nene.

48. Graham, *Hindu Nationalism and Indian Politics*, p. 66.

49. For an analysis of the new RSS constitution and a summary of its major points, see, Baxter, *The Jana Sangh*, pp. 44–49.

50. The constitution itself can be found in *Organiser* (6 September 1949). The original constitution was adopted on 1 August 1949 and was amended on 1 July 1972.

51. Amshekar email.

52. *The Times of India*, 'Bharat Mata Ki Jay Will Influence Politics in Goa: Chief Subhash Velingkar', 13 November 2017, https://timesofindia.indiatimes.com/city/goa/bharat-mata-ki-jay-will-influence-politics-in-goa-velingkar/articleshow/61620759.cms (accessed 30 November 2017). Velingkar was politically isolated when his campaign ally, the MGM, joined the BJP-coalition government.

53. A review of the notion of a 'Congress system' in Rajni Kothari, 'The Congress "System" in India', *Asian Survey*, December 1964, vol. 4, no. 12, pp. 161–73.

Chapter Fourteen: Bihar Elections 2015

1. For an analysis of the significance of the 2015 Bihar Assembly vote, see, Milan Vaishnav and Saksham Khosla, 'Changing Alliances, Caste Arithmetic: Bihar Polls Explained', *Hindustan Times*, 9 October 2015, http://www.hindustantimes.com/india/bihar-polls-explained-changing-alliances-caste-arithmetic/story-ujzxZ63J6zJG2IxhpZDfgK.html (accessed 5 December 2017).

2. Rahul Kanwal, 'Inside Story of How Amit Shah's Redrawing Bihar's Caste Map', *India Today*, 17 July 2015, http://www.dailyo.in/politics/amit-shah-bjp-bihar-assembly-polls-narendra-modi-lok-sabha-election-2014-congress-lalu-prasad-yadav-nitish-kumar/story/1/5024.html (accessed 5 December 2017).

3. The primary voter base of the RJD consisted of the landowning Yadav caste while that of the JD(U) was made up of the lowest levels of the Hindu caste hierarchy (Most Backward Castes or MBCs) comprising traditionally landless labourers or tenant farmers. These Yadav and MBC communities have traditionally been antagonistic to each other because of their respective positions in the caste hierarchy.

4. Rahul Verma and Pranav Gupta, 'Good Arithmetic but No Chemistry', *The Hindu*, 23 September 2015, http://www.thehindu.com/opinion/op-ed/bihar-assembly-elections-2015-good-arithmetic-but-no-chemistry/article7678191.ece (accessed 5 December 2017).

5.   DNA web team, 'RSS to Decide BJP Strategy for Bihar Polls after Delhi Drubbing?', *DNA*, 17 February 2015, http://www.dnaindia. com/india/report-rss-to-decide-bjp-strategy-for-bihar-polls-after-delhi-drubbing-2061703 (accessed 14 March 2018).

6.   Ibid.

7.   Mohan Bhagwat, 'Strengthening the Weakest Link Will Lead Nation to Development', *Organiser*, 21 September 2015, http:// samvada.org/2015/articles/bhagwat-interview-organiser/ (accessed 29 April 2018).

8.   Indrani Basu, 'Lalu Prasad Yadav Dares BJP, RSS to End Reservations', *Huffington Post*, 21 September 2015, http://www.huffingtonpost. in/2015/09/21/lalu-dares-bjp-reservations_n_8171196.html (accessed 5 December 2017).

9.   The Citizen Bureau, 'RSS Is BJP's Supreme Court, Says Bihar CM Nitish Kumar', The Citizen, 23 September 2015, http://www. thecitizen.in/index.php/en/newsdetail/index/1/5252/rss-is-bjps-supreme-court-says-bihar-cm-nitish-kumar (accessed 29 April 2018).

10. For an analysis of how the BJP was able to mobilize support from upper-caste voters after the implementation of the Mandal Commission report, see, Pavithra Suryanarayan, 'When Do the Poor Vote for the Right-Wing and Why: Hierarchy and Vote Choice in the Indian States', *Comparative Political Studies*, https://pavisuridotcom. files.wordpress.com/2012/08/bjp_paper_latest3.pdf (accessed 3 May 2018).

11. Nistula Hebbar, 'BJP Backs Off from RSS Chief's Remarks on Quota', *The Hindu*, 22 September 2015, http://www.thehindu.com/ news/national/bjp-backs-off-from-rss-chiefs-remarks-on-quota/ article7674916.ece (accessed 13 December 2017).

12. Shyamlal Yadav, 'Why RSS Changed Its Stand on Reservation', *The Indian Express*, 3 November 2015, https://indianexpress.com/article/ explained/why-rss-changed-its-stand-on-reservation/ (accessed 12 July 2018).

13. Pradeep K. Chhibber and Sandeep Shastri, *Religious Practice and Democracy in India* (New York: Cambridge University Press, 2014), p. 131.

14. Prashant Jha, 'How Does BJP Succeed in Relentlessly Acquiring Power, State after State?', *Hindustan Times*, 16 September 2017, http://www.hindustantimes.com/books/what-you-need-to-know-

about-the-bjp/story-8UgwXeNznIdE5lTExmyOAJ.html (accessed 5 December 2017).

15. Paul R. Brass, *Factional Politics in an Indian State: The Congress Party in Uttar Pradesh*, (London: Cambridge University Press, 1965), pp. 50–70.

16. Simone Chauchard and Neelanjan Sircar, 'Courting Votes without Party Workers: The Effect of Political Competition on Partisan Networks in Rural India', unpublished paper, http://www.simonchauchard.com/wp-content/uploads/2014/02/politicalbrokerage_20171113.pdf (accessed 3 May 2018).

17. Indian Census Bureau uses relatively stringent criteria for classifying a location as urban. The relative generosity of fiscal transfers to rural areas and lower incidence of land taxes incentivizes localities to remain rural. Researchers using satellite data contend that almost half of India is urban. For more details on methodology, see, Ajai Sreevatsan, 'How Much of India is Actually Urban?', LiveMint, 16 September 2017, http://www.livemint.com/Politics/4UjtdRPRikhpo8vAE0V4hK/How-much-of-India-is-actually-urban.html (accessed 5 December 2017).

18. Reserve Bank of India, 'Per Capita Income by State', Database on the Indian Economy.

19. Ravish Tiwari, 'Bihar Poll Strategy: BJP Picks 3 RSS Men, Amit Shah's Aide to Lead the Electoral Battle', *The Economic Times*, 4 August 2015, http://articles.economictimes.indiatimes.com/2015-08-04/news/65204857_1_pracharak-amit-shah-s-party-leaders (accessed 5 December 2017).

20. Panini Anand, 'Battle for Bihar: How the RSS Is Helping the BJP Fight the Election', Catch News, 13 October 2015, http://www.catchnews.com/politics-news/battle-for-bihar-snapshot-of-how-the-rss-is-helping-the-bjp-fight-the-election-1444360753.html (accessed 12 July 2018).

21. Ibid.

22. Archis Mohan and Satyavrat Mishra, 'Meet the Backroom Boys in the Battle for Bihar', *Business Standard*, 22 September 2015, http://www.rediff.com/news/report/bihar-polls-meet-the-backroom-boys-in-the-battle-for-bihar/20150922.htm (accessed 5 December 2017).

23. Milan Vaishnav, 'The Merits of Money and "Muscle": Essays on Criminality, Elections and Democracy in India', Columbia University PhD thesis, 2012.

24. Dhirendra Kumar, 'Infighting in Bihar BJP over CM Candidate', *Millennium Post*, http://www.millenniumpost.in/infighting-in-bihar-bjp-over-cm-candidate-61813 (accessed 5 December 2017).

25. Binod Dubey, 'Bihar: BJP "Factions" Put Up Own Names for CM Candidates', *Hindustan Times*, 30 June 2015, https://www.hindustantimes.com/patna/bihar-bjp-factions-put-up-own-names-for-cm-candidates/story-g52QYaozSCkzeLxIW3adoJ.html (accessed 26 February 2018).

26. Binod Dubey, 'RSS Has Its Say in BJP's First List for Bihar Elections', *Hindustan Times*, 17 September 2015, http://www.hindustantimes.com/india/rss-has-its-say-in-bjp-s-first-list-for-bihar-elections/story-UTaHFTvmAVt4EafcdRLXIK.html (accessed 5 December 2017).

27. *The Indian Express*, 'Bihar Polls: RSS Sends Its Muslim Wing to Woo Community', 28 September 2015, https://indianexpress.com/article/india/politics/bihar-polls-rss-sends-its-muslim-wing-to-woo-community/ (accessed 12 July 2018).

28. Vasudha Venugopal, 'Bihar Polls 2015: RSS Steps Up Help to BJP, Invokes "Hindu Self-Esteem"', *The Economic Times*, 27 October 2015, http://economictimes.indiatimes.com/news/politics-and-nation/bihar-polls-2015-rss-steps-up-help-to-bjp-invokes-hindu-self-esteem/articleshow/49545370.cms (accessed 5 December 2017).

29. Ibid.

30. Subsequent to the 2015 Bihar election, Lalu Prasad Yadav was convicted in three more corruption cases and has been imprisoned at Birsa Munda Central Jail since 23 December 2017.

31. Vishwa Mohan, 'Dump Maa-Bete ki Sarkar, It Works Only for Jijaji: Modi', *The Times of India*, 22 April 2014, https://timesofindia.indiatimes.com/news/Dump-maa-bete-ki-sarkar-it-works-only-for-jijaji-Modi/articleshow/34067230.cms (accessed 5 December 2017).

32. For example, Lalu Prasad, the president of the RJD and the BJP's main competitor in Bihar, was convicted of graft charges and sentenced to five years in prison. As of 2018, he is out on bail, pending appeal.

33. Muzamil Jaleel, 'Bihar Polls: From RSS Shakha to Jan Sampark, "Invisible" Ways to Promote BJP', *The Indian Express*, 29 September 2015, https://indianexpress.com/article/india/politics/bihar-polls-

from-rss-shakha-to-jan-sampark-invisible-ways-to-promote-bjp/ (accessed 12 July 2018).

34. Bhagwat had said in March 2014 that 'we [the RSS] are not in politics. Our work is not to chant "NaMo, NaMo". We must work towards our own goal.' See, India Today Online, 'RSS Can't Cross Limit, Chant "NaMo, NaMo" for BJP: Mohan Bhagwat', *India Today*, 11 March 2014, http://indiatoday.intoday.in/story/mohan-bhagwat-rss-can-not-cross-limit-chant-namo-namo-for-bjp/1/347791.html (accessed 5 December 2017).

35. Jaleel, 'Bihar Polls: From RSS Shakha to Jan Sampark', *The Indian Express*.

36. Ibid.

37. See, for instance, Venugopal, 'Bihar Polls 2015: RSS Steps Up Help to BJP', *The Economic Times*.

38. For details on campaign rules, see, Election Commission of India, http://eci.nic.in/eci_main1/the_function.aspx#campaign (accessed 10 December 2017).

39. Ibid.

40. Rakesh Sinha, 'Dr Keshav Baliram Hedgewar', Publications Division, ministry of information and broadcasting.

41. Anand, 'Battle for Bihar: How the RSS Is Helping the BJP Fight the Election', Catch News.

42. India Today Online, 'RSS Can't Cross Limit, Chant "NaMo, NaMo" for BJP: Mohan Bhagwat', *India Today*.

43. Jaleel, 'Bihar Polls: From RSS Shakha to Jan Sampark, "Invisible" Ways to Promote BJP', *The Indian Express*.

44. For instance, see, Anand, 'Battle for Bihar: How the RSS Is Helping the BJP Fight the Election', Catch News.

45. Kumar Shakti Shekhar, 'Bihar Is Now Bringing the Best (and Worst) out of Modi', *India Today*, 26 October 2015, http://www.dailyo.in/politics/bihar-polls-narendra-modi-nitish-mann-ki-baat-lalu-yadav-geeta-reservation-obcs-dalits-muslims/story/1/6998.html (accessed 5 December 2017).

46. Ibid.

47. Venugopal, 'Bihar Polls 2015: RSS Steps Up Help to BJP, Invokes "Hindu self-esteem"', *The Economic Times*.

48. Ibid.

49. Rahul Shrivastava, 'RSS Steps in with Hindutva Strategy for Last Lap of Bihar Election', NDTV, 29 October 2015,

http://www.ndtv.com/bihar/after-amit-shahs-crackers-in-pakistan-remark-gloves-are-off-in-bihar-poll-campaign-1237913 (accessed 5 December 2017).

50. Ibid.
51. Venugopal, 'Bihar Polls 2015: RSS Steps Up Help to BJP, Invokes "Hindu Self-Esteem"', *The Economic Times.*
52. Ibid.
53. Ibid.
54. Salman S.H., '98% of Connected Rural Users Men; 79% from the City: Report', *Medianama*, 16 August 2016, https://www.medianama.com/2016/08/223-rural-internet-usage-pattern/ (accessed 5 December 2017).
55. Venugopal, 'Bihar Polls 2015: RSS Steps Up Help to BJP, Invokes "Hindu Self-esteem"', *The Economic Times.*
56. Rahul Varma and Sanjay Kumar, 'How the Grand Alliance Won', *India Seminar*, http://www.india-seminar.com/2016/678/678_rahul_&_sanjay.htm (accessed 18 February 2018).
57. Press Trust of India, 'Lalu Backs Nitish on Call for Opposition Unity against BJP, RSS', *Deccan Chronicle*, 19 April 2016, http://www.deccanchronicle.com/nation/politics/190416/lalu-backs-nitish-on-call-for-opposition-unity-against-bjp-rss.html (accessed 5 December 2017).
58. The eighth state, Mizoram, long dominated by the Congress, goes to polls in late 2018. As elsewhere in the Northeast, the RSS and its 'family' are gearing up to assist the BJP. The BJP has a government in Assam (led by Sarbananda Sonowal), Arunachal Pradesh (Pema Khandu), Manipur (N. Biren Singh) and Tripura (Biplab Kumar Deb), and is part of the government in Meghalaya (led by Conrad Sangma) and Nagaland (led by Neiphiu Rio). The regional party that governs Sikkim (Sikkim Democratic Front, led by Pawan Kumar Chamling) is a BJP ally and a part of the North Eastern Democratic Alliance.
59. Smriti Kak Ramachandran, 'Assembly Election Results: How RSS Helped BJP in Nagaland, Tripura and Meghalaya', *Hindustan Times*, 3 March 2018, https://www.hindustantimes.com/india-news/how-rss-helped-bjp-in-nagaland-tripura-and-meghalaya/story-uGB72XgWMZTXVF7Pb0XaGJ.html (accessed 16 March 2018).
60. Eram Agha, 'North East Elections: Rise, Reach and Outreach of the Sangh', CNN-News18 https://www.news18.com/news/

politics/north-east-elections-the-rise-reach-and-outreach-of-the-rss-1677851.html (accessed 1 May 2018).

61. Pratul Sharma, 'Rise of the Sangh: How RSS Scripted BJP's Victory in Tripura', *The Week*, 9 March 2018, https://www.theweek.in/news/india/2018/03/09/rise-of-the-sangh-how-rss-scripted-bjp-victory-in-tripura.html (accessed 1 May 2018).

62. Ibid.

63. Tamanna Inamdar, 'Formed Meghalaya Alliance in Ten Minutes, Says BJP Master Strategist Himanta Biswa Sarma', Bloomberg Quint, 6 March 2018, https://www.bloombergquint.com/politics/2018/03/06/formed-meghalaya-alliance-in-ten-minutes-says-bjps-master-strategist-himanta-biswa-sarma (accessed 5 May 2018).

64. Express Web Desk, 'BJP Leader Sunil Deodhar Says His Party Will Not Impose Beef Ban in Tripura', *The Indian Express*, 14 March 2018, https://indianexpress.com/article/india/bjp-leader-sunil-deodhar-says-his-party-will-not-impose-beef-ban-in-tripura-5096613/ (accessed 12 July 2018).

65. Kumar Uttam, 'How BJP Tweaked Its Campaign for Christian-Majority Meghalaya', *Hindustan Times*, 25 February 2018, https://www.hindustantimes.com/india-news/how-bjp-tweaked-its-campaign-for-christian-majority-meghalaya/story-nXIqbgYk6VqFN3Ld383tkM.html (accessed 16 March 2018).

66. Simantik Dowerah, 'Rise of Hindutva in North East: Christians in Nagaland, Mizoram May Weaken BJP Despite RSS' Gains in Tripura, Meghalaya', Firstpost, 21 April 2017, https://www.firstpost.com/politics/rise-of-hindutva-in-north-east-rss-bjp-face-challenge-in-nagaland-and-mizoram-better-off-in-meghalaya-tripura-3369560.html (accessed 5 April 2018).

67. Anusha Ravi, 'It's Official, RSS Helps BJP Up the Game in Coastal Karnataka', *The New Indian Express*, 24 April 2018, http://www.newindianexpress.com/states/karnataka/2018/apr/24/its-official-rss-helps-bjp-up-the-game-in-coastal-karnataka-1805542.html (accessed 2 May 2018).

68. Stanley Pinto and Asha Rai, 'RSS Active in Karnataka Polls to Influence LS Elections', *The Times of India*, 1 May 2018, https://timesofindia.indiatimes.com/india/rss-active-in-karnataka-polls-to-influence-ls-elections/articleshow/63982066.cms (accessed 16 May 2018).

69. Sandeep Moudgal, 'Karnataka Election 2018: Boost for BJP, as RSS Swings into Action in Karnataka', *The Times of India*, 9 April 2018, https://timesofindia.indiatimes.com/city/bengaluru/karnataka-election-2018-boost-for-bjp-as-rss-swings-into-action-in-karnataka/articleshow/63675134.cms (accessed 1 May 2018).

70. Muralidhara Khajane, 'RSS Turns to Active Mode in Karnataka', *The Hindu*, 15 April 2018, http://www.thehindu.com/news/national/karnataka/rss-turns-to-active-mode-in-karnataka/article23544186.ece (accessed 1 May 2018).

71. Kumar Uttam, 'In Coastal Belt of Karnataka, BJP Banks on "Hindutva" Ahead of Election', *Hindustan Times*, 30 April 2018, https://www.hindustantimes.com/india-news/in-coastal-belt-of-karnataka-bjp-banks-on-hindutva-ahead-of-election/story-dDtSQawMKWSyaThbGD85XK.html (accessed 2 May 2018).

72. Smriti Kak Ramachandran, 'Karnataka Election Results 2018: RSS Says Congress' Lingayat Card Backfired', *Hindustan Times*, 15 May 2018, https://www.hindustantimes.com/india-news/karnataka-election-results-2018-rss-says-congress-lingayat-card-backfired/story-crTs1bGWj1Vn2Uuq08Kb8H.html (accessed 16 May 2018).

73. Roshan Kishore, 'A Big Hindutva Imprint in BJP's Karnataka Election Performance', *Hindustan Times*, 16 May 2018, https://www.hindustantimes.com/india-news/in-karnataka-election-results-a-big-hindutva-imprint-in-bjp-s-performance/story-nhBafBnIGDVf5wdyfdHcUO.html (accessed 16 May 2018).

74. Roshan Kishore, https://twitter.com/Roshanjnu/status/996656432052424704 (accessed 16 May 2018).

75. Ibid.

76. Kanchan Gupta, 'I Too Need to Speak Up Now!', ABP News, 28 September 2017, http://www.abplive.in/blog/i-too-need-to-speak-up-now-585940 (accessed 5 December 2017).

77. Neena Vyas, 'Advani to Step Down, Criticises RSS', *The Hindu*, 19 September 2005, http://www.thehindu.com/2005/09/19/stories/2005091907280100.htm (accessed 5 December 2017).

78. Interview with Praful Ketkar, editor of *Organiser*, in New Delhi on 29 June 2016.

79. Vinay Kumar, 'Chidambaram Warns against "Saffron Terror"', *The Hindu*, 25 August 2010, http://www.thehindu.com/news/national/

Chidambaram-warns-against-saffron-terror/article16144675.ece (accessed 5 December 2017).
80. Ibid.
81. Rupam Jain Nair and Frank Jack Daniel, 'Battling for India's Soul, State by State', Reuters, https://www.reuters.com/article/us-india-rss-specialreport/special-report-battling-for-indias-soul-state-by-state-idUSKCN0S700A20151013 (accessed 5 December 2017).
82. Press Trust of India, '"World's Largest Political Party" BJP Crosses 10-Crore Membership Mark', NDTV, 20 April 2015, https://www.ndtv.com/india-news/worlds-largest-political-party-bjp-crosses-10-crore-members-mark-756424 (accessed 4 May 2018).
83. Election Commission of India publishes a booklet of registered voters. A panna pramukh (literally, page chief) is a party activist who is responsible for persuading voters on one page and to ensure that BJP supporters turn out on election day.
84. Prashant Jha, *How the BJP Wins: Inside India's Greatest Election Machine* (New Delhi: Juggernaut, 2017), pp. 90–91.

Conclusion

1. There is an immense and unsettled body of literature on national identity issues in India. Two of the better compilations in our view are Bidyut Chakrabarty (ed.), *Communal Identity: Its Construction and Articulation in the Twentieth Century* (New Delhi: Oxford University Press, 2003) and T.K. Oommen, *State and Society in India: Studies in Nation-Building* (New Delhi: Sage Publications, 1990).
2. Vinayak Damodar Savarkar, *Hindutva*. This book was first published in 1923 in Nagpur, and Savarkar, who was in prison at the time, used the pen name Maratha. It was published by V.V. Kelkar. We referred to a later edition of this book published by Veer Savarkar Prakashan (Mumbai, 1967).
3. These bills sought to homogenize the widely different elements of civil law among a group which the government defined as Hindu. These bills included the Hindu Marriage Act, the Hindu Succession Act, the Hindu Minority and Guardianship Act and the Hindu Adoptions and Maintenance Act. For a discussion of the significance of these acts in homogenizing Hinduism, see, Kumkum Sangari, 'Politics of Diversity', in Chakrabarty, *Communal Identity*, pp. 200–02.
4. For a discussion contrasting these two visions, see, ibid., ch. 4.

5. The notion of a national soul, first systematically articulated by romantic European nationalism, analysed in, Anthony Smith, *National Identity* (London: Penguin, 1991). Also see an analysis of this phenomenon in India in, Bhikhu Parekh, 'Discourses on National Identity', in Chakrabarty, *Communal Identity*, ch. 5.

6. The foundation stone of the much enlarged RSS Delhi headquarters at Jhandewalan was laid on 3 October 2014. Besides official, living and meeting spaces, several of the publishing arms of the RSS and its international outreach cell will be located in the new facility.

7. We were told by Prakash Mithbhakare, district karyavah (secretary for a part of Pune district in Maharashtra and attendee at the 2009 ABPS conclave), that the then sarsanghchalak (K.S. Sudarshan) responded to accusations of the home minister that the RSS was engaged in what he called 'Hindu terrorism' by calling on the RSS to participate fully in the 2014 elections in order to vote the Congress government out of power 'to protect the dignity of Hindu civilization'. Interview with Mithbhakare in Chicago on 14 September 2017. The new RSS sarsanghchalak, Bhagwat, after assuming office told a press conference on 5 December 2009 that the RSS would work '*shat pratishat*' (100 per cent) in the forthcoming parliamentary election to change the government. The YouTube video of his speech can be accessed at www.youtube.com/watch?=8xp2JGND88Y.

8. The process of this canvassing was initiated by forming teams of the cadre at the local booth level (1000 voters) to meet voters to find out their political views. Then the results went up through the RSS hierarchy to reach the central leadership in Nagpur. At every level of the RSS, there is communication with the affiliates, including the BJP, and the strong support for Modi by the cadre was in addition communicated up the BJP hierarchy—and to Modi himself. This created an atmosphere of popular support among the RSS cadre for Modi.

9. Many swayamsevaks told us that the charges against Modi for alleged involvement in the 2002 communal rioting were not substantiated by legal inquiries and he was ultimately exonerated on 10 April 2012 by the Supreme Court. Moreover, they considered the highly publicized 2005 US travel ban on Modi an insult to India. We were told by senior RSS functionaries that the membership became infuriated when sixty-four members of the Indian Parliament from a range of political parties signed a letter dated 12 November 2012 to

US President Barack Obama to continue to deny a US visa to Modi, a reaction that they say made Modi a victim.

10. Ram Madhav, a BJP general secretary, told us that the RSS has committed itself 'fully' to a national election only twice, once in 1977 at the end of the 1975–77 Emergency and then in 2014. Interview with him in Washington DC on 21 November 2016. He further informed us that the BJP has launched a massive programme to train its cadre in preparation for the forthcoming 2019 parliamentary elections.

11. Lokniti CSDS, Lokniti-CSDS-ABP News Mood of the Nation Survey, May 2018, http://www.lokniti.org/pdf/Lokniti-ABP-News-Mood-of-the-Nation-Survey-Round-3-May-2018.pdf (accessed 25 May 2018).

12. Opposition parties rest their hopes on consolidating the votes of the popular majority who voted for them.

13. Milan Vaishnav argues that the Modi government, unable to meet its economic expectations, seems to be creating a new narrative referred to as a 'New India' for the 2019 elections that focuses on it stabilizing the uncertain economic situation it inherited and laying the groundwork for future growth, while addressing the issue of corruption and asserting Indian power on the world stage. See, Milan Vaishnav, 'For BJP and Modi Government, Dominance and Doubt in an Uncomfortable Embrace', *The Indian Express*, 10 September 2017, https://indianexpress.com/article/opinion/dominance-and-doubt-in-an-uncomfortable-embrace-4836661/ (accessed 12 July 2018).

14. The sarsanghchalak's annual Vijayadashami speech is the major public statement of RSS priorities. See the full 2017 speech at, 'Read Full Text of RSS Chief Mohan Bhagwat's Vijaya Dashami Speech', News18, 4 October 2017, http://www.news18.com/news/india/read-full-text-of-rss-chief-mohan-bhagwats-vijaya-dashami-speech-1532625.html (accessed 2 October 2017).

15. Ibid.

16. See our discussion of this distancing from politics in our earlier work, Walter Andersen and Shridhar Damle, *The Brotherhood in Saffron: The Rashtriya Swayamsevak Sangh and Hindu Revivalism* (Boulder: Westview Press, 1987), pp. 237–38.

17. Ram Madhav told us that the RSS has only rarely involved itself fully in support of the BJP as it did in 2014, and it is not likely to do so in 2019 because the BJP itself is creating a dense network of booth-level

workers. Interview with him in Washington DC on 21 November 2017. The RSS has worked to maintain cordial relations among the various affiliates and the government by setting up opportunities for them to meet and discuss policy issues, and to work out compromises if possible. At the same time, the RSS has encouraged the various affiliates to act as pressure groups to restrain 'government arrogance', but without the violence and the harsh condemnation of the government that happened frequently when Vajpayee was the prime minister.

18. Narendra Modi is the choice for 34 per cent of voters and Rahul Gandhi for 24 per cent. No other politician comes close to these two in the CSDS poll. Lokniti CSDS, 'Lokniti-CSDS-ABP News Mood of the Nation Survey', May 2018, p. 15, http://www.lokniti. org/pdf/Lokniti-ABP-News-Mood-of-the-Nation-Survey-Round-3-May-2018.pdf (accessed 25 May 2018).

19. Prashant Jha, 'Rajasthan By-Polls Loss Should Worry BJP, Vasundhara Raje as State Election Nears', *Hindustan Times*, 2 February 2018, https://www.hindustantimes.com/analysis/rajasthan-bypolls-loss-should-worry-bjp-vasundhara-raje-as-state-election-nears/story-ioG5hDQLMbvXGkzQGRxyTP.html (accessed 3 February 2018).

20. Quotes from Bhagwat's 2017 Vijayadashami speech, 'Read Full Text of RSS Chief Mohan Bhagwat's Vijaya Dashami Speech', News18.

21. Staff Reporter, 'All Indians Are Hindus, Says RSS Chief', *The Hindu*, 26 February 2018, http://www.thehindu.com/todays-paper/tp-national/all-living-in-india-are-hindus-rss-chief/article22853514. ece (accessed 18 March 2018).

22. An excellent analysis of the non-religious nature of Hindutva in, Arun R. Swamy, 'Hindu Nationalism—What's Religion Got to Do with It?' (Honolulu: Asia-Pacific Center for Security Studies, March 2003).

23. Modi, when chief minister of Gujarat, was also irritated at the VHP's opposition to the Gujarat government's removal of temples that blocked his programme of road expansion. The VHP was later to oppose a similar programme of temple removal by the BJP government of Rajasthan. Mahim Pratap Singh, 'Demolition of Temples in Rajasthan: RSS Goes Ahead with Its Protests against Government', *The Indian Express*, 7 July 2015, https://indianexpress. com/article/india/india-others/demolition-of-temples-in-rajasthan-

rss-to-go-ahead-with-its-protest-against-government/ (accessed 12 July 2018).

24. Ashutosh Varshney, 'India's Watershed Vote: Hindu Nationalism in Power', *Journal of Democracy*, October 2014, vol. 24, no. 4, pp. 34–45. In 2014, the BJP won sixty-six of the 131 parliamentary seats reserved for Dalits and tribals, far ahead of any other party and more than twice its performance in 2009. Note that all registered voters in a constituency are eligible to vote, even though the candidates must be Dalit or tribal.

25. Varghese K. George, 'In 2014, Hindutva Versus Caste', *The Hindu*, 26 March 2014, http://www.thehindu.com/opinion/lead/In-2014-Hindutva-versus-caste/article11426711.ece# (accessed 23 September 2017).

26. Ashis Nandy, 'Hinduism Versus Hindutva: The Inevitability of a Confrontation', *The Times of India*, 18 February 1991, http://www.sscnet.ucla.edu/southasia/Socissues/hindutva.html (accessed 28 September 2017). We believe Nandy has it wrong, however, when he argues that Hindutva's attack on Hinduism is an attempt to protect a minority consciousness which democracy is threatening to marginalize. Rather, its goal is to get the support of the popular majority and do so in a way that unifies them socially.

27. An analysis of the RSS's equal treatment of low-caste Hindus, including Dalits and tribals in, Ramesh Patange, *Manu, Sangh aani mee* (Mumbai: Hindustan Prakashan Sansta, 2012), in Marathi.

28. See report of this in, *Sree Guruji Samagra* (New Delhi: Suruchi Prakashan, Hindu year 5016), vol. 3, in Golwalkar's article on BJS founder Syama Prasad Mookerjee.

29. Donald Eugene Smith, *India as a Secular State* (Princeton: Princeton University Press, 1963), pp. 470–71. Some RSS figures argue that Smith does not adequately distinguish the state from the nation. The state is by necessity secular, they argue, and the nation survives because of its 'national soul'. The analogy often used is the state of Israel and Jewish Zionism.

30. Ibid., p. 471.

31. For instance, K.S. Sudarshan, the fifth sarsanghchalak (2000–09), said, 'ALL MUSLIMS [sic] living in India are Hindus. All Sikhs are Hindus'. See, Nonica Datta, 'Are the Sikhs Hindus?', *The Hindu*, 4 March 2003, http://www.thehindu.com/2003/03/04/stories/2003030400951000.htm (accessed 18 March 2018).

32. For a discussion of the RSS–BJS positions on language, see, Bruce Graham, *Hindu Nationalism and Indian Politics: The Origins and Development of the Bharatiya Jana Sangh* (Cambridge: Cambridge University Press, 1990), pp. 128–38.

33. Golwalkar himself (like Prime Minister Jawaharlal Nehru) initially had reservations about the creation of linguistic states, fearing that it could enhance linguistic subnationalism that would weaken the central government. But Golwalkar's silence on the issue after the reorganization of the states on a linguistic basis indicated his aim to keep the RSS out of this language issue once the BJS indicated its support. The BJS and the RSS, on the other hand, have backed the notion of small states, referred to as *janapad*, as more administratively efficient.

34. See discussion of this effort at Hinduizing regional customs in Gujarat in Christophe Jaffrelot, 'Narendra Modi between Hindutva and Subnationalism: The Gujarati Asmita of Hindu Hriday Samrat', *India Review*, 2016, vol. 15, no. 2, pp. 202–03.

35. Ketan Alder, 'How the BJP Has Come to Dominate Lower-Caste Politics', Al Jazeera, 13 April 2017, http://www.aljazeera.com/indepth/ opinion/2017/04/bjp-dominate-caste-politics-170412085718269. html (accessed 1 October 2017).

36. Balveer Arora, 'The Distant Goal of Cooperative Federalism', *The Hindu*, 22 May 2015, http://www.thehindu.com/opinion/op-ed/the-distant-goal-of-cooperative-federalism/article7232184.ece (accessed 2 October 2017). Modi has used the notion of 'competitive federalism' to give the states room to innovate and serve as a model for other states to emulate. Two examples are the legislation to provide more business-friendly laws on land and labour. Competitive federalism builds on the development model introduced in China in the late 1970s; Modi has expressed admiration for its role in the rapid growth of the Chinese economy.

37. M.S. Golwalkar, *Bunch of Thoughts* (Bangalore: Vikram Prakashan, 1966), chs. XII-1 (for Muslims) and XII-2 for Christians. Ranga Hari, a senior RSS figure and an editor of the complete works of Golwalkar, told us that *Bunch of Thoughts* was in fact a collection of Golwalkar's speeches. The original titles given to the chapters on Muslims and Christians in *Bunch of Thoughts* had a political orientation and the new edition will rename them 'Muslim Fundamentalism' and 'Christian Evangelism' to distance itself

from the associated political controversy and focus instead on the cultural differences. Information on this from an email from him on 6 April 2016.

38. Interview with Saji Narayanan, president of the BMS, with us in New Delhi on 14 January 2018.

39. Varshney, 'India's Watershed Vote', *Journal of Democracy*, p. 38.

40. Varshney develops this theme in, *Ethnic Conflict and Civic Life: Hindus and Muslims in India* (New Haven: Yale University Press, 2001).

41. 'RSS Annual Report-2017', RSS website, http://rss.org// Encyc/2017/3/23/rss-Annual-Report-2017-English.html (accessed 8 October 2017). RSS workers also include vistaraks, young men who usually complete the first level of training and serve for about a year as a kind of intern. If they decide to go on to become a pracharak, they then go to the second- and third-year camps. The mukhya shikshak at the shakha usually goes to first- and second-year camps. The RSS also runs one-week introductory camps (referred to as Prathmik Shiksha Varg) for people who will be eligible for various positions at the shakha, milan and mandali. The 2017 report notes 1059 such camps in 2016–17 with 1,04,127 participants coming from 29,127 shakhas, about half the number of shakhas in the country. The RSS has also started special first- and second-year camps for members over forty-five years to address specialized needs, like providing help in natural disasters or organizing community projects. The 2017 report notes 1891 participants in the first-year special camp and 1527 in the second.

42. Bhagwat's Vijayadashami speech. The two most controversial government policies were demonetization and the GST and, while they are not specifically mentioned in the speech, Bhagwat very likely had these two measures in mind as representing the 'same old economic "isms"' that the government must rethink.

43. Ibid.

44. 'GST Council Meet: Rates for 27 Items Slashed; E-Wallet for Exporters, Quarterly Filing for Small Business Approved', MSN, 6 October 2017, https://www.msn.com/en-in/money/topstories/gst-council-meet-rates-for-27-items-slashed-e-wallet-for-exporters-quarterly-filing-for-small-businesses-approved/ar-AAsZHuK?li=AAggbRN (accessed 8 October 2017).